DATE DUE

			PRINTED IN U.S.A.

METHOD ACTORS

◆ ◆ ◆

METHOD ACTORS

◆ ◆ ◆

THREE GENERATIONS OF AN AMERICAN ACTING STYLE

◆ ◆ ◆

STEVE VINEBERG

SCHIRMER BOOKS
A Division of Macmillan, Inc.
New York

Collier Macmillan Canada
Toronto

Maxwell Macmillan International
New York   Oxford   Singapore   Sydney

Acknowledgments for quoted materials appear on page 349, which shall be considered a continuation of the copyright page.

Portions of this book have appeared in slightly altered form as follows: "American Revival," "Initiation and Discovery: The Career of Blythe Danner," and "Drama as Monument" in *The Threepenny Review;* "The Gleeful Subversive" in *The London Guardian;* "Willy Loman and the Method" in *Journal of Dramatic Theory and Criticism;* and "The Many Jacks," "Man of the '80s?: A Case for Paul Newman," "A Method to Their Madness," and "Head of the Class" in *The Boston Phoenix.*

Schirmer Books
A Division of Macmillan, Inc.
866 Third Avenue, New York, N.Y. 10022

Collier Macmillan Canada, Inc.
1200 Eglinton Avenue East, Suite 200
Don Mills, Ontario M3C 3N1

Library of Congress Catalog Card Number: 90-9004

Printed in the United States of America

printing number
1   2   3   4   5   6   7   8   9   10

Library of Congress Cataloging-in-Publication Data

Vineberg, Steve.
Method actors : three generations of an American acting style /
Steve Vineberg.
p.   cm.
Includes bibliographical references and index.
ISBN 0-02-872685-5
1. Method (Acting)   I. Title.
PN2062.V56   1991

792′.028—dc20   90-9004
                                                 CIP

For my parents

CONTENTS

◆ ◆ ◆

Illustrations

ix

Preface

xi

Acknowledgments

xv

1

Moving Toward the Method

1

2

Passionate Moderates

22

3

The Reality Quest

51

4

Psychogropings

85

5

Texts for Method Actors

114

CONTENTS

6

The Method Actor as Movie Star:
Montgomery Clift and Marlon Brando
142

7

Mystical Communion: James Dean and Julie Harris
186

8

The Neurosis Kids
206

9

Method Sanity
223

10

Jason Robards: The Method as Instinct
249

11

Submerging Technique and Other Options
274

Notes
323

Selected Bibliography
335

Index
351

ILLUSTRATIONS

◆ ◆ ◆

Illustrations follow page 142.

1. John (then Jules) Garfield and Morris Carnovsky in *Awake and Sing!*
2. Stella Adler and Morris Carnovsky in *Paradise Lost.*
3. John Garfield and Jeffrey Lynn in *Four Daughters.*
4. Montgomery Clift and Elizabeth Taylor in *A Place in the Sun.*
5. Frank Sinatra and Montgomery Clift in *From Here to Eternity.*
6. Marlon Brando and Elizabeth Taylor in *Reflections in a Golden Eye.*
7. Marlon Brando and Maria Schneider in *Last Tango in Paris.*
8. James Dean, Edward Platt, Jim Backus, and Ann Doran in *Rebel Without a Cause.*
9. Brandon de Wilde, Ethel Waters, and Julie Harris in *The Member of the Wedding.*
10. Julie Harris and James Dean in *East of Eden.*
11. Sandy Dennis in *Come Back to the 5 & Dime, Jimmy Dean, Jimmy Dean.*
12. Maureen Stapleton and Warren Beatty in *Reds.*
13. Marlon Brando and Eva Marie Saint in *On the Waterfront.*
14. Kim Hunter and Marlon Brando in *A Streetcar Named Desire.*
15. Juano Hernandez and Rod Steiger in *The Pawnbroker.*
16. Rip Torn and Dana Hill in *Cross Creek.*
17. James Robards in *Long Day's Journey into Night.*
18. Jason Robards and Colleen Dewhurst in *A Moon for the Misbegotten.*
19. Paul Newman and Piper Laurie in *The Hustler.*
20. Paul Newman and Edward Asner in *Fort Apache, the Bronx.*

21. Arthur Kennedy, Winifred Cushing, and Lee J. Cobb in *Death of a Salesman*.
22. Blythe Danner and Anthony Perkins in *Lovin' Molly*.
23. Blythe Danner and Frank Langella in *The Sea Gull*.
24. Randy Quaid, Jack Nicholson, and Otis Young in *The Last Detail*.

PREFACE
◆ ◆ ◆

Most books on American Method acting are either textbooks written by acting teachers, or chronicles of the Group Theatre or the Actors Studio—the two chief institutions in this country associated with the principles of Konstantin Stanislavski, whose "system" acquired the popular name "the Method" when it reached these shores in the 1920s. This book is a kind of history, too—not of institutions, but of an approach to acting and of three generations of Method performers who have personified it.

From the time Americans began to practice it professionally, in the 1930s, there has been strenuous argument about exactly what the Method is. In the middle of the decade during which the Group Theatre—which introduced the Method to Broadway audiences—led its beleaguered existence, its acknowledged queen bee, Stella Adler, returning from a tutorial in Paris with Stanislavski himself, collided with Lee Strasberg, who was in charge of the Group acting classes. The issue was the relative value of the most controversial of all Method techniques, affective memory (also known as "emotional recall"). Almost all Method teachers since have lined up on one side or the other of the crack left by the Strasberg–Adler debate, so it's impossible to get a consensus on how the Method's supposed to work. Furthermore, though Adler and her fellow Group alumnus Sanford Meisner share a point of view about affective memory, on other fronts their approaches to the teaching of acting are so resoundingly different that even graduates from Meisner's Neighborhood Playhouse and students at Adler's studio can't agree on a definition. That's why there's been so much confusion about the Method—why most people still don't know exactly what the term means, even though we see examples of it all the time in our theaters, in our moviehouses, and on our television screens.

This book's definition of the Method is based on what Method actors have done since the days of the Group Theatre. That is, it's based on what we actually *see* when we watch actors whose work is dominated by the interior, psychological, naturalistic paths Stanislavski marked as the most fruitful for *his* repertory troupe and Americans were drawn to subsequently, by temperament and by culture. Often by training, too, though not always—an actor's affiliations can be misleading. Performers who never took a class in Stanislavski techniques have often arrived at them instinctively, as Barbara Stanwyck did. And sometimes actors who disdain the idea of the Method and think of themselves as representatives of other, older traditions give performances indistinguishable from those of Actors Studio regulars: Jason Robards's interpretations of the great O'Neill roles provide one potent example.

What I hope to suggest in this book is not only what Method acting is, but how American culture has led our actors straight to it—how the Method, because of its link with realism, its affirmation of Freud, and its focus on adolescent rebellion as the core of much adult behavior, is a natural dramatic expression of the way Americans understand and define themselves. I'm also fascinated by the way American playwriting has built itself up around the Method and, by becoming part of the Method scene, has inevitably contributed to its development. Many of our classic plays, beginning with Clifford Odets's *Waiting for Lefty* and *Awake and Sing!* (both produced in 1935), can be seen as texts for actors who bring Method concerns to their performances.

It's the actors, though, who are at the heart of this exploration of the Method. The work of John Garfield and Lee J. Cobb, Montgomery Clift and Marlon Brando, Julie Harris and James Dean, Sandy Dennis and Eva Marie Saint, Jason Robards, Paul Newman and Dustin Hoffman, Blythe Danner and Jack Nicholson is far more eloquent about what the Method is (and in what significant ways it's changed in the more than half a century since American audiences first caught a glimpse of it) than any teacher, any handbook could hope to be.

I first began to sense what Method acting was when, at fourteen,

I saw Montgomery Clift in the 1951 George Stevens movie *A Place in the Sun* on TV and his performance broke my heart. As a teenager who felt himself a bewildered receptor of all kinds of terrifying (and thrilling) stimuli, I was responding not only to the forceful erotic charge of Clift's love scenes with Elizabeth Taylor, but also to his laconic expressiveness, his gift for communicating the feelings of a hypersensitive and inarticulate character. I'd never seen an actor convey the intensity of an emotional life so powerfully and poetically; I didn't know actors could *do* that—could actually recreate feelings I recognized in myself. Up to that point, I'd been under the delusion that acting was about big symbolic gestures and romantic flourishes and had to be loud and insistent; but here was this wonderful actor, speaking softly, saying almost nothing, and I was locked into every word he *didn't* say. After that night, I started watching for acting that could draw me inside a character that way, finding it tougher and tougher to accept performances that failed to illuminate anything underneath the surface. Later I recognized that, for Americans at least, the Method is most often the means of penetrating that surface. This book is my way of explaining a vision of acting that has given me more pleasure and excitement, as a spectator and as a critic, than any other single element in the theater, in movies, or in television.

ACKNOWLEDGMENTS

♦ ♦ ♦

This volume's six-year journey from first research to publication has left me indebted to many people for their generous assistance, and I would like to express my gratitude here.

The Social Sciences and Humanities Research Council of Canada, the Mabelle McLeod Lewis Memorial Fund, and the Research and Publications Committee at College of the Holy Cross greatly eased the financial demands of the research process. And since so much of that process consisted of viewing films, videotapes, and kinescopes, I would like to thank those individuals who permitted me access to movies I couldn't find at revival houses or my local video store: in Los Angeles, Eleanore Tanin of the UCLA Film, TV and Radio Archives; in New York, Betty Corwin, director of the Theatre on Film and Tape Collection at the Library and Museum of the Performing Arts. In San Francisco, Mark Collopy extended the use of a private collection without question to a virtual stranger. His tapes filled in a few embarrassing gaps in my notes.

A number of people read all or part of the manuscript, at various stages, and provided both valuable counsel and welcome encouragement: at Stanford, Charles Lyons, William Chace, and Wendell Cole; at Holy Cross, Dale Bauer and Robert Cording; Wendy Lesser at *The Threepenny Review;* Pauline Kael, Ray Sawhill, and Polly Frost. Charles Taylor, my valued associate at *The Boston Phoenix,* read every page as I completed the final draft; his sharp eye for the kinks and traps of academic writing and his pointed but good-humored comments kept me honest. And my editor, Robert Axelrod, who championed this book from the outset, has been gracious, helpful, and consistently supportive.

Just as I rounded the turn into the chapter on Jason Robards's O'Neill performances, I had the good fortune to teach a remarkable group of Holy Cross students in a class on Eugene O'Neill and Tennessee Williams: Amy Amatangelo, Chris Capot, Steve Gambino, Kate Gibson, Susan Jones, Susan Lennon, Kristen McCue, Katie Marshall, Lisa Moore, Tim O'Keefe, Laura Panzarino, Joe Saab, Michelle Slysh, Frank Taplin, and Mike Tosca. Their incisive intelligence and their enthusiasm for Robards were inspiring, and they provided a dynamic testing ground for my ideas.

Whatever I've learned about scholarship, I owe to Eleanor Prosser, who taught as much by the example of her own work as by her instruction in the classroom. And three Stanford colleagues—Lorne Buchman, David McCandless, and Frank Murray—have, as always, filled many roles during the course of this project: dedicated friends, bottomless sources of emotional support, challenging intellectual companions.

My brother, David Vineberg, unconsciously planted the seed of this book thirty-five years ago when he began to share with me his own love for the Method rebels of the 1950s, Marlon Brando and James Dean. I've often felt his presence in these pages, as a kind of silent collaborator.

Steve Vineberg

METHOD ACTORS

◆ ◆ ◆

1

MOVING TOWARD THE METHOD

◆ ◆ ◆

There are times when you pick up your shoes and see through them your whole life.[1]

—Lee Strasberg

In 1953 the young Rod Steiger, who'd received training at the Actors Studio, the home of the American Method, made his mark in the title role of Paddy Chayefsky's "Marty" on "Goodyear Television Playhouse," under Delbert Mann's direction. Two years later, Mann filmed a slightly expanded version of the teleplay, starring Ernest Borgnine. If you look at these two performances side by side, you immediately see a few significant differences between a Method and a non-Method approach to a role. Steiger reproduces the natural cadence of conversation as closely as possible and refrains from large-scale emotional displays. He conveys the unhappiness of Chayefsky's Bronx butcher, a reluctant but nearly defeated bachelor, suggestively: He gives the character a low-frequency whine, he talks a little too quickly (out of discomfort because his solitariness is so much the focus of his family and neighbors), he stutters occasionally. When Marty's attempt to find a date for Saturday night fails, as on so many other occasions, and he's greeted by yet another neighborhood well-wisher who comments on his brother's recent wedding and wants to know when *Marty's* planning to tie the knot, Steiger tamps down Marty's immediate impulses. Instead of exploding, he replies with a touch of irony while his eyes tell us he's reached the end of his patience.

Rather than barreling toward the big scenes, or inflating the performance so that it's all high points, Steiger emphasizes Marty's everyday efforts to cope with his interior struggle, and the way his

1

sweetness and gentleness—qualities he underrates in himself—rise to the surface in even the most exasperating circumstances. When his anxious old Italian mama (Esther Minciotti) coaxes him to visit the Waverly Ballroom because it's "loaded with tomatoes," Steiger controls the dramatic outburst Chayefsky has written for him, refusing to yield to the temptation of shedding tears. He even ends the scene by kissing his mother's hand. "Loaded with tomatoes . . . boy, that's rich," he mumbles, deriving obvious pleasure from his mother's incongruous use of an American phrase. It's a surprising coda; you feel the actor must have thought of it during performance, spinning off the character's deep affection for his mother rather than the stock dramatic confrontation between them.

Ernest Borgnine approaches the same pair of scenes in a more traditional, histrionic manner. When he's rejected by a potential Saturday night date, he falls back on the theatrical platitude of squeezing his eyes shut to indicate the intensity of his pain. He stutters, too, though not casually—it's a set-piece stutter. At the dinner table with his mother, he plunges into a big-deal exhibition of actorish bravado, expending all his reserves of emotional energy at once, so that his only out at the end is to shut his anger off abruptly like a faucet. Marty's painful confessional speech ("Blue suit, gray suit, I'm still a fat little man. A fat little ugly man") sounds carefully rehearsed rather than unexpectedly arrived at, because Borgnine stresses all the obvious key words. And since he hasn't balanced the character, as Steiger did, by setting up a tension between Marty's sweet-souled modesty and his accumulated frustration and rage, when Borgnine echoes his mother's phrase at the end of the scene he comes across as unnecessarily sarcastic and bitter.

It would be preposterous to claim that the only reason Steiger is so much better in the part than Borgnine is that he's a Method actor. What this comparison shows, though, is that Steiger's Method-trained style is able to call forth something meaningful in the material—a four-square slab of American realism—that Borgnine's more traditional approach fails to. Without the fine shadings and contrasts of Steiger's performance, Chayefsky's play sounds as flat, banal, and undifferentiated on the screen as it reads on the page. Yet the TV production, seen nearly four decades later, retains its freshness. We recognize at once how worn, even condescending the script is, but the easy understatement of Steiger's performance works against the basic fraudulence of

Chayefsky's representation of the "little man" hero. What Steiger accomplishes here is the double task of making the theatrical familiar and making the familiar dramatically interesting. And if I had to sum up the aim of the American Method in a single phrase, that would be it.

American Method acting actually began in Russia with Konstantin Stanislavski, who, in collaboration with Vladimir Nemirovich-Danchenko, opened the Moscow Art Theatre in 1898. The Moscow Art is the company we associate with the premiere productions of Chekhov and Gorki—with the signal achievements, in other words, of Russian dramatic realism. Basing it on his own observations of the best acting he'd seen on the stages of Europe, Stanislavski evolved an approach to the teaching of acting that became known as the "Stanislavski system." In fact it was less a system than a series of experiments, since his ideas about what stimulated the process of good acting remained in flux throughout his life. However, perhaps because of his powerful—almost tyrannical—personality, Stanislavski tended to turn his students into disciples, eager to take him at his word even though he might alter that word radically later on. The result is that you can almost always find something in Stanislavski's acting textbooks (*An Actor Prepares, Building a Character*, and *Creating a Role*) that contradicts the schools of thought about acting that sprang up under the guidance of his own students.

In his first handbook, *An Actor Prepares,* published in Russia in 1926 and in the United States in 1936, he divides his own persona in two. There's the teacher, Tortsov, who demands total physical, emotional, and spiritual commitment from the members of his classes; and the gifted student, Kostya Nazvanov, whose passion for acting and faith in Tortsov's leadership make him the model repository for (and reflection of) Tortsov's lessons—Tortsov's words personified on the classroom stage. If Kostya is Stanislavski the pupil, still learning his craft, then Tortsov is Stanislavski the instructor, who's mastered his, and no one who dares to challenge his authority is dealt with kindly. (As the teacher, Stanislavski doesn't permit his pupils to see the doubts and questions he may struggle with in his private hours. He places those in Kostya's mouth.)

What's amazing about *An Actor Prepares* is the unwavering assurance with which Tortsov calls forth an apparently endless store of ideas on the art of acting. Tortsov inspires the same confidence in a

3

reader as, you might imagine, Stanislavski did in his students; we identify with Kostya, wide-eyed, dedicated, devouring all he can of Tortsov's wisdom. *An Actor Prepares* reads as so definitive that you're a little shocked to find, in *Building a Character* (not published in the United States until 1949, eleven years after Stanislavski's death), Tortsov changing the accent of his teachings, stressing vocal and physical exercises ("external" work) rather than the psychological ("internal") preparation he preached with unswerving conviction in *An Actor Prepares*.

There are two things that Stanislavski, importantly, did *not* do. First, he never professed the ability to instill talent. He claimed it couldn't be taught, only nurtured with constant hard work. But he believed that a system of acting, working in league with natural talent, could at least result in consistency of performance, in the maintenance of certain standards. Second, he never denied the presence of great actors in the theaters of his own country and other countries. Far from it—he incorporated his perceptions of the working methods of actors he admired into his design. What his insistence on the importance of developing a system implied, however, was that there wasn't *enough* good acting to be seen, and no efficient manner of passing on to novices the wisdom a handful of prodigies had found on their own.

"Truth on the stage," Tortsov explains to his students in *An Actor Prepares*, "is whatever we can believe in with sincerity, whether in ourselves or in our colleagues."[2] And that, in a sentence, is the center of Stanislavskian acting technique. Stanislavski didn't initiate this quest for truth in the theater, but he was the first to identify it as the aim of all good acting by codifying it into a system. He practiced his profession at a time when all the arts—especially literature and drama—were moving toward a greater realism (or naturalism), and so in his view there was a strong implied link between the concept of "truth" in theater and verisimilitude, the attempt to present an image of actual life on the stage.

This movement toward verisimilitude in drama had been preoccupying theater people in other parts of Europe since the eighteenth century, but it was much more of a recent development in Russia, which was, after all, a late addition to the company of modern nations. One of Ostrovsky's plays had caused a minor sensation in 1853 (ten years before Stanislavski's birth) because the leading actress appeared in a simple dress and without a wig, opting for realism rather than glamor. The emphasis that Irina Arkadina, the actress in Chekhov's *The Sea Gull*, places upon being fashionable on stage (much to the annoyance of her aspiring-playwright son) confirms Stanislavski's complaint that the Moscow theater was still, in his time, too often a place of *haute couture* rather than reproductions from life. In the spirit of Russia's new age (the First Revolution occurred in 1905–1906), Stanislavski and Nemirovich-Danchenko were conducting their own small-scale theatrical revolution. Influenced by the realistic ensemble performances of Germany's Meiningen Players, whose tour had stopped in Moscow in 1885, they strove to put on the Moscow Art stage the kind of truth they found lacking in the work of most of their theatrical contemporaries.

American actors didn't get to read Stanislavski until 1936, but long before that a handful began to feel the effects of his teachings. In 1923 Richard Boleslavsky, a graduate of the Moscow Art Theatre school, emigrated to New York, where he founded The Laboratory Theatre (renamed The American Laboratory Theatre two years later). It was through Boleslavsky and his fellow M.A.T. alum Maria Ouspenskaya, who taught in his school, that young Americans received Stanislavski's system second-hand.

In America in the 1920s, the teaching of acting was still in its infancy, and still a highly individualized process. Moreover, the concept of ensemble acting that Stanislavski aspired to—the complete interdependence of actors in a company—was alien to the American acting world. For Americans, acting meant climbing toward stardom: The locus of professional theater in this country was the completely commercial, star-topped hierarchy forged by the iron claw of the Theatrical Syndicate, which managed almost all of the professional houses across the nation in the late nineteenth and early twentieth centuries. So what Boleslavsky was offering to his students was really a startling new approach. And among those who learned it were Stella Adler and Lee Strasberg, who in 1931 became founding members of the Group Theatre—the first ensemble troupe in America, as well as the first theatrical organization to espouse what they believed to be Stanislavski's system. Americanized, the "system" became known popularly as "the Method." By the 1950s, under the influence of the first Method

5

school for professional actors, the Actors Studio, and Strasberg, its guru, the Method had established itself as the preeminent acting style of Americans.

Because there has been so much debate among defenders and detractors, and infighting among teachers, about what the Method is and isn't, no one has ever drawn up an official list of the tenets of Method acting. What I propose here, in the interest of cutting through some of the confusion, is an *un*official list, based on a reading of such acting texts as Robert Lewis's *Method—or Madness?* (1958) and *Advice to the Players* (1980), Charles McGaw's *Acting Is Believing: A Basic Method* (1966), Edward Dwight Easty's *On Method Acting* (1966), and Uta Hagen's *Respect for Acting* (1973). It's based, too, on my own observations of Method actors' tactics.

1. The Method sees as the actor's essential task the reproduction of recognizable reality—verisimilitude—on stage (or screen), based on an acute observation of the world. Few Method teachers believe this focus restricts actors to one particular style of production, but it clearly links the Method to American naturalism, which has the same aim.
2. The Method seeks to justify all stage behavior by ensuring that it is psychologically sound. In order to provide a unifying motivation for this behavior, each actor establishes a single overall purpose for the character, known as a "super-objective" (or "through-line" or "spine"). This larger movement is divided into smaller, playable units called "objectives" or "actions."
3. It places a high premium on the expression of genuine emotion, which may be evoked by the use of a technique called "affective memory." (In its most popular version, "emotional recall," affective memory is an extremely controversial device that, more than anything else, has factionalized the community of Method teachers.)
4. It identifies the actor's own personality not merely as a model for the creation of character, but as the mine from which all psychological truth must be dug.
5. It encourages the use of improvisation as a rehearsal aid, and even in some cases as part of the performance, in an effort to keep acting spontaneous (and therefore lifelike).
6. It promotes intimate communication between actors in a scene,

6

and therefore moves toward the performance ideal of a true ensemble.

7. It stresses the use of objects both for their symbolic value and as emissaries from the solid, material world.

8. Finally (though this last consideration is more often implied than stated), it demands an almost religious devotion on the part of an actor, based on what seems to be a mystical belief in the power of truth in acting.

These concerns weren't invented by Stanislavski or his American successors; they emerged naturally out of the two-thousand-year history of Western acting. Perhaps the best way to begin looking at the Method would be to elaborate on each of these tenets, and take a cursory glance at how each fits into that history.

Versimilitude

> The actor does not have to learn to act—he already knows how; he does it all the time, naturally, spontaneously, and convincingly. The process of acting on stage is not fundamentally different from that which he uses automatically in ordinary life. In a very real sense, then, the actor's training is nothing more than his learning to do consciously—in the unreal world of the stage—what he already knows how to do unconsciously in the real world outside the theatre.[3]

There's a strong tradition in both European and American theater of attempting to reproduce reality on stage; it goes back amazingly far. In his comprehensive study of the history of stage performance, *The Length and Depth of Acting*, Edwin Duerr cites an attempt by British directors Charles Macklin and David Garrick, as early as 1741, to do away with the accepted stage mannerisms of their day—"an elevated tone of voice, a mechanical depression of its tones, and a formal measured step in traversing the stage"[4]—and substitute a more natural approach to speaking and acting. The notion of the "fourth wall," which we normally associate with the realism of Ibsen and Strindberg, was actually suggested by Diderot in the mid-eighteenth century as advice to the actor:

7

Think no more of the audience than if it had never existed.
Imagine a huge wall across the front of the stage, separating
you from the audience, and behave exactly as if the curtain
had never risen.[5]

It wasn't until a century later, however, that the first great strides
were made toward naturalism in acting. They were clearly linked to
the new popularity of naturalism in literature and drama. In 1853
Adolphe Montigny, director of the Gymnase in France, made a daring
departure from the semicircular staging popular at the time: He posi-
tioned a table downstage center, grouped his actors around it, and
directed them to play to each other and ignore the audience. At around
the same time, the English actor Charles Fechter broke with convention by playing *Hamlet* as a contemporary melodrama in a modern
setting, with Shakespeare's dialogue spoken in conversational tones
rather than declaimed. Meanwhile, his countryman Thomas Robertson, working with the Bancrofts at the Prince of Wales Theatre, was
employing practical sets and props, coaching the actors to underplay,
and working for ensemble effects. (In Arthur Wing Pinero's affectionate 1898 parody of acting styles, *Trelawny of the "Wells,"* Robertson
shows up as the renegade playwright Tom Wrench.) Drama critic
William Archer, writing in 1888, praised stars like Edmund Kean,
W. C. Macready, and Ellen Terry for conscientiously researching their
roles by observing the death throes of executed murderers and the
agonies of the insane in Bedlam. The most profound influences on
Stanislavski's way of thinking about acting, though, were certainly the
Duke of Saxe-Meiningen, whose Meiningen Players first performed in
Berlin in 1874, and André Antoine and his Théâtre Libre (begun in
1887).

By the time Richard Boleslavsky exported Stanislavski's technique
to the United States, American actors had been primed to receive it by
nearly seventy-five years of progress toward stage naturalism. Edwin
Booth, an actor known for his unmannered acting, rose to stardom as
early as 1856. In the 1880s the comedian and theater manager Edward
Harrigan, famous for the vaudevilles he starred in with Tony Hart,
came up with the innovation of employing non-actors (often street
bums) to put the stamp of authenticity on his low-life street comedy.
Clara Morris, dubbed "the queen of spasm," took pride in reproducing
on stage the horrors she saw outside the theater; her performances

8

featured elaborate lunatic fits and death scenes and gruesomely detailed make-up. And William Gillette, the actor and playwright whose *Sherlock Holmes* played to packed houses for decades, wrote a lively, much-quoted essay on the "illusion of the first time in acting," where he stressed the importance

> for an actor who knows exactly what he is going to say to behave exactly as though he didn't; to let his thoughts (apparently) occur to him as he goes along, even though they are there in his mind already; and (apparently) to search for and find the words by which to express those thoughts, even though these words are at his tongue's very end.[6]

By 1900, this emphasis on stage realism had reached the doors of the American Academy of Dramatic Art, where a newly installed "department of life study" required all students to perform monologues based on the observation of role models.

In the opening decade of the twentieth century, the first Russian actors carried their skills to American audiences. The St. Petersburg Players specialized in Ibsen and were managed by Paul Orlenev, in a style he claimed was modeled on Stanislavski's. Orlenev's star was an intense, astonishing actress named Alla Nazimova, who—breaking away from the company before long—dazzled New York as Hedda Gabler and Nora in *A Doll's House*. Critics, accustomed to the reign of stage personalities who were easily recognizable in role after role, marveled at this chameleon. Nazimova, who predated Boleslavsky's American Laboratory Theatre by nearly twenty years, provided an early model of the naturalistic actors' art of submerging themselves in roles—what Stanislavski called loving the part in yourself rather than loving yourself in the part.

The first homegrown American acting company to strive for something like naturalistic acting was the Provincetown Players. A democratic organization without an established hierarchy (at least in its debut year, 1915), it boasted the most intellectually exciting membership of any cultural group in the country: Eugene O'Neill, Susan Glaspell, George Cram Cook, Hutchins Hapgood, Robert Edmond Jones, and Kenneth Macgowan, among others. Amateurs all, they flaunted their lack of professionalism proudly. Professionalism meant technique, they argued; technique called attention to itself; and that kind of self-consciousness marred the psychological authenticity of the play. O'Neill's biographers, Arthur and Barbara Gelb, describe how O'Neill's father, the matinee idol James O'Neill (renowned for playing the lead in *The Count of Monte Cristo*), tried to pass on his old-school ideas about acting to the Provincetown amateurs he directed in his son's one-act *Before Breakfast*, while his son paced and glowered and muttered in the background.[7]

It's ironic that what the Provincetown Players reached for instinctively is what the Method teaches as technique. For the Method actor concentration, observation, and sense memory (the memory of sights, sounds, smells, tastes, and textures) are the chief means of bringing the pulse of actual life onto the stage or screen. The exercises Boleslavsky set for his students to sharpen their observation and their recall of sensory impressions became a permanent part of the Method program, beginning with the Group Theatre.

Justification and Super-Objective

The term "justification" originated with Stanislavski. He wrote in *An Actor Prepares* that "action, motion, is the basis of the art followed by the actor,"[8] and "all action in the theatre must have an inner justification, be logical, coherent, and real."[9] To unify an actor's individual actions in terms of overall character, he proposed the idea of a "super-objective," which would articulate a character's motivation from first entrance to final exit. Boleslavsky defined a role as " 'a long string of beads . . . of action' following 'one after another, sometimes overlapping each other but always clear and distinct.' The 'spine' of the part is the cord upon which the 'beads of action' are strung."[10] The small, separate actions the Method actor engages in, each one carefully linked to the super-objective, are now called "beats"—probably because Boleslavsky's American students, struggling to penetrate his thick Russian accent, misheard what was meant to be the word "beads."

The forward thrust of action was perhaps the most exciting and most revolutionary of Stanislavski's ideas. It put an end to the stodgy, consecutive structure of declamatory acting, where the actors each held the stage separately, one after another. Stanislavski didn't believe in actors' waiting to take their turns in a play. The actress and teacher Uta Hagen tells a story about her early exposure to Stanislavski's system when she rehearsed with the German actor Albert Basserman for a production of *The Master Builder*.

> There was such a vibrant reality to the rhythm of his speech and behavior that I was swept away by it. I kept waiting for him to come to an end with his intentions so that I could take my "turn." As a result, I either made a big hole in the dialogue or desperately cut in on him in order to avoid another hole. I was expecting the usual "It's your turn; then it's my turn." At the end of the first act I went to his dressing room and said, "Mr. Basserman, I can't apologize enough, but I never know when you're through!" He looked at me in amazement and said, "I'm *never* through! And neither should you be."[11]

Genuine Emotion

Always a controversial subject, the concept of real emotion in performance has given rise to some of the most heated writing on acting in the last century and a half. The classical critics recommended it, but then it fell out of favor, and stayed out until the early years of the eighteenth century. The argument between the "Emotionalists" and the "Anti-Emotionalists" began in earnest in the 1830s. Denis Diderot's *The Paradox of Acting*, published posthumously in 1830, contends that a true actor, far from experiencing genuine emotion while he is playing it, is actually absorbed in self-reflection: "At the very moment when he touches your heart he is listening to his own voice. . . ."[12] This may sound to us like the sheerest vanity, but Diderot's idea of emotion on the stage is actually much like Wordsworth's notion, in poetry, of emotion recollected in tranquility. And two great French actors embodied Diderot's ideas. Talma is said to have made a mental note of his own cry of grief upon his father's death, so he could reproduce it in performance; and Coquelin divided the actor into two parts: a primary, intellectual self, which keeps tight control, and an emotional alter ego.

But while Coquelin practiced the cool-headed French method of calculating emotion, in England W. C. Macready was drawing, in performance, on his own grief over his daughter's death; and in Amer-

11

ica Clara Morris was insisting, "You must feel, or all the pretty and pathetic language in the world won't make other people feel. I never go on the stage but that about four o'clock in the afternoon I begin to suffer."[13] And in Italy one of Stanislavski's idols, Tommaso Salvini, made this unofficial response to Coquelin:

> An actor lives, weeps, and laughs on the stage, and all the while he is watching his own tears and smiles. It is this double function, this balance between life and acting that makes his art.[14]

Coquelin's twin selves—one emotes, the other plans strategies in advance and reins in the performance—and Salvini's "double function" *sound* like two interpretations of the same process. But the coexistence of emotion and thought in Salvini is quite different from Coquelin's emotional detachment, where no actual feeling takes place on stage. Between them, Coquelin and Salvini define the distance between acting that's all technique, and Stanislavski's system, which calls for "natural emotions *at the very moment* in which they appear before you in the flesh."[15]

Method actors' usual tool for channeling their own emotions is the device known as "affective memory." According to both Stanislavski and Boleslavsky, the turn-of-the-century psychologist Théodule Ribot coined the term, but there's a difference between what Boleslavsky means by "affective memory" and the way Method teachers like Lee Strasberg employ it. According to Boleslavsky:

> After having decided what is the feeling necessary for a certain part of his role, the actor tries to find in his affective memory a recollection similar to that particular feeling. He may use all kinds of means in order to bring that feeling to life, starting with the actual lines of the author and finishing with experiments from his own life, recollections from books and finally using his own imagination. Then by a series of gradual exercises and rehearsals he brings himself into a state, enabling him to arouse in the strongest degree the necessary feelings by a mere thought of it and to retain it for the necessary period of time.[16]

Boleslavsky is distinguishing between "affective memory" (you could substitute a benign phrase like "memory bank") and "memory of emotion," the most powerful of the exercises he refers to. But because "affective memory" had an appealing sound for the Americans he taught, it gradually came to represent his "memory of emotion."

Here's the great Method teacher Robert Lewis's definition of affective memory:

> The theory is that if, quietly relaxed, you think back over a certain incident in your life which moved you strongly at the time, and if you can remember and recreate in your mind the physical circumstances of that moment (where you were, who was there, what happened, the time of day, the place, surroundings) and start reliving it . . . it is possible that a feeling similar to what you felt at that time will recur.[17]

Americans tend to champion this particular exercise to the exclusion of the other facets of Boleslavsky's affective memory—in fact, to elevate the ability to elicit genuine emotion to the supreme achievement possible in naturalistic acting. And this preference isn't original with us. In *An Actor Prepares*, Stanislavski (in the role of Tortsov) admits, "I incline toward the *emotional side of creativeness* . . . purposely because we are too prone to leave out feeling."[18] However, between the time Stanislavski prepared his notes for the publication of *An Actor Prepares* and the time he began work on *Building a Character*, his ideas changed, and he shifted to stressing a more thoroughgoing physical and vocal training for the actor. The Method emphasis on the psychological/emotional side of acting comes from the attention the Group Theatre paid to Stanislavski's earlier book (which was, after all, the only one they had available to them in the 1930s). And Lee Strasberg made the quest for true emotion his personal crusade in his classes at the Actors Studio in the 1950s.

Robert Lewis, in *Method—or Madness?*, tried to redress the balance by describing the perils of affective memory. Twenty years later, in *Advice to the Players*, he repeated his warning:

> In choosing experiences from our own lives, we risk the chance of dredging up personal emotions that may not be apt for the character's feeling at all. They may be very true, but

13

rather reflect the way *you* would feel at that moment rather than the way the character would feel. You have to be very clever to find experiences that serve up the emotions analogous to the character and the situation in the play.[19]

Others outside the Method have been harsher. Charles Marowitz, the director and theorist, sees affective memory (which he calls by its popular alternate title, "emotional memory") as extremely dangerous:

> . . . an artificial and disruptive technique which can produce stunning results in the classroom but is chemically unsuited to the needs of performance. No technique which encourages an actor to introduce an emotional non-sequitur into his performance can be anything but misguided.[20]

Drawing on the Self

It was the Roman rhetorician Quintilian who first suggested that an actor "get to know his own peculiarities and . . . consult not merely the general rules of technique, but his own nature as well with a view to forming his delivery."[21] In the twentieth century the extent to which an actor ought to draw on that nature has become a fiery topic. Some argue that it's absurd for an actor to restrict the exploration of Othello or Blanche DuBois to his or her own puny personality. But in *An Actor Prepares*, Tortsov asks his students, "Do you expect an actor to invent all sorts of new sensations, or even a new soul, for every part he plays? How many souls would he be obliged to house? . . . You can borrow clothing, a watch, *things* of all sorts, but you cannot take *feelings* away from another person."[22] Robert Lewis, Charles Marowitz, and acting teachers Michael Chekhov and Robert Benedetti (among others) lay the blame for the frequent charge that Method actors tend to give the same performance over and over again to their habit of looking only within themselves for the role they're playing. But it's Stanislavski himself who calls for

> a super-objective which is in harmony with the intentions of the playwright and at the same time arouses a response in

the soul of the actors. That means that we must search for it not only in the play but in the actors themselves.[23]

This advice also—and importantly—implies that no actor is suited for every role.

Of all American Method teachers, Morris Carnovsky is the most passionate about the validity of "self" in acting, and his most eloquent defense of it comes in the form of an anecdote. He remembers a matinee of Clifford Odets's *Awake and Sing!*, one of the landmark productions of the Group Theatre, when he decided, "Today I'm going to relate to Stella Adler (who was playing my daughter in the play) not as my daughter, Bessie Berger, but as Stella Adler. I know it's Stella. . . . I don't have to say that's Bessie Berger. I don't have to do her creation for her." Carnovsky assumes Stella Adler's work in building the character of Bessie, as well as his own in playing Jacob; clearly he wouldn't attempt an experiment of this kind in an early rehearsal, before they'd both found their characters. This stripping-down to a basic dialogue between two actors who care about each other, which he swears brought greater relaxation and intimacy to their scenes together, is based on their common recognition that

> within that particular image [of Bessie Berger] there is an essential Stella whom I know and to whom I relate with my eyes, with my ears, with my senses, with my attitude. She at the same time is doing so to me in the same way—I hope. And this is what makes a scene. This is what makes it pulse.[24]

Of course, the critical complaint that an actor or actress always gives the same performance has become, especially since the sixties, not just a familiar accusation levelled against students of the Method but a whip for flogging *all* American actors, who are constantly being compared to the classically trained technicians of Great Britain and found wanting. It's been said of most of our greatest performers: Katharine Hepburn, Marlon Brando, Dustin Hoffman (perhaps less so since *Tootsie* and *Death of a Saleman*), Diane Keaton. It's rarely said of Robert De Niro, who gained fifty pounds to play Jake La Motta in *Raging Bull*, or Meryl Streep, because of her fiendish gift for duplicating accents.

15

The accepted wisdom in this case seems to me misguided. In *Respect for Acting,* Uta Hagen comes up with a more useful, common-sense distinction. Answering the student actor's question "If I must use myself, won't I be the same in every part I play?" Hagen draws a line between the actor who uses himself imaginatively and one

> who is *really* the same in every part he plays. . . . Because they are always the same does not mean that they are truly using themselves. They are simply playing the identical few notes in themselves over and over again without a real search or selection. . . . Often, after an initial success, these "personality" actors simply copy from themselves, imitating moments and effects which have worked for them before.[25]

Improvisation

A Method teacher who stresses the importance of staying in character at all times is effectively repeating the advice Albert Basserman gave the young Uta Hagen. In *Method—or Madness?*, Robert Lewis explains how difficult it is to train for this kind of consistency in the classroom, since student actors tend to choose big scenes to work on that aren't likely to soar without the firm foundation of the smaller scenes that precede them. Besides, in order for a performance to make complete sense, it has to take into account what the playwright omits as well as includes. (Anyone who's tackled Chekhov understands this principle.)

Stanislavski's answer to this problem was improvisation—another case in which he identified a device good actors had been employing for some time. The nineteenth-century American actress Minnie Maddern Fiske said that in preparation for playing Hedda Gabler she "staged in my own ghost theater" Hedda's first encounter with Lovborg, and all their subsequent meetings;[26] and Uta Hagen claims that even staunchly anti-Method performers like Alfred Lunt and Lynn Fontanne indulged in their own improvisations—such as playing an entire off-stage supper scene during Act IV of *The Sea Gull.* But Robert Lewis, always the pragmatist, warns that improvisation can "encourage a lack of form" and "a disrespect for the author's lines."[27] When he began to lecture publicly on the Method in the late 1950s,

16

Lewis found himself in the uncomfortable position of having to defend it against the attacks of critics (and actors, too) whose misunderstanding of it was largely based on the excesses they'd witnessed in bad, self-indulgent Method actors. And if you've seen bad Method— "Methody"—actors (and who hasn't?), you know that uncontrolled improvisation can have exactly the effect Lewis is afraid of.

Ensemble

Both the Meiningen Players and the Bancroft–Robertson team were high on the idea of ensemble as a performance ideal, and it's often been spoken of dreamily by Americans. A perilously difficult goal to attain, ensemble acting means more than just consistently good acting by all the members of a cast: It generally implies that everyone on stage is acting in exactly the same style, and it requires the delicate orchestration of group scenes. Unfortunately, the history of American drama and film actually contains few examples of it, though the Group Theatre certainly worked toward it. It may be the sad case that for American actors, who strive to create theater in a highly commercial context (one that supports the star system and is hostile to a democracy of performance), moments of intimate connection between individuals are often the closest they come to ensemble acting. I'd say that the best American examples of ensemble are Francis Ford Coppola's first two *Godfather* films and Robert Altman's winning streak of pictures in the early seventies, culminating in *Nashville*.

The Prop as a Method Instrument

The use of three-dimensional objects on the stage (as opposed to two-dimensional ones painted on the backdrop) predates not only Stanislavski but the realist movement itself. It began as an extension of the Romantic notion of drama as spectacle, which encouraged more and more elaborate set designs. Eugène Scribe, Victorien Sardou, and other authors who popularized the "well-made play" in the nineteenth century, employed stage objects selectively, creating an aura of meaning around them by making them essential to the unfolding of the plot. The realists, like Zola and Ibsen, adopted Scribe's dramatic focus on objects along with his entire well-made play structure, which they used as a convenient skeleton to be fleshed out by psychological realism and social issues. The result was the "social" or "problem" play, a drama dealing with a significant issue (the role of women in marriage in *A Doll's House,* slum housing in Shaw's *Widowers' Houses*, and so on).

As these playwrights deepened Scribean melodrama by adding thematic and psychological layers to it, the stage prop began to acquire new levels of meaning. And as naturalist philosophers campaigned for a complete reliance on the scientific method to understand, predict, and even control human behavior, man became the central natural object, fit to be examined under the scientist's microscope. So the stage object in these plays is not only a representative of the solid, three-dimensional world of cause and effect the realists wished to evoke, but also a symbol for that greater object, man. In Strindberg's *Miss Julie*, the boots belonging to Julie's father the Count take on a special significance when Jean, his valet, first polishes and then kicks them: Strindberg wants us to see Jean's enslavement to his employer, which even his supreme act of rebellion (degrading the Count's daughter by sleeping with her) can't alter. There are countless marvelous examples in Ibsen: the macaroons in *A Doll's House*, the books that shock Pastor Manders in *Ghosts*, the manuscript and the pistols in *Hedda Gabler*, the camera and the duck in *The Wild Duck*, to name just a few. When he looked for ways to help actors to illuminate the psychology of a character, Stanislavski naturally turned to the prop.

Mysticism in Acting

The notion of a mystical element in modern acting originates with Stanislavski, in some of his more elusive terminology (such as "irradiation," meaning communication between actors—a process a later generation would call "giving vibrations") and especially in his belief that great acting conjures up magic. That's really not as peculiar an idea as it sounds. Casting around for words to describe something wonderful we've seen at the theater or the movies, many of us tend to fall back on mystical words like "magical" or "miraculous." Most actors, amateur or professional, can recount the experience of feeling that, for one scene or even an entire performance, they seem drawn into all the right paths by forces they can't define. That is when an actor says, "I couldn't do anything wrong on that stage today."

Though we may substitute the word "instinct" or (Stanislavski's choice) "inspiration," or try to justify an actor's highest flights by the most commonplace, day-by-day training, still actors will tell you that, just as no can teach talent, so no amount of hard work can explain the most extraordinary moments in drama. Certainly the theater has always been a storehouse of superstitions, and since classical times performers have often considered themselves lucky targets for the mysterious gifts of the muses. But, though Stanislavski cautions against waiting for inspiration, it's a characteristic of some Method actors that they seem to incorporate the *expectation* of magic into their work, struggling to bring themselves to a feverish state in which they're prepared to receive it. This high degree of nervous intensity explains some of the excitement in the performance of Actors Studio prodigies like Julie Harris and James Dean.

Esthetically, the Method's roots are clearly in nineteenth-century realism, which, traveling from Europe, made its earliest contact in the United States with painters like Whistler and Thomas Eakins, and novelists like Dreiser and Frank Norris. In a *New Yorker* column on Eakins's work, appropriately titled "The Truth of Appearances," art critic Calvin Tomkins describes the 1871 painting "Max Schmitt in a Single Scull" as

> an almost perfect realization of the pragmatic ideal—of the evocation of the general through the particular. By paying infinitely close attention to precise details—to the way these men in their boats looked at that moment, on that river, in that light—Eakins achieved an image that goes beyond the moment and into the collective consciousness.[28]

Eakins's work, Tomkins argues, expands far beyond the accuracy of superficial details; a precise recreation of the familiar world allows us to see more and more behind its face. (Proust, of course, made the same discovery.) For Eakins, the reproduction of authentic details has a double function, situating us in the real world (his source) while it becomes an emblem of the emotional richness with which we endow the smallest details in our own lives, thereby allowing us to reach out to others who respond to the paintings in the same way. Tomkins reports that when Eakins was asked to counsel young artists, he advised them to "peer deeper into the heart of American life."

> The haunting presence in so many of his later portraits is the presence of the artist, who has looked so long and so unflinchingly at the surface of things that he has gone right through to the heart of them.[29]

When Lee Strasberg told one of his classes at the Actors Studio, "There are times when you pick up your shoes and see through them your whole life," he was expressing something much like the paradox Tomkins identifies in Eakins's paintings.

When fledgling director Joshua Logan visited Stanislavski in Moscow in 1931, he received the following advice:

> Our methods suit us because we are Russian. . . . You are American, you have a different economic system. You work at different times of the day. You eat different food and your ears are pleased by different music. You have different rhythms in your speech and in your dancing. And if you want to create a great theatre, all these things must be taken into consideration. They must be used to create your own method, and it can be as true and as great as any method yet discovered.[30]

The Method isn't merely an approach with which a small group of performers have experimented at one or two junctures in the recent history of American acting. It has been the locus of American acting since the late forties, and long before that it was the goal toward which serious American acting was striving. When you watch the 1930s movies of Barbara Stanwyck and Burgess Meredith, neither of whom ever performed with the Group Theatre, it's tough to distinguish what they do from the acting of the best Group players. That so strong a parallel exists between trained and untrained Method actors suggests that acting in this country had been geared toward the Method for some time, as does the movement toward greater realism in this country since the nineteenth century. When we define the Method, then, we really are defining modern American acting.

Not that Americans are alone in the attention they've paid to Stanislavski's work. When the English actress Billie Whitelaw describes the experience of performing Samuel Beckett's *Not I* as "a terrible inner scream, like falling backwards into hell . . . the scream that I never made when my son was desperately ill,"[31] she's speaking about acting in a way no one did before Stanislavski. His books validated psychological terminology as a vocabulary for working actors. And, despite Laurence Olivier's celebrated remark that he knew he'd found his character when he'd chosen the right nose, it would be as absurd to claim Olivier as an "external" actor as it would be to call Brando a purely "internal" one who ignores the vocal and physical differences between the characters he plays. However, it's undeniable that the manner in which Method acting approaches performance (particularly its concentration on verisimilitude, genuine emotion, and the use of the actor's own personality) has proven most amenable to American actors. I hope to suggest why.

Harold Clurman of the Group Theatre called the Method "a codified formalization of the technique of acting."[32] Following from Clurman's definition, Robert Lewis set out, in his 1957 lectures, to demystify it and discuss it in a reasonable, common-sensical, working actor's manner, as though it were nothing more than carefully observed process—technique rather than style. But, as film critic Hal Hinson has said, "Although Lewis' statement is in itself accurate, in retrospect his words ring with the naive assurance of a Baron Frankenstein who, having left his monster safely in chains, is unaware that it is ravaging the countryside."[33] A technique doesn't change; a style does—and we have only to compare the performances of John Garfield in the forties, Marlon Brando in the fifties, and Robert De Niro in the seventies to see that the distance between generations of Method actors chronicles the history of an American acting style.

2

PASSIONATE MODERATES

◆ ◆ ◆

We saw a very good movie, with Wallace Beery. He acts like life, very good.
—Bessie Berger, in *Awake and Sing!*[1]

The Group Theatre, where Stanislavski received his first professional workout in America, was mostly the inspiration of one person: Harold Clurman. But it resulted from a series of fortuitous encounters among a crowd of zealous, argumentative young theater people. Clurman's first stage experience was as an extra at the Provincetown Playhouse in 1924, where he saw Richard Boleslavsky in action as the replacement director for a Stark Young play called *The Saint*. After Clurman had begun to work for the prestigious Theatre Guild (initially as a stage manager and bit player and then, beginning in 1929, as a play reader), he enrolled in Boleslavsky's directing classes at the American Laboratory Theatre—partly at the urging of Lee Strasberg, a Guild friend who shared his discomfort at the current state of directing and acting on Broadway. At the Lab, Clurman met Stella Adler, daughter of the celebrated Yiddish Theatre performer Jacob Adler.

Clurman and Strasberg made their first (and unsuccessful) attempts at organizing their own theater as early as 1928. Then, when producer Theresa Helburn suggested to Clurman the formation of a supplementary Guild company to produce less conventional plays for a Sunday matinee subscription series, he enlisted Strasberg, as well as Cheryl Crawford (a friend working as an assistant stage manager for the Guild). The Theatre Guild Studio was short-lived—the Russian drama *Red Rust* was its only production, in 1929—but it did constitute a sort of training ground for the Group

Theatre, which began in 1931 under the shared management of these three.

In order to understand the aims and achievements of the Group Theatre, it's important to recall where America stood in the early days of the Depression. The official unemployment figure for 1930 was 3,500,000; by the end of the Group's first season (1931–32) it had almost quadrupled. And with the purchasing power of the average farmer reduced to half of what it had been ten years earlier, and with the Dust Bowl drought that ravaged the Midwest beginning in 1933, rural America was submerged even deeper in economic disaster than the cities were. Strikes and riots flared up everywhere—among farmers, longshoremen, truckers, auto workers, taxi drivers (the subject of *Waiting for Lefty*, which Clifford Odets wrote for the Group in 1935). Moreover, since management normally employed scabs to replace strikers, and stooges to smash picket lines, and since even this early in American labor history some unions were already corrupt, infected with gangsterism, strikes often resulted in shocking outbreaks of violence.

Chronicling these troubled times was America's first generation of left-wing writers: novelists, poets, journalists, and playwrights. Some boasted membership in the Communist or Socialist Party, others proudly called themselves fellow travelers. Some were self-proclaimed "proletarian" writers, others just shocked observers of the desperate social and economic scene. Leftist periodicals published the writing, vivid and immediate at its best, of Albert Maltz, Tom Kromer, Robert Cantwell, Grace Lumpkin, Michael Gold, Edward Dahlberg, Edward Anderson, Kenneth Fearing, Dalton Trumbo, Humphrey Cobb, Mary Keaton Vorse, John Howard Lawson, Erskine Caldwell—and some whose fame would outdistance this concerned epoch: Ernest Hemingway, John Dos Passos, John Steinbeck, Richard Wright, Edna St. Vincent Millay.

Out of this cacophony of literary protest and pleading—the fervent efforts of alarmed intellectuals to put the country on an S.O.S. alert—new clichés grew up. The country, even the world, was now seen to consist of two factions: the virtuous workers and the evil Fascist bosses. Suddenly the American masses were the subjects of a great collective melodrama; their past sins of ignorance and pettiness and greed (recorded in the naturalist literature of the previous thirty years) washed miraculously away, they became symbols of what had been

done to them and what must be done to counteract it. In a characteristic report on the San Francisco longshoremen's strike of 1934, Tillie
Lerner described "a pregnant woman standing on a corner, outlined
against the sky, and she might have been a marble, rigid, eternal,
expressing some vast and nameless sorrow."[2]

Educated middle-class men and women, who had previously
maintained a cautious distance from those whose socioeconomic
status they had risen above, now craved identification with them.
"I'm not the civilized type, Mr. Fayette," exclaims the lab assistant
who refuses to be a company spy in Clifford Odets's crowd-pleaser
Waiting for Lefty. "Nothing suave or sophisticated about me."[3]
Broadway audiences cheered the International Ladies' Garment
Workers' Union chorus in the opening number of Harold Rome's
Pins and Needles:

> *VARIOUS MEMBERS OF THE*
> *ENSEMBLE:*
> *We're not George M. Cohans or*
> *Noel Cowards*
> *Or Beatrice Lillies*
> *Or Willie Howards.*
>
> *We've never played in stock or*
> *studied at the Playhouse*
> *And the only line we've ever said*
> *in a Broadway house is:*
>
> *GIRL:*
> *Which way to the gallery?*
>
> *VARIOUS MEMBERS OF THE*
> *ENSEMBLE:*
> *The dancing we've done has been*
> *for fun at the Savoy or Webster*
> *Hall.*
>
> *And our singing too. . . .*

24

It's the bathtub kind and rough
But it's always been good enough
For meetings, parades and for
Picket lines.[4]

As glaring and insistent as a political cartoon, the worst of this writing was insufferably repetitive, haranguing, peppered with editorial comment, and burdened with a sanctimonious, salt-of-the-earth pose: Authors tended to banalize their diction by infusing it with a fraudulent plain-folksiness. Proletarian literature strained for the impossible—it wanted to embrace the masses and romanticize them at the same time, which meant keeping an esthetic distance while seeking to eliminate it. (This peculiar mixture of affectations reached its apotheosis with the publication of Steinbeck's *The Grapes of Wrath* in 1939.) No wonder so much of the prose of the period is more lumpy than *lumpen*.

There were some writers, though, who broke through with a vibrant new style that truly expressed something akin to revolutionary fervor, or else genuine sorrow. Occasional patches of exciting prose validated the creaking agit-prop structure of much leftist periodical literature. In the hands of the best recorders of the Depression, the freedom to employ street vernacular energized the writing and forged a bond between the author and the readers, who could plunge into the recognizable cadence of workaday dialogue and rejoice that it had given value to their experience. When this happened a new tone, a national feeling exclusive to the 1930s, found a voice—as it did in novels like Horace McCoy's *They Shoot Horses, Don't They?* and Edward Anderson's *Thieves Like Us*, and in the best plays of the Group Theatre's Clifford Odets.

Rejoicing was actually a significant (if generally the least convincing) part of the literature of the Depression. Optimism held a firm place in the Marxist ethic and, of course, in the rhetoric that poured forth from the White House during Franklin Roosevelt's tenure. "I'm a child of the thirties," director Elia Kazan, who began as a supporting player at the Group Theatre, has said in interviews. "There's still something in me of the thirties which says, 'There will be a better world some day. We are going through a terrible struggle now, but it's not for ever and it's not inevitable.' "[5] And perhaps the most zealous optimists were the European Jewish immigrants who made up a large and vocal part of the radical–intellectual population in the thirties. According to Irving Howe, "An infection of hope had seized these Jews, not really for themselves (a possibility their sardonic realism taught them to discount), but hope at once passionate and abstract, fixed equally upon America and their children. Whatever their faith or opinions, they felt that here in America the Jews had at least a chance. . . ."[6] The flavor of intellectual discourse in this country in the 1930s was distinctly Jewish—for example, in the *Partisan Review*, which occupied an influential position in American literary and political intellectual circles. The temperament and upbringing of these first- and second-generation American Jews equipped them for involvement in the Left. Howe reports that he "felt awed by this outpouring of language"[7] at the first Socialist meeting he attended: The rhetoric appealed to his Talmudic side, and the extroverted, openly emotional nature of Socialist debate must have struck a deep chord in him as well.

This was the world that gave birth to the Group Theatre, a world to which, as artists and intellectuals and—in most cases—as Jews, they responded. (Among the best-known members of the Group, and the ones who carried the most weight in decisions, Kazan, an immigrant Greek from Turkey, was perhaps the only non-Jew. Harold Clurman, Stella and Luther Adler, Morris Carnovsky, Lee Strasberg, Clifford Odets, John Garfield, Robert Lewis, and the set designer Mordecai Gorelik all emerged from European Jewish stock.) As men and women of the theater, of course, they resided in another world as well; and what they felt to be its inadequacies prompted their rebellion in the form of the Group Theatre.

In the early thirties, as at any other time in the history of American theater, most commercially successful Broadway fare was purely escapist. Among Broadway's hits between 1929 and 1931 were the musicals *Fifty Million Frenchmen, Flying High,* and *The Band Wagon;* the prison melodrama *The Last Mile;* the Victorian weeper *The Barretts of Wimpole Street;* a retelling of the Old Testament as a Negro folk fable, *The Green Pastures;* and a spate of comedies, including *Strictly Dishonorable, Sons of Guns, Once in a Lifetime,* and the Noel Coward import *Private Lives.* Most theater of a weightier bent was doled out solemnly by the Theatre Guild, which had seized the role of cultural minister to the New York theater in 1919. Its first fifteen seasons featured plays by Shaw, Molnar, Andreyev, Kaiser, Capek, Ibsen, Claudel, Toller, Pirandello, Jonson, Goethe, and Turgenev, and Jacques Copeau's adaptation of Dostoevski's *The Brothers Kara-mazov*. Among the American works the Guild produced were Elmer Rice's *The Adding Machine*, Sidney Howard's *They Knew What They Wanted* and *The Silver Cord*, DuBose and Dorothy Heyward's *Porgy*, Lynn Riggs's *Green Grow the Lilacs*, Philip Barry's allegorical *Hotel Universe*, Rodgers and Hart's parodic *Garrick Gaieties* revues, and three of Eugene O'Neill's most elaborate experiments: *Marco Millions*, *Strange Interlude*, and *Mourning Becomes Electra*.

There's much to be said in favor of a company pledged to bring the most provocative new plays, both American and European, to Broadway audiences. But Clurman deals harshly with the Guild in his Group Theatre chronicle, *The Fervent Years*:

> They were admirers rather than makers. They were imitators rather than initiators, buyers and distributors rather than first settlers or pioneers. . . . [They] had no blood relationship with the plays they dealt in. . . . They didn't want to say anything through plays, and plays said nothing to them, except that they were amusing in a graceful way, or, if they were tragic plays, that they were "art." And art was a good thing. . . . As a result they chose plays of the most conflicting tendencies, and produced them all with the same generalized Broadway technique, though in better taste than the average. All the productions were rather pretty (with a kind of disguised middle-class stuffiness) and they nearly always lacked passion or pointedness. . . . The Guild's tone was almost always undifferentiatedly correct or standard, according to the nearly latest models, because back of it was no individual drive, only a dilettante acceptance of something someone else—eminently worthy—had first created.[8]

It was the aim of the Group Theatre to provide precisely the kind of theater the Guild, according to Clurman, had failed to: a theater where the choice of plays reflected social and political values shared by the Left-leaning members of the Group and were performed in a style both distinctive to the Group and consistent with their values. With that end in mind, the three directors set up a structure that would allow the free exchange of ideas among the actors, playwrights, designers, and themselves. This plan resulted, unsurprisingly, in a kind of besieged democracy. Arguments ran rampant and tempers high, and somebody (usually one of the directors) was invariably under attack.

The cornerstone of the Group style was to be the Stanislavskian acting technique several of them had been exposed to for the first time in Boleslavsky's classes at the American Laboratory Theatre. Deeply conscious of their role as cultural innovators introducing this new approach to performance into the American theater, the company spent a great deal of time studying acting, and often months preparing their productions—a length of time unprecedented in professional theater (where a show is usually put up in a month), and divided evenly among lectures on theater history and Group Theatre philosophy (by Clurman and Strasberg), workshops (generally conducted by Strasberg), and rehearsals.

Before the Group, American repertory theater had been largely restricted to the little (amateur) theaters, such as the Provincetown Playhouse. The only professional repertory was Eva Le Gallienne's Civic Repertory Company, which opened in 1926 and closed in the early thirties. Political theater, too, was restricted to amateurs in the pre–Group days; the Workers' Laboratory Theatre, the Proletbuehne, and other Socialist troupes performed only for union meetings and labor rallies. The Group's commitment to produce plays of social significance came out of a collective impulse among politically conscious theater people, the same impulse that accounts for the proletarian writers. It yielded more radical fruit than the Group Theatre: the Organization of the League of Workers Theatres (1932), which was the professional wing of labor theater; the Theatre Union (1933), founded by Sherwood Anderson and others—a self-proclaimed "proletarian theater" proclaiming bigotry as its target and pacifism as its credo; and the Federal Theatre Project (1936), the theatrical branch of the government-subsidized Works Progress Administration, most famous for producing *The Living Newspaper*. Then there was the New Theatre League, an organization that attempted to unify the rapidly growing number of amateur and professional groups (by 1935, it was handling some three hundred) and published *New Theatre Magazine*, the major leftist drama journal of the decade.

The Group Theatre was actually the least radical of these theaters and leagues, with no stated allegiance to any leftist organization. Clur-

28

man claims that when the Group started out in 1931, no one had any specific political agenda. But by 1932 a "sudden preoccupation with social, economic and political matters was like a fever running through our camp,"[9] and though the Group's three directors—Clurman, Cheryl Crawford, and Lee Strasberg—continued to keep the company itself free of ties to political organizations, by the mid–1930s some of the Group members had joined the Communist Party (including, briefly, Clifford Odets), and all of them had been drawn into political activity in some way. Group members found themselves directing plays for the Theatre of Action, giving classes at the Theatre Collective School, fighting Actors Equity battles, studying economic and social conditions in Cuba, boycotting Japanese products, raising funds during the Spanish Civil War. And, inevitably, this political concern colored the productions of the Group Theatre, which had dedicated itself from the outset to producing drama of social conscience, and whose dedication seldom wavered in the years of its existence.

> The question which naturally arose in sensitive people's minds was, "What are we doing here? In what way are we members of our time? In what way are we contributing to the contemporary theatre?" . . . Suddenly they [the Group actors] found that life was a rather bitter thing; it was sometimes pitched in a minor key. It was not possible then for us of the Group Theatre to accept a play like *Dinner at Eight*, good as it may be. . . . That was not our kind of play.[10]

Morris Carnovsky's reference to "our kind of play" begins to explain the choices the Group made when putting together its seasons. Mordecai Gorelik made the oft-quoted remark that all of the Group plays shared a common theme: "What shall it profit a man if he gain the whole world and lose his own soul?"[11] The theater's premiere production was Paul Green's *The House of Connelly*, which dealt with a post-bellum South struggling to rid itself of the corruption of its past; and subsequent plays took a firm stand against capitalistic greed (*Success Story*, *Gold Eagle Guy*); war (*Johnny Johnson*); fascism (*Night Over Taos*, *The Gentle People*, Odets's *Till The Day I Die*); and the wage slavery of the common man (*1931—*, *Waiting for Lefty*). Others preached the virtues of personal integrity (*Gentlewoman*, Odets's *Golden Boy*), professional integrity (*Men in White*) and political activ-

29

ism (*Thunder Rock*). Still others articulated the sorrows of the working class (*The Case of Clyde Griffiths*, adapted from Theodore Dreiser's *An American Tragedy*), the lower middle class (Odets's *Awake and Sing!*), the solid middle class (Odets's *Paradise Lost*), and the unemployed (Odets's *Night Music*). Carnovsky says, "Early on we heard our directors assert that every good play is propaganda for a better life,"[12] and the Group sought only plays that would answer that description.

In his book *The Drama of Attack*, Sam Smiley divides leftist theater of the 1930s into four categories (plays of individual, social, collective, and revolutionary protest), and lists four different methods of dramatic protest (to depict, to exhort, to accuse, to censure). He includes at least one Group play as an example of each.[13] Consistent with the demands of revolutionary theater that a play end affirmatively (usually with a "call to action"), the Group even insisted from time to time that a playwright change his original ending if they felt it was too downbeat. *The House of Connelly*, *Men in White*, and even the homegrown *Awake and Sing!* all passed through considerable final-act alterations to make them consistent with this principle.

Norris Houghton, writing in 1938, expressed the Group Theatre credo as follows: "We believe that art has to have a close and immediate relationship to the people from whom it springs."[14] In that spirit, the company restricted itself to American plays on American themes. Clurman stated repeatedly, in answer to his critics, that the Group would happily have scheduled revivals of European classics among their seasons of new American plays if they'd been able to find backers. But his dismay (mentioned more than once in *The Fervent Years*) that playwright Maxwell Anderson tended to veer away from American subject matter and to seek a verse style that couldn't support American diction suggests that the Group felt little affinity with European drama. In 1939, with the search for a new script so far unsuccessful, Clurman and Stella Adler did begin work on a production of *The Three Sisters* (a project they eventually abandoned). But Clurman's view of the play, preserved in his notes, reveals an idiosyncratic American vision:

> To me *The Three Sisters* is a very American play because it deals with young people. This reminds me of an American town, with its high school, its teachers, its Rural Board—much of the atmosphere in a small town in 1925. Main

30

Street, U.S.A., has a general relationship to the small town life of this play. [15]

Almost all the Group's productions were set in large American cities or their suburbs, and many contained a variety of ethnic types. Leftist literature not only acknowledged the melting pot, it celebrated it—for this was the era in which a slang reference to a man's racial background could be intended not as a slur but as an affectionate tribute to the individual strain he contributed to the immense *lumpen-proletariat*. No audience in 1935 would have thought these lines from *Waiting for Lefty* racist:

> That Wop's got more guts than a slaughter house. Maybe a traffic jam got him, but he'll be here. . . . We gotta make up our minds. . . . It's plain as the nose on Sol Feinberg's face we need a strike.

Men in White and Group Theatre Technique

A theatrical troupe of white, middle-class Americans, vitally concerned with the moral and social issues of their time but without a collective commitment to any one political group, would tend naturally toward the kind of drama Sidney Kingsley's *Men in White* represents. (*Lefty* became a popular favorite among proletarian theaters, but it was an exception; the audience for Group plays—the Broadway audience— was overwhelmingly middle class. And Clifford Odets, the author of *Lefty*, came from the middle class and was most comfortable writing in that milieu.) Conscientious and worthy, but reduced by its overstated good intentions to a kind of bland inoffensiveness, *Men in White*, produced in 1933, rallied the Group's sinking financial resources and remained its longest-running production. It was an early example of the American "problem" play. Like their European precursors, American playwrights such as Kingsley and Elmer Rice (*Street Scene*) focused on moral questions. These were the more moderate, thoughtful cousins of the overheated proletarian writers—but they shared with them a strictly high-school civics-class iconography with clear demarcations for good and evil, triumph and defeat. Their reluctance to present an issue in all its ambiguity was, of course, a product of a time

31

that disliked clouded moral pictures. But long after the Depression was over, American problem drama continued to do the audience's work for them, sorting out all the arguments and underscoring the correct one.

It's not difficult to see why such a pedantic approach has always attracted audiences. After watching a play like *Men in White*, in which a gifted young intern (played by Alexander Kirkland) must decide between marrying an empty-souled socialite fiancée who cares only for amusement, and apprenticing to a brilliant surgeon who urges him to devote himself to study, we can congratulate ourselves for applauding the moral rectitude of the intern's final decision—as if the play gave him any real choice!—and for having spent a "serious" evening at the theater. Playwrights like Kingsley and Rice were neither poets nor journalists, but they did possess enough skill to stir up some genuine feeling. *Street Scene* is a very effective slice of ghetto life; and a banal drama on the order of *Men in White*, when it's as well acted and directed as Lee Strasberg's original production reportedly was, can work up considerable power—the power of the familiar. *Men in White* was a hit, and an influential one: The first hospital drama, it resurfaced in movies throughout the thirties and forties, and finally in the fifties and sixties on television, the perfect, the *inevitable* medium for the American problem play. Closer to home, it probably suggested the "Interne Episode" in *Waiting for Lefty*. (When Hollywood picked up the rights to Kingsley's play in 1934, the director assigned to the film turned out to be none other than Richard Boleslavsky.)

Carnovsky claims that "the kind of inner technique that we were acquiring made us the logical people to do that particular play."[16] *Men in White* really made the Group's reputation, even though their first show, *The House of Connelly*, had received an enthusiastic press. For it was *Men in White* that first provided the company with an opportunity to exercise the acting values Strasberg had been communicating to them in his workshops.

In the course of writing *Men in White*, Kingsley had spent many hours in hospitals, observing operations and building up an acquaintanceship with doctors and nurses in order to reproduce the details of their everyday lives. Taking their cue from him, the cast visited hospitals, too, and doctors attended rehearsals to instruct them on medical procedure. "The Group Theatre built up a set of actors and actresses who were extraordinarily reliable in small parts," Clifford Odets later recalled. "You'd give somebody five lines and say this woman is a nurse, and the actress would go away and she would become a nurse to the life. She thought about how a nurse waddles, what kind of shoes she would wear, why she walks the way she does, and what her professional mannerisms are."[17] The high point of the production was evidently Act II, Scene 4 (the "operating room" scene), which begins, in the published edition of the text, with three pages of stage directions. Critics claimed that the clarity of detail and the purposefulness of the action increased the tension of the scene and made this long passage without dialogue riveting on the stage.

This sequence must have benefited from Strasberg's talent for keeping explosive emotional scenes under tight rein. According to Clurman:

> He is the director of introverted feeling, of strong emotion curbed by ascetic control, sentiment of great intensity muted by delicacy, pride, fear, shame. The effect he produces is a classic hush, tense and tragic, a constant conflict so held in check that a kind of beautiful spareness results. . . . Above everything, the feeling in Strasberg's production is never stagy. Its roots are clearly in the intimate experience of a complex psychology, an acute awareness of human contradiction and suffering, a distinguished though perhaps a too specialized sensibility.[18]

This "too specialized sensibility" is connected to Strasberg's most salient—and controversial—quality as both a director and a teacher:

> Strasberg was a fanatic on the subject of true emotion. He sought it with the patience of an inquisitor, he was outraged by trick substitutes, and when he had succeeded in stimulating it, he husbanded it, fed it, and protected it. Here was something new to most of the actors, something basic, something almost holy. It was revelation in the theatre; and Strasberg was its prophet.[19]

The reports on *Men in White* seem to agree that the production demonstrated a new level of emotional verisimilitude and spontaneity. Edith Isaacs, writing in *Theatre Arts Monthly*, said it was "as revealing as a group photograph,"[20] and Helen Westley, the character actress, compared it to watching an accident.[21]

The spontaneity, of course, was directly related to the central element in Strasberg's workshop sessions, improvisation. He'd already made it a production element in *The House of Connelly* by giving the leading actor, Franchot Tone, a series of choices rather than set directions for a particular scene. The fact that Tone changed his performance slightly every night, and the rest of the company didn't know which route he would take, was meant to keep the acting fresh. According to Robert Lewis, all of Act II, Scene 1 of *Men in White* (the meeting of the hospital's board of directors) was improvised in rehearsal, Kingsley sitting in the audience and jotting down all the best lines and bits of business the actors came up with. Although whatever freshness this scene may have had on stage never translated well onto the page, its stiff, satirical portraits of the money-minded hospital directors, meant to contrast with those of the nobly intentioned doctors and nurses encountered in the previous act, are of some historical interest. They hint at what the political sketches the Group performed in class, at fund raisers for various causes, and on the bill with *Waiting for Lefty* at its first press performance in 1935 might have been like.

The name "Group Theatre" underscores one of Clurman's primary goals: a company without stars, in which the level of acting would be consistently high throughout. The Group's usual procedure was to choose plays with large casts, then work on vivifying each small portion of the group picture. *Men in White* had a cast of twenty-eight. The most enormous shows the company performed were *Gold Eagle Guy*, with sixty roles; *Johnny Johnson*, with fifty-eight speaking parts and a chorus; and *1931—*, with forty-five speaking parts and assorted extras. A fat roster like this demanded a high level of ensemble playing (as well as some double casting), especially since, in the philosophy of the Group, each role, no matter how small, is distinctive. Part of the director's job was to emphasize these vignettes without sacrificing the integrity of the strong main plot, or else the drama would play like a series of blackout sketches and its point, about professional ethics and lifestyle values—the reason the Group selected the play to begin with—would be lost. Strasberg's knack for creating an authentic atmosphere apparently solved the problem of dramatic balance: He provided a vivid milieu that motivated (and therefore unified) the actions of everyone on stage. His attentiveness to individual actors in large group scenes was famous; sometimes he would spend half an hour coaching one extra.

The surgery pantomime at the bottom of the second act of *Men in White* depended as much on the actors' deftness with physical objects as it did on their psychological preparations. In the light of the heightened emotional context (the patient on the operating table is a young nurse, pregnant by the intern hero), the tools in the hands of the medics take on more significance. And the deliberate exclusion of dialogue as a dramatic element throws the weight of the scene on the physical actions to which these props are linked.

So Kingsley's play, with its whirling simultaneous-plot structure, its constantly shifting focus, its presentation of men and women whose commitment to medicine makes them try (with varying success) to suppress their instincts to lead normal lives, offered Strasberg and the Group an ideal vehicle for the emotionally "true," painstakingly researched ensemble technique they were striving to refine. Other Group plays, such as the previous season's failure, *Night Over Taos*, and the next year's *Gold Eagle Guy*, presented difficulties for actors trained to home in on contemporary American realities. *Men in White* showed off what they did best.

Clifford Odets

The youth of the Group—the average age at the outset of the first season was twenty-seven—made their overwhelming reforming energy possible. Almost everyone who's written about the Group has stressed that it was, in Clurman's words, "an experiment in living."[22] The kind of probing and self-questioning carried on in acting class and rehearsal forged an intimacy too intense to be shut off afterwards; and anyway, the thinking was that whatever concerned an actor privately automatically became a potential creative fuel source. The Group was training completely sensitized Stanislavskian actors. Many of them lived in a communal house known as Groupstroy (the Russian moniker is a reminder of the pervasive Soviet influence on the liberal Left of the thirties), where they shared cooking and other household duties and eked out a scarcely solvent existence which their camaraderie, and their consciousness that they were attempting something bold and new, turned into an adventure. Stella Adler has said that the actors "responded to the social situation, to the group quality of not being alienated or alone."[23] Unfortunately, this need for a communal experience in the midst of the Depression is one aspect of the Group Theatre historians have neglected to acknowledge.

In a sense Groupstroy, waging its daily battle against economic hardship, paralleled the Group Theatre itself, whose "piecemeal, bread-line existence,"[24] Clurman claims, is the chief reason the Group experienced so much inner turmoil and finally collapsed of exhaustion in 1941. What Clurman fails to see is that this constant struggle also explains, to a great extent, the energy and excitement of the Group enterprise, which sketched way past the decade in which the company actually performed. You can hear these qualities in the reminiscences of the Group actors, and—more importantly—you can see it in their performances on film and kinescope, almost all of them given after the demise of the Group itself.

Clifford Odets was the only playwright the Group Theatre had—could ever have had—with a complete and intimate knowledge of their way of working. He began as an actor in the company, living in Groupstroy. Clurman's dream for this theater incorporated playwrights into the group structure: They would observe rehearsals, engage in dialogue with the actors, and change text according to the needs of the performers as much as to the specifications of the director. This redefining of the playwright as only one part of a theatrical whole apparently began as early as the improvised boardroom scene in *Men in White*. But only Clifford Odets, caught up early on in the Group's building process, was the ensemble–naturalist–Method playwright they needed. When the Group achieved its greatest critical success in 1935, it was with a trio of Odets plays (*Waiting for Lefty*, *Awake and Sing!*, and *Paradise Lost*). Stanislavski reportedly advised Harold Clurman, "Tell Mr. Odets for me not to give up acting. It will always help him in his playwriting."[25]

"When I write," Odets once said, ". . . what comes out is something that is very natural and very easy for actors to speak because it has always been spoken."[26] Odets's influence on American acting began early in 1935 when audiences heard, for the first time, the astonishing opening line of *Waiting for Lefty*: "You're so wrong I ain't laughing." The strategy of starting a play *in medias res* was established by the Greeks, but no one before Odets had begun a play at the climax of a scene, with all the characters already on stage. For once, a play-

36

wright was really testing the realists' notion of the audience as a fourth wall by plunging us into the middle of a heated debate. You can see the superficial influence of the German Expressionist playwrights and the epic theater of Bertolt Brecht on this play in the short, cinematic scenes, the attempts (however unconvincing) at an editorial chorus, the direct address to the audience. But Odets's loyalty is clearly to the naturalistic camp. He breaks down the barrier between actors and audience in order to make us part of the dramatic action, not distance us from it. The characters acknowledge onlookers straight through the play, but as if they were fellow cab drivers in a union hall; Odets tests the fourth wall by exploding it and then rebuilding it on the far side of the theater.

Some of what made *Lefty* such an immediate experience for Depression audiences—Odets's choice to draw his subject matter from recent headlines (the New York cabbies' strike in February and March of 1934)—is no longer available to us. But the startling use of the vernacular in the opening speech, instantly establishing a milieu for the play, and the quick, broad-stroke painting of the corrupt union chief, Harry Fatt (who speaks those first words), still have the power to establish the immediate emotional contact with the viewer (or reader) that made the play a scandalous success in 1935. Left-wing acting troupes all over the country, mostly amateur, made *Lefty* part of their repertory in the thirties. At one point thirty-two companies were performing it simultaneously; and, since some cities refused to license productions of such an incendiary play, the New Theatre League was constantly engaged in court battles over it—thirty-five by 1939. A figure too large, and equipped with too many human markings, to remain in the realm of the political cartoon, Harry Fatt is both caricature and flesh, custom-built for an actor who will awaken him to life.

Odets wrote two one-act and five full-length plays for the Group: *Waiting for Lefty, Awake and Sing!, Paradise Lost, Till the Day I Die, Golden Boy, Rocket to the Moon,* and *Night Music,* all produced between 1935 and 1940 and all illustrating a constant awareness of the actor's problems and the actor's perspective. He even goes so far, in his prefatory stage directions for *Awake and Sing!,* as to provide a "spine" or "through-line" for the play: "All of the characters . . . share a fundamental activity: a struggle for life amidst petty conditions."

One of the best specific examples of the way Odets incorporates the acting process into his texts can be found in the second act of

Paradise Lost, in a scene written for Stella Adler, the Group's leading actress. This is the last in a series of three episodes illustrating the pathetic condition of the middle-aged, middle-class Gordons, Leo and Clara. First, Leo's partner, Sam Katz, concerned about the financial strain on their business, suggests they hire an arsonist, Mr. May. When Leo, outraged, throws the arsonist out, Sam confesses to embezzling funds from the company. Leaving the Gordons alone to contemplate this latest in a series of disasters, Odets shows how Clara, a decent woman, moves slowly from anger and despair to a willingness to make a moral compromise. Odets doesn't announce Clara's emotional changes, but a careful reading of the scene shows how Odets has calibrated it to set in motion an actor's attention to beat shifts:

> **CLARA:** For God's sake, do yourself a personal favor and listen to me! What will *we* do, *now?*
>
> **LEO:** We'll go on living.
>
> **CLARA:** Oh, I married a fool. (Prowls and picks up article. Puts it down.) I married a fool. (Picks up another article; replaces it.) Yes, a fool.
>
> **LEO:** Yes . . .
>
> **CLARA:** (picks up card left by MAY): What is this?
>
> **LEO:** He left a card.
>
> **CLARA:** Who?
>
> **LEO:** The man to make the fire. (CLARA reads the card. Puts it down, walks to fix windows for the night; goes back to card.)
>
> **CLARA:** Beaumont? Where is that?
>
> **LEO:** What?
>
> **CLARA:** Beaumont 6922—
>
> **LEO:** Across the river. (Upstairs PEARL begins to range over the keyboard in light fleet exercises.)
>
> **CLARA:** What kind of name is that, May?
>
> **LEO:** I don't know.
>
> **CLARA** (putting down card): Tomorrow you'll go over the books?
>
> **LEO:** The accountant.
>
> **CLARA:** (after arranging another detail, at other end of room. Goes

back and re-peruses card. Finally brings it forward to LEO whose back is to her): What did you say to him?

LEO: To who?

CLARA: To him. . . .

LEO (in a low voice): I said no.

CLARA: Leo, we live once. . . . [Act II]²⁷

Odets uses Clara's restlessness, her habitual fidgety way of arranging the house, to trace a path back to the central prop—Mr. May's calling card—and as a metaphor for the psychological journey that brings her to a grim realization of their circumstances. (The scene is also a two-minute Marxist object lesson in how economics undermines ethics.) Clara travels an enormous distance in the course of this passage, yet there isn't a line or action that seems odd or intrusive. Odets piles detail upon commonplace detail, in Clara's words as well as her movements, to build a dramatic moment that is anything but commonplace.

The most successful episodes in *Lefty*, "Joe and Edna" (an acting-class perennial), "The Young Hack and His Girl," and "The Young Actor"—which Odets later unwisely removed—work because each depicts a shared human connection. Odets's dialogue advances and recedes with his characters, always reminding the actors to listen to each other. Only the tacked-on grandstanding scene endings demanded by the rules of Left-wing theater—"For a moment EDNA stands triumphant" (when she's persuaded Joe to commit himself to the strike), and the Stenographer's tip to the starving young actor to go out and read *The Communist Manifesto*—seem dated. When Odets breaks the rules, leaving "The Young Hack and His Girl" with a downbeat ending, he does his most honest writing in the play.

Because his dialogue has such an authentic urban ring, even the play's speechmakers have human dimensions. Odets mixes realism with a kind of jagged poetry: "They'll tear Christ off his bleeding cross. They'll wreck your homes and throw your babies in the river. You think that's bunk?" And he combines earthiness with propaganda: "These slick slobs stand here telling us about bogeymen. That's a new one for the kids—the reds is bogeymen! But the man who got me food in 1932, he called me Comrade!" He finds the music in street jargon: "You're so wrong I ain't laughing. Any guy with eyes to read knows it."

He introduces irony in the midst of crisis—"Christ, we're dyin' by inches! For what? For the debutant-ees to have their sweet comin' out parties in the Ritz!"—shifting the rhythms of the language to keep both the actors and the audience constantly engaged.

Odets's dialogue was his greatest gift to American acting. He built breathing spaces into it, so that it speaks even on the page: "But Fatt's right. Our officers is right. The time ain't ripe. Like a fruit don't fall off the tree until it's ripe." His best plays—*Lefty*, *Awake and Sing!*, *Paradise Lost*, and *Night Music*—feature a highly varied verbal landscape. Hopeless when he makes a concerted effort to be "poetic" (as in much of *Golden Boy*), Odets is most genuinely poetic when he draws on his homegrown talents for reproducing the vernacular ("His hands got free wheeling" [*Awake and Sing!*]); for redeeming the ungrammatical ("In business 'intimately' don't grow hair on a bald man's head" [*Paradise Lost*]); for infusing everyday conversation with colorful metaphor and hyperbole ("But we're stalled like a flivver in the snow," "Honey, I rode the wheels off the chariot today" [*Waiting for Lefty*]); for punching lines by abbreviating them (the opening lines of *Awake and Sing!*: "Where's advancement down the place? Work like crazy! Think they see it? You'd drop dead first"); or by injecting them with a distinctly Jewish brand of sarcasm, as in this key speech by Bessie Berger, the mother of *Awake and Sing!*:

> Ralphie, I worked too hard all my years to be treated like dirt. It's no law we should be stuck together like Siamese twins. Summer shoes you didn't have, skates you never had, but I bought a new dress every week. A lover I kept—Mr. Gigolo! Did I ever play a game of cards like Mrs. Marcus? Or was Bessie Berger's children always the cleanest on the block?! [Act III]

Odets validates the ensemble ethic by writing distinctive dialogue for each character. For Moe Axelrod, the hard-boiled World War I veteran in *Awake and Sing!*, he provides this entrance line: "Hello, girls, how's your whiskers?" Hennie Berger's pitiful husband, the immigrant Sam Feinschreiber, talks in Yiddish pidgin English: "I fell in the chair like a dead." Siggie, the cab driver in *Golden Boy*, tells his wife affectionately, "Shut the face, foolish."[28] In *Night Music*, Steve

Takis's diction reflects his proudly forged individual style: "A morato-
rium on the eating! Please!," "Your whole manner's anti-cupid!"[29] This
detailed attention to supporting characters extends the lesson Odets
learned from Strasberg when playing small roles in Group productions:
that every actor on the stage needs to develop a complete and truthful
inner life. In these plays the minor characters often are as memorable
as the protagonists, and the reminiscences of the men and women who
were involved in these shows are peppered with fond recollections of
Elia Kazan's portrayal of the homosexual gangster, Fuseli, in *Golden
Boy*, Robert Lewis's Mr. May, John Garfield's Siggie.

The best dialogue in Odets tends to be the most specifically Jewish. Like a well-trained Method actor, Odets reproduces snatches of
his own past, especially in *Awake and Sing!* (In her Freudian biography of Odets, Margaret Brenman-Gibson points out that certain key
phrases in *I Got the Blues*, the preliminary draft of *Awake and Sing!*,
came directly from the mouths of Odets's parents.[30]) Odets draws on
Yiddishkeit, the Jewish penchant for self-deprecation ("Who am I? Al
Jolson?" Ralph Berger asks his mother when she claims he's too good
for the girl he loves) and on the colorful English of Jewish immigrants—
even in *Waiting for Lefty*, where only one of the characters (Dr.
Benjamin in the "Interne Episode") has a specific ethnic identity. For
example, Edna tells Joe, "I heard worse than I'm talking about," and
the Stenographer in "The Young Actor" calls down-on-their-luck actors
"phoney strutting 'pishers'."[31]

Much of the emotional power in *Awake and Sing!*, in *Paradise
Lost*, and in "I Can't Sleep" (a monologue Odets wrote for a Marine
Workers Industrial Union benefit in 1930) derives from its Jewish
diction, the way it pins down a precise time and place and style. The
following excerpt from "I Can't Sleep" demonstrates the ability of his
diction to evoke a specific world:

> Listen, you think I never read a book? "Critique of the
> Gotha Programme," Bukharin, Lenin—"Iskra"—this was in
> our day a Bolshevik paper. I read enough. I'm speaking
> three languages, Russian, German, and English. Also Yid-
> dish. Four. I had killed in the 1905 revolution a brother. You
> didn't know that. My mother worked like a horse. No, even
> a horse takes off a day. My mother loved him like a bird, my

41

dead brother. She gave us to drink vinegar we should get sick and not fight in the Czar's army. Maybe you think I didn't understand this.[32]

It's not hard to imagine how strongly Morris Carnovsky, the actor who performed "I Can't Sleep," must have related to the language—how immediate an affinity all the Jewish members of the Group had with his early plays. Here was a case of a playwright whose private use of emotional recall in his own work both encouraged actors to follow suit and made it easy for them to do so. No wonder the actors in the Group greeted *I Got the Blues* with such enthusiasm. (Odets had to struggle with the Group's directors to get the play produced—oddly enough, Strasberg himself was the major obstacle—but the actors were on Odets's side.) The original cast of *Awake and Sing!* included Carnovsky, John Garfield, J. Edward Bromberg, Sanford Meisner, and Stella and Luther Adler—who had received their early training in the Yiddish Theatre, where their father, Jacob, was a star.

It's Odets's brilliant recreation of the Jewish–American family life of the Depression that remains his signal contribution to the American theater. As the critic Robert Warshow writes, "Jews are never commonplace to him—they are never commonplace to any Jew—but neither are they prodigious, either of absurdity or of pathos or of evil. [Odets] has perceived that they are human beings living the life which happens to be possible to them."[33] The economic constraints of life require that "they live on top of one another, in that loveless intimacy which is the obverse of the Jewish virtue of family solidarity"[34]—as exemplified by the Berger family in *Awake and Sing!* (Odets's secondary theme, the claustrophobia of the urban experience, became an obsession for the generation of American playwrights that followed him. Think of *The Glass Menagerie, A Streetcar Named Desire, Death of a Salesman.*) Here they live in constant terror of poverty, "as if soon the walls would disappear, and they would remain naked and alone on the cold empty street of a night without a morrow"[35]—as Harold Clurman describes his own parents' fears during the Depression.

The behavior of the Jewish lower middle class in response to their environment is comic and touching, and in *Awake and Sing!* Odets catches both aspects. He depicts the exclusiveness of the Bergers, who, whatever their inner conflicts, always band together against the rest of the world. Bessie epitomizes this attitude. Her father exasperates her, but she's quick to defend him when she feels the apartment superintendent has been rude to him; and she firmly believes that no outsider is good enough for her children—not Ralph's neighborhood friends ("those tramps on the corner") or his girl friend ("Miss Nobody should step in the picture and I'll stand by with my mouth shut"), not Hennie's husband ("a man like a mouse"), or even Moe Axelrod ("my daughter ain't in your class, Axelrod").

Odets locates the emotional core of the Jewish household at the dinner table, where the play begins, food being a symbol of stability in this scary, uncertain world. And perhaps his most unusual observation is seen in the vague, ominous threats the Bergers make to one another. "I mean something," Ralph mutters to his mother when he complains about how little of his wages he gets to keep for himself. "All you know, I heard, and more yet," Jacob tells Bessie. "What you mean, I know . . . and what I mean I also know," Bessie warns her son cryptically. In these lines we hear the brave cry of the frightened soul whose bravado is all that's left. These are the echoes of Lear's "I will do such things— / What they are, yet I know not; but they shall be / The terrors of the earth."

Odets seems to fall apart, however, whenever he strays too far from the Jewish middle class. The language dies in the "Lab Assistant Episode" of *Waiting for Lefty*, when Fayette, the industrialist, speaks, because Odets either doesn't know or can't reproduce how successful businessmen converse. (In the tradition of leftist theater, Fayette isn't a human being anyway. He's a stage Fascist.) Similarly, Dr. Benjamin, in the "Interne Episode," sounds fraudulent until Odets reveals the character's Jewish roots and allows him to relax into more familiar diction. He has a tin ear for other kinds of dialect: Joe Bonaparte's Italian papa in *Golden Boy* is a caricature, and Frenchy in *Rocket to the Moon*, who is supposed to be Swedish, occasionally slips into Yiddishisms ("I should worry who").[36] It's an unhappy fact that in the years following the Group's demise, Odets lost the knack of converting his own experiences, both in the theater (*The Country Girl*) and in Hollywood (*The Big Knife*), into dialogue that had the ring of truth.

Since Stanislavski and the Moscow Art Theatre represented a dramatic ideal for the Group, Chekhov, the Moscow Art's signal playwright, was a heroic figure to the Group actors. They were inspired by his subtlety in suggesting the turbulent world inside his characters' minds, and the extent to which his technique suited actors trained in

43

Stanislavski's system. Odets aimed for a Chekhovian subtext in his own plays; he strove to be an American Chekhov. And so, even though at various times in his career Odets attempted to play down his dramatic heritage, or give most of the credit for the shaping of his work to another Group play, John Howard Lawson's *Success Story* (a tough one to swallow if you've read *Success Story*), it's Chekhov's influence you find in almost every scene of Odets's *Awake and Sing!* and *Paradise Lost*. You can see it in the skillful drawing of minor figures; in the tendency of the characters to wander aimlessly about the house (especially in *Paradise Lost*); in the way the dialogue, in Brooks Atkinson's phrase, "gets at the truth of characters by indirection."[37]

Odets's "indirect" dramaturgy often takes the form of non sequiturs; they provide a glimpse of the private world running on in Myron Berger's head (*Awake and Sing!*) or Gus Michaels's (*Paradise Lost*)—touching, pathetic men who can't stop thinking but have somehow been cut off from the rest of the world. "Why'd I come in here?" Myron asks himself in the second act of *Awake and Sing!* He has a vague notion that his family's in trouble, but he always arrives a moment too late to see where the trouble started. And he usually fails to grasp the meaning of the situations he stumbles into: When he enters at the end of the last act to tell his daughter goodnight, he has no idea she's about to abandon her husband and child and run away with Moe Axelrod. No, he's preoccupied with some item he read in a magazine that says people with thick tongues are feeble-minded, and he's recalling the events of the year Hennie was born. Finding the present a puzzle he can't unravel, he turns repeatedly to the past, when Valentino held sway over women's hearts and people had better manners, just as Gus Michaels reminisces over "the old Asbury Park days" and "the shore dinners at old Sheepshead Bay." Like Myron, Gus remembers how beautiful his daughter was as a baby, but he can't fix her unhappy marriage or prevent her from cheating on her husband.

On a plane directly above these helpless nostalgics—the Sorins of Odets's world—are the intellectuals, the Andreis, who read and philosophize but are just as powerless to effect change as Myron and Gus are. Jacob Berger, in *Awake and Sing!*, rails against capitalism and religion and the petty *bourgeois* obsessions of his tyrannical daughter, Bessie, but he doesn't stand in the way when she traps Sam Feinschreiber into marrying Hennie, or when she tries to break up Ralph's romance with his girl friend. Leo Gordon, so utterly self-absorbed that he has no idea how oppressive labor conditions are in his own shop ("Oh, you sleep, Boss," one of his workers tells him), sits alone at the conclusion of Act I, lost in thought—a Chekhovian end-of-act image if ever there was one. Leo's not disconnected, exactly, but what he *is* connected to is inside himself, and we can't see it. (It's something the actor has to work out during rehearsal.)

Odets's most moving characters, like Chekhov's, fail to communicate with each other not because they're adrift, but because their thoughts and sensitivities turn in on themselves like a Möbius strip. Whenever two characters do manage to forge some temporary link with each other—when Trepleff tells his mother he loves her in *The Sea Gull*, or when Clara Gordon's invalid son Julie confesses to her that he's frightened in *Paradise Lost*—it's an epiphany, because we've grasped how difficult it is for human beings to get loose, even for a moment, from the cord that leads them back into themselves.

Just as Masha's famous interjection "My foot's asleep" in *The Sea Gull* and Chebutykin's smashing of the clock in *Three Sisters* make interior rather than narrative sense, so many of the lines and actions in Odets either mean the opposite of what they seem to mean, or else suggest another level of subtext altogether. Ralph's complaint that he's never had a pair of black-and-white shoes expresses a lifetime of deprivation and a lifelong feeling of worthlessness. *Awake and Sing!* contains an entire love scene played by indirection: Hennie and Moe bait and deride each other because they're terrified of revealing their true feelings—commitment to love is too frightening in a world where the roof seems perpetually on the verge of caving in. (Steve's treatment of Fay in *Night Music* follows the same pattern.) Hennie's revulsion toward weak, fawning Sam derives from her own fear of appearing weak, and her own need for assimilation. She calls him a "mockie," which would be an anti-Semitic insult in the mouth of a Gentile, because his broken English and old-world mannerisms remind her of bonds she'd rather deny. (She wants to break free of her family; she's afraid of turning into her mother.) In *Paradise Lost*, Sam Katz turns on his wife because he's impotent and an embezzler and has to blame *some*one; and (though this is less clear) Ben Gordon's insensitive remarks to her about the children he knows she can't have project his bitterness about his own failing marriage. The most powerful and fascinating example of indirection occurs late in the second act of *Awake and Sing!* Here's Robert Warshow again:

In a brilliant climax, Bessie Berger reveals the whole pattern of psychological and moral conflict that dominates her and her family: when Ralph discovers that his sister's husband was trapped into marriage, Bessie, confronted inescapably with her own immorality, and trembling before her son's contempt, turns upon her *father*, who has said nothing, and smashes the phonograph records that are his most loved possessions and the symbol of his superiority. This act of fury is irrelevant only on the surface: one understands immediately that Bessie has gone to the root of the matter.[38]

"The root of the matter" is Jacob's guilt for having fathered Bessie and given her no better life than this.

At his very best (in *Awake and Sing!* and the first two acts of *Paradise Lost*), Odets travels a long way toward the kind of subtextual richness he and his colleagues in the Group admired in Chekhov. The expansive depiction of character in his plays was part of his generosity to actors. Odets employed his gift for writing dialogue to their advantage—to help them listen to each other; recreate the drama of genuine human connection on the stage; shape distinctive, memorable characterizations; and evoke a specific, detailed milieu. In all these ways Odets both reflected the concerns of actors trained like himself in the Method, and contributed to the movement of American acting toward a greater realism. And he made another contribution as well, one that could not have seemed as significant at the time as it would turn out to be. He invented the Method prototype: the rebel without a cause.

In Odets's America, the America of the Depression, the few remaining innocents (like Ralph Berger and Joe Bonaparte in *Golden Boy*) receive an abrupt rite of passage into a cynical adulthood (symbolized, in *Awake and Sing!*, by Moe Axelrod), where they quickly learn how to live with their backs against the wall (as the characters in *Paradise Lost* must). Once they've arrived, they find they're part of a confederacy of males who show a steel-plated exterior to the rest of the world and to each other, converting the psychological damage the world has done them into wisecracks, insults, and a frank, callous approach to sex. Moe gives Ralph a taste of this men's-club sensibility when he taunts him for being a virgin; Ben and Kewpie in *Paradise Lost* are charter members, as are the prizefighters in *Golden Boy*.

Since it is dangerous to reveal how much he wants to escape from his world, or how badly he hungers for the love of a particular woman, Odets's tough guy often says the opposite of what he means, activating the playwright's penchant for communicating feelings by indirection. And this world isn't necessarily dominated by men: The women, too, are survivors. The hard-edged, defensive behavior of characters like Bessie and Hennie Berger, Libby Michaels in *Paradise Lost*, and Lorna Moon in *Golden Boy* results partly from their understanding, won with difficulty and pain, that "when one lives in the jungle one must look out for the wild life" (*Awake and Sing!*)—and partly from habitually taking the traditional male role to fill in for weak husbands or lovers (like Myron Berger or Tom Moody in *Golden Boy*).

Odets's men and women *are* vulnerable, though; they fall into the same sucker's traps again and again. The insidious popular songs that run through their heads (Moe Axelrod, Ben Gordon, and Tom Moody all sing to themselves) plant the vision of an exotic land now lost to them forever: Paradise Lost, the "O Paradiso!" that Caruso sings about on Jacob's shattered record. The movie stars they admire reside in an earthly Paradise of wealth and success, an Eden they dream of being able to steal a corner of, somehow. Alienated from the life they were born into—alienation is what both *Paradise Lost*, with its characters roaming aimlessly around the house, and *Golden Boy*, which ends in twin suicides, are mainly about—they are pushed into rebellion.

But their choices are limited. According to Elia Kazan:

> We used to say in the Communist Party that in American society you can either become a revolutionary or a gangster: both are bred by the same anger and the same resentment. . . . But there was a third possibility: to become an artist.[39]

Ralph Berger, the "boy with a clean spirit," becomes a revolutionary, as does Joe Bonaparte's brother Frank. But the most interesting characters in Odets are the ones who rebel by courting success—in Kazan's terminology, by becoming gangsters. In *I Got the Blues* Odets made Moe's underworld connections more explicit, and ended the play with his arrest for illegal gambling operations. In *Paradise Lost* Ben Gordon, a one-time boxing champ, sells his medals, and while his younger brother Julie, dying of sleeping sickness, makes fantastic paper profits

47

on the stock market (sleeping sickness and paper stock profits: a stunning pair of Depression symbols for stagnation and waste), Ben gets himself killed in a robbery set up by Kewpie. (Odets's concern with the corruption of heroism suggests he learned something from Sean O'Casey, too.) And in *Golden Boy* the rebel, Joe Bonaparte, throws away his violin and becomes a prizefighter, choosing to embrace the American dream and declare loyalty to commerce rather than art. Odets and Kazan come from the same world: Odets makes clear what kind of choice Joe's made by having a gangster, Fuseli, buy up his contract once he starts winning big.

Harold Clurman, who directed the original Broadway production of *Golden Boy* in 1937, defined the spine of the play as "how to deal with the problems of life in a world where success is the criterion."[40] For Joe, boxing represents both a way of escaping the ghetto he grew up in, and a license to fight back, to avenge the psychic injuries he suffered as a child. But his sensitive side refuses to leave him alone, pulling him into a kind of emotional shadow boxing every time he climbs into the ring:

> You're a miserable creature [Lorna tells Joe]. You want your arm in *gelt* up to the elbow. You'll take fame so people won't laugh or scorn your face. You'd give your soul for those things. But every time you turn your back your little soul kicks you in the teeth. [Act I, Scene 4]

In Odets's plays, music is an important symbol: It represents the finest impulse in a human being—his redemption. But life is rough, and continually threatens that impulse. The purest thing in *Paradise Lost*, the love between two musicians (Pearl Gordon and Felix), can't survive: Felix has to leave New York to look for work, Pearl's piano is repossessed, and both must resign themselves (like Sid and Florrie, the young hack and his girl in *Waiting for Lefty*) to the sad truth that, in their world, economics takes precedence over love. In *Till the Day I Die* the Nazi officer, Schlegel, smashes Ernst's fingers so he can no longer play the violin. And in *Golden Boy*, Joe breaks his hand winning a fight and shouts, "Hallelujah! It's the beginning of the world!" Here "the world" is a synonym for compromise, commerce, corruption—the army Joe enlists in when he leaves his music behind. This world brings him death: first his opponent's, at his hands; and then his own by suicide when the part of him that music once expressed (his sensitivity, his soul) torments him beyond endurance.

> That's right—I didn't mean it! I wouldn't want to do that, would I? Everybody knows I wouldn't want to kill a man. . . . But I *did* it! That's the thing—I *did* it! What will my father say when he hears I murdered a man? [Act III, Scene 2]

Fascinatingly, *Golden Boy* represents the playwright's own compromise—the Hollywoodization of Clifford Odets. He had been writing for the movies in 1936 and 1937, and in *Golden Boy* he abandoned the long, Chekhovian group scenes of *Awake and Sing!* and *Paradise Lost* for a more cinematic structure: a dozen relatively short scenes ending in fade-outs. The real influence of Hollywood, though, emerges in the content of the play—in the more sentimental and generalized treatment of character and environment. Odets wrote, after *Golden Boy's* successful opening in New York, "It is about time that the talented American playwright began to take the gallery of American types, the assortment of fine vital themes away from the movies. This was attempted in *Golden Boy*."[41] Half the characters in *Golden Boy* are ethnic stereotypes in the Warner Brothers tradition. And in portraying Joe's home life, Odets substitutes for the bitter domestic truths of his earlier work a cozy, artificial picture, common in American movies right up to the 1960s, of a purely warm, supportive family environment: the harmless squabbling of Joe's loving sister and brother-in-law; the comfortable relationship between his Italian father and a Jewish neighbor; the homemade wine (a popular cliché in the depiction of Italian–Americans); the transcendent wisdom of Papa Bonaparte, who knows instinctively which of his son's friends are decent and which destructive.

Joe Bonaparte is a Hollywood type, too—the sensitive prize fighter. But here Odets turns a convention on its head and exposes what's underneath. When *Golden Boy* was filmed (it was the only one of Odets's Group Theatre plays to make it to the screen), Hollywood sanitized it, changing Joe's and Lorna's suicide drive into an implausible happy ending. The death of his opponent, the Chocolate Drop, shakes Joe to his senses. He and Lorna decide that his gangster manager, Fuseli, bears responsibility for turning Joe into a killer (an accusation the screenplay never explains), and walk out on him with apparent impunity—returning home to Joe's papa and the certainty that, as soon as Joe's hand heals, he will once more take up the violin. What this cheery conclusion does is violate Odets's single significant contribution through this play: his portrayal of boxing as a form of rebellion, and the boxer as a schizoid recruit for the American dream.

The conflict between art (or personal ideals) and commerce (or the American dream) would resonate throughout American drama after *Golden Boy*, most loudly in Arthur Miller's *Death of a Salesman*. And, though Hollywood obviously couldn't handle this aspect of *Golden Boy* in 1939, in the 1940s and 1950s Joe Bonaparte would resurface again and again—often as a fighter, sometimes in other incarnations. And always, as if a reminder of Bonaparte's origins, a famous Method actor would play the role.

3

THE REALITY QUEST
♦ ♦ ♦

Self-proclaimed revolutionaries in the field of acting, the members of the Group Theatre had strong feelings about others in their profession. Elia Kazan dismissed Orson Welles, for example, as "a terrific 'ham,' [who] made deep and terrifying sounds with his voice. At the Group, we thought very little of him."[1] Gifted and witty as he was, Welles was an actor of the old school—a matinee-idol type, a declaimer. Perhaps we can't fully understand the innovations the Group Theatre made without examining the kind of acting it was trying to get away from.

If you think of some of the most memorable movie performances of the thirties and early forties—James Cagney in *Public Enemy, A Midsummer Night's Dream,* and *Yankee Doodle Dandy*; Gary Cooper in *A Farewell to Arms*; Clark Gable in *It Happened One Night*; Bette Davis in *Marked Woman, Jezebel,* and *The Letter*; Jean Arthur in *Mr. Deeds Goes to Town, Mr. Smith Goes to Washington,* and *Easy Living*; James Stewart in *Destry Rides Again* and *The Shop Around the Corner*; Margaret Sullavan in *Three Comrades* and *The Shop Around the Corner*; Cary Grant in *Holiday* and *The Philadelphia Story*; Ginger Rogers in *Stage Door* and *Bachelor Mother*; Humphrey Bogart in *The Maltese Falcon* and *High Sierra*; Katharine Hepburn in *Little Women, Alice Adams,* and *Holiday*—what comes to mind first is the eccentric *personalities* of these actors. That's what made them stars, and that's what accounts for much of the pleasure we take in watching them in film after film—even in very bad pictures, where their quirkiness often provides the only spark.

There's a famous anecdote about Katharine Hepburn's reaction to the one Group meeting she attended. She sat quietly through a lecture by Harold Clurman, listened to the enthusiasm it generated in the rest of the room, and finally excused herself, explaining, "That's all right for you people, but you see, I want to be a star." That story may sound like a barb directed at Hepburn's snobbishness, but in fact she was quite perceptive: The Group wasn't for her. They neither promoted nor indulged in star performances, and in Hepburn's case, working with them would have been constricting—she wouldn't have had the freedom to express her brilliant idiosyncrasies, as she has throughout her career.

The Group in fact hated Hollywood, even though several of them screen-tested in the late 1930s, and most ended up there during the war. It wasn't just that the Hollywood hierarchy, with stars on its crown, was undemocratic, a slap in the face to the Group's good liberal Left principles—though certainly that was a factor.

Group actors felt that the quality of self-containment that made a star was simply a display of ego, and that the luminous distance of the star image was an insurmountable obstacle to any real connection with other performers, and to the baring of the soul that Strasberg had taught them was the cornerstone of all great acting. There's no indication that, as a collective, they recognized any kind of range in these stars—that, for example, they distinguished between a Bette Davis and a Cary Grant. The Group would have been appalled at the notion of a Method movie star; Brando and James Dean belonged to another generation of Method actors. Characteristically, when one member of the Group, John Garfield, did migrate to Hollywood to become the first Method star, most of his former colleagues treated him as a defector.

Part of what infuriated Clurman and Strasberg in their days of working for the Theatre Guild was the self-consciousness of the stage stars they saw in action. The early talking films provide us with a number of examples of stage-trained actors from this era whose style—bold, bigger than life, every speech and movement carefully underlined so it could be read from the balcony—may seem peculiarly broad and overstated to us because by now several generations of actors have moved so far away from it. Even the best of these performers seem to belong to another world, a world we foolishly think must have been a simpler one because their reactions seem a little slower and they usually display only one emotion at a time.

Of course, early talkie technique exacerbates the problem: Sound pictures didn't discover their own tempo until around 1931, and right up to 1933 or 1934 there still were directors who clung to the conventions of stage timing. (In the less deft stage-to-screen translations of the time, such as the atrocities committed on Philip Barry's plays *Holiday* and *The Animal Kingdom* in 1930 and 1932, the pauses and takes are agonizing.) But even the best early-thirties movies have strange *longeurs*. In Lewis Milestone's marvelous 1931 film of the Charles MacArthur–Ben Hecht classic *The Front Page*, the large cast playing the raucous, hard-boiled corps of newspapermen delivers the rapid-fire, overlapping dialogue with enormous skill; yet in the smaller scenes, involving only two or three characters, the action slows down, punctuated by pauses unfamiliar to our sense of rhythm. Sometimes these long takes can be satisfying in themselves, the way a grand moment in a vaudeville turn is. When Adolphe Menjou (playing the sly, dictatorial editor, Walter Burns) grins knowingly into the camera as his best staffer, Hildy Johnson (Pat O'Brien), passes out of the room with his fiancée (Mary Brian), he holds the pose several seconds longer than we need to understand that Burns intends to outmaneuver the woman who dares to steal his star reporter away from him. And occasionally they can be minor irritations: Menjou's face comments on his speeches after he's completed them, so in effect we get the gist of every speech twice.

Most actors—even very fine ones—who began their careers on the stage in the pre–Group days never lost that stagy self-consciousness about their movement and voice. Paul Muni's early movie performances in *Scarface* and *I Am a Fugitive from a Chain Gang* (both 1932) are vivid, electric, peppered with wit (qualities that vanished from his acting once he began to play impressive historical figures like Emile Zola and Louis Pasteur). But when he strikes a match on a cop's badge in the opening scene of *Scarface*, the speed and depth of what happens in his face, the way he registers his enjoyment of his own bravado, are no different from what a member of a stage audience would have seen if his performance had been live.

The handsome young matinee idol Fredric March illustrates the same broad-faced, straight-ahead quality in his early–1930s screen appearances. In the 1934 *Death Takes a Holiday* (derived from plays by Alberto Casella and Maxwell Anderson and betraying its theatrical origins in every scene), March plays Death, who disguises himself as a foreign count on a visit to the villa of an Italian noble so he can learn why all human beings fear the grave. There are many wonderful moments in March's performance—like his response when a beautiful young woman pins a fresh rose to his jacket and, miraculously, the flower doesn't wither from the contact with death. But on the whole the emotions he projects seem slightly outsize for the camera (especially in a scene that calls for him to laugh and cry in quick succession).

When March learned to relax on camera and lessen the appearance of effort in his acting, he became subtler and more naturalistic. His portrayal of the alcoholic Norman Maine in *A Star is Born* (1937) may be the first indication of his maturity as an actor. But he never lost that slightly-larger-than-life presence; it was his style, and much of his strength in movies like *The Best Years of Our Lives* derived from it. In his final—possibly his best—screen performance, as the salty, stubborn saloonkeeper Harry Hope in John Frankenheimer's 1973 film of Eugene O'Neill's *The Iceman Cometh*, the girth of March's acting is what makes it so joyous. Amazingly alive in every pore of his being, March wears the physical details of Harry's character the way Harpo wears the apparatus he keeps tucked away in his jacket. They pop out everywhere: the sodden smile, the tired, self-pitying shuffle, the chronic blinking of the eyes (as if he were forever waking out of a drunken stupor), the tendency to rush his words so he keeps swallowing a fat portion of them. And the antiquated style of March's acting (by 1973, twenty-five years after Brando's appearance on the scene) is perfect for Harry, an old-school barkeep who lives happily—even gracefully—in the past.

John Barrymore also acquired his immense vocabulary of facial expressions on the stage. He went to Hollywood late in his career (as a matinee idol in the last days of the silents), when he was already as famous for his drinking as for his acting. And though his movies have often been dismissed as trivial self-parody, he was witty enough to tease that affectation into a full-blown comic style, most memorably in the Hecht–MacArthur screwball comedy *Twentieth Century* in 1934.

Barrymore's neglected performances in *Svengali* (1931) and *Counsellor-at-Law* (1933) offer a glimpse of what the most imaginative stage acting was like before the influence of the Group Theatre. His acting here is a series of wonderful physical and vocal tricks: He's entertainingly hyperbolic in *Counsellor at Law*, and in the Gothic crowd-pleaser *Svengali* he's often hilarious, in a mad-eyed theatrical fashion. His performance is a cartoon extension of the *outré* make-up and costumes he wears: Sporting thick, bushy eyebrows, a Pinocchio nose, a trident-edged beard, and a wig which sticks out at the back and sides like glued straw, he manages to make this megalomaniacal mesmerist both frightening (staring at Marian Marsh's Trilby, hypnotizing her into submission) and pathetic (when, exhausted, he realizes that his hold on her is weakening). What dazzles you about Barrymore's acting is the enormous scale he worked on.

It's from watching Walter Huston in *Dodsworth*, however, that we can learn the most about the generation of actors that preceded the Group. When Huston starred in this vehicle on Broadway in 1934, playing the role of Sinclair Lewis's retired auto-industry millionaire, who takes his *poseuse* wife on a trip to Europe and loses her there, he made it the most famous of his career. In a rare fit of common sense, Hollywood invited him to repeat it in the 1936 film version for Samuel Goldwyn, under William Wyler's superbly intelligent direction. (Of course, by that time Huston was already a movie star, so there wasn't much risk.) And since neither the performance nor the play itself seems to have been reshaped for the movies, *Dodsworth* affords us the privilege of seeing a preserved stage performance—and a splendid one—in the pre–Method style.

As Huston plays him, Sam Dodsworth is most comfortable tinkering with machines—or sending off cables, because the clipped language perfectly expresses his all-American love of speed. And though his rough-hewn energy embarrasses and finally repels his pretentious wife, Fran (Ruth Chatterton), it's what attracts us to him. Huston sends out this energy in enormous theatrical flashes, like his excitement over his first peep at England from the ship. He physicalizes Dodsworth in the fashion of a supreme stage craftsman: His walk, for instance, is a comical amble. And he gives a sage, self-knowing line like "It makes us look like the hicks we are" (his admonition to his wife not to get above her American self) a humorous, deliberately provincial rhythm, pausing after "hicks" as if he were reading a line of music that demanded a rest in mid-bar, while tilting that lanky, Lincolnesque frame like a scarecrow about to topple, holding his pose in wait for the blackout.

Huston has a genius for tableaux like this one. His face may register nostalgic sadness, or tender affection, or enthusiasm so great it lights him up like an electric bulb, and then he'll freeze—isolating that feeling, making it the point of the scene. The stilted angle of his body as he sits listening to Fran's pleas that he return home without her (which Gregg Toland's expressionistic lighting, cloaking Huston in shadow, emphasizes); the unsurprised displeasure on his face when he sees she's acquired a set of Jean Harlow curls in a shameless attempt to please a lover; his last look at her as the train carries him away—these moments of high, stylized emotion really are signposts telling us how to read Sam Dodsworth, and they're very carefully prepared, just like his line readings or his comic fit at the way his daughter and son-in-law have altered the house in his absence. There's not a moment of spontaneity in Huston's performance, but it would be grossly unfair to say he lacks feeling; he just orchestrates it differently, in his body and his voice, than the Method actors to whose style we've now become accustomed.

What Huston represents here are the last glories of nineteenth-century acting. (Ralph Richardson's impression of James Tyrone in *Long Day's Journey into Night*, a character modeled on Eugene O'Neill's stage-star father, is much like this.) And, like it or not, the Group Theatre actors were stuck with the legacy of this style: They made huge alterations in acting, but even they couldn't get away from theatrical flourish entirely.

The work of the Group actors looks particularly impressive when you compare them to many of the Broadway stars of the 1920s who brought to the movies an odd vocal mannerism that sounds to our ears like an artificial English cocktail party accent. (Amazingly, it's still taught in some of our acting schools, where it's known as standard English or standard American.) Even in what is probably her best film performance, as the social climber chasing her youth in *Dodsworth*, Ruth Chatterton's line readings give the impression of having been worked out beforehand on a tape recorder. (What makes the performance work is how appropriate that kind of self-consciousness is for Fran Dodsworth.) Similarly, Ann Harding seems stilted and distracted as the supposedly free-spirited heroines of *Holiday* (a role later transformed by Katharine Hepburn) and *The Animal Kingdom*. And Helen Hayes—famous, like Chatterton, for playing noble, long-suffering women in movies—never tries anything on screen that wouldn't milk applause from a Broadway audience. The mechanics of her acting are transparent, but everything else remains opaque: She's got a tough skin the camera can't penetrate. (Hayes's entire career is a series of variations rung on a single worn irony: that such an elf could be so resilient.) She plays wise, loving Catherine Barkley in A *Farewell to Arms* (1932) with a misty-eyed spiritual gaze, but there's no actual depth underneath. Twenty-one years later, in the paranoid Cold War melodrama *My Son John*, she's the mother of a Communist spy (Robert Walker), a woman whose suspicions of her son's activities have caused her nerves to unravel, a sort of middle-American Ophelia. You can't find a muted moment in this display of histrionics, or an emotion that wasn't born in a trunk.

There were others, however—film actors the Group admired and felt some kinship to. One was Edward G. Robinson. Robinson's tough gangster image, introduced in *Little Caesar* in 1930, is etched so strongly on the popular imagination that he might seem a peculiar role model for Group actors. But unlike Cagney, he did tend to efface his own personality, and he didn't reprise *Little Caesar* as often as most people think. (Cagney, though, was finally the more exciting actor of the two.)

In a movie like the 1935 comedy *The Whole Town's Talking*, Robinson demonstrates a finely modulated subtlety. He plays a dual role: Arthur Ferguson Jones, a meek bank clerk; and the hoodlum "Killer" Mannion, whom Jones so closely resembles that Mannion, seeing a good thing, forces him into an unholy partnership, sharing his identity and providing a cover for Mannion's underworld activities. The picture is an adaptation (by Jo Swerling and Robert Riskin) of a novel by W. R. Burnett, who also wrote *Little Caesar*; the connection may have clinched the project for Robinson, who could parody himself deftly. And the fact that he was on loan to Columbia from Warner Brothers, and working with a director (John Ford) who had a gentler, more expansive touch with actors than anyone at Warners, may have permitted Robinson to try something unusual that he wouldn't have gotten away with at his home studio.

You wouldn't call Robinson's portrait of Rico in *Little Caesar* a character study, but "Killer" Mannion is, and so, in a very different way, is Arthur Ferguson Jones. In the most memorable scene, Jones returns home to find Mannion asleep and, seeing his opportunity at last, reaches for the gangster's gun. Mannion wakes up suddenly, and

Jones, rather than pressing his advantage, politely hands over the weapon. Here Robinson turns a stock comic bit (the milquetoast intimidated by the thought of violence) into a quiet demonstration of gentility; his performance draws a line between the man who lives by violence and the man whose nature rejects it as poison. (*The Whole Town's Talking* is a far more effective statement about the distance between savagery and humanism than its gabbier contemporary, *The Petrified Forest.*)

Burgess Meredith almost joined the Group Theatre, but the directors failed to vote him in when he refused to swear an oath of loyalty that placed the Group above all other concerns in his life. (The Group's evangelical self-absorption could be insufferable.) Without false modesty, Meredith describes his own approach to acting, in an interview in Helen and Lillian Ross's 1962 book *The Player:*

> As Marchbanks in "Candida," I probably had a kind of vitality and realism that were just beginning to come into the theatre. Looking back, I remember that the words used about me were "realistic" and "sensitive." What I did was to believe absolutely in the circumstances that I found myself in onstage, so that the play was an actual experience for me and the emotions were real to me. We didn't have Methodology at that time, but later on I sought it. In 1937, after I had started in "Winterset," I studied with Benno Schneider, who gave lessons much like the ones given at the Actors Studio now.[2]

Watching Meredith in *Winterset* (1936), a faithful transcription of the play and the role that made him famous on stage, you can easily see why the Group actors admired him. Maxwell Anderson's verse drama about gangsterism and the Sacco–Vanzetti case is a curio now, a fascinating sample of what Depression theatergoers applauded as high art. It's crammed with half-digested thoughts and impossibly high-flown language, but Meredith manages somehow to bring this purple melodrama down to earth. He plays Mio, a young man haunted by the specter of his unjustly executed father, with passion and (miraculously) without affectation; even the heavy demands of the verse present no apparent obstacle. It's interesting that though Clurman spoke out against Anderson's search for an American tragic verse style, the Group counted itself among *Winterset*'s admirers; and Clurman later said it was a play he wished he could have produced—no doubt because of the subject matter. *Winterset* is really a glorified "problem" play—an aberrant example, maybe, but an example nonetheless. The Group must have spotted this. And Meredith's lucid reading of the working-class protagonist role must have struck Group actors as a model of the kind of acting they favored, both emotionally and politically.

His finest performance may be as George, the itinerant ranch hand, in Lewis Milestone's 1939 film version of *Of Mice and Men* (also a filmed play). It's another seamless piece of naturalistic acting in another proletarian role. In this mounting of John Steinbeck's frequently performed drama, George's relationship to Lennie (Lon Chaney, Jr.), the mentally handicapped companion he protects, is obviously paternal and more openly affectionate than in many other productions. Meredith's George has a sweet, attentive patience with Lennie that his brief bouts of bad temper don't taint for very long. When he talks about the farm he and Lennie plan to own someday, you can see why Lennie asks for this story so often. The dream softens Meredith's face; it transforms him. This is a deeply felt piece of acting, with effects so understated that you never see him reach for them— either in the scene where he discovers the body of a woman he knows Lennie must have killed, or when he shoots his friend to save him from being lynched, or at the end, when he hands his gun silently to the sheriff, the pain of what he's had to do raging in his face. (If you've never understood George's final act as a suicide, Meredith's performance of this scene will make it indelibly clear to you.)

Meredith has remained a highly respected realist actor throughout his career, giving modest, soft-spoken performances in films like the 1945 *The Story of G.I. Joe*, in which he slips without fuss into the frame of the balding, good-natured journalist from Albuquerque; and receiving renewed attention later in life for his crusty characterizations in the mid-seventies movies *The Day of the Locust* and *Rocky*. It's intriguing to see his attempt to bring his naturalistic instincts to bear on theater of the absurd when he plays Vladimir in the 1961 "Play of the Week" version of *Waiting for Godot*, opposite Zero Mostel's Estragon. The production, directed by Alan Schneider, is an unqualified fiasco. The only sane way to watch would be to close one eye and pay attention to only one of the two actors at a time, because Mostel's music-hall antics definitely don't belong in the same frame as what Meredith is doing.

Meredith is painful to watch at first; his performance seems mistimed, like those takes in early sound films, before actors had found the right rhythm for talkies. But gradually you see a vaudevillian coarseness begin to emerge that gives his acting some purpose. He gets at vaudeville in a very Method way (not, say, with the raucousness of a Bert Lahr, who actually came out of vaudeville), but he gets there. So while Mostel is engaged in vaudeville, Meredith is actually *playing* a vaudevillian (the way he would in *Day of the Locust*). It's a very weird combination. You certainly wouldn't call Meredith's Vladimir a success, but his effort to find, in true Method style, a subtext for every scene at least guarantees some variety, and an occasional poignant surprise. One comes when he stops Estragon from beating Godot's messenger boy by saying, "Extraordinary the tricks memory plays"; it's clear he's reminding his comrade that he was a child once, too, and that he too has been abused. For anyone interested in the application of the Method to non-naturalistic, non-American drama, this performance is probably essential viewing.

Spencer Tracy thought the Method was nonsense, yet Group actors saw in his performance in the lyrical 1933 romance *A Man's Castle* something like their own approach. Probably what impressed them were the no-fuss, workmanlike attitude toward acting, his ease with the vernacular (he plays an obstinate, softhearted tramp living in a Hooverville), his naturalness on camera, and his economy of means. (They might also have been responding to the quality in Tracy's acting that limits it, makes it seem a little bland and even condescending: his folksiness. Tracy was usually cast as the kind of hero the leftist theater of the Depression adored: rugged, straightforward, solidly working-class). And like Robinson, he could be quite effective when he played very quiet, a virtue better seen in *Edison the Man* (1940). The later film also contains Tracy's most Method-like preparation: In the final scene, a pedantic speech by the aging Edison, Tracy's tremulous ancient voice eerily recalls Edison's own on his first recordings.

Frances Farmer's Hollywood career was a celebrated disaster, but in her first starring role, in *Come and Get It* (1936), she showed a tough, authentic presence. She plays a dual part—a saloon singer in the first half of the movie, her ambitious daughter in the second—and, like Robinson in *The Whole Town's Talking*, she keeps each character distinct from the other. When she sings "Aura Lee" in an early scene, her earthiness flavors the ballad without sacrificing its nostalgic tenderness; years later, when her daughter sings the same song, she lends it the veneer of a concert piece. (We know immediately the mother would have laughed at her daughter's genteel manner.)

There's a sentimental side to Farmer's acting here, a weakness for sobs in the throat. But you keep marveling at the originality of her temperament (her lusty glamor is tinged with melancholy) and the promise of her acting. And then you feel let down again when you remember she never had the opportunity to realize that promise. Her performance in *The Toast of New York* the following year, as a chorus girl loved by both Edward Arnold and Cary Grant, feels truncated, but it was the last decent role Hollywood allowed her. Playing a middle-class heroine, she's far too much of an aristocrat, and she seems a little too pleased with the melodic quality in her sultry contralto voice. Still, she brings the film its few legitimate emotional moments. Clurman and Odets were impressed with Farmer in these two movies; in 1937 she came east at their invitation to play Lorna Moon in the Group production of *Golden Boy*.

The other actress who came to the Group from Hollywood was Sylvia Sidney, who'd already had a brief career on stage in the late 1920s (when she was still in her teens) before winning a film contract. By the time she returned to the theater in the Group production of Irwin Shaw's *The Gentle People* in 1939, she'd given a series of delicately affecting performances in such films as *Street Scene, Merrily We Go to Hell*, Hitchcock's *Sabotage*, Fritz Lang's *Fury* and *You Only Live Once*, and *Dead End*. With her eggshell mandarin face, her undisguised New York street accent, and her skill at expressing pain quietly through her slight, sweet presence—the sad smile, the way she held her hands, the angle of her hat—she was Hollywood's only true proletarian tragedienne, the ideal actress for the social-problem plays transposed to film in the thirties, as well as the dramas the studios themselves manufactured on the same structure.

Both *Street Scene* and *Dead End* are theses on the crushing effects of a cruel environment; *Fury* is about mob madness; and *You Only Live Once*, an early, romanticized version of the Bonnie and Clyde story, is about the relationship between class and justice. In *Sabotage*, Hitchcock's version of *The Secret Agent*, Sidney turns Winnie Verloc, the frail, victimized wife of the Joseph Conrad novel, Americanized for her, into another of her working-class heroines, a woman alienated by an unhappy marriage. To these roles she brought a doomed beauty and a touching conviction—touching because she always looked too fragile and waif-like to survive the blighted marriages, the lecherous bosses, the debilitation of poverty she faced in film after film, and yet the women she played were always fighters.

No one in this era could suggest the desperation of a woman with a normal emotional range more persuasively than she could. (The dinner scene in *Sabotage*, where she kills her husband with a kitchen knife after learning he was responsible for her brother's death, is the most famous example.) In *You Only Live Once* the depth of her devotion to her convict husband (Henry Fonda) is neurotic and frightening; it shakes her diminutive frame. When she thinks he's about to be executed, she tiptoes into the kitchen, pours a drink of water, and empties an envelope of poison into the glass. Then the phone rings. It's Fonda, free and on the lam—and her tremulous voice as she calls out his name is pitched right on the line between agony and joy. Sidney shows you she's already moved beyond the ordinary bounds of experience by the time she hears his name; emotionally she's a fugitive herself, so to join the man she adores in an outlaw existence is only a small step for her.

In this beautiful film, in which an emigré German director brings his Expressionist style to socially conscious Hollywood material, destiny hovers above the day-to-day interchanges of ordinary human beings; their fate may depend on the placement of a pilfered fedora or a chance recognition by a passerby. The movie is all about small steps that are irrevocable and lethal. And here's where Sidney's gift for realism comes in: Since the character she plays seems clearly to live in our world, the distance between our safe lives and her tormented one can suddenly strike us as a small step, too.

Though Sidney's film career belonged mainly to the Depression, she still shows up occasionally, and in sharp form—in the TV movie *An Early Frost*, for instance, and in *Beetlejuice*. Looked at today, her 1930s work seems like a series of moments, potent small scenes that make the filmmakers' points for them: Rose Maurrant, at the end of *Street Scene*, walking sadly away from the tenement where her father has murdered her mother, while the neighbor children sing, "The farmer killed the wife . . . / The wife killed the child"; the miserable heroine of *Merrily We Go to Hell* (one of her few non-working-class roles, as a woman who takes a lover as revenge on an unfaithful husband) hesitating at the top of a stairway before plunging into her first party as a "modern" woman; Joan in *You Only Live Once* breaking a shop window to steal food because she and her fugitive husband are starving. These moments are as compressed and emblematic in their way as Walter Huston's tableaux in *Dodsworth*, but Sidney plays them as fully and complexly as if they were complete scenes while the director holds and frames them (or we do ourselves, in recalling them). You wonder whether this was the approach the Group Theatre had in mind when they attempted a Brechtian piece like *1931*—or *The Case of Clyde Griffiths* or the Paul Green–Kurt Weill musical *Johnny Johnson*: naturalism shaped by a director to make an ideological point.[3] It's interesting to note that when Hollywood made its one attempt at a Brechtian musical drama in the thirties, *You and Me* (which had music by Weill), Sidney played the female lead.

It's not surprising to find movie actors like Robinson, Tracy, Farmer, and Sidney discovering on their own what the Group Theatre attempted to put on the stage only after months of careful study. After all, the Group, like Stanislavski himself, was part of an unconscious movement toward greater realism in acting which had begun in earnest as early as the mid–nineteenth century. And film, with its close-up, all-revealing camera, is the natural home of naturalism. An actress like the magnificent young Barbara Stanwyck seemed to understand that instinctively. Though she received her training on the stage, Stanwyck sensed even in her first screen roles that muted reactions would register most realistically in the movies. Her performances in early-1930s pictures like *Ladies of Leisure*, *The Miracle Woman*, *Night Nurse*, *Baby Face*, and *The Bitter Tea of General Yen* haven't lost their clarity and freshness through the years. Compared to most of the motion-picture acting in the early talkies, which didn't take the intensifying presence of the camera into account, they seem mysteriously subtle and spontaneous and emotionally complex.

The 1930 *Ladies of Leisure*, the first of a series of movies Stanwyck made for the young, still unsentimental Frank Capra, is *Camille* with a happy ending. Stanwyck plays Kay, a "party girl" (a common euphemism for "prostitute") who falls in love with the painter (Ralph Graves) she poses for. When his mother begs her to free him, she throws herself off a boat—but Graves rescues her in time for the final fade-out. Stanwyck's utter commitment to this trite dramatic situation redeems the movie, with the help of her character's earthy sense of humor and the occasional 1920s snap in Jo Swerling's dialogue. (*Sample*: When Stanwyck meets Graves for the first time, in soaked flapper clothes, her mascara bleeding down her face and her dark hair mussed after swimming to shore from a yacht party, she asks him, "You don't happen to tote a flask, do you? You know, medical aid to the injured?") A tough hide and a vulnerable core became Stanwyck's trademark combination. If Sylvia Sidney was a working-class tragedienne, Stanwyck in this period was usually a working-class survivor who neither forgot her wounds nor let them destroy her. Maybe *Ladies of Leisure* resurrected Kay at the end because, even that early in her career, suicide seemed the wrong choice for a Stanwyck heroine.

Stanwyck's fame as one of the toughest women on the screen expanded in her *film noir* period (in the forties), when she played *femme fatales* like Phyllis Dietrichson in *Double Indemnity*—shimmering beauties who are heartless bitches underneath. No one ever cracked as wise as Stanwyck: In *Baby Face*, when a greasy politician makes a pass at her in her father's beer joint, she pours a pot of coffee over his head and quips, in a sarcastic voice with its own built-in New York been-around lilt, "My hands shake so when I'm around you." But in early hard-boiled roles like Kay, or Lora Hart in *Night Nurse*, or the shrewd, promiscuous Lily in *Baby Face* (or, a few years later, her roles in *Golden Boy, Remember the Night, Meet John Doe,* and *The Lady Eve*), her cynicism masks an underlayer of emotional generosity or hurt or desperation. Lora's toughness enables her to deal with the people who present obstacles to her work: She cares for a couple of children, neglected by their alcoholic socialite mother, deliberately undernourished by her chauffeur (Clark Gable), who wants to get at their trust fund, and ignored by the corrupt society doctor on the case, who's been paid off to turn a blind eye. When one of the kids falls into danger, Stanwyck's Lora crashes the mother's party and tries to lead her forcibly into the nursery. When the woman collapses from drink, Stanwyck looks down at her, hands on her hips, and says, underplaying her disgust in that hard-as-nails voice, "You mother."

On the other end of the scale, she gives a fascinating performance in *Baby Face*, as a woman whose treatment at the hands of her father (who turned her into a tramp, expecting her to service his friends—after, it's implied, having molested her himself) has damaged her and turned her into a manipulative man-hater. There's a disturbing scene where her father dies when the still behind his bar burns up. Stanwyck's silent reaction is unmistakably satisfaction. You can read her thoughts: "The bastard got exactly what he deserved." Later, when she's slept her way into a soft, penthouse life and a servant asks her if she's planning to spend Christmas with her family, her sour "No" is lined with pain.

In Capra's sensational *The Miracle Woman*, an uplifting drama with a terrific cynical streak, Stanwyck plays Florence Fallon, a character modeled on Aimee Semple Macpherson. Jo Swerling's script saves Sister Florence through the love of a good blind man (David Manners), but Stanwyck's portrayal of the circus-show evangelist, whose suckering of her congregation is fueled by her hatred of the hypocrites who drove her pastor father to an early grave, is much too complex for simple salvation. This character belongs to the real world of human dilemmas, not the melodramatic realm of heroines and villainesses.

So does Megan, the missionary's fiancée kidnapped by a Chinese chieftain in *The Bitter Tea of General Yen* (also directed by Capra). The story, which chronicles a repressed young white woman's sexual awakening under the hand of her captor, was bold and strange for Hollywood. The casting was, too: Stanwyck plays opposite the Swedish actor Nils Asther (whose acting was inspired by Richard Barthelmess's Oriental in *Broken Blossoms*). Stanwyck's performance is an astonishingly modern exploration of sexual tensions and sexual release. When she awakes to find herself in Yen's carriage with Asther's eyes surveying her with appreciation, she slowly draws a blanket up over her dress; but by the last third of the picture she has completely abandoned herself to her passion for him.

The romance builds to a demi-*Liebestod*. Yen, learning that his troops have deserted him and he will certainly lose his province, poisons his own tea and dies in Megan's arms. Our last glimpses of Megan, on a ship carrying her away from China, show us a woman whose life has collapsed with the death of her lover. It's an ironic study in sexual energies: When Yen liberates Megan's repressed passions, he brings her tremendous happiness; but he also destroys her by robbing her of the strength she brought with her from her New England upbringing—the strength of resistance. When he's dead she passes into a frozen state, officially alive but psychically removed from the world of the living.

65

There's a moment in *Baby Face* when one of Lily's spurned boy friends swears to her that if she doesn't marry him, he'll kill himself, and she answers disdainfully, "Stop acting!" Considering her uncluttered, uncalculated approach to acting—acting that doesn't announce itself as acting—that's the perfect Barbara Stanwyck line. There are no effects in a great Stanwyck performance; it's like a two-hour burst of fresh air. Even in a movie like *The Bitter Tea of General Yen*, which depends on the careful layering of emotion, the fine tuning of sexual strings, you never see those strings.

Stanwyck is even more extraordinary in *Stella Dallas*, directed by King Vidor in 1937. The Olive Higgins Prouty chestnut about mother love and self-sacrifice had already been filmed once, in 1925, with Belle Bennett and Ronald Colman. But Stanwyck transforms the role of the working-class girl who wins a society husband (John Boles), then loses him when he can no longer stand her vulgarity. Relaxing into the thickest New York accent she's ever had, Stanwyck makes Stella's brassiness funny: We see her wait, with exaggerated patience, for Boles's Stephen to open the front door for her, or lean against the bedroom door after a dance at the club, anticipating the lecture she knows is coming to her for her behavior.

It's not a comic performance, though. When Stephen takes Stella to a movie, her eyes grow shiny as, sucking on her finger, she gets wrapped up in the romance on the screen. The characters in the film are well-bred, refined, and that's what Stella wants to be. But she can't refine anything—whatever she feels, whether it's the pleasure of a good joke, or the desire to be introduced to a stranger, or enthusiasm over a proposed outing, her emotions leak all over the place. Stanwyck makes this overeagerness, her inability to tuck feelings in neatly, so genuine it's almost embarrassing to watch. You keep wanting to tell her to cover up her face, to lower her voice, to compose herself, because you can see the effect she's having on Stephen (and on other people). The performance becomes devastating when Stella starts realizing it too, and still can't help herself: when she overhears her daughter's friends bad-mouthing her, or when, realizing she can never make herself attractive enough to Stephen to override her essential vulgarity in his eyes, she wipes the lipstick off her mouth. Stella is a kind of country cousin to Booth Tarkington's Alice Adams, whom Katharine Hepburn had played on screen two years earlier, and the performances share that emotional nakedness. It's funny to think of these two actresses together: Their styles could hardly be more different.

The Group Actors

It is unfortunate that no filmed record exists of any of the Group Theatre performances, except for the excerpts they used for their screen tests in the late 1930s. However, since several of its most celebrated alumni went on to long careers as character actors in movies and on television, we can get a sense, in glimpses and snatches, of what Group acting must have looked like from observing their later work. The Group penchant for playing small roles "to the life," as Odets described it, is evident in the distinctive qualities they so often show in undistinguished dramas—and frequently in barely written roles. Actors like Luther Adler, Roman Bohnen, and Lee J. Cobb consistently convey a sense of substance on camera; their presence demands our attention. The urgency of their acting is partly the result of stage training that teaches actors to establish their space in a play, to give the audience a reason to watch them; and partly it's an outgrowth of the kind of material the Group liked to perform: drama with a clearly stated moral to which the actors were expected to give physical and vocal weight and immediacy.

The working-class or (more often) middle-class milieu of the plays the Group produced was essential to an understanding of the issues, and so the actors acquired a proficiency at depicting the characters' roots. Elia Kazan, the Agate of *Waiting for Lefty*, the Fuseli of *Golden Boy*, and the Steve Takis of *Night Music*, is a case in point. Kazan's career as a movie actor was short-lived: Within a year he left Hollywood to become a stage director. But he brought an urban sharpness and a fiery street wisdom to his two film roles—Googi, the gangster in *City for Conquest* (1940), and Nicky, the law student who opts to play jazz, in *Blues in the Night* (1941). Here's Kazan's assessment of his own abilities as a young actor:

> I was intense, an intensity that came from all the pent-up anger in me. I didn't have much range. I was like an instrument with only three or four very strong notes. I was re-

ferred to in one review as "the proletarian thunderbolt."
This kind of talent fitted the plays that Odets was writing. In
Paradise Lost I played a gangster [Kewpie] and in *Night
Music* a resentful, dammed-up boy. In some peculiar and
symbolic way the next step in the development of the "pro-
letarian thunderbolt" was to play gangsters in films.[4]

The key word is "proletarian." Googi, in *City for Conquest* (a
boxing picture starring James Cagney), has just been released from
prison and, eager to make up for the time he has lost, he plunges into
the rackets, entering high society by the back door. Garbed like a
Damon Runyon character in pinstripe suits and flashy ties, his hat
tilted cockily, he's tight as a bullet, and he looks as if he were struggling to stretch his diminutive size up to full stature. All that energy
concentrated in such a small mass makes him a conspicuous comic
presence in each of his few scenes. You can see exactly why Warner
Brothers, which specialized in city pictures, signed him up: Kazan is a
witty little fireball who can make a terrific joke out of the contrast
between his fancy clothes and his second-generation immigrant New
York accent. In one scene, Kazan arrives to congratulate Cagney after
a win, with a heap of chorus girls from *George White's Scandals* on
both arms, every one of them taller than he is. When Cagney asks him
where he's been, Kazan quips, "The same stinkin' place you came
from—Forsythe Street and Delancey!" In *Blues in the Night*, under
the same director, Anatole Litvak, he simply shifts that crackling intensity from one hot milieu (the underworld) to another (the world of
jazz).
　　Other Group actors had a special talent for ethnic roles. Robert
Lewis was famous for playing Asians, and Luther Adler for Europeans
with imaginatively wrought accents. It was part of the character actor's
baggage Adler brought with him from the Group stage (where he'd
created such roles as Moe Axelrod, Sam Katz, and Joe Bonaparte) to
Hollywood, where he made himself sound like a gypsy in the 1949
D.O.A. and, for *Under My Skin* the same year, came up with an Italian
accent tinged with Magyar. His alert patience stands out in *D.O.A.*, a
tacky *film noir*, where he reads his dull lines slightly off the beat and
manages to find peaks and hollows in them. In both these movies, as
in the 1945 thriller *Cornered*, he shows a knack for playing oily characters and for suggesting extreme psychological states (he's a Fascist in

Cornered, an underworld chieftain in *D.O.A.* and *Under My Skin*) with just a few strokes—like opening his eyes unnaturally wide or measuring his speech a little too carefully.

But nothing Adler did in movies or on TV suggests the quality of his acting on the stage during the Group years. Nothing, that is, except his 1937 screen test, which, miraculously, still survives, along with five others by Group actors. Adler's shows him and Phoebe Brand (she's silhouetted, her back to the camera) in the crucial scene between Moe and Hennie in *Awake and Sing!,* and he holds the camera the way he must have held audiences in this role in 1935. He's invigorating, powerful, cocked from the moment he starts speaking; and his stage technique is so rock-solid and confident that the scene builds to an almost unbearable tension without our being made aware of exactly how he does it. He has qualities here you don't pick up in his later, stock character roles—a dangerous balance of hard experience and romantic longing, a gambler's almost masochistic ferocity about giving himself over to the game. It's a breathless, winner-take-all scene.

Morris Carnovsky was the most distinguished member of the Group, creating such roles as Jacob Berger, Leo Gordon, Mr. Bonaparte, Ben Stark in *Rocket to the Moon.* However, Hollywood ignored his talents and tossed him into a series of nondescript character roles (like Le Bret in *Cyrano de Bergerac,* 1950), and this phase of his career, unlike Adler's, is marked by perfectly adequate, unmemorable performances. In the 1950s he returned to the stage, mostly playing Shakespeare. (Carnovsky has devoted the greater part of his life as an actor to proving, on stage and in the classroom, that the Method has significant applications to the classics.)

It wasn't until a 1959 TV production of *The World of Sholom Aleichem* (on "Play of the Week") that any camera captured Carnovsky showing what he could do. *Sholom Aleichem* consists of three episodes—"A Tale of Chelm," "Bontche Schweig," and "The High School"—and he appears in all three. As the Rabbi in "A Tale of Chelm," and especially as Father Abraham in "Bontsche Schweig" (who holds court in Heaven to judge newly arrived souls), he employs his rich, regal voice to full stage effect. It's amusing to see that Carnovsky, a rebel against the matinee-idol style of acting, comes across as a little old school here. He doesn't strike attitudes, but you catch a few emblematic looks held for the camera. (He's more restrained in the modern-dress folk fable, "The High School.") Don't misunderstand me: If Carnovsky's manner of presenting himself smacks of the stage, it's not merely artifice. Actually, he's so good in these roles that you get the sense that on other occasions, when his mellifluous, creamy voice seems overly solemn for the role (in *Cornered*, for example), it's because he has too much class for the flimsy material. Even in a conventional wartime melodrama like *Cornered*, where he plays an anti-Fascist, he resists the temptation to sentimentalize the character.

Father Abraham is an ideal part for the aging Carnovsky. As he and Luther Adler grew older, they became grand old men of the theater; the combination of their experience, their stage-trained bearing, and their background in the Group's social drama lent them an aura of wisdom. In the kinescopes of fifties teleplays they strike you as men who, after struggling with issues of conscience in their youth, suffering under the yokes of the Depression and the war, have eased into a kind of understanding and acceptance and serenity. There's a rabbinical calm in their acting. Indeed, Adler's ideal role from this period may be Molotov in "The Plot to Kill Stalin" (on a 1958 "Playhouse 90"), the willfully blind bureaucrat—one of the few old Bolsheviks left in Stalin's government—who makes the mistake of remaining loyal to his old master. Adler's slightly pedantic eastern European style is the cornerstone of his work here; it gives him both background authenticity and sympathetic weight.

Roman Bohnen (Gus Michaels in *Paradise Lost*, Tom Moody in *Golden Boy*) had only one major role in movies: Candy, in *Of Mice and Men*, in 1939. Like Burgess Meredith, Bohnen was at home with this sort of material—dialogue originally written for the stage, proletarian drama of the thirties. Candy is the foolish, eager farm hand who has become little more than a messenger boy since an accident crippled him. One of the most insistent symbols in Steinbeck's play is Candy's identification with a scruffy, stinking, sick old mutt that follows him around everywhere, until Candy's bunkmates vote to put the animal out of its misery. Bohnen suffuses the role with so much humanity—a high, hoarse, chattering voice, bright little eyes that betray his excitement when he makes a new friend or proves he's still of some use to somebody, a bashful self-effacement, the crumpled mien of a working-class son who hasn't forgotten the manners his mother taught him—that he embodies the symbol and transcends it at the same time by imbuing it with so much life (a Group specialty). The scene where his dog is shot is the best example. We don't see the animal die. Instead

Lewis Milestone, the director, trains his camera on Candy, lying on his back in the bunk with his face pierced by pain and his eyes focused on the ceiling, waiting for the gun to go off. He's tensely, unsettingly alive, but you're afraid that what he hears is going to kill him. When the shot rings out he pulls in his stomach muscles—then his body relaxes and he rolls over on his side, as if he'd taken the bullet in his own belly.

Bohnen's only other role of interest is a brief stint in William Wyler's *The Best Years of Our Lives* (1946) as Pat, the tippling father of returned serviceman Fred Derry (Dana Andrews). In his first scene, Pat welcomes Fred home in a cracked, slightly sodden voice, with a weak alcoholic tentativeness. The phrase "My boy"—his affectionate name for Fred—sounds a little foolish in Pat's mouth, a little too gallant and old-fashioned for this poor, sweet, sloppy man. We don't see him again until Fred comes to say goodbye to him, and then once more there's that strange, touching formality in the way he tells his son he'll treasure the citations Fred has passed on to him as souvenirs. Derry trembles when he shakes his son's hand, and his voice quavers as he reads one of the citations aloud to his wife (Gladys George). The screenwriter, Robert Sherwood, dropped this role into the picture perfunctorily, mostly as a means of sketching Fred's rough background (drunken father, slum upbringing), but Bohnen builds an entire character out of about five minutes on the screen.

Of all the character actors the Group turned out, Lee J. Cobb, who played only small roles in Group productions, became the most famous. He had a very unusual career. At twenty-eight he was cast in the Morris Carnovsky part, Mr. Bonaparte, in the 1939 film version of *Golden Boy*, and for the next decade continued to play men several decades older than himself (such as the white-haired town doctor in *The Moon Is Down*, 1943). He capped this young/old career in the original Broadway production of *Death of a Salesman*, under Elia Kazan's direction, in 1949. Only in his late thirties did he begin to get romantic leads, and then only briefly, in modest films like *The Man Who Cheated Himself* (1950). Approaching fifty, Cobb returned to old-men roles on television, and in 1966, at fifty-five, he dusted off Willy Loman for a famous TV production of *Salesman*, directed by Alex Segal.

A glance at Cobb's work in *Golden Boy* tells us why he didn't land large roles during his time with the Group: He simply wasn't ready.

71

His bushy stage moustache is meant to make him seem older than he is, but he's almost amateurishly unconvincing as the Italian papa, and his accent is a stage conceit. (Unlike Luther Adler, Cobb never mastered accents.) In the centerpiece sequence where Bonaparte refuses to give his son Joe (William Holden) his blessing, Cobb indulges in stage-bound hysterics. It's only in his quieter scenes that his training with the Group shows through. Visiting Joe in his dressing room before a fight, Bonaparte watches his bitter exchanges with his manager, Tom Moody (Adolphe Menjou). Cobb's ability to listen with rapt intensity draws our attention away from all the shouting and excess movement, and we begin to see the scene through his eyes. When another boxer taunts Joe we feel ashamed for him, because we can't forget his father is hearing the insults.

Cobb had such a long career, and one so well documented by the camera, that we can observe his virtues as an actor and his manner of approaching a role more thoroughly than we can with Carnovsky or Adler or Bohnen. His performances are invaluable in assessing the results of Group training. Cobb's acting always resides equally in his face, his body, and his voice—unlike that of many movie and TV actors, who've had inadequate vocal training or tend to show everything in their faces and neglect to use their bodies as well. Cobb has a great bull face that he can turn either into a guard against threatening external forces or into a blank, flabby mass. He uses it both ways in *Twelve Angry Men*, the 1957 film in which he plays a juror in a murder case who finally breaks down and reveals his bias against the accused teenager on trial. He's famously adept at the clouded brow and the bowed head, and his personal code for emphasizing a phrase is to close his eyes, cluck his tongue, and throw back his head. He inhabits his make-up, so that even his *outré* facial job in "I, Don Quixote" (a 1959 "DuPont Show of the Month") becomes an extension of his performance. As Cervantes/Don Quixote (one of his best roles), he has certain moments of high emotion—like a lyrical flight in which he pays homage to his dream lady, Dulcinea—when he tosses his head back, aiming his pointed beard toward heaven.

Cobb employs not only his oversized face but also his football player's body for character effects. He gives both Don Quixote and the unnamed juror in *Twelve Angry Men* a lumbering strength, using his girth to express the juror's stubbornness, physicalizing the wall that's inside this miserable man; and to show an untrained athletic force

72

when Don Quixote confronts his enemy, the Knight of the Mirrors. Quixote lopes across the room, sword in hand: Cobb always reveals a little unexpected bounce in the over-the-hill men he plays, who move restlessly on the balls of their feet. (Dr. Joe Pearson, the old-fashioned pathologist in "No Deadly Medicine" on "Studio One," practically hops and dances around his lab.) And, just as the character life in his face extends to the peculiarities of his make-up, so the character energy in his body carries into the props he handles. After his portrayal of the corrupt union boss, Johnny Friendly, in *On the Waterfront*, a cigar becomes practically a Cobb trademark; we see it in later gangster roles (in *Party Girl*, for example) and in "No Deadly Medicine."

Like Carnovsky and Adler, Cobb holds an enormous store of strength in his voice. Even when he's speaking in a persuasive working-class vernacular (*Twelve Angry Men*), his vocal range is impressive and his training unmistakable. He returns to the chief vocal resource of the matinee idols, the tremolo (Bohnen does this, too, in both *Of Mice and Men* and *The Best Years of Our Lives*), but modifies it, reining it in so it never flies off into sentimentality, using it as a tool for expressing pride or exhaustion. When it doesn't serve him well—when one of his scenes flops (like Don Quixote's vigil prayer)—it's usually because he's concentrating too much on his vocal technique.

The Group Theatre trained its actors to convey both emotion and thought on stage, but without resorting to nineteenth-century melodramatic clichés. Since the art of thinking dramatically (giving the act of thought dramatic substance) is crucial in the drama of social conscience, a leading actor like Morris Carnovsky became highly skilled at playing thinkers and idealists—liberal, educated men who face moral dilemmas. Although Cobb's strength lay more in the proletarian camp, he gave a Carnovsky-like performance in "I, Don Quixote," in the role of a man for whom emotion and intellect are one and the same.

What unites the characters Cobb plays, though, whatever their intellectual range, is their innate nobility and the constant struggle they wage to retain their dignity. When Quixote, defeated by the Knight of the Mirrors, lies on the ground, one hand to his shaking head, it's the loss of his dignity that moves us. In the iconography of the story, it means he's lost his sanity. Morris Carnovsky went on to become one of the most celebrated Lears in American theatrical history. So, in his way, did Lee J. Cobb: There's a little bit of Lear in his performances in *Twelve Angry Men* and "I, Don Quixote," and his

73

approach to Willy Loman in *Death of a Salesman* is to play him as a contemporary Lear who's given his kingdom away to his sons.

Cobb shares with other Method actors of both his generation and the Actors Studio generation a special gift for isolating an important moment in a scene, lending it added weight. This technique bears a relationship to Walter Huston's tableaux (it's probably an outgrowth of that kind of acting), but because the goal of Method acting is emotional realism, it doesn't draw attention to itself; you have to study the performance to see how it works. Cobb becomes very still just before or just after these moments, as if he were creating spaces in time to contain them. "A Patch on Faith" (on TV's "Alcoa Hour") offers one striking example: The schoolmaster Cobb plays grows impatient with one of his students and slaps him, then takes a hard pause before framing his next line with surprising tenderness.

But Cobb's way of shaping a speech has a theatricality which the generation that followed him began to lose. *Twelve Angry Men*, a later version of the "problem" plays Cobb appeared in as a young man, is full of big scenes that the author, Reginald Rose, intends us to see as signposts to this juror's psyche. And when Lee J. Cobb takes the floor we listen, because he can call forth a lot of emotional power from inside that bulky frame, and because there's an old-time beauty in the skills of construction he brings to a major speech. In the climactic scene in *Twelve Angry Men* he begins by defending his stand against the boy on trial, and ends by exposing his bitterness toward his own son. In the banquet sequence in *Party Girl*, where he pays mock tribute to a rival gangster, his raucous laughter turns scarily quiet and his jokes turn bitter before he finally explodes.

In the last scene of "No Deadly Medicine," Cobb's Dr. Pearson gives advice to the young doctor (William Shatner) who is set to take over Pearson's post. Laughing and reminiscing about his years at the hospital, he warns the younger man not to get tired, because then (like Pearson himself) he won't be able to keep up with the times. Here, tempo is everything. Cobb performs much more slowly in this scene than actors generally do on television under the constraints of time slots. Up to this point his acting has seemed oddly lacking in energy and concentration, but this scene illuminates the rest of his performance. Suddenly we realize he's been playing deliberately against the grain of this fast-paced hospital drama in order to underscore the fact that Pearson occupies a different world—the world of his past, which still runs according to twenty-year-old speed limits. Arthur Hailey's teleplay is set rigidly in the *Grand Hotel* pattern, rushing through characters and past them to the melodramatic action, but in the midst of all this hype and platitude there's Cobb's daring approach: He waits patiently for the play to come around to him, and then slows it down to his character's own pace.

Only one Group Theatre actor ever became a movie star: John (originally Jules) Garfield. One of its youngest members, he arrived without the basic stage training that Carnovsky, Luther and Stella Adler, and most of the others had under their belts by the time they joined the company. Garfield first met Harold Clurman and Cheryl Crawford when he was cast in a small role in *Red Rust*, the sole production of the short-lived Theatre Guild Studio venture; but his real introduction to the Group came through Clifford Odets. According to Garfield's biographer, Larry Swindell, Odets believed Garfield had a natural gift for acting, that he'd already attained the level of emotional realism the Group actors were striving for, and that all he needed to tap into his own resources was a basic understanding of the Stanislavskian process. So it was Odets who first tutored Garfield in Method acting, laying the strongest emphasis on emotion memory.[5]

Garfield stayed with the Group for four years before signing a Hollywood contract, and during that time he played only one leading role: Ralph Berger, in *Awake and Sing!* Casting himself as Garfield's mentor, Odets wrote Ralph with Garfield in mind, as well as Julie Gordon in *Paradise Lost* and Joe Bonaparte in *Golden Boy*—but the Group directors insisted on other actors in the latter two parts. (Garfield's anger over the casting of Luther Adler in *Golden Boy* was probably a major factor in his breaking away from the Group.) Garfield received wonderful reviews in *Awake and Sing!* and in the small comic role of Siggie in *Golden Boy*, and he got to play Sid in the "Young Hack and His Girl" episode of *Waiting for Lefty* in the 1935 New Theatre League benefit production. Without a doubt his work with the Group filled in some of the gaps in his theatrical education. It showed him how to work on a part—how to search for role models and research a character. In the mid–1940s, preparing for *Pride of the Marines*, the biography of Al Schmid (a World War II hero blinded in action), he spent some time living with Schmid. And he learned how to play the violin for *Humoresque* so his concert scenes (dubbed by Isaac Stern) wouldn't look fake.

The most significant contribution the Group made to Garfield's career, however, was to confirm what Odets had already begun to teach him: the importance of drawing on himself when he acted. Raised in the streets and saved by the guidance of a high-school principal from the underworld life he seemed destined for, this cocky slum kid carried around inside him a rich supply of life experiences, an imaginative life based on the kind of personal history that the plots of dozens of Depression movies derive from. In other words, his four years with the Group taught him how to play himself—no mean feat for an actor. And when he made his movie debut in 1938, in *Four Daughters*, he became the first official Method star in Hollywood.

When we watch John Garfield in *Four Daughters* we're seeing two new things enter film acting: a new dedication to finding emotional truth, and a new kind of tension. *Four Daughters* began life as a Fannie Hurst novel about the loves of a quartet of sisters. In the Warners film version, directed by Michael Curtiz, it acquired a WASP-ish blandness with the casting of the Lane sisters and Gale Page as the heroines, and Jeffrey Lynn in the primary juvenile role of Felix Deitz, the young composer set to marry Ann Lemp (Priscilla Lane). Garfield signed on as Mickey Borden, Felix's gifted orchestrator, who's informally adopted by the Lemp family and then falls in love with Ann. When she discovers just before her wedding that Emma (Gale Page) also loves Felix, she elopes with Mickey to leave the field free for her sister. After a year of marriage Mickey realizes he can't make Ann happy, and kills himself. Emma outgrows her schoolgirl crush on Felix, who's finally reunited with Ann.

In structural terms, Mickey Borden is just a device inserted to present an obstacle to Ann and Felix's union, and his suicide is the film's way of disposing of him in order to hasten a happy ending. But the peculiarly independent nature of the role (Mickey is an outsider, never truly integrated into the family) liberates Garfield. Unshaven, his eyes half-closed, his hair mussed, his hat battered and his tie loose, he makes such a striking first entrance that it's probably not an exaggeration to say he was a star by the end of the reel. (He reportedly based Mickey on his pal Oscar Levant.) It's a theatrical entrance: He thrusts himself into the Lemps' living room, bums a cigarette from

Felix, and starts right in on the wisecracks, disdaining everything in the Lemp household as "normal" and "domestic."

What Garfield does is bring Odets's street-wise rebel, with his dark Semitic looks, into a small-town, middle-class house full of Gentiles. Borden isn't *written* as Jewish, of course: Because of Hollywood's Jewish studio heads' obsession with assimilation (their terror of anti-Semitism), Garfield wasn't allowed to play specifically Jewish characters until after the war. But in a sense he never played anything else, because he was always drawing so closely on himself. In this early performance you can spot a slight staginess, a trace of theatrical self-consciousness, but he's got more dynamic presence and genuine banked energy than anyone else on screen, and his acting carries infinitely more wit and authority than that of his dimpled costars. *Four Daughters* is a carefully cultivated Norman Rockwell fantasy, but Garfield is an emissary from the *real* world: It's only when he's on screen that we believe there's a Depression going on outside the Lemp household.

The screenplay saddles Mickey with an overwritten cynicism. He refers to "the Fates working overtime against me," and broods through the film like a ghetto Heathcliff. Garfield carries this stuff off by displaying a bright-eyed, tough-hide sincerity (and he's most successful when he throws his lines away). In his scenes with Priscilla Lane he's a boy from the wrong side of the tracks, eager to make a good impression but not sure how to go about it. Ann tries to straighten Mickey out, to infect him with her wholesome optimism, but he stays resolutely bent. Even his manner of sitting on a couch—his hip thrown sideways, his leg twisted—has a renegade quality to it, and he seems to live with a cigarette dangling out of his mouth. In *Daughters Courageous* (made the following year with the same cast to capitalize on the first film's runaway success), Garfield is still bumming cigarettes, and they become a trademark of his, a suggestion of something darkly anti-establishment—as well as of sexual potency (especially in *The Postman Always Rings Twice*).

Garfield plays outsiders like Mickey Borden brilliantly—injured men with restless, brooding minds and a feeling of entrapment that amounts almost to paranoia. In fact, he rarely plays anything else. Mickey touches us most when he's standing apart from the other characters, watching the Lemp family hijinks around the Christmas tree; though they've tried to include him, he feels naturally left out.

"Friends, nothing! Nobody's got any friends!" is a typical John Garfield line. (It comes from *They Made Me a Criminal*.) "You don't have to worry, Captain," Garfield's George Leach tells the master he hates, Wolf Larsen (Edward G. Robinson), in the 1941 film of Jack London's *The Sea Wolf*, "this kind of blood never cools off." (Garfield stars opposite Ida Lupino: Both dark, vivid, and brooding, they're unusually well matched, physically and temperamentally.) In the wartime propaganda adventure *Air Force*, Garfield plays the sour, authority-bucking member of the bomber crew, Sergeant Winocki—though, since there's no room for rebels in the war effort, Winocki ends up (unpersuasively) a hero.

Ironically, it was Garfield's working-class authenticity that propelled him into the Hollywood aristocracy. The unrefined New York accent, the quick defensiveness, the cockiness (always a little less forthright than Cagney's) epitomized a sharply contemporary urban persona that connected directly with audiences in the thirties and early forties. Garfield always appears most comfortable when playing someone who's either on the dole or fighting to stay off it—when, exhausted, he wanders onto May Robson's farm in *They Made Me a Criminal*, or when he brings his drifter's unfussy likableness into the roadside diner owned by Lana Turner's husband in *The Postman Always Rings Twice*. He belongs as much to the Depression as Sylvia Sidney or Barbara Stanwyck. In fact, he's inseparable from it, which is partly why some of his forties pictures (like *Body and Soul*) feel a little retro when you watch them. In *Dust Be My Destiny* (1939), his voice has a distant, almost nostalgic timber when he speaks of the future. The character he plays, Joe Bell, is fleeing from a murder charge, and he and his girl friend (Priscilla Lane again) seem to have no chance at happiness. As a movie, *Dust Be My Destiny* is completely lacking in individuality; it's built on a Depression melodramatic grid—the lovers try to escape, their dreams growing smaller and smaller as the world closes in around them. But its very impersonality accentuates Garfield's authenticity: He's a real hard-times hero whose struggles against a mean world, which can only be hinted at in one bad movie after another, provide a powerful emotional undertow. Even the absurd happy ending of *Dust Be My Destiny* can't invalidate the reality of John Garfield.

Ann elopes with Mickey in *Four Daughters* in the spirit of self-sacrifice, but in *Daughters Courageous* Priscilla Lane's attraction to Garfield (who plays an Italian ne'er-do-well named Gabriel Lopez) is a clear-cut response to his unconventionally undisguised sexuality. This was the heyday of Hollywood's popularity, when the studios pumped out one quickie after another; *Daughters Courageous* was Garfield's fifth picture, and he looks far more relaxed. Lopez is a role that already capitalizes on Garfield's anti-authoritative image (and it's a role he hated), but he understates it, and his dark charm, insouciance, and sexual force emerge much more clearly and believably than before. Gabriel gave audiences an early glimpse of the low-down con man appeal Garfield would maintain throughout his career—in *Force of Evil* (1948), for example, where he's a crooked attorney making a pass at his brother's secretary (Beatrice Pearson). (The way he plays this low-life, you can't help thinking of Sky Masterson in *Guys and Dolls*.) When this seductiveness was combined with the boyish bravado Garfield had begun to demonstrate in *Four Daughters*, it could be very touching, as in *Body and Soul* (1947), where you see the insecurity and fear underneath Charley Davis's aggressiveness. Garfield's best moment in *Body and Soul* may be his incredulous reaction when Lilli Palmer agrees to go out with him: He projects sexual readiness and emotional innocence at the same time. Garfield certainly wasn't the first actor in Hollywood to announce his sexuality on screen, but he may have been the first to use it as a conscious part of the acting process.

Garfield's sexual presence has both an emotional and a physical component. Looked at another way, it's an example of his faculty for physicalizing a complex emotional state without stylizing it, without making it unreal. He can generate suspense just by standing still, by the way he holds his body in check: In *The Postman Always Rings Twice*, when he tells Lana Turner he loves her so much that nothing else matters, his taut frame expresses a desperate eroticism. To use the vocabulary of the Method, Garfield's personal truth as an actor is partly this amazing tension, which is so potent that when the always-threatened violence inside him finally explodes, we experience a sense of tremendous release along with the character. (No actor until Marlon Brando ever seemed more apt to play a boxer.) And partly it's what explains the tension—the rich store of emotional experience that he carried around with him, as if every Garfield character was cursed with the inability to forget, even for an hour, any pain or injury he had ever borne. His eyes are always alert, even when he half closes them. Laurette Taylor once said of them, "It's as if he's looking inside himself."[6] Close-ups of Garfield draw us in more forcefully than close-ups of other stars of the era, because his characters always seem to be receiving sensory messages through their skin.

By the late 1940s Garfield was allowed to admit his heritage and play overtly the Jews he'd been playing covertly all along. In *Humoresque*, *Body and Soul*, and *Gentleman's Agreement*, his characters have not only Jewish looks and temperaments, but Jewish names as well. The war against Hitler was over, and some American writers and journalists were discovering the scourge of anti-Semitism at home: It became a favorite fighting issue for liberals in popular fiction and in film. In 1947 Elia Kazan and screenwriter Moss Hart turned *Gentleman's Agreement*, a best-selling novel by Laura Z. Hobson, into an Academy Award–winning movie. The picture focuses on Phil Green (Gregory Peck), a magazine writer who passes for Jewish in order to pen an exposé of anti-Semitism in America. As Dave, Phil's lifelong best friend whose experiences Phil draws on, Garfield doesn't make an appearance until the film is half over. And he easily wins the acting honors. He's so much more vivid and robust than anyone else on screen that the film acquires an accidental subtextual message—that Jews live fuller emotional lives than the thin-blooded WASPs who hate them so much. Kazan and Garfield, colleagues from the Group days, link forces here in a special way in a drama that is of course formally derived from the plays they grew up doing during the thirties.

The Postman Always Rings Twice (made in 1946) may have been the first movie in which Garfield really began to listen to the other actors in a scene in that intense, almost sensual manner that came to mark Method actors through the next generation. And, under Kazan's direction in *Gentleman's Agreement*, his attuned silence became the most powerful force in the film. (In a 1945 guest lecture at the Actors Laboratory in Hollywood, Garfield had said, "Talking to people [in movies] is very difficult. Once I looked at an actor and he got scared—he thought I was crazy."[7]) And he acted with an economy he'd never shown before. Called an ugly name by a stranger in a restaurant, he passes from indignation to fury and shame in a single take. When Phil's son is beaten up by neighborhood toughs for (allegedly) being a Jew, Garfield compresses Dave's entire emotional past in one precise line reading: "Now you even know that. You can stop the series [of articles] now. You know everything now."

Garfield had far from a smooth ride in Hollywood—he died before reaching his fortieth birthday. In the end, only a handful of his movies were worthy of his talents. Warner Brothers used him for his image, throwing him a series of badly written copies of Mickey Borden and the first underworld role he played, in *They Made Me a Criminal*. Until he worked with Kazan on *Gentleman's Agreement*, he had to rely on his natural, undertrained skills to dodge the obstacles of big-studio movie acting (like lousy directors) as best he could. It wasn't always easy, and he didn't always make it. We find him, in *They Made Me a Criminal*, sketching the contours of a clichéd drunk scene rather than personalizing it; or, in *Daughters Courageous*, playing to the camera instead of actually looking at Claude Rains, in a long scene between them. In the sentimental scenes in *Criminal* he just melts, not having acquired the knack later Method actors would have of playing against obvious emotional moments. And at times he falls into the old Hollywood trap of striking poses which are only *symbols* of emotions—shock in the folksy Steinbeck picture *Tortilla Flat*, or fear in the fatuous wartime spy drama *The Fallen Sparrow*, where he relies on a facial tic to show us his terror of the Nazi who tortured him. (He never gave a worse performance than in *The Fallen Sparrow*.)

In his last films (after 1947), Garfield's acting became a case of either trying too hard or not trying hard enough. In the 1948 *Force of Evil* the director, Abraham Polonsky, strives for a 1930s agit-prop atmosphere, but everything in the movie looks strained, and Garfield is miscast, both as a lawyer and as a vice figure. (He's the "force of evil" of the title, corrupting every decent character he can get to.) Polonsky's overheated style—all the actors hit the peak of their anger a second or two into every scene—and the impossible, sloganeering script he and Ira Wolfert provided leave Garfield stranded. He tries to rely on his old youthful energy, but he didn't look especially youthful by 1948, and his speeches, reeled off too fast, sound like cant. Whenever he gets mad here he stiffens his body, points it in the direction of his adversary, and sputters out his lines. Maybe he's working for an expressionistic style (maybe the whole picture is), but he's definitely the wrong actor for it.

By *Under My Skin* and *The Breaking Point* (both released in 1950), the middle-aged exhaustion in his face has burnished into character once more, but his acting has become loose, sagging. He wears an obsequious smile in *Under My Skin*, where he has an eleventh-hour speech about how the crooked jockey he plays (who's expected to throw the next day's race) is going to change his life around. But he'd already done this scene in *Body and Soul*, and here it comes across as self-imitation. He's not quite as flat in *The Breaking Point* (based on Hemingway's novella *To Have and Have Not*), but he's still uninspired; you sense that by this time acting in Hollywood had become a joyless exercise for him.

When Garfield is really on, one of his signal traits is a rapid verbal tempo: He speeds up for intensity. In *Humoresque* (which Clifford Odets wrote for him in 1946) he plays Paul Boray, a violinist whose performance, according to his friend Sid Jeffers (Oscar Levant), is "a little too broad, a little over-brilliant—you need more restraint." Levant also tells him, though, that his "personal style" could skyrocket him into the front rank, because that kind of brashness is a key component in the making of a great American artist. When Boray refers to himself as "the dynamo that makes it all tick," Odets is evoking Yank in O'Neill's *The Hairy Ape*, but the real source of the role is an earlier Odets character, the one Odets had written for Garfield as his consummate act of friendship—Joe Bonaparte in *Golden Boy*.

Paul's genius isn't as important to Odets as the violinist's ambition to pull himself out of the poverty he grew up in. "You're suffering from the all-American itch: you want to get there fast, and you don't want to pay for the ride," Jeffers tells Paul. Boray is a Joe Bonaparte who banks on his soul rather than his fists, a rebel (to return to Elia Kazan's system) who chose to become an artist rather than a gangster or a revolutionary. In the first close-up of Garfield, his cheeks fleshier now than in his early Hollywood years and his brow grown into a permanent overcast, we sense that he hasn't just expanded into the role the Group Theatre never gave him the opportunity to play—he's taken it into maturity. Unfortunately, Warner Brothers parlayed Odets's script (out of a Fannie Hurst story) into a vehicle for Joan Crawford. After the first half hour, the steamy, preposterous love story takes over the picture and Odets's hand just about disappears. You can spot him, of course, in the purplish dialogue that blights so much of his writing after his heyday in the Group Theatre.

Odets and Garfield were tightly bound up throughout Garfield's career. When Garfield returned to the stage in the late 1940s, the second role he accepted was in an Odets play, *The Big Knife* (1949), directed by Lee Strasberg, with another Group alum, J. Edward Bromberg, in the cast. Once again the part was obviously written for

Garfield: Charlie Castle is a movie star who's wrecked his talent on dreadful movie roles ("In your last ten pictures you were electrocuted four times!" his wife complains), who womanizes compulsively, who collects paintings but by his own admission doesn't know one painter from another, who still believes in F.D.R.—all documented Garfield biographical data. And he finally got to play Joe Bonaparte, too, on TV in 1950 (opposite Kim Stanley), and starred in a revival of *Golden Boy* at the ANTA Playhouse in L.A. in 1952, with Lee J. Cobb repeating his screen performance as Mr. Bonaparte. The ANTA production was the last piece of acting Garfield did before he died—an appropriate send-off.

Actually, Garfield played Joe Bonaparte throughout his career. As early as 1939, in *They Made Me a Criminal*, Warners cast him as a fighter who becomes entangled with mobsters. By the time he made *Body and Soul*, nearly a decade later, he'd done so many versions of this character that the role no longer seemed fresh, although Garfield freaks usually claim it to be his finest performance. It certainly covers all the old *Golden Boy* ground: Charley Davis is a charmingly nervy youngster, sore at the world. He makes a conquest of a woman (Lilli Palmer) much more sophisticated than he; his boxing brings him in contact with unsavory types, and going into partnership with them corrupts his values; he hurts an opponent, who eventually dies as a result. The only significant additions—the fixed fight and the happy ending—take Odets's play back to its Hollywood origins, the urban pictures of the early and mid-thirties.

Garfield did better work than in *Body and Soul*, but in a Hollywood sense it is his consummate performance, because it is the quintessential statement of the John Garfield persona. And that persona is three-quarters Joe Bonaparte. Odets ended up paying Hollywood back for the tough/sensitive boxer type he'd stolen—he rang a new, potent variation on it that became *de rigeur* in fight movies forever after.

Of all the actors whose work is available to be seen, John Garfield best epitomizes the Group Theatre approach. Distinctly American, distinctly of the Depression era, distinctly naturalistic, he played Clifford Odets's rebel hero over and over again. Engaging with other actors in a way that film audiences hadn't seen before, he carried his Group training from New York to Hollywood. He reached his zenith as an actor in his only collaboration with Elia Kazan, who was about to become famous for introducing the two emblems of the Actor's Studio generation of Method actors, Marlon Brando and James Dean, to American audiences. It's fitting that Garfield's work with Kazan should climax his career. The Method intensity sharpened by his Group years, and the strong sexual presence that was his own private contribution—the two qualities that made Garfield a cultural phenomenon—were also his legacy to Marlon Brando and the Actors Studio actors.

4

PSYCHOGROPINGS

◆ ◆ ◆

RICHARD SCHECHNER: Does Method training inevitably result in a Method style of playing?
LEE STRASBERG: Training the actor has nothing to do with style.[1]

The Method, as any acting instructor who teaches it will tell you, is a technique, a means, a codification of acting values. Lee Strasberg used to remind his classes that there were good actors before Stanislavski; that he merely translated what they did into a vocabulary novice actors could use as a basis for learning: "It's like Monsieur Jourdain in *Le Bourgeois Gentilhomme*, who was overjoyed and even a little horrified when the man told him he spoke prose, because he hadn't realized that he did."[2] But though *technically* it's accurate to call the Method a process rather than a style, the truth is a lot more complicated: The insistence of Group-trained teachers like Strasberg on seeing themselves as clinicians indicates a peculiar naïveté about what's happened to acting in this country largely as a result of their work.

When the Group Theatre began, the men and women who formed it may have had a common vision, but, as Elia Kazan has pointed out, they came from vastly different backgrounds: "Carnovsky was from the Theatre Guild, Luther Adler from the Yiddish theatre, Russell Collins from the Cleveland Playhouse, I was from Yale and from the street, and Garfield and Bromberg from Eva LeGallienne, and so forth."[3] The second generation of Method actors, however, all received their training from teachers who had worked with the Group, and almost all the young performers who brought a new excitement into American acting in the late 1940s and early 1950s and familiarized Broadway, film, and television audiences with the Method—Marlon Brando, Montgomery

Clift, James Dean, Julie Harris, Eva Marie Saint, Rod Steiger, Kim Hunter, Maureen Stapleton, Paul Newman—studied at one time at the Actors Studio under either Elia Kazan or Lee Strasberg. So, whatever its teachers had *intended* it to be, the Method inevitably picked up the markings of the Group actors, Kazan's priorities, Strasberg's obsessions, and the concerns of the postwar era in this country. What emerged was unquestionably a style, the trademark style of American actors.

Viewed from the perspective of the 1990s, the 1940s appears as the most dramatic and decisive of decades—an abrupt, shocking succession of events that scarred the face of our moral and political landscape. The first casualty of World War II was the optimistic liberalism of the 1930s. In the face of the Holocaust, the popular convictions that, given a benevolent environment, human beings would incline toward the greatest good, and that we always had the power to alter our environment, dissipated quickly. During the war, political positions were shifted, the battle lines drawn horizontally (in terms of borders) rather than vertically (in terms of class); only diehard Socialists continued to believe that the fight against fascism was essentially a class struggle. And the schematic humanistic politics of the Depression gave way to the even more simplistic politics of wartime jingoism.

Other factors contributed to the end of Depression-era liberal thought, too. The decade had been distinguished by a bonding of leftists and liberals, in Leslie Fiedler's words,

> not only by a passionate revulsion from war and the inequities of capitalism, but more positively, too, by certain tastes in books and in the arts, by shared manners and vocabulary—and especially by the sense of moral engagement that used to be called "social consciousness."[4]

But this commonality—which led to a sentimental solidarity, an inability to "believe that a man of liberal persuasion is capable of wrong,"[5] and to a blind trust in Russia—weakened at several points in the days before the war, first when the initial wave of Stalinist purges was revealed and then in the wake of the Soviet–German pact. It sickened and died with the first chill of the Cold War and the establishment of the House Committee on Un-American Activities to deal with the possible treason of the thirties' liberal Left.

In Europe existentialism, a philosophy for a time when the sky rained unanticipated and arbitrary horrors, had already caught the educated imagination as the new barbarism, fascism, began to take hold. America felt the emotional effects of the Holocaust late, and only at second hand, when survivors of the concentration camps made their way here, bringing the experience with them; and of course through the reverberations of the Nuremberg trials. What signaled the permanent change in American consciousness was the dropping of the bombs on Hiroshima and Nagasaki—an act that, at the time, was enthusiastically endorsed by an overwhelming majority of Americans. The protest of the Depression years had been an attempt to deal on a personal and human level with the suffering of groups of individuals; our new understanding that death could be dealt anonymously and instantaneously to enormous numbers of human beings had the inevitable effect of blurring the victims' faces.

Not surprisingly, the young Americans whose writing reflected the new mood of their country adopted the brave fatalism of the existentialists. Saul Bellow in *Dangling Man* and Norman Mailer in *The Naked and the Dead*, to select two vivid examples of late–1940s literature, threw out the tremulous optimism of the previous decade of writers and forged a raw, personal, nerve-exposed fiction that painted us all as Lears abandoned on the heath and unable to stop (or even comprehend) the storm. The movement to darker fiction focusing on individuals rather than communities had actually begun even earlier. Robert Penn Warren published *Night Rider* in 1939, the same year as the most celebrated—and last—of the proletarian novels, *The Grapes of Wrath*; and the following year Carson McCullers's *The Heart Is a Lonely Hunter* and Walter Van Tilburg Clark's *The Ox-Bow Incident* adopted a more psychological and fatalistic approach to social topics. As soon as the boys came home, the American theater made its own transition—from the patriotic and escapist productions of the war years to a more troubled drama. These were the years of psychological darkness on the American stage, the years of *The Glass Menagerie* and *A Streetcar Named Desire* and *Summer and Smoke*, of *All My Sons* and *Death of a Salesman*, of *The Iceman Cometh* and *A Moon for the Misbegotten*, of *Deep Are the Roots*, *Home of the Brave*, *Truckline Cafe*, *Detective Story*. Within a few years it would seem to some critics, including the *Partisan Review*'s Eleanor Clark, that success in the theater was "due largely to the feeling of depression with which one makes for the exit. The idea is that anything that can make you feel that glum must be good, true and above all important. . . ."[6]

This national recognition of the dark side of the human psyche was unprecedented in the American culture of the twentieth century. And it coincided with the widespread acceptance of psychiatry in this country. During World War II the military was forced to cope for the first time with appallingly large numbers of psychologically disturbed or maladjusted young men; more than 10 percent of all registrants were classified as unfit for service for "neuropsychiatric" reasons, and nearly 10 percent of those who were admitted ended up in psychiatric wards (500,000 received psychiatric discharges).[7] The influx of European psychoanalysts fleeing Hitler in the thirties had triggered a trend for Freudian therapy in certain intellectual circles, but suddenly the pressing needs of psychically damaged soldiers made the services of these immigrant psychiatrists and their American students and colleagues indispensable rather than just fashionable.

When this treatment met with some success the press publicized it with theatrical flair, and many Americans became convinced they'd found a psychological cure-all. Psychiatry achieved the status of a rapidly and thrillingly advancing science, like television technology. (Bruno Bettelheim suggested that the reason American translations of Freud don't use one of his favorite words, "soul," is that talk of souls doesn't sound scientific enough for American Freudians.) Writing in 1945, Dr. Otto Fenichel asserted, "Psychoanalysis represents . . . a definite step toward the aim of scientific thinking in psychology—away from the magical,"[8] and "Scientific psychology explains mental phenomena as a result of the interplay of primitive physical needs . . . and the influences of the environment on these needs. There is no place for any third factor."[9] The tone of scientific definiteness is so reassuring; it implies that a good dose of therapy can send our little psychic troubles packing the way an aspirin eradicates a headache. So the generation that put self-help books by Dale Carnegie and Norman Vincent Peale repeatedly on the best-seller list applauded the advent of psychiatry in the same spirit. And the number of psychiatric outpatient clinics in this country more than doubled between 1940 and 1950. President Truman signed the National Mental Health Act in 1946, granting new power to the Mental Hygiene Division of the Public Health Service and officially endorsing the growing number of psychiatric bodies: the American Psychiatric Association, the Psychiatric Foundation, the National Mental Health Foundation, and the National Committee for Mental Hygiene.

Each stride made in this arena was the source of fascinated coverage in the popular magazines, and the cause for national pride. And the more "scientific" they were, the better. In his biography of Frances Farmer, the one-time Group Theatre actress institutionalized in the 1940s in the Western State Hospital at Steilacoom, Washington, William Arnold explains that the overwhelming public and governmental approbation of unconstrained psychiatric research made it possible for the Steilacoom physicians to subject Farmer to a succession of experimental drugs, and to perform the transorbital lobotomy operation developed in 1935 by Dr. Antonio Moniz. (Moniz won the Nobel Prize for Medicine in 1949—an indication of the attitude of the Western world at the time toward the kind of work he was engaged in.)

The United States had become a nation of Freudians, devouring Mary Jane Ward's 1946 novel *The Snake Pit* (which started a trend for psychiatric novels) and newly attentive to psychological detail in the theater, at the movies, and on TV. The first generation of analysand playwrights—Arthur Miller, Tennessee Williams, and William Inge most prominent among them—were only too happy to oblige; so were the best directors. After his first experience with psychoanalysis in 1945, director Elia Kazan "began handling darker, riskier material and started gravitating toward deeply troubled characters whose behavior ranged beyond their own understanding and control," according to Thomas Pauly.[10] And Kazan's concerns directly influenced his students at the Actors Studio, who were learning that most psychologically focused of acting techniques, the Method.

According to David Riesman, writing in 1950, "the tremendous growth in counseling services, including psychotherapy, also testifies to people's need for group adjustment."[11] For the advanced technology of the forties had transformed forever the relationship of individuals to each other. Riesman's important sociological study *The Lonely Crowd* covers the transition from the "inner-directed" society of earlier centuries, in which parent and teacher figures are central to a child's moral, social, and psychological development, to the "outer-directed" society of the twentieth century, where the most powerful educational tools are in the hands of the media. Defining and spreading popular culture, the media assumes (and therefore creates) a peer group of viewers and listeners to which every individual is made to feel the need to conform. When television suddenly usurped the mainstream of popular culture in the late forties and early fifties, it gave unthought-of strength to the tyranny of the peer group. Riesman writes:

> To say that judgments of peer-groupers are matters of taste . . . is not to say that any particular child can afford to ignore these judgments. On the contrary he is, as never before, at their mercy. . . . The child is . . . exposed to trial by jury without any defenses either from the side of its own morality or from the adults. All the morality is the group's.[12]

And the chief agenda of the TV-invented peer group was

> the task of telling members of large groups of mobile people what they can expect of each other and what they should expect of themselves. The inner-directed man learned what he needed to know of these matters in a primary group, or by a purposeful internalization of his schooling and reading. The mass media today are expected to perform ten-minute miracles of social introduction between people from a variety of ways of life and background. The entertainment fields serve the audience today less and less as an escape from daily life, more and more as a continuous sugar-coated lecture on how to get along with the "others."[13]

It's amazing: The media, having created a peer group of unprecedented psychic power, now ensures its continued existence by directing its attention not to the real needs of Americans (poverty or social injustice or insufficient education) but to an imagined new need—the need to conform, to share the tastes and the thinking of the group. The natural movement Fiedler talked about, from shared tastes to a feeling of human connection, has been replaced by a synthetic process: The media creates popular tastes and encourages the audience to adopt them and thereby make connection with the "others." The media has become the Blob.

This media-propelled drive for conformity produced a strange dichotomy of responses from Americans as the Truman era segued into the Eisenhower years. On the surface of the country was a blank smile, a wash of complacency that found its most popular expression in the image of the commuter spending a peaceful Sunday afternoon mowing his lawn (the suburban pastorale) and its most vicious shape in Joe McCarthy, the Red scares, xenophobia. But locked in an unresolvable tension with this national complacency was a national uneasiness—not just at the fringes, where the beatniks lived, where Norman Mailer wrote "The White Negro" and Paul Goodman wrote *Growing Up Absurd*—but in the very heart of the American family: its teenagers.

The postwar era practically invented the American adolescent—at least as a figure to be reckoned with, feared, and analyzed. For Riesman, the teenager is the ultimate victim of the mad conformity of his age, which he or she instinctively struggles to buck or devalue. And the literature and drama of the fifties bears out Riesman's thesis, most clearly in the oppressive boarding-school atmosphere of J. D. Salinger's *Catcher in the Rye*, Calder Willingham's *End as a Man*, and Robert Anderson's *Tea and Sympathy*. The teenager's newfound, unconcealed sexuality is a source of terror to the repressed adults around him (the focal adolescent in this period is almost always male), as in William Inge's *Picnic*, where the protagonist, Hal, is a slightly superannuated (just post–college-age) version of a typical hell-raising teen. Often, in this Freudian era, he's seen as a repository for the sins of his parents (who carry all the blame for the young heroes' troubles in the movie *Rebel Without a Cause*, for example).

Television, with bland predictability, propagated the image of the adolescent as Andy Hardy (Bud Anderson, Wally Cleaver, David and Ricky Nelson), an image pitifully at odds with the more realistic one of rock 'n' rollers out there jiving to Elvis Presley and Little Richard. Much closer to them emotionally was the figure in movies who heaved desperately against the pull of conformity: the tough/vulnerable, semi-articulate rebel without a cause who had come down in a direct line from Joe Bonaparte in *Golden Boy* through all the post–Odets roles John Garfield played in the late 1930s and 1940s. The single factor most responsible for the popularity of the Method in the Eisenhower years was that the rebel without a cause was the exclusive turf of Method actors.

The Actors Studio: Elia Kazan and Lee Strasberg

When the Group Theatre disbanded in 1941, many of its members remained active in the New York theater scene. Some made a home for themselves in Hollywood—John Garfield (of course), Morris Carnovsky, Luther Adler, Robert Lewis, Ruth Nelson—with others, such as J. Edward Bromberg and Stella Adler, taking occasional professional trips to the West Coast. Lee Strasberg (briefly), Harold Clurman, and Elia Kazan (after his brief acting stint in pictures) continued to direct on Broadway.

Among Clurman's most notable productions in the forties and fifties were *Truckline Cafe* (Maxwell Anderson), *The Member of the Wedding* (Carson McCullers), *The Autumn Garden* (Lillian Hellman), *Bus Stop* (William Inge), and *Orpheus Descending* (Tennessee Williams). Kazan catapulted into a phenomenally successful directing career: He staged ten plays on Broadway between 1941 and 1947, including Thornton Wilder's *The Skin of Our Teeth*; the Kurt Weill–Ogden Nash–S. J. Perelman musical comedy *One Touch of Venus*; *Deep Are the Roots* (d'Ussau and Gow); and *All My Sons* (Arthur Miller), while at the same time establishing himself as one of Hollywood's most dynamic young moviemakers. He made his film directing debut in 1945 with a highly acclaimed adaptation of Betty Smith's best seller *A Tree Grows in Brooklyn*, and in 1947 won the Academy Award for *Gentleman's Agreement*.

However, except for Kazan on both coasts and Garfield before the cameras in Hollywood, the graduates of the Group Theatre had their most powerful influence on American acting in another forum altogether: the classroom. The master acting instructor was still a relatively new concept in this country; prior to Boleslavsky's American Laboratory Theatre, men and women of the professional theater didn't teach. In the early 1940s Erwin Piscator, the German emigré director whose play *The Case of Clyde Griffiths* had been staged by the Group in 1936, invited Lee Strasberg, Stella Adler, and Sanford Meisner to give classes at his Dramatic Workshop in the New School in New York, where Marlon Brando, Rod Steiger, Montgomery Clift, and Maureen Stapleton were enrolled. By the 1950s, all three had moved on to other, permanent homes: Stella Adler to form her own Conservatory, Sanford Meisner to take over the Neighborhood Playhouse, and Lee Strasberg to run the already established Actors Studio. Meanwhile,

Phoebe Brand found work teaching in the Actor's Laboratory in Hollywood, and later with her husband, Morris Carnovsky, at the American Shakespeare Festival Theatre and Academy, the American Theatre Wing, and the American Academy of Dramatic Art.

The Actors Studio opened on October 5, 1947, under the direction of Elia Kazan, Cheryl Crawford, and Robert Lewis. It was a unique proposition: All the students, who had been carefully chosen after a series of interviews and auditions, were professional actors—a stipulation the Studio has maintained as a basic rule in the more than four decades of its existence. According to Kazan, the purpose of the institution was to promote "a common language so that I can direct actors instead of coach them . . . so that we have a common vocabulary. It's not a school. Actors can come and actors can go. It is a place to work and find this vocabulary."[14] Kazan taught the beginners' class: twenty-six students, including Julie Harris, Steven Hill, Cloris Leachman, Nehemiah Persoff, James Whitmore, Warren Stevens, Rudy Bond, Jocelyn Brando, and, before the first season was out, Kim Hunter and Martin Balsam. Lewis was in charge of the advanced workshop. Among the fifty-two names on his roster were Marlon Brando, Montgomery Clift, Mildred Dunnock, Eli Wallach, Maureen Stapleton, David Wayne, John Forsythe, Tom Ewell, Anne Jackson, Sidney Lumet, Karl Malden, E. G. Marshall, Patricia Neal, Kevin McCarthy, Jerome Robbins, William Redfield, Beatrice Straight, and Herbert Berghof (who went on to open a well-known acting studio of his own in the 1950s).

Crawford's contribution to the Studio was strictly that of an administrator and businesswoman; Lewis walked out after a year as the result of a private quarrel with Kazan. The spirit of the Studio in its fledgling days was really defined by Elia Kazan. "Kazan was a symbol to me of the daring, exciting part of the theatre," June Havoc, an early member, has said.[15] According to Martin Ritt, who was Kazan's assistant at the Studio before his own career as a filmmaker took off, Kazan's classes were "exercises in imagination, concentration, faith, and a sense of truth."[16] Kazan was certainly the Studio's drawing card, even before Lewis left. Given the chance to work with the hottest young director on two coasts, what young actor would say no—especially since, if Kazan liked your class work, chances were he'd cast you in one of his ventures? To men and women starting out in theater during this era, Kazan represented the fervent energy of the postwar American stage; at their best his movies transported that energy to the screen.

93

By the mid-forties Hollywood movies had become glossy, manicured, essentially fake. Sure, there were exceptions: John Huston, Preston Sturges, Orson Welles, William Wyler, Robert Siodmak, and occasionally William Wellman, Howard Hawks, and John Ford still made movies worth watching. But the power of the studios, which had been run by colorful tyrants dispensing ironclad contracts, was on the wane, and after the experience of World War II American audiences craved some fresh air at the movies—something a little daring, something contemporary. The best pictures of these years cut boldly across the complacent sheen of the big-studio products: Wellman's *The Story of G.I. Joe*, with its melancholy, understated, highly personalized vision of war; Wyler's *The Best Years of Our Lives*, with its un-Hollywood-like frankness about marriage; Huston's brutal psychological study *The Treasure of the Sierra Madre*. Kazan was in the new wave of directors who caught fire in the postwar years, each adding a distinctive voice to the movies: the cynical ironist Billy Wilder (*Double Indemnity*, *The Lost Weekend*, *Sunset Boulevard*), the poetic humanist–realist Fred Zinnemann (*The Search*, *The Men*, *The Member of the Wedding*, *From Here to Eternity*), and Mark Robson, who located the temperaments of young men at war in *Home of the Brave* with the sensitivity of the best Vietnam coming-of-age pictures of our own epoch (like *Casualties of War* or *Hamburger Hill*), but whose promise was short-lived.

Kazan's first experiences in filmmaking were on documentaries with the photographer Ralph Steiner in the 1930s, and his comradely interest in "real" people, the salt of the earth, continued through his career as a movie director, long after he'd abandoned the leftist politics of his youth. He tended to employ as extras the citizens of the small cities and towns where he shot his pictures—as early as *Boomerang!* (his third picture, made in 1947), in *A Face in the Crowd* and *Wild River*, and most memorably in *Baby Doll*, where the undisguised delight of the locals, black and white and Asian, at Karl Malden's clownish inability to take charge of the sexy bride he hasn't yet bedded (Carroll Baker) is the movie's running gag. (The moment in *Baby Doll* more people may have retained than any other is the most unexpected one: An old black woman in a hash joint bursts into a chorus of "I Shall Not Be Moved." She has one of those amazing old-time blues voices— thin but sinewy, with a powerful resonance—that could never be duplicated by a trained singer.) Actual longshoremen turn up in the dock scenes of *On the Waterfront*.

94

This impulse toward documentary truth translates, in Kazan's work with professional actors, into a knack for finding performers who are "experientially" right for their roles, and even for encouraging personality conflicts on the set that enhance those in the script. Over and over again in his autobiography, *A Life*, Kazan furnishes examples: the casting of alcoholic James Dunn as the hard-drinking ne'er-do-well Johnny Nolan in *A Tree Grows in Brooklyn*, and of infuriating, rebellious James Dean as Cal Trask in *East of Eden*, using Raymond Massey's personal distaste for Dean to step up the tensions between father and son in that picture. (Evidently he did the same thing in his stage productions: He cast Barbara Bel Geddes as Maggie in *Cat on a Hot Tin Roof* because of the way he read the actress's own character; and he swears that the unconcealed enmity between Tallulah Bankhead and Florence Eldridge in *The Skin of Our Teeth*, present from the outset, made the show work.)

It took Kazan a decade of filmmaking to master the art of merging professionals and nonprofessionals, but the vivid, smoking mix that resulted is one of the trademarks of a Kazan picture. At first he wasn't great at directing crowd scenes or throwaway bits: A montage in *Boomerang!* depicting the response of citizens to the slowness of police in apprehending a murderer has a quaint, prewar theatricality. (It's like the tenement set pieces in an early-thirties picture like *Street Scene*.) And his first movies, to a greater or lesser extent, are bowed under the yoke of big-studio sentimentality and complacency. His debut film, *A Tree Grows in Brooklyn*, about the indomitability of a child raised in poverty, is full of clichés, though as it goes on, the performances solidify and melt your resistance to the undercurrent of banality. *Boomerang!* is a good, unpretentious picture, but there must be half a dozen stock scenes, like the one where the hard-working D.A. (Dana Andrews) persuades the besieged police chief (Lee J. Cobb) not to throw in the towel; or the one where the D.A.'s loving wife (Jane Wyatt) mops her husband's psychological brow and quietly sets him back on track.

Gentleman's Agreement, which won Kazan his first Academy Award, has thorny, unresolvable issues churning around in it, but like the polite anti-Semites it wants to expose, it has a veneer of niceness that wants to suffocate the real drama in it, and often succeeds. Even when the hero's girl (Dorothy McGuire) reveals her racist streak; even when Kazan and the screenwriter, Moss Hart, play with the suggestion

95

that the writer (Gregory Peck) is becoming a self-righteous pain, the movie is quick to subdue all that rocky, discomfiting material to a convenient, unwrinkled conclusion. What distinguishes these movies is the performances Kazan is able to get from a variety of actors— Dorothy McGuire and Joan Blondell and the kids (the intense, borderline-neurotic Peggy Ann Garner, and Ted Donaldson, with his peculiar, scratchy-voiced charm) in *A Tree Grows in Brooklyn*; John Garfield and Celeste Holm in *Gentleman's Agreement*; Dana Andrews and a cast full of idiosyncratic character actors in *Boomerang!*: Lee J. Cobb, Ed Begley, Arthur Kennedy, Sam Levene.

Kazan says he learned how to be a filmmaker while shooting *Panic in the Streets* in 1950, and you can see a striking difference between the pictures he released in the forties, which are still very much studio products, and the ones he made in the fifties, which are representations of an exciting personal style—especially *A Streetcar Named Desire*, *Viva Zapata!*, *On the Waterfront*, *East of Eden*, *Baby Doll*, and *A Face in the Crowd*. His movies suddenly acquired an unusual visual clarity: In *Streetcar* he collaborated with photographer Harry Stradling, and both *Waterfront* and *Baby Doll* were shot by the extraordinary Boris Kaufman, who had worked with Jean Vigo in France in the thirties. And a strong new focus on setting suggested a kinship with neorealist directors Vittorio De Sica, Roberto Rossellini, and the young Federico Fellini—all working in Italy at the same time.

These pictures don't feel as if they were made in a studio, and most of them weren't. Kazan's experiences in Hollywood in the forties, especially on *Sea of Grass* (his worst film, which starred Katharine Hepburn and Spencer Tracy), convinced him that he couldn't do the kind of work he wanted in an environment he found synthetic, and so, despite his amazing success in movies (he won a second Oscar for *On the Waterfront*), he remained a New York personality. As early as 1954, long before New York had become a second film capital, he insisted on shooting there; the city was a constant impetus to his imagination. The freezing docks and parks and alleys of Hoboken, where *Waterfront* was shot, authenticate the experience of the movie. And the same can be said of the more exotic locations Kazan chose for other films—like Benoit, Mississippi, where he shot *Baby Doll*, in a ramshackle old Southern Gothic mansion that functions as a glorious symbol of the disastrous marriage of Archie Lee and Baby Doll Meighan. Against the background of this sprawling antique—antebellum graciousness that's become overgrown and decrepit but still retains some of its implausible plantation beauty—Kazan stages Tennessee Williams's sly sex farce. The three principals (Silva Vaccaro, the Sicilian seducer, played by Eli Wallach, is the third, the catalyst) whoop and holler up and down the ancient staircases while, outside, the Meighans' neighbors, like a comic chorus, collapse in laughter at the couple's foolish antics.

Kazan is practically a genius at this juicy mixture of realism and stylization, at finding exactly the right naturalistic detail to ground—and set off—the poetry (in *Streetcar*) or the extravagant comedy (in *Baby Doll*) in the material. He's got one foot in each camp: Even a piece of *bona fide* naturalism like *On the Waterfront* has an achieved, close-in energy that reaches toward theatrical Expressionism. The rabble-rouser in Kazan—the child of the leftist drama of the thirties—loves the scrambling interplay of painterly tableau and mad movement. The crowd of longshoremen framed like Walker Evans figures against the docks, waiting to learn who'll work that day, shifts into a free-for-all when the foreman tosses a spare work tag onto the ground; a long, silhouetted exterior of the Meighan house is juxtaposed with an interior montage of close-ups as characters chase each other from room to room. It's melodrama, though of a high style, and Kazan can never resist melodrama. Here he mocks his own penchant for it:

> I used to make every scene GO GO GO! mounting to a climax, and if I had sixty minutes in a picture there were sixty climaxes, *ready? CLIMAX! all right, rest a minute—CLIMAX!* That was what I used to do. And it's easy to do, you know, make somebody shout, or grab somebody by the neck or throw somebody out, or slam a door, or open a window, or hit somebody with a hammer, or eat something quick in disgust—it's easy to do.[17]

In his best movies (*Streetcar, Waterfront, Baby Doll*) the melodrama isn't a problem; it's mitigated, validated, or transformed by the depth and power of the performances. But in *Viva Zapata!*, large chunks of *East of Eden*, and especially *A Face in the Crowd* and *Splendor in the Grass*, melodrama—often a scalded stew of Freudian passions and violence with the volume cranked way up—tends to take the place of drama; though it keeps you watching, you know it's rigged, phony.

Kazan's chief contribution to movies is his work with actors. He sees movies as a possibility to extend the improvisatory process a Method director goes through with actors in rehearsal or in workshop:

> Another thing . . . I always stress a lot when I direct actors is what happened just before the scene. I not only talk about it, I sometimes improvise it. By the time the scene starts, they're fully in it, not just saying lines they've been given. Sometimes I do a scene that's unrelated to the scene in the script . . . so the actor knows what he's bringing into the scene that he plays. All these things are cinematic in that they take the reliance off the dialogue . . . and put it on activity, inner activity, desire, objects, partners. . . . All this can be photographed: the movement to achieve something can be photographed, what you are trying to achieve—the object—can be photographed, the partner and your relationship to him can be photographed. The lines are put into what I think is their proper place, into a secondary position.[18]

The kind of improvisation any director trained in the Method employs in rehearsal, or even on the set, tends to belong to one of two categories. Some is independent of the script; it's meant to loosen up the actors and establish a rapport (especially important if they haven't worked together before), as well as to strengthen their trust in the director. It may involve relaxation exercises or improvised scenes on stock setups. More often, though, the improvs are text-related, either indirectly (building on situations that parallel the circumstances in the script) or specifically: The actors may improvise scenes the playwright omits—scenes that help to establish or develop relationships—or they may replay actual scenes in their own words, as a middle step toward making the writer's words sound natural in their own mouths.

Of his generation, Kazan exerted the most powerful influence on younger filmmakers (Martin Ritt, Arthur Penn, and Sydney Pollack, among others, learned from him). The link he forges between improvisation and the use of the camera in his movies not only explains his success in American movies and the role he played in revitalizing them; it also suggests how this era managed to produce so many actors who were as comfortable in front of a camera as they were on a stage. This was one of the distinguishing features of the Actors Studio generation, which can be dated from 1947—the year the Studio opened its doors, the year Kazan made the picture that won him official recognition in Hollywood (that is, his first Academy Award), and the year he featured Marlon Brando in the Broadway production of *A Streetcar Named Desire*. Significantly, *Streetcar* went into rehearsal the week the Actors Studio held its first meeting.

The first season of Studio classes culminated in a workshop presentation from each of the two groups. Lewis's actors made a stab at *The Sea Gull*, with Maureen Stapleton as Masha, David Wayne as Medvedenko, Herbert Berghof as Dorn, and Mildred Dunnock as Paulina. (Montgomery Clift was originally cast as Treplev but withdrew after a fight with Lewis.) Kazan's class performed a first play by novelist Bessie Breuer, *Sundown Beach*, about World War II fliers convalescing in a psychiatric hospital. Delighted with the results, Kazan booked the show into two summer theaters and then, following an encouraging out-of-town critical reception, into a Broadway house at the top of the next season. (Unfortunately, the New York critics weren't as generous as the Westport and Marblehead press had been: The play closed after seven performances.) *Sundown Beach* is the earliest example of the Studio's efforts to reach beyond the classroom and into the professional theater, where its students were struggling to make a living.

When preparing his book on the Actors Studio, *A Method to Their Madness*, Foster Hirsch was told by an anonymous Group Theatre alumnus that, unlike the Group, "the Studio is a commercial enterprise, dedicated above all to creating stars."[19] That's a harsh judgment, but the fact is that the Actors Studio was conceived as a laboratory, not a rep company, in an age when—thanks to directors like Kazan—acting in the movies no longer seemed by its nature an undermining of the principles serious Method actors had learned to apply to their stage work. (Anyway, John Garfield had already proven that a serious Method actor could become a movie star.) The Group's idealism would have been incongruous behind the doors of the Studio. Besides, Kazan's position on both coasts necessarily connected his work at the Studio with the professional work he participated in outside. Despite Lee Strasberg's insistence during the 1950s and early 1960s that the Studio was a workshop protected from the crucible of the professional theater—a place where actors could be private and risk themselves in scenes that no public audience would ever see—it's never been possible to separate the fact of the Studio from the work of its students, and of Kazan, away from it.

Moreover, since its make-up was entirely professional from the start, it was inevitable that the Studio would involve itself in theatrical ventures again and again. Sometimes new plays began in workshop there (*The Rose Tattoo, Camino Real, A Hatful of Rain*) and ended up on or off Broadway. And in 1963 the Studio attempted to branch out into repertory, though with a marked lack of success. One of the first direct associations between the Studio and the professional theater, just weeks after *Sundown Beach* opened and closed, was the "Actors Studio" television series, which premiered in September 1948 with a production of Tennessee Williams's one-act play *Portrait of a Madonna*, starring Jessica Tandy. (Tandy never actually belonged to the Studio, but she was related to it through Kazan, who directed her on Broadway in *Streetcar.*) Sanford Meisner directed the second episode, "Night Club," with Maureen Stapleton, Cloris Leachman, and Lee Grant, and in the next two years such Studio actors as Mildred Dunnock, Martin Balsam, Eva Marie Saint, Julie Harris, Kim Hunter, E. G. Marshall, Kevin McCarthy, David Wayne, Eli Wallach, Jo Van Fleet, and Nehemiah Persoff made their TV debuts on the series. One of the earliest anthologies of live TV drama, "Actors Studio" established television as a third arena for this generation of Method actors.

Because of his efforts to integrate Studio workshops and public performances—his insistence on employing Method–trained actors in productions and films that made some of them famous—it's fair to say that Kazan had more to do with establishing the Method as the American acting style in the late forties and early fifties than anyone else. His work drew the attention of the press and their theatergoing and filmgoing readers to the Studio's existence. But by the time the publicity had reached its peak in 1955, when Brando and Eva Marie Saint had won Oscars for *On the Waterfront* and James Dean was creating a sensation in *East of Eden*, Kazan was no longer the most powerful force behind the Studio. Lee Strasberg had taken over in 1951, and as the decade wore on Kazan spent less and less time there.

Strasberg had been a conspicuous absentee from the Actors Studio faculty in 1947 because of the difficulty other Group members experienced in working with him—his volatile, unpredictable temper, his tendency to tyrannize actors, and his insistence, called fanatical even by his admirers, on exercising complete control in all situations. He and his colleagues had had philosophical disagreements, too, based upon his continued enthusiasm for affective memory after it had fallen out of favor in the Group. But when Lewis withdrew from the Studio in 1948, Kazan and Crawford cast around for teachers to alleviate Kazan's classroom load, and Strasberg accepted their invitation to conduct a few workshops. By the early 1950s, he'd moved into Kazan's old position at the helm. And somehow, under his tutelage, the Method changed from a fresh new way of working, representing the best impulses of a restless postwar generation, into a sacred calling. Perhaps this shift was in the cards anyway: Once Brando appeared on the scene, he became the idol of young actors across the country who dedicated themselves to finding their own "truth" in the same way he had. But Strasberg's personality, his pedagogical approach, and his offhand way of courting publicity (which tied in with his obsession with stars and stardom, as evidenced by his peculiar way of crowding Marilyn Monroe's limelight) accelerated the transformation and established him as high priest of this new religion.

"Lee is like the rabbi, he has this long-range point of view," Maureen Stapleton has said of him.[20] Other actors have spoken less kindly, like Celeste Holm, who decried the "cabalistic pomposity" of the Studio membership.[21] David Garfield, the author of *The Actors Studio: A Player's Place*, suggests:

> The facts that the workshop headquarters had once been a church, that Strasberg usually wore a clerical-looking dark suit and shirt, and that talk of the Method and "Methodism" had a quasi-doctrinal ring to it . . . served to reinforce the religious imagery.[22]

But mostly it was Strasberg's air of omniscience, his ecclesiastical style and patriarchal obstinacy, his presentation of himself as the chief nurturer of that most delicate plant, talent, and his fits of chastising fury—combined with his obvious gifts as an instructor of acting—that encouraged a worshipful response in his students (and gave many of them cause to rebel along the way, including his son John, who began a rival school in the sixties).

These characteristics were intensified holdovers from an earlier

101

era; they were the tools that feisty second-generation American Jews like Strasberg and Harold Clurman (whose lectures fostered the "religion" of the Group Theatre) had made use of during the Depression years. Irving Howe says it was the Talmudic love of argument that led Jews to Socialist meetings in the thirties. That same love must have led Clurman and Strasberg to the theater, where Clurman held small audiences of actors spellbound for hours while he spun dreams of the drama of the future, and where Strasberg, another great talker, became the Method's first guru.

Strasberg has certainly had his share of detractors through the years. Gordon Rogoff, who worked with him at the Studio, wrote a scathing article about him in 1964. George C. Scott, directed by him once (in a calamitous 1964 production of *Three Sisters*), used to refer him as "Lee you-should-excuse-the-expression Strasberg." James Baldwin, whose *Blues for Mister Charlie* was among the casualties in the ill-fated Actors Studio Theatre venture in the early sixties, satirized him mean-spiritedly in *Tell Me How Long the Train's Been Gone*. And the Method he promoted has come in for frequent attacks, too, especially in the fifties and sixties. Most of them target the Actors Studio stereotype, seen variously as a gum-chewing mumbler, a beatnik, or, in David Garfield's words, "a rebel against refinement, decorum and gentility, who, in his nonglamorous approach to acting, was attempting to appear 'proletarian.' "[23] This perception aligns the Method prototype with the beats, rock 'n' roll, hipsterism—the anti-establishment strivings of the Eisenhower era that were damned, depending on which end of the spectrum you tuned into, for subversive tendencies or bad manners.

Theodore Hoffman's description of the Method actor type, put forth in 1960, is funnier and more incisive:

> Method actors seem more intense than others. They like to get close to each other (closer than the traditional arm's-length). They are apt to speak low when there is distance between them and loud when they are close to each other. There is a tautness in their voices which makes them inaudible or gratingly monotonous. They don't seem to move much, and when they do it is with rapid, spasmodic movements. They like to scratch themselves, rub their arms, brush their hair, count their buttons. They keep on doing

these things even when other actors are the center of attention. They seem to alternate between assaulting each other
and retreating into themselves. They like to play scenes
wherever they choose, frequently in odd pockets of the
stage. They apparently don't like to deliver lines towards the
audience.

All the characters in a Method production seem to be
gifted with similar voice levels and similar speech patterns,
and they all behave alike. The play grips one at every moment, but seems to go on forever. There are long pauses
between lines. When a piece of business like lighting a cigarette or pouring a drink comes up, the play seems to stop
while the actor carefully examines the cigarette to find out
what brand it is or looks for germs on the glass. One gets the
impression that a great deal is happening to the characters
but one isn't always sure just what. And in the end one gets
a kind of cheated feeling, as if the actors were going through
all that rigmarole for their own pleasure and really weren't
the least bit interested in communicating anything to the
audience.[24]

It's only fair to say that this catalogue of "Methodisms" is, by
Hoffman's own admission, a list of "clichés, which can also be taken as
the mistakes, aberrations, and botched experiments that must somehow or other be gone through on the way to genuine achievement"[25]
and that though "it is possible, of course, to tell when you're observing
Method actors . . . it's easier when the actors are bad Method
actors."[26] Still, Hoffman was only stating, in a much wittier manner,
what a lot of other critics and acting teachers and (mostly older) theatergoers were complaining about, and his summary is a useful starting
point for an examination of the Actors Studio approach to acting.
Briefly, he's focusing on the following Method vices: a preoccupation
with "preparation," i.e., the steps the actor takes to get into character
but which the audience has no interest in seeing; an apparent working-
out of some internal psychological problem in performance; an exaggerated focus on emotionality that ignores the demands of dramatic
action; an inclination toward mannerism—the actor's insistence on
playing himself rather than the character; and a disregard of craft.

Preparation is a way for an actor who has trouble getting into character to focus concentration before launching into a scene. It's a luxury of the acting class, where the actors are free from the pressure of producing something authentic right off the bat and can take as much time as they need. Strasberg first employed this aid in the Group Theatre days, when he and his actors referred to it as "taking a minute." Of course, a workshop or class situation such as the Actors Studio sets up permits actors much greater ease than they could have had during rehearsals at the Group, since the Studio's emphasis isn't on product but on process. And although Strasberg himself has spoken against the tendency of Studio actors to incorporate preparation into professional performance, it's not difficult to see how the habit of indulging in preparation time in class could carry onto a professional stage. That's when, as Tyrone Guthrie complained, a Method actor seems to "over-prize the Search for Truth as opposed to the Revelation of Truth."[27] In other words, the personal satisfaction that the preparation exercise provides can lead a bad actor to mistake the means for the end.

When the demands of playing Stanley Kowalski in *A Streetcar Named Desire* led Marlon Brando into analysis, psychiatry received its official endorsement as a profession accessory to the theater. Strasberg had no first-hand experience with psychotherapy, but clearly he was one of its advocates. "If the actor cannot function well in his personal life," according to an unidentified Studio member, "Strasberg recommends psychoanalysis, to be undertaken simultaneously with his studio or class training."[28] This suggestion seems less peculiar if you recall Strasberg's obsession with genuine emotion in performance. An actor "must deal with deep, firm things inside himself,"[29] he believed, and any obstacle that stands in the way of that process must be removed. Strasberg claimed that analysis "often leads to a more direct possibility of expression, and the acting work often brings out things that help with the analysis."[30] But by defining the relationship between therapy and acting as a two-way street he implies that, as an acting teacher, he is in effect also playing the role of a psychoanalyst. One of Strasberg's students told Paul Gray, "In order to really relate to a teacher . . . you have to make an analyst or a god out of him,"[31] and Robert Hethmon's preface to the chapter called "Problems: Stopping Imagination" in his book of transcribed Studio sessions, *Strasberg at the Actors Studio*, describes Strasberg as a man with "the objectivity of the doctor who stands outside the body he is treating."[32] Furthermore, several of the exercises reproduced in Hethmon's book, and in Edward Dwight

Easty's *On Method Acting*, sound amazingly—alarmingly—like therapy.

Garfield and other sources list four kinds of exercises for "unblocking" emotion: "affective memory," "speaking out," "song and dance," and "the private moment." "Affective memory," as we have seen, is the inducing of an emotional state by probing one's past. In "speaking out," the actor vocalizes all the feelings he or she encounters while working through a scene, even if they seem to bear no direct connection to the scene itself. "Song and dance" begins with a song, during which the actor tries to remain sensitized to every feeling. This is followed by a dance version of the tune, with Strasberg directing the changes in the actor's movements and tempo; an increased consciousness of the emotions welling up under the song eventually forces them through the surface. "The private moment," an exercise Strasberg developed in the mid–1950s, is best described by Strasberg himself:

> I was rereading Stanislavski's books, and I came across the statement that the basic problem in acting is to learn to be private in public. . . . So I asked myself, "What would happen if I asked these actors to do something that they do in life, but which even in life is so private that . . . when anyone comes in, they have to stop doing it? . . . The exercise produced wonderful results in the actor's belief in what he was doing, and it led to a releasing of emotion and a degree of theatrical energy I had not previously seen in these particular actors. . . . People do things in life on a much wider and more vivid scale of expression than they will permit themselves to use on the stage, even at a moment of good acting. People who were inhibited in moving on the stage did private-moment exercises in which they behaved with startling abandon.[33]

"The private moment" has been a notorious target for Method detractors, who consider it an intrusion of the actor's privacy and an airing of dirty linen in public—though in fact nothing obscene has ever occurred, as far as I know, in an Actors Studio classroom. (The "private moment" Strasberg cited most often was one where a shy actress flung herself into a dance with sensual delight.)

Most of the criticism Strasberg has received for his psychoanalytic approach to acting comes from fellow members of the Group Theatre. "He assumes that he knows everything and that we know nothing," Robert Lewis says of him. "In the role that he has given himself he assumes the power of the minder of souls and prober into the unconscious."[34] "It's therapeutic, not artistic," according to Harold Clurman. "Actors don't need Freud to give them a psychology."[35] Sanford Meisner quips:

> I have had even more extensive experience with dentists than with psychoanalysts but that doesn't license me to pull a tooth. Of course, out of my dental experience I do recognize that a puffy jaw may dictate a certain type of mental attention, but I do not feel inclined to take the work upon myself. I humbly offer this as a precept.[36]

Stella Adler does recommend analysis for actors whose imagination can't be freed by a good teacher,[37] but it's not a role she feels she can fill herself. However, Marlon Brando, who was taught by Adler at Piscator's Dramatic Workshop in the 1940s, has said of her:

> Outside of her phenomenal talent to communicate ideas, to bring forth hidden sensitivity in people, she was very helpful in a troubled time in my life. She is a teacher not only of acting but of life itself. She teaches people about themselves. I wouldn't want to say that it's psychotherapy, but it has very clear psychotherapeutic results.[38]

Possibly any kind and sensitive teacher would respond to a gifted actor "in a troubled time," and even an actor as unsentimental as Brando, casting a backward glance on a difficult period in his life, might tend to see those who showed emotional generosity to him as "psychotherapeutic." However, his tribute to Adler is an indication of how tough it is to draw a firm line between acting training and therapy when the subject of acting is the internal workings of human beings. Though Meisner is sure he's never attempted to analyze his students, to a classically trained British actor of the 1950s even the more "objective" classes at Meisner's Neighborhood Playhouse might have seemed psychologically intrusive.

The most incendiary subject among Method acting teachers is affective memory. Strasberg, having introduced it to his colleagues in the early thirties, was the only one who continued to rely on it after the disbanding of the Group Theatre. In a 1964 interview with Richard Schechner he explains how sensory memory leads to emotional recall, asking Proust and Pavlov to go bail for him:

> The best description of affective memory is in Proust's *Swann's Way*. That's how it works. You do not start to remember the emotion, you start to remember the place, the taste of something, the touch of something, the sight of something, the sound of something, and you remember that as simply and as clearly as you can. You touch the things, in your mind, but with the senses alive. And we know from psychology that emotions have a conditioning factor. That's how we're trained, not from Freud, but from Pavlov. . . . By singling out certain conditioning factors, you can arouse certain results.[39]

Strasberg's fellow Group alumni have also been vocal on the subject. Kazan says he never used it in his classes at the Studio because "It's false. You see the worst misuse of emotional recall in actors who are really playing with something in themselves—not with the person in the scene. There is this glazed, unconnected look in their eyes and you know they're somewhere else."[40] Robert Lewis warns that "in choosing experiences from our own lives, we risk the chance of dredging up personal emotions that may not be apt for the character's feeling at all."[41] Phoebe Brand claims that the process "makes for a moody, self-indulgent acting style," and that in insisting that his actors concentrate on painful past incidents "Lee crippled a lot of people. . . . Acting should be joyous, it should be pleasurable and easy if you do it right; but it wasn't with Strasberg."[42] Sanford Meisner objects that "emotion . . . is a most elusive element. It works best when it is permitted to come into play spontaneously, and has a perverse inclination to slither away when consciously wooed."[43] (Strasberg's response to this last objection would likely have been a reminder that his "Pavlovian" technique of affective memory woos the senses and not the emotions.)

The most scathing condemnation of this technique comes from Stella Adler, who says that it "induces hysteria."

It's polluted water, and yet Americans, typically, continue to drink it. Stanislavski himself went beyond it. He was like a scientist conducting experiments in a lab; and his new research superseded his earlier ideas: the affective memory belonged to the older, worn-out ideas. But Lee always thought it was the cornerstone of the Method, and in this way he became a laughingstock.[44]

The Strasberg–Adler debate over affective memory began as early as 1934. Adler had just returned from several weeks with Stanislavski in Paris, where they worked together on scenes from John Howard Lawson's *Gentlewoman*, a play she'd done for Strasberg that year. Although reports of what actually occurred in Paris are contradictory, evidently Stanislavski criticized Adler for paying too much attention to emotion and neglecting two other crucial elements of acting: "given circumstances" (working to make the context of a scene—milieu, circumstances—fully believable) and "truthful action" (devising logical actions for the character inside that context). When Adler brought back this revised view from Stanislavski (*An Actor Prepares* does place the greatest emphasis on emotion), Strasberg refused to lend it credence in his productions, and his obstinacy was one of the factors leading to the rift between him and the rest of the Group. He left the company in 1937.

This quarrel over what Stanislavski *really* meant has its humorous side—you might think of the foolish old mother-in-law in *Uncle Vanya*, reading the latest pamphlet by some culture hero and discovering with horror and confusion that he's reversed the position he took during his youth. As it turned out, Stanislavski's fresh concern with action was the introductory step in a *new* theory of emotion he formulated, with Pavlov's help, shortly after Adler's visit (and then had insufficient time to test before his death in 1938). He called this theory the "Method of Physical Actions." It states that "all behavior is 'psychophysical,' and . . . if an actor selects appropriate physical actions and executes them with full belief and logic in the playing of the scene, he will automatically elicit an emotion in the process."[45]

All the other Method teachers from Strasberg's generation stress the importance of action, none more strongly than Sanford Meisner. Students in their first year at Neighborhood Playhouse are still taught that "to act is to do or to live truthfully under imaginary circumstances."[46] Originally the Actors Studio classes emphasized action, too—in the days when Kazan taught them. Strasberg did teach actors to search for an objective (or action), but it seems to have occupied very little of class time: Hethmon's lengthy book mentions only one reference to it,[47] and Strasberg is on record as saying that if an actor experiences every one of the character's emotions, "the action of the scene will result almost without your knowledge"[48]—exactly the opposite of Stanislavski's "Method of Physical Actions."

The aim of all Method teachers, whatever their means, is to produce genuine emotion on the stage, but Strasberg's actors have been accused of displaying *emotionalism*, as a result of his prodding and pushing at their feelings. It was Robert Lewis who made the famous remark, "Crying, after all, is not the sole object of acting. If it were, my old Aunt Minnie would be Duse!"[49] But it isn't likely that Strasberg was simply incapable of recognizing the distinction between exhibitions of emotion and real acting. Hethmon records him telling one actor, "You have great sensitivity, but almost too much. Your sensitivity does not have a base,"[50] and another, "You have too much emotion, and it functions at times when it is not needed."[51] Strasberg often took tension as a sign of emotional excessiveness, and his relaxation exercises fought against it.

Besides, if it's fair to offer Strasberg's own acting as evidence of his understanding of the role of emotion in acting, his portrayal of the mafioso Hyman Roth in *The Godfather, Part II* is a remarkable example of the "strong emotion curbed by ascetic control" Harold Clurman applauded him for in Strasberg's directing days. In one superb scene, Michael Corleone (Al Pacino), investigating an anonymous attempt on his life, visits the ailing Roth in his Miami home, and what he sees is a sick, depleted old Jewish guy slumped in front of his TV set, munching on a sandwich. Only when Roth mentions one of his protégés, murdered years before on Michael's say-so, do we catch a glimpse of the steel beneath his benign fallen-patriarch manner. As he grows more excited, a click rises in his throat. It suggests the imagined sound of a pacemaker as his burdened heart starts to race, but it's creepy, too, like a snake's rattle. You can't find a moment of wasted emotion in this scene, or for that matter in Strasberg's whole performance. It's the best

109

promo anyone could ever have done for his approach to Method acting.

Strasberg's ideal conception of great acting as "a true relation between impulse and expression"[52] is vague and, finally, incommunicable. He claimed he'd seen it in only a handful of actors (Duse, Grasso, Jacob ben Ami, the singer Feodor Chaliapin, and in the early work of Laurette Taylor and Pauline Lord). He probably meant that there's a deep mystery about the greatest acting—you don't see the process at all—and he was right to believe that unteachable. What he did make clear was his belief that good actors work directly out of their own neuroses, so "when there is something in an actor's experience that makes him afraid of a particular kind of event, that is a sure sign that there exists in him wonderful material for dealing with that event."[53]

This point of view reflects the traditional romantic notion of the relationship between pain and the creation of art (which Lionel Trilling deals with in "Art and Neurosis" and Edmund Wilson takes into other directions in "Philoctetes: The Wound and the Bow"). And it may have led Strasberg to "sometimes confuse a disturbance with a gift," as Estelle Parsons says of his admiration for Marilyn Monroe.[54] Monroe's performance in John Huston's *The Misfits*—coached by Strasberg's wife Paula—might be a parody of the Method: sighs, strange pauses, sudden and distracted sidelong glances, bewildering mood shifts, fuzzy, broken line readings, a flood of unmotivated, undifferentiated feeling. (And talk about excess of "preparation"! Even her most straightforward line is heralded by a full battery of emotion.) It may have led him to endorse the kind of neurasthenic acting that raised the hackles of some observers. Stanislavski's student Vera Soloviova proclaimed, "Convulsions such as the ones in *Hatful of Rain* . . . belong in a hospital."[55] And the London reviews for Strasberg's 1964 revival of *The Three Sisters* suggest it was a shower of neurotic outpourings.

Writing about *The Three Sisters* during its New York run, Robert Brustein castigated the actors for their "inability to subordinate personal mannerisms to the requirements of Chekhov's characters."[56] Actors Studio actors have always fought the criticism that they never play anything but themselves. Strasberg distinguishes between actors who "can go on on stage and always be themselves, and by being themselves they can be the character" (his example is Duse) and those who "in order to act fully on the stage . . . have to feel that there is a mask" (Chaliapin, Paul Muni, Stanislavski himself). But though he says that "both approaches are perfectly plausible,"[57] it's obvious which one he *really* endorses when he asks an actress worried about confusing her own emotions with those of the character she is playing, "What the hell does that mean? How can I paint unless I am willing to confuse my own feelings with what I am doing?"[58]—and instructs another to use her nervousness to fill out the character instead of struggling to hide it.

Robert Lewis, a "mask" actor himself, disputes this inner-directed approach to playing a role, but for most Method teachers it's the cornerstone of truthful acting. Think of Morris Carnovsky's description of the personal way he related to Stella Adler in *Awake and Sing!* Elia Kazan writes, in his director's notebook for *A Streetcar Named Desire*, "The only way to understand any character is through yourself."[59] He believes that in order for an actor to play a role successfully, the director has to "find a little river of experience in the person that's like the thing in the part,"[60] so, rather than casting from conventional auditions, he likes to "take the actor for a walk or . . . to dinner or I watch him when he doesn't notice it and I try to find what is inside him."[61] And once he's chosen his performers, he tends to "create values around the events of the scenes that are meaningful to the actors. . . . [You] touch elements in their lives that make the scene so real and specific to them that it takes on a life of *its* own."[62] In Method terminology this technique is called "personalization."

Theodore Hoffman offers the popular response to the role of personalization in the Method: "The main psychological tenet of The Method is that each man is somehow universal and that the actor can find the ingredients of any role within his own personality, and use them to transform himself into the character he wishes to play."[63] But Kazan's casting strategies (including the use of "ringers" in small roles) contradict this interpretation, and nowhere does Strasberg suggest that any actor has the potential to play all roles. The fact is that for American actors—and not just Method actors—versatility has never been the ideal it is for European actors. Blame the cult of personality that goes back to the days of the matinee idols, or blame Hollywood, but we love to recognize our stars in role after role, and we feel a little cheated if they hunker down so deep inside a role that nothing of *them* is visible. We expect chameleon-like transformations from Olivier, but if we couldn't see links between Dustin Hoffman's three roles in that great comic paean to the Method, *Tootsie*, the movie simply wouldn't work. American acting teaches us a different concept of range, one that allows for the expression of personal quirks, and those critics who persist in thinking that Brando, Hoffman, and Diane Keaton show no range just don't get it.

Range is only one possible virtue in an actor (and, the way movies get made and plays get cast, it's the one most seldom tested in this country, anyway). Brando's got it; Montgomery Clift didn't have much; James Dean played only one role, over and over, in his brief career. What these performers share is a combination of indelible personality and emotional depth. American acting has attained its most spectacular peaks when a gifted actor has connected in a personal way with a character. All American acting assumes what would be sacrilege to a classically trained English or French actor: that the actor and not the text is the most important element in a play or movie. Only an American could have written these lines (they're by Norman Mailer):

> How disagreeable then, even brutal, is the situation of the actor when his role is not adequate to him, when he cannot act with some subtle variations of his personal style. But, indeed the actor, living uncomfortably in that psychic ground between the real and the unreal, consummate creature of modern anxiety, can find his reality only in a role worthy of his complex and alienated heart.[64]

What about the Actors Studio's neglect of craft—the frequent accusation that Studio actors slouch and mumble? Clearly that's an exaggeration, though you can see where it comes from: You have to adjust your focus to listen to Brando, who couldn't care less about enunciating every word, just as you have to get used to the overlapping dialogue on the multi-tiered soundtrack of a Robert Altman movie. And the more convinced you are of the sacredness of the text, the harder it is to give yourself up to this process. Strasberg did urge his classes to study voice and movement, and teachers specializing in these fields have found occasional employment at the Studio. But he was primarily concerned with the soul of a performance, not with its form; he fought against what he characterized as "reality hidden under a veil,"[65] i.e., carefully crafted copies of true emotion. And he had a model for the kind of acting he deplored: What the British were doing.

If Stanislavski's system represented a rebellion against the artificial emotion he observed on the stages of Russia; if the Group Theatre strove to break away from the sedate, mannered drawing-room style of the Broadway theater of the twenties and the romantic excesses of the matinee idols; then the Actors Studio set up an alternative to the beautifully rhythmed declamation of British actors, which has always had an appeal for Americans. In *A Method to Their Madness*, Foster Hirsch contrasts the American and English styles:

> Against British poise the Studio espouses countervalues, in which British formality is answered by American spontaneity, British reserve is smashed by American intensity. Militantly anti-classical, the Studio style is rough-and-ready, instinctive, improvisatory, proletarian, physically active, and defiantly emotional.[66]

Kazan argues that the American actor's appreciation for Stanislavskian acting derives from his empathy with the "Russian idea of the profound soul of the inconspicuous person [which] also fits the American temperament. We have not got the burden that everybody should be noble, or behave heroically, that the English used to have."[67] He goes on to say, "We helped them get out of it"—and he's right. Look at Billie Whitelaw in her Beckett monodramas, or Albert Finney in *Shoot the Moon*: What you see is the Method with an English accent.

5

TEXTS FOR METHOD ACTORS

♦ ♦ ♦

What is the purpose of histrionic truth when it serves nothing but dramatic falsehood? . . . Unlike Stanislavski, who invented a new acting technique in transforming the Russian theater, Strasberg has been the interior decorator of a crumbling structure whose foundations he has done nothing to change.

—Robert Brustein[1]

The fundamental fault of The Method is that it always seems to be producing the same play, a play about the tragically frustrated desires of well-intentioned, deeply feeling failures—of Strindberg's characters living a Chekhovian life amid Ibsen's social problems.

—Theodore Hoffman[2]

These harsh words were written to decry the state of the American theater in the Actors Studio years—the period from the late 1940s through the early 1960s, before the focus of serious theater shifted away from the Broadway stage. Brustein and Hoffman made these comments at the latter end of that stretch, when the shortage of interesting new plays had become epidemic; they might have seemed inappropriate to the booming, energetic Broadway of the late forties and early fifties, when the Studio was at its young peak. Still, they're useful in making a direct connection between the Method and the kind of plays that actors trained in it tended to be comfortable in.

Brustein and Hoffman disagree about cause and effect: Brustein finds the Method inadequate to the task of refurbishing the Broadway theater because the plays themselves are so paltry, while Hoffman blames the Method for the paltriness of the plays. And in a way, both men are right. For though the Method teachers like to think their approach is applicable to any kind of play, what they don't see is that

114

a style has limitations that a technique doesn't have, and that the Method long ago ceased to be mere technique. (To the extent that it *is* technique, it's suitable for any style of play; that is, the *mechanics* of the Method—individual exercises, the focus on communication between actors, the sharpness of sensory memory, etc.—probably are useful in any context.)

As a style, the Method instinctively seeks out its own kind: drama which attempts to reproduce a recognizable American reality on the stage. Plays that fall into this category are the most obvious texts for Method actors. But most American naturalism, unfortunately, is no more inspired than *Men in White:* It's banal, obvious, prosaic, and message-laden, and it tends to hover around a few worn themes (the American Dream, the American way of business, the tension between reality and illusion, the entrapment of family life, loss of innocence). The fact that there are a handful of great plays on these subjects—*A Streetcar Named Desire, Long Day's Journey into Night, The Member of the Wedding, The Iceman Cometh, Awake and Sing!*, and perhaps half a dozen others—is the impetus that keeps driving playwrights back to mine the old terrain again and again. That, and the undeniable fact that familiar themes cast in a familiar idiom (American naturalism) often can call up the best imaginative resources of American actors, whose performances transform them: Rod Steiger in Paddy Chayefsky's "Marty" (on TV), Shirley Booth in William Inge's *Come Back, Little Sheba* (on stage and screen), Gene Hackman and Melvyn Douglas in the film version of Robert Anderson's *I Never Sang for My Father*, the cast Robert Altman directed in his film of Ed Graczyk's *Come Back to the 5 & Dime, Jimmy Dean, Jimmy Dean*, or (most recently) James Whitmore, Aidan Quinn, Michael Learned, and Joan Allen in Jack O'Brien's TV production of Arthur Miller's *All My Sons*. All of these are bad plays, but the performances turn them into memorable theater.

Arthur Miller

If you drew a line directly from Odets's plays for the Group Theatre era to the drama of the Actors Studio years, it would end right at Arthur Miller's doorstep. Even Miller's first plays, produced at the University of Michigan, apparently showed a strong Odetsian influence,[3] and you can certainly see it in his first two Broadway hits, *All My Sons* (1947) and *Death of a Salesman* (1949)—both of which were directed by Elia Kazan.

In these plays Miller is concerned with close family ties. Joe Keller, in *All My Sons*, lives through his boys, indirectly causes the death of one (Larry commits suicide out of disillusionment with his father's ethics), and finally kills himself when he feels he's lost their love and respect. Biff Loman, in *Death of a Salesman*—which also culminates in a father's suicide—has spent his life trying to live up to his dad's inflated image of him. Both Larry and Biff are heroic figures, the war pilot and the high-school football star, who crash (like Odets's Ben Gordon and Joe Bonaparte) because the values on which they built their lives turn out to be rotten. (In both cases it's the *father's* values that are threadbare. For Miller, a child of Ibsen as much as of Odets, the sins of the father are always transmitted in full force to the son.) *All My Sons* reverts to the Odets debate of commerce versus ethics, and in *Death of a Salesman* we get the same question again, in the form of whether or not we should subscribe to the American Dream. Odets's hand is more clearly visible in the earlier play because, though it doesn't end on an optimistic note (American plays seldom did in the postwar years), its "brotherhood of man" credo echoes the idealism of the thirties.

There's another, less obvious, link between Odets's early plays and Miller's: Both deal with distinctly Jewish characters. Miller tries to generalize his men and women, to make them into something symbolically all-American, but what he ends up with is a bunch of Jews with WASP names—a "crypto-Jewish" milieu, to borrow Leslie Fiedler's phrase.[4] Several critics have commented astutely on the patently Jewish roots of the characters in *Death of a Salesman*. George Ross claimed that the first Yiddish translation of the play (in 1951) felt more like the original text than the English-language original did.[5] Morris Freedman saw the Gentile names of the characters and the language, free of Odets's Yiddishisms, as symbols of the assimilation of American Jews in Miller's generation.[6] And, more recently, Julius Novick (in *The Threepenny Review*) called *Salesman* a kind of sequel to *Fiddler on the Roof*, with Willy Loman representing the transplanted Jew who tries— and fails—to assemble a new set of values his people can live by in the new world.[7]

116

The cadence of Miller's dialogue bears all these critics out:

With scholarships to three universities they're going to flunk him? [Act I][8]

Your father came to me the day you were born and asked me what I thought of the name of Howard, may he rest in peace. [Act II]

Attention, attention must be finally paid to such a person. [Act I]

And Miller sprinkles his characters' speeches with Jewish folk wisdom:

Biff, a man is not a bird, to come and go with the springtime. [Act I]

Can't we do something about the walls? You sneeze in here, and in my house hats blow off. [Act I]

Who liked J. P. Morgan? Was he impressive? In a Turkish bath he'd look like a butcher. But with his pockets on he was very well liked. [Act II]

Like Odets, Miller allows his characters to speak in the vernacular, which reveals their class origins while making rapid contact with an audience that recognizes their speech patterns immediately. Linda Loman talks in homilies: "Well, dear, life is a casting off" (Act I); "he's only a little boat looking for a harbor" (Act II). Willy's language is occasionally ungrammatical—"that boy of his, that Howard, he don't appreciate" (Act I); "The average young man today . . . is got a caliber of zero" (Act I)—and (like Joe Keller's) littered with "y'knows" and "y'understands," as well as with go-getter, self-help phrases like "make the grade" and "personal attractiveness."

The banalities of the language in both *All My Sons* and *Salesman* have a resolute quality; Miller waves his characters' commonness of speech and lowbrow tastes like a flag. This excerpt comes from the opening scene of *All My Sons*:

KELLER (indicating the sections beside him): Want the paper?

FRANK: What's the difference, it's all bad news. What's today's calamity?

KELLER: I don't know, I don't read the news part any more. It's more interesting in the want ads.

FRANK: Why, you trying to buy something?

KELLER: No, I'm just interested. To see what people want, y'know? For instance, here's a guy is lookin' for two Newfoundland dogs. Now what's he want with two Newfoundland dogs?

FRANK: That is funny.[9]

Miller lays his thematic bricks with clanging efficiency here: We'll learn soon enough that Keller's lack of interest in the news is an indication of the parameters of his narrow, family-centered world. But this brief exchange between neighbors smacks of plain-folksiness, too. The fact that Miller provides mostly undifferentiated, unleavened dialogue for everyone on stage suggests a defensive attitude toward these people's "smallness." He struggles to transform their banalities into poetry (a feat Odets accomplished in *Waiting for Lefty* and *Awake and Sing!* and *Paradise Lost*) by giving them symbolic weight, as in the opening lines of *Salesman:*

LINDA: (hearing Willy outside the bedroom, calls with some trepidation): Willy!

WILLY: It's all right. I came back.

LINDA: Why? What happened? (Slight pause) Did something happen, Willy?

WILLY: No, nothing happened.

No verbal interaction between Pinter characters could be more deliberate, more fraught with significance, but there's an absence of wit in Miller, and a lack of mystery: First he underscores every word of this late-night conversation between two exhausted middle-aged, lower-middle-class, implicitly Jewish Brooklynites and then, in the course of the play, spells out what each word means. In tandem with his Ibsen-like reliance on objects as symbols (the felled tree in *All My Sons*; Biff's silver athletic trophy in *Salesman*), Miller's insistence on commonplace dialogue constitutes what Robert Warshow dubs "mechanical realism,"[10] and it's Miller's chief tool in building his so-called "tragedy of the small man."

Too much has already been written about Miller's efforts to discover an authentic American tragic form by scaling tragedy down to the common man. (Miller himself has brought forth two essays on the subject.) In play after play he tries to inflate drama by redefining it as tragedy—in *All My Sons*, where Joe Keller's petty crime acquires the status of a sin against mankind; in *Death of a Salesman*, where Willy Loman is supposed to stand in for all "low men"; in *A View from the Bridge*, which usurps some of the conventions of Greek tragedy; in *After the Fall*, where Miller lays down the shards of his own life in the hope that they'll reflect most of the major concerns of this country in the twentieth century (Freudian/family issues, sex and marriage, the Holocaust, the death of the political Left, business ethics, the price of fame).

Whatever you may think of his point of view, it's clear that the resoundingly successful *Death of a Salesman*, which proclaims the nobility of the common man's struggle to preserve his dignity (Miller's candidate for the American tragic burden), cemented the popularity of the small-man-as-emblem drama that invaded the theater, movies, and television in the late forties and fifties. It ensured (for a time at least) the livelihood of such minor playwrights as William Inge and Paddy Chayefsky. It provoked Leslie Fiedler to cry out against these "gray [images] of suffering inaction,"[11] and Robert Brustein to describe the American theater as a crumbling structure. And it provided most of the texts for training the Actors Studio generation. Miller's idea of the tragic hero as a recognizable lower-middle-class American corroborates the Method emphasis on personalization and emotion memory.

The enthusiastic reception the American public has given Miller, Inge, and Chayefsky is the result not only of the pleasure of recognition, but also of what Michael Paul Rogin, in his discussion of Joe McCarthy, calls "the devotion of Americans to concrete detail"[12]—our confidence that anything solid enough and presented in enough specific detail must be real. To be fair, there's more to Miller than just surface realism. With Ibsen as his teacher, Miller learned his lessons in structure brilliantly. Both *All My Sons* and *Death of a Salesman* are shrewdly crafted, well-made plays erupting with eleventh-hour revelations, and both embody Ibsen's idea of psychological realism by presenting conflicts in the

119

present as inevitably rooted in the past. In terms of the history of the American theater this is a new development, a fresh wrinkle on the problem play familiar to American audiences since the late twenties. What impressed Miller and his contemporaries (like Arthur Laurents in *Home of the Brave*, William Inge in *Come Back, Little Sheba*, and even old-timer Sidney Kingsley in his 1949 hit *Detective Story*) was that Ibsen's home truth fit the new psychoanalytic model perfectly.

In *Home of the Brave* a young Jewish soldier, paralyzed on his return from battle in the South Pacific, is cured by an army psychiatrist who links the boy's psychological injury to the anti-Semitism he's dealt with all his life and to his guilt over not saving the life of a fellow soldier. In *Come Back, Little Sheba* an alcoholic on a tear threatens his wife with a knife, blaming her youthful, seductive ways and resulting pregnancy for his wrecked life. In *Detective Story* a cop discovers that his wife was once another man's mistress and can't forgive her; his second (double) revelation—that his moral intolerance stems from his hatred of his father, and that in reality he's just *like* his father—arrives late in the play and drives him to suicide. *Death of a Salesman*, the most celebrated and one of the most compelling of these Freudian problem plays, exposes the adolescent agony at the heart of Biff Loman's fury at his father: A high-school senior, he surprised Willy and a female buyer in a hotel room in Boston.

The psychological substance of *Salesman* is more complex (and more interesting) than the revelatory structure indicates. Dr. Daniel Schneider defined the play as "visualized psychoanalytic interpretation woven into reality."[13] He was referring to the attention Miller insists must be paid to the disintegration of Willy's psyche as he tumbles from the unbearable present into a series of pasts, some of them idyllic (and probably fictionalized), some of them as horrifying and assaultive as anything he shrinks from in his present. It's well known that Miller originally planned to call the play *The Inside of His Head*, and that he wanted Jo Mielziner to design a set that looked like a man's skull, with platforms within it. What Mielziner finally came up with was a house with a trick facade (a transparent fourth wall)—actually a variation on Robert Edmond Jones's set for Eugene O'Neill's 1924 Freudian–mythic drama *Desire Under the Elms*. It was a metaphorical edition of what Miller first had in mind. The allusion was most appropriate, since O'Neill was the first American playwright to set up house in Freud country, and his late masterpieces—*The Iceman Cometh, Long Day's Journey into Night, A Moon for the Misbegotten*—are the most sublime examples of the American psycho-problem play of the postwar era.

Miller poses an interesting problem for the actor. Though his plays ask for rigorous attention to realistic detail, *Death of a Salesman* introduces a second level of dramatic action—what goes on in Willy's head—juxtaposed with the linear narrative; sometimes the two levels alternate, and sometimes Miller presents them simultaneously. Willy's not the only character on stage who feels the tension of belonging to two worlds at once (though his is obviously the most extreme case): Biff's behavior in the present is always motivated by the turbulence of his past. So the very structure of the play demands acting that is fully informed by an understanding of the psychology of Miller's characters; it's tailor-made for the kind of interior acting students of the Method are prepared for. (The 1964 *After the Fall* is Miller's most ambitious attempt at psychoanalytic drama: It takes the form of a single long therapy session.)

Lloyd Rose is the only critic who has pointed out that Willy Loman is the prototype of the rebels of the 1950s, the angry young men flailing desperately against the tyranny of conformity who represent, for most audiences, the Method stereotype.[14] He's the missing link between the John Garfield characters of the thirties and forties and the roles Marlon Brando and James Dean would play in the fifties in movies like *On the Waterfront, The Wild One, East of Eden*, and *Rebel Without a Cause*. The Garfield figure—the Joe Bonaparte type—is a potential artist who chooses to be a gangster. In his trenchant essay "The Gangster as Tragic Hero," Robert Warshow demonstrates that the gangster is an outcast, a rebel, because he's successful:

> Success is always the establishment of an *individual* preeminence that must be imposed on others, in whom it automatically arouses hatred; the successful man is an outlaw. The gangster's whole life is an effort to assert himself as an individual, to draw himself out of the crowd, and he always dies *because* he is an individual; the final bullet thrusts him back, makes him, after all, a failure. . . .
>
> At bottom, the gangster is doomed because he is un-

121

der the obligation to succeed, not because the means he employs are unlawful. In the deeper layers of the modern consciousness, *all* means are unlawful, every attempt to succeed is an act of aggression, leaving one alone and guilty and defenseless among enemies: one is *punished* for success.[15]

The gangster has the fleeting, heady experience of success before he is hurled inevitably into failure in the form of a violent death. But Willy Loman courts success and can't win it; he's one outcast, one rebel against conformity, whose path leads him straight to failure, with no stops along the way. Willy's tragedy is not that he subscribes to a set of values which a handful of other men (like his brother Ben) have managed to live by, but that he doesn't understand that the very act of seeking success, of worshipping it, carries within it the seeds of failure—of destruction. *Salesman* is usually read as an indictment of middle-class American values, but in fact it's a cautionary tale about the dangers of the quest for success that most middle-class Americans (like Charley and Bernard) don't engage in. It warns us, just as surely as those Warner Brothers gangster pictures did, not to try to stand out from the crowd.

As a man who is, in Thomas Allen Greenfield's words, "entirely at odds with the unwritten philosophies and laws of behavior that his society has established for itself,"[16] Willy experiences the city, the heart of society, as an adversary, suffocating him, just as for the gangster "the final meaning of the city is anonymity and death."[17] Miller builds on the urban claustrophobia motif that Odets put forward in *Awake and Sing!*: For Miller, the city is both a just cause for rebellion (since part of him believes in the frontier dream Willy cherishes) and a symbol of Willy's moral displacement. If this sounds like a contradiction, it is; *Death of a Salesman* is littered with contradictions, beginning with the fact that it simultaneously justifies and condemns its protagonist. It's difficult to know what Miller intended—the play may be most interesting for what Miller presents unconsciously, i.e., as a psychoanalytic examination of the playwright himself. But Miller's ambivalence toward his central character is exactly what makes Willy a middle-aged precursor of the conflicted, antisocial heroes of the next few years, young men who often behave in a repugnant fashion but plead successfully for our sympathy.

Tennessee Williams

The greatest challenge *Death of a Salesman* posed for its director, Elia Kazan, was how to move his actors (especially Lee J. Cobb as Willy) from one level of reality to another without sacrificing the root naturalism Miller's dialogue and milieu called for. This was a problem he'd already dealt with two years earlier with Jessica Tandy as Blanche DuBois in Tennessee Williams's *A Streetcar Named Desire*. The original Broadway production of *Streetcar* established a connection between Williams and Kazan, and Williams and the young Method actors, that remained a constant into the early sixties: Kazan also directed *Camino Real*, *Cat on a Hot Tin Roof*, and *Sweet Bird of Youth* on the New York stage, and *Streetcar* and *Baby Doll* for the movies; and Williams's plays and movies featured such performers as Geraldine Page, Paul Newman, Maureen Stapleton, Joanne Woodward, Eli Wallach, Jo Van Fleet, Rip Torn, and Madeleine Sherwood. *The Rose Tattoo* and *Camino Real* even received their initial workshop productions at the Studio, while Williams was still in the process of finishing the scripts.

Like Arthur Miller, Williams continues the line from the social conscience drama of the Depression. The link isn't as clearly visible as it is in Miller's plays—the poetic language and the southern Gothic trappings of Williams's style tend to obscure it. Still, the remnants of prewar leftist drama surface in the opening monologue of *The Glass Menagerie*, where Tom Wingfield provides the social and political background of the play. The cramped quarters of the Wingfield apartment, where Tom feels trapped by his life, and the tiny flat that houses both Blanche and the Kowalskis in *Streetcar*, forbidding both the privacy they so badly need, both recall the Berger home in *Awake and Sing!*, where Ralph can't phone his girl in peace.

As in Odets, the soul of a man shrivels in the workplace: Tom, the poet, cries out against the constrictions of the warehouse job he ekes out a meager living at in order to support his mother and sister. In Williams's 1953 resurrection play, *Camino Real*, the optimism of the thirties makes a surprise comeback. Even the Odets theme of the corruption/rebellion of the athlete hero reemerges in Williams's work. In *Cat on a Hot Tin Roof*, Brick Pollitt, one-time college football star, turns to alcohol as a rebellion against his wife, his family, and his unfaceable homosexuality. When he makes a drunken attempt to relive

123

the days of his football glory, he ends up with a broken leg. And, in a curiously upbeat variation on Odets, Kilroy in *Camino Real*, who wears a pair of golden boxing gloves around his neck, outwits the Street-cleaners (the messengers of Death) by remaining true to his romantic ideals.

Williams's characters are firmly rooted in Freudian soil; their pasts control their present lives as tyrannically as Ibsen's ghosts. Blanche DuBois, who can't shake the "Varsouviana" out of her head until she imagines the sound of the gunshot that killed her young husband; Brick Pollitt, who drinks until he hears the "click" that shuts out the suicide of his friend Skipper; Amanda Wingfield, who still lives in the gracious southern girlhood of wealthy beaux and rooms full of jonquils; her son Tom, who travels farther than the moon to escape his family yet sees his sister's image everywhere he turns—these are the theatrical children of the postwar years.

Otherwise, Williams hardly falls into the Arthur Miller category. He's not a realist, even to the extent Miller is in *Salesman*, and his language isn't the language of the Brooklyn Jewish middle class, or in fact of any recognizable American group—even his fellow southerners. In his first play to be produced in New York, *The Glass Menagerie* (1945), Williams called for devices (projections; direct address to the audience) culled from epic theater, and touches (Jim's voice ringing through Laura's memory, just as the "Varsouviana" would haunt Blanche in *Streetcar*) inspired by Proust. His stage directions in *Glass Menagerie* insist at one point on lighting "satirical as a Daumier print" (Scene 4);[18] at the beginning of *Streetcar* he asks for "a peculiarly tender blue, almost a turquoise [sky], which invests the scene with a kind of lyricism and gracefully attenuates the atmosphere of decay" as well as a " 'blue piano' [that] expresses the spirit of the life which goes on here."[19] His characters have names like Baby Doll Meighan, Heavenly Finley (who lives in St. Cloud), and Valentine Xavier, and they meet at the Paradise Dance Hall, Moon Lake Casino, and Tiger Tail Road. Williams displays his symbols with pride: the fragile glass animals and the portrait of the departed Father Wingfield in *The Glass Menagerie;* the anatomy chart in *Summer and Smoke;* the iguana in *The Night of the Iguana.* And his dialogue, magnificent at its best (in *Streetcar, Camino Real,* and *The Eccentricities of a Nightingale*), gaudy and purple at its worst (in *Sweet Bird of Youth* and *Orpheus Descending*), is always heightened, poetic, feverous.

So much has been written about Williams's use of language that I won't devote much space to it here. Many of his characters are poets: Tom Wingfield, who describes the Depression as an era where "sex . . . hung in the gloom like a chandelier and flooded the world with brief, deceptive rainbows" (Scene 5); Blanche, for whom an hour in New Orleans in the rain "isn't just an hour—but a little piece of eternity dropped into your hands" (Scene 5); John Buchanan in *Summer and Smoke*, who explains to Miss Alma that "space . . . turns back onto itself like a soap-bubble, adrift in something that's even less than space" (Part I, Scene 4).[20] In Williams, a single word can transform a vernacular sentence into poetry—"resurrected" or "sashayed" or "Della Robbia" employed as an adjective. (Blanche says her dress is "Della Robbia blue" [Scene 11].) Repetition and redundancy can intensify and alter a line by transposing it into a delicately balanced musical rhythm: "Well, Stella—you're going to reproach me, I know that you're bound to reproach me . . ." (*Streetcar*, Scene 1); or "The Gulf wind has failed us this year, disappointed us dreadfully this summer" (*Summer and Smoke*, Part I, Scene 1); or "There must be a flood, there must have been a tornado!" (*Menagerie*, Scene 1). These sentences are like a word game invented by poets, in which the players have to keep finding new and more extravagant ways to say the same things, building on the musical structure of a sentence without ever changing its syntax.

Hyperbole erupts, and it can be potent ("Daylight never exposed so total a ruin!" [*Streetcar*, Scene 1]) or comic ("They call me Killer, Killer Wingfield, I'm leading a double-life, a simple, honest warehouse worker by day, by night, a dynamic *czar* of the *underworld*, Mother" [*Menagerie*, Scene 3]). And though not everyone in a Williams play speaks poetically, in his best plays everyone has a distinctive turn of phrase. Jim, the gentleman caller in *The Glass Menagerie*, justifies Tom's reference to him as an emissary from the world outside the Wingfield apartment by talking in clichés: Within a few pages of text he uses the phrases "stumble-john," "way off the beam," "I've—got strings on me," "she's a home-girl," "being in love has made a new man of me," "the power of love is really pretty tremendous," and "Love is something that—changes the whole world" (Scene 7). Stanley Kowalski's diction in *Streetcar* is a triumph of wit and invention; not only does it contrast with Blanche's fragile, allusive language, but it's also unlike the way any other character in drama speaks—messy, crabbed, ungrammatical ("And wasn't we happy together? Wasn't it all okay? Till she showed here. Hoity-toity, describing me as an ape" [Scene 8]), but inflated with oddball word choices ("Let me enlighten you on a point or two, baby" [Scene 2]) and aggravated with extended words or phrases that threaten to collapse the spine of the sentence (". . . when you been exercising hard like bowling is" [Scene 1], and "It's gonna be all right again between you and me the way that it was . . ." [Scene 8]).

Another idiosyncrasy of Williams's language provides a clue to the approach Studio actors—and directors such as Kazan—would take to material that on the surface seems to defy a Method reading. The dialogue often contains italics, and a sort of built-in ellipsis in the form of dashes separating abbreviated, abruptly punctuated phrases:

> I'm so—*proud!* Happy and—feel I've—so much to be thankful for but—Promise me one thing, son! [*Menagerie*, Scene 4]

> Crumble and fade and—regrets—recriminations . . . [*Streetcar*, Scene 9]

> Well, I!—just remarked that!—one of th' no-neck monsters messed up m' lovely lace dress so I got t'—cha-a-ange. [*Cat on a Hot Tin Roof*, Act I][21]

This peculiarity in Williams's dialogue is one element in his style. It should be looked at in connection with the episodic structure of the early plays (*The Glass Menagerie, Streetcar, Summer and Smoke, The Rose Tattoo*, and *Camino Real* are made up of mostly short scenes); with individual moments like Stanley's physical attack on Stella in Scene 3 of *Streetcar*, where the main action is obscured and what we get is a collage of exploded sensory strands (screams, curses, objects crashing, men and women packed in close, blows delivered, clumsy drunken attempts to pull Stanley off his wife); with the allusions to Van Gogh (in the stage directions for Scene 3 of *Streetcar*) and Proust (in *Camino Real*, which lists the Baron de Charlus among the characters).

The world Williams creates is lit by lightning and Japanese lanterns and searchlights that either filter and shade and suggest, or else illumine abruptly and expose. It's an impressionistic world, and impressionism is heightened realism in which time, place, and character are often telescoped yet the details focused on are presented vividly, sensuously, with tremendous depth of feeling. *Camino Real* is the most extreme example of Williams's impressionism. Here he chooses a completely nonrealistic setting, a Cocteau-esque afterlife, a no-man's-land where figures plucked from a dozen different fictions wait with increasing desperation while street theater erupts around them and earthly substance passes suddenly, chillingly into shadow. Because none of the action in *Camino Real* transpires on anything even resembling a realistic level, each of the characters, each of the sixteen "blocks" or episodes, possesses a poetic purity, existing solely on a symbolic plane. But Williams's use of symbolism doesn't reduce his characters, because his symbols, his characters, throb with inner life. And that's where his dramaturgy intersects with that of psychological realists like Arthur Miller, and where a Method actor can enter an extraordinary freak of a play like *Camino Real.*

Kazan wrote, in his director's notebook for *Streetcar*, "Stylized acting and direction is to realistic acting and direction as poetry is to prose. The acting must be styled, not in the obvious sense. (Say nothing about it to the producer and actors.)"[22] His understanding that he bears the burden of finding a dramatic form for Williams's nonrealism suggests that, for his cast, the acting process is essentially the same as in a play by Arthur Miller. Each actor searches for a spine (superobjective) to pursue from scene to scene; each tries to personalize his or her character, to plumb the layers of turmoil and contradiction under the surface. (This process is just as important for Stanley as it is for Blanche.) For Kazan, direction is always a practical process that "finally consists of turning Psychology into Behavior."[23] That is, his responsibility is to help his actors discover physical ways of communicating the psychology of their characters so even the strangest and most poetic of them comes across as utterly real. His idea for Jessica Tandy is to "find an entirely different character, a self-dramatized and self-romanticized character for Blanche to play in each scene. She is playing eleven different people. This will give it a kind of changeable and shimmering surface it should have."[24] In this way Blanche expands into a tangible role on the stage, instead of being diminished to a conceit.

The work of directors like Kazan and Harold Clurman on Tennessee Williams's plays and on Carson McCullers's *The Member of the Wedding* had a powerful effect on the development of the Method in the Actors Studio era. It released the capacity for poetry in gifted actors like Brando and Julie Harris; it poeticized the Method style itself. I'm not talking about actors' learning to appreciate the beauty of Williams's language, though that's certainly part of it; reading his lines didn't immediately compel Americans to give greater attention to voice training. But the "poet's weakness for symbols" that Williams's alter ego, Tom Wingfield, speaks of in *The Glass Menagerie* challenged actors to find ways to physicalize symbolic gestures.

When Strasberg insisted that "[One] gesture of the actor must show the audience his entire personality,"[25] he was referring not only to the importance of economy in acting but to the symbolic value of a single action. Robert Lewis calls these actions "psychological gestures," crediting Stanislavski's great student, Michael Chekhov, with coining the term. Lewis's example is a scene from *The Deluge* in which Chekhov, to express his love for a friend, burrowed into the man's chest with his finger as he spoke. Not all psychological gestures are so extravagant. When Brando in *A Streetcar Named Desire* picks a piece of lint off Kim Hunter's blouse, this tiny motion illuminates an entire area of Stanley Kowalski: that he thinks of his wife as a prize he's snatched off the pillars of her genteel southern childhood, and that if she looks presentable, she's doing him credit. That's physical poetry.

Clifford Odets and the Group Theatre actors understood the value of stage props; in the scene from *Paradise Lost* that climaxes with Clara pleading with Leo to hire the arsonist, the card with Mr. May's phone number on it, which keeps drawing Clara back to it as she prowls restlessly through the living room, operates as a tangible symbol. Williams reinforced the symbolic weight of props and brought it onto a new, more vivid level. When a playwright provides his actors with such marvelous objects as Laura's glass animals and her Victrola, Blanche's Japanese lantern, and the statue called Eternity that Alma admires in *Summer and Smoke*, he'd have to increase their awareness of the poetic possibilities of props, of their potential as a medium which both the inner life of a character and the thematic concerns of a writer can be projected onto. Kazan claims that, even before he began to work with Williams, he got the idea from watching the movies of the Russian director Dovzhenko that

a film can be both true—realistic—and completely poetic. And that became the ideal of my aesthetic—to the extent that I was conscious of my aesthetic. Suddenly you look at it and it's as plain as a loaf of bread, and it's completely poetic at the same time. It has overtones, it has suggestions, it has poetry all around it, but then, it can also be just nothing, a loaf of bread.[26]

Strasberg learned the same lesson from Van Gogh: "There are times when you pick up your shoes and see through them your whole life."[27]

If Williams's plays affected the development of an American acting style, it's equally fair to say that the Method influenced the development of his writing. As he deepened his association with Kazan and with the Studio, he began to incorporate more and more Method exercises into his work. *Camino Real* specifically calls for improvisation at one point, and both it and *The Night of the Iguana* are built on the most basic group improv premise: Gather a group of disparate characters together in a provocative setting and see how they interact with each other. And when Williams writes of Stanley, "He sizes women up at a glance, with sexual classification, crude images flashing into his mind and determining the way he smiles at them" (Scene 1), or when he gives John Buchanan in *Summer and Smoke* a speech in which he describes the sensation of seeing his mother's corpse, he demands sensory recall—a crucially important technique for the Method actor (especially in Strasberg's classes, where it's the first step toward emotional recall). *Camino Real* could almost be called a series of sense memory exercises in which all the transplanted romantic figures use the past they've brought with them to this strange locale as a shield against their fear of the unknown.

Even more prevalent in Williams is the confirmation of the animal exercise (actors reproduce the physical behavior of different animals as a way of suggesting qualities in the characters they're playing) that Strasberg borrowed from Maria Ouspenskaya's classes at the American Laboratory and introduced to the Group Theatre. Williams's plays abound with references to characters as human embodiments of animal traits. He describes Stanley as "a richly feathered male bird among hens" (Scene 1), and Mitch as "a dancing bear" (Scene 3), and writes of Blanche, "There is something about her uncertain manner, as well as her white clothes, that suggests a moth" (Scene 1). When Stanley and Stella make love, "they come together with low animal moans" (Scene 3). Stanley calls Blanche "canary bird" (Scene 7), while she characterizes the poker players as a "party of apes" (Scene 4), and herself (ironically) as a tarantula luring her victims to the Hotel Flamingo (Scene 9). In *Summer and Smoke*, Alma "makes a sound in her throat like a hurt animal" (Part I, Scene 6) and John speaks of himself as sliding downhill (morally) "like a greased pig" (Part I, Scene 7). Mae and Gooper's children in *Cat on a Hot Tin Roof* are "pigs at a trough" (Act I), and one of them "shrieks like a monkey gone mad" (Act II); Big Mama enters "huffing and puffing like an old bulldog" (Act I). And the title of the play—an allusion to Maggie—introduces a symbolic level in the animal exercise, as does the title *The Night of the Iguana*, with its reference to Shannon.

By the mid–1950s, Williams was employing his skills more and more to accommodate actors. In *Cat on a Hot Tin Roof* and his screenplay *Baby Doll*, he streamlines thick, tantalizing roles for actors—roles that call for juicy southern accents, tantrums, horseplay, grandstanding, and (in *Cat*) provide sizable monologues. The plays of Williams's middle period, which also includes *Orpheus Descending*, *Sweet Bird of Youth*, the one-act *Suddenly, Last Summer*, and *The Night of the Iguana* (his last commercial success, in 1961), mix melodrama and psychodrama; he lays the psychological subtext out on the prop table right next to Brick Pollitt's liquor bottles, Silva Vaccaro's whip, and Val Xavier's snakeskin jacket.

Cat's structure signals the switch to this overheated Freudian drama of revelations: Instead of the short scenes of his earlier plays, we get long acts consisting largely of encounters between two characters at a time. The stage directions indicate he's chiefly concerned with setting tasks for his performers, especially for the actress cast as Maggie the Cat (the talented, Studio-trained Barbara Bel Geddes in the original production): "MARGARET's voice is both rapid and drawling. In her long speeches she has the vocal tricks of a priest delivering a liturgical chant, the lines are almost sung, always continuing a little beyond her breath as she has to gasp for another . . ." (Act I), and—significantly—"[she] has to capture the audience in a grip so tight that she can hold it till the first intermission without any lapse of attention" (Act I).

The Williams of *The Glass Menagerie* and *Streetcar* didn't write in such bald terms of the relationship between actors and audience. Williams was working so closely with Kazan by this time that he even rewrote his third act in response to Kazan's actor-centered criticisms:

One, he [Kazan] felt that Big Daddy was too vivid and important a character to disappear from the play except as an
off-stage cry after the second-act curtain; two, he felt that the
character of Brick should undergo some apparent mutation
as a result of the virtual vivisection that he undergoes in his
interview with his father in Act Two. Three, he felt that the
character of Margaret, while he understood that I sympa-
thized with her and liked her myself, should be, if possible,
more clearly sympathetic to an audience. [From "Note of
Explanation" to the published text. *Both* versions of Act III
appear in the published edition of the play.]

The central image in early Tennessee Williams is the delicate
shade that transforms a harsh light into something soft and magical—
the mirror ball in the Paradise Dance Hall and the floor lamp with its
rose-colored silk shade in *The Glass Menagerie*, the Japanese lantern
that Stanley rips down and hands to Blanche at the end of *A Streetcar
Named Desire*. Blanche distinguishes between these two elements—
the harsh light and the medium through which it's filtered—when she
insists, "I don't want realism. I want magic!" (Scene 9). And most of the
commentary on Williams also divides them up, not very helpfully, into
"reality" and "illusion," implying a bias Williams himself doesn't share.
I prefer to think of them as conflicting realities, contrasting visions of
the world. After all, Williams gives Blanche's candles no less credence
than Stanley's colored lights (until she goes mad), just as he allows that
Stanley's behavior toward Blanche, brutal and insensitive on one level,
is perfectly sane and reasonable on another (until he rapes her). The
critic Normand Berlin writes:

> The scales are balanced so finely that when Stanley con-
> demns Blanche for her sexual looseness and Blanche con-
> demns Stanley for his apishness, each seems *both* right and
> wrong, right in the light of truth, wrong in the light of
> understanding.[28]

Berlin calls *Streetcar* "a play with balanced sides built in, dra-
matizing an attitude toward life based on duality and complementarity."[29] And it's not the only Williams play that can be described

in this way: To a greater or lesser extent, all of his work is built on the tension between warring realities. In *Summer and Smoke*, Alma's angel and her name (which means "soul" in Spanish) fight against John's anatomy charts; at the end, in Alma's words, "[The] tables have turned with a vengeance" (Part II, Scene 11)—John has come to believe in the soul, and Alma to acknowledge her capacity for sexual desire. The scene between Jim and Laura in *The Glass Menagerie*, "the climax of her secret life" (Scene 7), gives equal weight to her gracefully idealized adolescent image of him and the fumbling, unpoetic pitchman we see walk into the parlor holding her mother's candelabra. In *Camino Real*, Gutman's cynicism and the lewd whispers of the decaying whore Rosita are balanced against the imperishable dreams of Don Quixote, Jacques Casanova, and Kilroy. The horn-locked realities in *Cat on a Hot Tin Roof* are the two views of Brick's friendship with Skipper—the one Brick drinks to preserve, and the one Skipper killed himself to avoid confronting. This tug-of-war between conflicting realities is the key element that makes Williams's plays ideal texts for the Actors Studio generation; it's the cornerstone of this phase of Method acting.

Theodore Hoffman talks about the proliferation of "characters who alternate between roughhouse and despair"[30] in American plays of this period. Edward Dwight Easty, whose book *On Method Acting* is an effort to translate Lee Strasberg's lessons into a textbook for actors, urges, "Only by contrast . . . will . . . [a] role become alive and fairly breathe truth on stage."[31] Elia Kazan says that "the ambiguity in character . . . is the *truth* for me. . . . As I began more and more to assert my own view of life, I expressed these contradictory impulses in my films. I found repeated in them a sort of psychological gesture. . . ."[32] Thomas Atkins, analyzing the troubled sexuality of Hollywood's movies of the 1950s, writes:

> Method acting is the perfect style for the self-conscious and divided mood of the fifties. . . . Brando, Montgomery Clift, Julie Harris, Eli Wallach, Patricia Neal, Kim Hunter, Anthony Perkins, Rod Steiger and the other Method performers are best in divided parts based on the unresolved tension between an outer social mask and an inner reality of frustration that usually has a sexual basis.[33]

Tennessee Williams was the poet of the divided consciousness, and the Actors Studio actors, with Marlon Brando at their head, were the crippled warriors in its cause.

Carson McCullers

The Member of the Wedding, Carson McCullers's 1950 dramatization of her novel about a twelve-year-old girl's coming of age, is another example of how the extraordinary language of the southern Gothic writers brought poetic realism to the American stage in the postwar years. Like Williams, McCullers creates a kind of theatrical impressionism out of dialogue, music (the offstage wail of Honey's horn), and structure. But whereas Williams's technique in his early plays is to chop the action into short, vivid scenes, then flash it across the stage in a series of ecstatic bursts, McCullers actually shapes the form of her play to approximate the way we perceive the movement of time—specifically, the way her protagonist, Frankie Addams, experiences it.

Acts I and II are solid, unbroken chunks of dialogue, almost all shared among three characters: Frankie; her seven-year-old cousin John Henry, who lives next door; and Berenice Sadie Brown, the black housekeeper whose special charge Frankie is. The length of their conversations, set against the unchanging background of the Addams kitchen and arbor and accentuated by the heaviness of the dog days of summer, suggests the unrelieved stillness of the childhood environment that Frankie seeks to escape, as well as the morass her restlessness and impatience make of the week before her brother Jarvis returns with his bride-to-be, Janice, to marry in the Addams house. Looking for an outlet for the terrible alienation she feels—from Berenice and John Henry, who represent the childhood she's no longer a part of; from the older girls of the neighborhood, who exclude her from their club—Frankie fastens onto the wedding as the event that will alter her life irrevocably and propel her out of her baby world. Irrationally, she hatches a scheme to go off with Janice and Jarvis after the ceremony, to weld her lonely, amorphous life to their (as she sees it) exciting, purposeful one.

Frankie's life does change with the wedding, but not in the way she anticipated. Her inevitable rejection by the newlyweds brings on an emotional crisis that, in tandem with the other unexpected events of the days that follow (John Henry contracts meningitis and eventually dies; Berenice's half-brother, Honey, is thrown in jail for stabbing a white man, and hangs himself in his cell) forces a measure of growth in her.

Act III is made up of three short scenes, with the explosions of action (Frankie's failed attempt to insinuate herself into the honeymoon car; Honey's fight; John Henry's death) occurring offstage, usually between the scenes. The drama is concerned not with events but with perception and reflection. Frankie says to Berenice at the end of Act III, Scene 2, "The wedding—Honey—John Henry—so much has happened that my brain can't hardly gather it in. Now for the first time I realize that the world is certainly—a sudden place."[34] And Berenice, whose life has gathered itself around that stillness Frankie abhors, replies, "Sometimes sudden, but when you are waiting, like this, it seems so slow."

Frankie is no teen rebel without a cause, but her struggle to squeeze her outsize frame into adolescence in a small, hot, dead southern town in the mid-forties is perhaps the most lyrical expression in American letters of the agonies of puberty. If J. D. Salinger's Holden Caulfield is one strain of the American variety of adolescent alienation (and the one most closely connected to the work of Brando and James Dean), then Frankie (always associated with Julie Harris, who played her on Broadway under Harold Clurman's direction, and again in Fred Zinnemann's beautiful 1952 film) is the other: She is McCullers's portrait of the artist as a young girl. "Frankie, you got the sharpest set of human bones I ever felt," Berenice tells her as she settles her head on Berenice's shoulder (Act II), but it's really the sharpness of her sensibilities that digs into Berenice, unsettling her and measuring the increasing distance between them.

Frankie has the soul and vision of a poet; she can't fathom the mysteries occurring in her body and her mind, but, unlike the James Dean heroes, she has the words to describe them. "I feel just exactly like somebody has peeled all the skin off me," she says in Act I. And, left behind after the wedding, she cries, "Oh, my heart feels so cheap!" (Act III, Scene 1). She has a poet's gift for personification:

> We've worn these old cards out. If you would eat these old
> cards, they would taste like a combination of all the dinners

of this summer together with a sweaty-handed, nasty taste. [Act I]

and for reproducing the quality of her own sensations:

> Jarvis talked about Granny. He remembers her very good. But when I try to remember Granny, it is like her face is changing—like a face seen under water. [Act I]

The most astonishing moments in the dialogue occur when Frankie describes her sense of the passage of time, or projects the movement of the world upon the rapid shifting of her own moods, or identifies the power of a single, dim image to bring a precious memory flooding back:

> I was walking along and I passed two stores with a alley in between. The sun was frying hot. And just as I passed this alley, I caught a *glimpse* of something in the corner of my eye. A dark double shape. And this glimpse brought to my mind—so sudden and clear—my brother and the bride that I just stood there and couldn't hardly bear to look and see what it was. It was like they were there in that alley, although I knew that they are in Winter Hill almost a hundred miles away. (There is a pause.) Then I turn slowly and look. And you know what was there? (There is a pause.) It was just two colored boys. That was all. But it gave me such a queer feeling. [Act II]

No dramatist before McCullers had given a voice to this universal experience. And, amazingly, she has it articulated by a twelve-year-old girl, in language that is at once poetic, expansive, and somehow perfectly reasonable in the mouth of a child. (Often Frankie's verbal style is as comically inflated as Stanley Kowalski's; it's sprinkled with colorful phrases she's chosen for the way they charge up her sentences—"[It] is immaterial with me," "as the irony of fate would have it," "I am sick unto death.") McCullers draws Frankie Addams as a kind of adolescent Proust.

The American theater was about to be deluged with plays about how teen-agers see the world—*Picnic; Tea and Sympathy; The Dark at the Top of the Stairs; Look Homeward, Angel; End as a Man. The Member of the Wedding* was the first, and without doubt it's still the finest. It was a landmark for the Method, too, because during the Actors Studio era the Method found its emotional focus in adolescence, and not only because the Freudian drama of the period so often located the source of adult neurosis in the teenage years (Biff in *Death of a Salesman* is the most obvious example). The tension between opposites that's at the root of the Method approach to acting has no better parallel than adolescence, where we feel the pull between childhood and adulthood. That's the root of Frankie's pain, so McCullers immediately establishes the setting of her play as the grey, troublesome area between these two poles.

The opening line of *Member of the Wedding* is Jarvis's: "Seems to me like this old arbor has shrunk. I remember when I was a child it used to seem absolutely enormous." Frankie longs to swing over to Jarvis's side of the gulf between childhood and adulthood; to be able to feel a nostalgia for her growing-up years, instead of being imprisoned inside them. (When she does get sentimental about her past—in Act I she reminisces about the good times she used to have with a friend who's since moved to another town—she is saddled with the additional pain of not yet having left it behind.) So she mimics the adults she's studied, pretending she's drunk when she accidentally takes a sip of her brother's spiked lemonade, sneaking a drag on Berenice's cigarette, repeating words she heard Jarvis speak, buying a grown-up dress for the wedding, exploding at Berenice for refusing to finish an anecdote in Frankie's presence because she's too young to hear it. (When Berenice apologizes, explaining that "[It] was just one of them things I suddenly realized I couldn't tell you and John Henry," Frankie answers, "You could have sent him out of the room and told me" [Act II]. Yet her untutored suspiciousness about the activities of the older kids in the neighborhood has already betrayed her naiveté about sex.) When she's removed from Jarvis's car after the wedding, Berenice and Mrs. Addams both suggest activities that might cheer her up. But they're childish pastimes, and Frankie aches to think that's all that awaits her now. "Those baby promises rasp on my nerves," she says (Act III, Scene 1).

Frankie's life is a continual twisting and turning between extremes. A precocious ability to express the workings of her own emotions alternates with childish behavior; her desire to assert her individuality (like cutting her hair tomboyishly short) wars with her yearning to be accepted by the other girls, who laugh at her because she's tall and odd-looking. "Why can't I be a member?" she cries out when they don't elect her to their club (Act I). And that leads her to think about her brother and sister-in-law, who, she decides, are members of a number of clubs, of the whole world, in fact—the world outside her kitchen. "Somehow they're just so different from us" is her sense of Janice and Jarvis (Act I). ("Us have a good time? Us?" she says to John Henry, as if the idea were absurd.) Searching for connection, Frankie visits her need on her brother and the bride:

> Not to belong to a "we" makes you too lonesome. Until this afternoon I didn't have a "we," but now after seeing Janice and Jarvis I suddenly realize something. . . . I know that the bride and my brother are the "we" of me. So I'm going with them, and joining with the wedding. . . . I love the two of them so much and we belong to be together. I love the two of them so much because they are the *we* of me. [Act 1]

And for most of the play she proclaims her difference from Berenice and John Henry, so she can associate herself with *them*.

Magically clicked in to the world of adolescent thought (a friend once told me her response to *The Member of the Wedding* when she read it at twelve was "How did she *know*?"), McCullers charts the movement of Frankie's mind. Sometimes Frankie's shifts seem abrupt on the surface, but if you look closely at the sequence of her lines they make perfect sense, and an actress attuned to the progress of her through-line should find McCullers has laid it out for her. For instance, in Act I Frankie looks at herself in the mirror and says, "The big mistake I made was to get this close crew cut. For the wedding, I ought to have long brunette hair. Don't you think so?" She doesn't listen to Berenice's reply, but continues with her physical worries: "Oh, I am so worried about being so tall. I'm twelve and five-sixth years old and already five feet five and three-fourths inches tall. If I keep on growing like this until I'm twenty-one, I figure I will be nearly ten feet tall." Then, after a pause, she thinks out loud: "I doubt if they ever get married or go to a wedding. Those freaks. . . . At the fair. The ones we saw there last October."

This last remark only *seems* like a non sequitur. Unlike John

Henry, Frankie doesn't think the circus freaks were "cute"; she's terrified that she's on her way to becoming one herself, and she needs to be consoled—to be told she's pretty. We can make similar sense of Frankie's shift from nostalgia about her friendship with Evelyn Owen, who moved to another town, back to Janice and Jarvis ("It was just so queer the way it happened this afternoon. The minute I laid eyes on the pair of them I had this funny feeling"): Her sense of abandonment by Evelyn leads her to seek new objects of affection.

Berenice, loving and kind, the companion of Frankie's childhood, isn't much help to her now. She can't keep up with the growth in Frankie's perceptions, and the girl's intensity makes her nervous. When Frankie needs to know she isn't going to grow up a freak, Berenice tells her, "I think when you fill out you will do very well" (Act I)—which is as infuriating as Mrs. Webb's response in *Our Town* when her daughter Emily fishes for a compliment on her looks: "You're pretty enough for all normal purposes." Berenice can cradle Frankie in her arms, giving her temporary respite from the exhausting pull of her pubescent energies; but she can't stretch her mind around most of what Frankie says, and she isn't sensitive enough to Frankie's agonies to know better than to kid her about having a "crush on the wedding."

Berenice's pragmatism limits her in her dealings with Frankie: She's sympathetic, but not capable of extending herself to understand what the child is going through. When Frankie declares she plans to leave home but doesn't know where she's headed, Berenice says she's not making sense. When Frankie talks about accompanying Janice and Jarvis after the wedding, Berenice reminds her of the "two by two" rule of Noah's ark and urges her to find herself "a nice little white boy beau" (Act II). Berenice keeps trying to force Frankie's eccentricities into the vise of conventional solutions; she doesn't realize how inappropriate her suggestion is in Frankie's case. There's a lovely moment in Act II when McCullers catches these two characters on the same wavelength—when Frankie's recounting of her alley experience with the "dark double shape" triggers a recognition in Berenice—but most of the time they're far from each other, and growing farther by the minute. At one point Frankie, expressing her wish for connection with everyone in the world, says, "When I see all these soldiers milling around town I always wonder where they came from and where they are going," and steady, church-going Berenice answers, "They were born and they going to die" (Act II). That vision of the world must have satisfied Frankie once when, motherless and hungry for a child's portion of love, she learned spirituals at Berenice's knee. Now it isn't enough.

Honey Brown, Berenice's rebellious half-brother, is Frankie's double. Her alienation from the rest of the world is her age; his is his blackness. Honey is one possible grown-up version of Frankie—the one that builds on her angriest, most antisocial self. Honey's poetry is in the blues he plays on his horn; and he draws on his rich sense of irony to keep himself at a distance from other people. The climax of Frankie's young life is the explosion after the wedding. For Honey, it's the moment when he pulls a razor on a white man: "I know now all my days have been leading up to this minute" (Act III, Scene 2). But Honey implodes, killing himself in his jail cell. Frankie rushes off with her father's pistol, planning to run away to Hollywood or join the Merchant Marine or die, but she recovers from the melodrama of her "child plans that would not work" (Act III, Scene 2) and goes on—to other rites of passage, to an infatuation with piano-playing Mary Littlejohn and life in a new neighborhood. As Harold Clurman has said, *The Member of the Wedding* is "the lyric drama of Frankie's growth."[35]

Michael V. Gazzo

One final play deserves mention. During the 1950s, several playwrights tested out early drafts of new plays at the Studio; by 1960 Strasberg had incorporated a Playwrights Unit which included such rising luminaries as Edward Albee and James Baldwin. Tennessee Williams brought both *The Rose Tattoo* and *Camino Real* to the Studio before preparing them for Broadway production; Calder Willingham's *End as a Man*, adapted from his novel about a sadistic bully who holds sway over a southern military school, started as an unofficial Studio project and moved off-Broadway from there. (The play made a star of Ben Gazzara, who portrayed the bully, a role he repeated in the 1957 movie *The Strange One*. Jack Garfein, a Studio member, directed both versions, each with an all-Studio cast.)

But the most celebrated of the Studio-initiated projects was *A Hatful of Rain*, written by actor–playwright Michael V. Gazzo (who much later played Frankie Pentangeli in that grand conference of Method celebrities, Francis Coppola's two-part *Godfather* epic) and produced in 1955. This harrowing portrait of a Korean War veteran hooked on heroin began as "Pot," a scene Gazzo wrote for some of his fellow actors to work on in class. Encouraged by director Frank Corsaro, also a Studio member, Gazzo expanded it into a play, trying out scenes from it in class and allowing different actors to improvise extensions on what he had written. (When it opened on Broadway, Ben Gazzara and Shelley Winters played the central roles, Johnny and Celia Pope.)

Controversy still hangs over the project: At the time it was widely assumed to have built up largely from those improvisations, while Gazzo claimed the lines were his alone. The truth about how much of Gazzo's dialogue began in the actors' mouths is not only undiscoverable but meaningless, since whether or not he actually recorded the improvisations of his fellow actors, he certainly was influenced by them, and by the *technique* of improvisation. His play, even on the page, comes across clearly as an attempt to introduce the spontaneity of that process into a dramatic text, with the double aim of creating a new, surpassing brand of naturalism and giving the actors the kinds of roles that their training has equipped them ideally to play.

A Hatful of Rain begins strikingly *in medias res*, like *Waiting for Lefty* or *Awake and Sing!*, with Johnny's father telling Johnny an anecdote about an umbrella he bought in Palm Beach. The story isn't important in itself, but the cadences of the speech are unusually lifelike:

> I almost missed the plane up because of this umbrella . . .
> it's made of Japanese silk, the handle is ivory . . . and it was
> designed in Germany . . . and they make the damn things in
> Peru. This guy down in Palm Beach who sold me the thing
> . . . Anyway, I kept looking at my watch. He wouldn't tell
> me how much it was . . . I thought he was crazy until he told
> me the price. Twenty-seven dollars for an umbrella . . .
> Seven minutes from plane time he tells me the price. . . .[36]

The abundance of ellipses (all Gazzo's—I haven't left anything out), the untheatrical, digressive style, even the pointlessness of the speech—Johnny's father is working hard to fill awkward pauses, to deny the gap between him and his son—all suggest that the actor playing this role (Frank Silvera in the original cast) might have improvised it. And the casual way Gazzo chooses to open the drama plays believably against the grain of the sordid dramatic situation at its center. You can certainly argue that Gazzo's dialogue is banal, that the vernacular he insists on is uninteresting to the ear (especially in these years of Tennessee Williams and Carson McCullers), that his kitchen-sink realism is grim and constricted. But there's something genuine about a play in which the protagonist's wife, learning her husband is a dope addict, replies, "That's silly" (Act II, Scene 3)—a reaction so basic and so human that it undercuts the sensationalism of the revelation. (That line, too, *sounds* improvised.)

Gazzo's characters shift focus constantly during their long speeches, and the emotional dynamics of both the monologues and the dialogue exchanges seem to have no prearranged pattern; but oddly enough, that's exactly what makes them compelling. This approach is most effective in the climatic scene, where Johnny's rising anger at his father over childhood wrongs shifts into a replay of a wartime nightmare under the pressure of his need for drugs. Johnny's delirium sounds scarily real.

In a way, *A Hatful of Rain* was one of the roads that led to the experimental theater of the sixties, where improvisation would be a key element, replacing the notion of the sacred text and reestablishing the actor as a human being, physically and emotionally involved in performance and central to the theatrical experience. When Richard Schechner, who formed the Performance Group in 1968, speaks of "our struggle to expose our feelings, to reveal ourselves, to be open, receptive, vulnerable; to give and take hard and deeply; to use impulse and feeling in our work,"[37] you can hear in his words the voiced concerns of Elia Kazan and Lee Strasberg. Michael V. Gazzo and his group of actors, striving to bring the rhythms of everyday conversation and the terror of actual experience onto the stage in *A Hatful of Rain*, were unheralded pioneers.

6

THE METHOD ACTOR AS MOVIE STAR: MONTGOMERY CLIFT AND MARLON BRANDO

◆ ◆ ◆

You can tell by looking in a person's eyes if he has real talent.
—Lee Strasberg[1]

Montgomery Clift and the Poetry of Reticence

Montgomery Clift was twenty-eight when his first film, *The Search*, came out in 1948, but he looked much younger. Playing an American soldier in Germany immediately after the war who befriends a child survivor of the concentration camps, he had a sweet, soulful, boyish presence, and a lifelike rhythm in his line readings that made even the most unaffected of his contemporaries—Dana Andrews or William Holden—look slightly theatrical. The fact was, he'd been a stage actor for fourteen years, first in summer stock and then on Broadway (where he appeared in the Cole Porter musical *Jubilee* in 1935). But his performances in *The Search* and the Howard Hawks western *Red River* (the same year) give the impression of a young man who had never acted professionally before—in the best sense. He had no bag of tricks, no carefully honed theatrical strategies to fall back on, and his diction was fairly awful: He always sounded as if he was choking back the remnants of an eastern European accent. (He was born in Nebraska.) But he acted with a lean intensity and an emotional immediacy that weren't quite like anything film audiences had seen before, even from John Garfield.

In *The Search* Clift speaks so informally that he might be talking for his own amusement. In one scene he reads a letter out loud, and his slow, choppy diction, made even muddier by gum-chewing, is so lifelike it puts us at ease right away. Clift shares all his scenes with Ivan

Getting at the truth by indirection: John (then Jules) Garfield and Morris Carnovsky as Ralph and Jacob Berger in the Group Theatre production of Clifford Odets's *Awake and Sing!* (1935).

Billy Rose Theatre Collection, The New York Public Library at Lincoln Center, Astor, Lenox, and Tilden Foundations

Stripping down to a basic dialogue between two actors who care about each other: Stella Adler and Morris Carnovsky as Clara and Leo Gordon in the Group Theatre production of Clifford Odets's *Paradise Lost* (1935).

Billy Rose Theatre Collection, The New York Public Library at Lincoln Center, Astor, Lenox, and Tilden Foundations

A street-wise Jewish rebel in a house full of Gentiles: John Garfield makes his screen debut as Mickey Borden (with Jeffrey Lynn) in *Four Daughters* (1938).

"Mama! I just met her!": Montgomery Clift's George Eastman with Elizabeth Taylor as Angela Vickers in George Stevens's *A Place in the Sun* (1951).
© *Paramount/A Gulf and Western Company*

The subtle interplay between hard and soft elements: Montgomery Clift as Robert E. Lee Prewitt, with Frank Sinatra as Sergeant Maggio in Fred Zinnemann's *From Here to Eternity* (1953).
© *RCA/Columbia Pictures*

Perhaps the most complex and disturbing portrait of sexual repression by an American film star: Marlon Brando's Major Pendleton with Elizabeth Taylor as Leonora in John Huston's film of Carson McCullers's novel *Reflections in a Golden Eye* (1967).
© *Warner Brothers/A Warner Communications Company*

An anguish so private that nothing we've seen before prepares us for it: Marlon Brando (Paul) with Maria Schneider (Jeanne) in Bernardo Bertolucci's *Last Tango in Paris* (1973).
© *MGA/UA Pictures*

His whole body responds to the weight of each episode in Jim Stark's story: James Dean, the apotheosis of adolescent "sincerity," with a sympathetic cop (Edward Platt) and Freudian-monster parents (Jim Backus and Ann Doran) in *Rebel Without a Cause* (1955).

Adolescence as a constant workout: 24-year-old Julie Harris as 12-year-old Frankie Addams, with Brandon de Wilde (John Henry) and Ethel Waters (Berenice) in the stage production of Carson McCullers's *The Member of the Wedding* (1950).

Billy Rose Theatre Collection, The New York Public Library at Lincoln Center, Astor, Lenox, and Tilden Foundations

Two completely intuitive actors, playing off each other with the fervor of great jazz musicians: Julie Harris as Abra and James Dean as Cal in Elia Kazan's *East of Eden* (1955).

© *Warner Brothers/A Warner Communications Company*

As Mona, playing emotional
hopscotch on the shreds of half
a dozen shattered personalities:
Sandy Dennis's sagging face,
puffed up with moldy emotion,
in Robert Altman's *Come Back
to the 5 & Dime, Jimmy
Dean, Jimmy Dean* (1982).
© *Cinecom International Corporation*

Maureen Stapleton as Emma
Goldman (with Warren Beatty
as Jack Reed) in Beatty's *Reds*
(1981): illuminating the fabled
revolutionary's warmth and the
grip of her intelligence as well
as her dogmatic, obstinate side.
© *Paramount/A Gulf and Western
Company*

Awkward in the unfamiliar
milieu of the saloon: Eva
Marie Saint as Edie Doyle
with Marlon Brando as Terry
Malloy in Elia Kazan's *On the
Waterfront* (1954).
© *RCA/Columbia Pictures*

Narcotized by sex: Kim Hunter
(as Stella Kowalski) with
Marlon Brando (as Stanley) in
Elia Kazan's *A Streetcar
Named Desire* (1951).
© *MGM/UA Entertainment
Corporation*

More pain than it seems any human could bear: Rod Steiger as Sol Nazerman
with Juano Hernandez in *The Pawnbroker* (1965).

Comic nobility and passionate expansiveness: Rip Torn as Marsh Turner with Dana Hill as Ellie in *Cross Creek* (1983).
© *Thorn Emi Films*

Jamie Tyrone's fourth-act confessional: Jason Robards in Sidney Lumet's film of Eugene O'Neill's *Long Day's Journey into Night* (1962).
Billy Rose Theatre Collection, The New York Public Library at Lincoln Center, Astor, Lenox, and Tilden Foundations

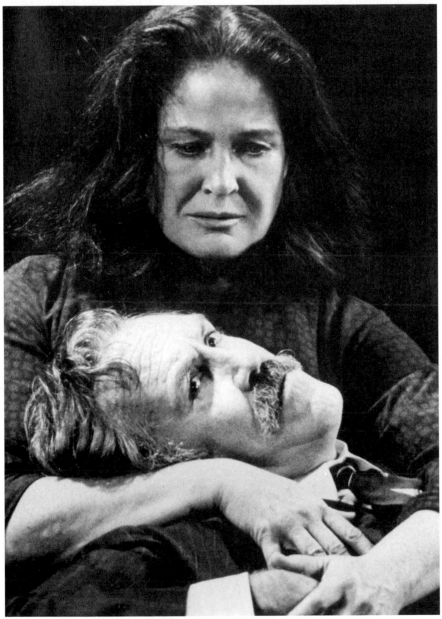

The *Pietà* at the end of Act Three of Eugene O'Neill's *A Moon for the Misbe-gotten:* Jason Robards as Jim Tyrone with Colleen Dewhurst as Josie Hogan in José Quintero's production (1973).
Photograph © 1984 Martha Swope

Paul Newman, with traces of the Actors Studio polish on him, as Eddie Felson
(with Piper Laurie as Sarah Packard) in *The Hustler* (1961).
© *CBS/Fox Company*

Living the kind of character he could only guess at in his early years: Paul
Newman as Murphy (with Edward Asner) in *Fort Apache, the Bronx* (1981).
© *Vestron Pictures Incorporated*

Always conscious of how he carries his oversized body: Lee J. Cobb as Willy Loman, with Arthur Kennedy as Biff and Winifred Cushing as The Woman in Elia Kazan's production of Arthur Miller's *Death of a Salesman* (1949).
Photograph © Eileen Darby, Point Lookout, New York

Displaying the kind of full-
blown, independent woman's
energy American movies
seemed ripe for: Blythe Danner in the title role of Sidney
Lumet's *Lovin' Molly*, with
Anthony Perkins (1973).
© *RCA/Columbia Pictures*

Blythe Danner as a vibrantly
innocent Nina in Act One of
Chekhov's *The Sea Gull* (a
PBS transcription of the
Williamstown Festival pro-
duction), with Frank
Langella as Treplev (1974).
*Billy Rose Theatre Collection, The
New York Public Library at Lincoln
Center, Astor, Lenox, and Tilden
Foundations*

Sitting on top of the Method like a peacock: Jack Nicholson as Buddusky, with
Randy Quaid as Meadows and Otis Young as Mulhall in Hal Ashby's *The Last
Detail* (1973).
© *RCA/Columbia Pictures*

Jandl, a child actor, and you can't spot a trace of falseness or conde-scension in any of them; playing straight man for this boy, he gives a completely charming performance. It's effortlessly warm acting, guided by an innate modesty. In the difficult scene where he has to tell the boy, Jim, that he has reason to believe his mother is dead, Clift lets his emotion slip out, almost with embarrassment: Breaking out of his usual light-humored repartee, he keeps smiling—but awkwardly, un-comfortably. Unashamedly undramatic and naturally understated, Clift was ideally suited to play the uncomplicated, openhearted, on-the-level G.I. American audiences still wanted to believe in after World War II (even after the publication of Norman Mailer's *The Naked and the Dead*).

In this first phase of his movie career, Clift was almost always blessed with directors known for bringing out the best in actors (William Wyler, Howard Hawks, George Stevens, Vittorio De Sica). If he was able to break through in his debut screen performance, much of the credit belonged to the director of *The Search*, Fred Zinnemann, who worked with him again in *From Here to Eternity* five years later. Zinnemann has never enjoyed the reputation he deserves in this coun-try, because his virtues—a delicate sensitivity, a poetic restraint, a fine hand with performers—are the kind of qualities that tend to escape notice. But his track record for this period is remarkable: He made splendid pictures and introduced to the screen the three most exciting young presences in movies—Clift, Marlon Brando (in *The Men*), and Julie Harris (in *The Member of the Wedding*).

The young Montgomery Clift infused his roles with an unusual, and unusually potent, sexuality. It's no surprise that he was the first member of the Actors Studio generation to become a movie star: He was the most attractive. Until the car accident he just barely survived shattered his face in the mid–1950s, he had almost unreasonably good looks that mesmerized the camera. Though he was adored by several screen belles in his films (Joanne Dru, Elizabeth Taylor, Jennifer Jones, Eva Marie Saint), he was actually more beautiful than handsome—angelic/seductive, an American Tadzio.

In a brilliant analysis of Clift's acting, in "Some Notes on Method Actors," Hal Hinson suggests that "the passion that Clift expressed was always an immature passion; it had the adolescent exuberance that we experience when we fall in love for the first time and are as infatuated with the idea of being in love as we are with the object of our

143

affection."[2] That immaturity came partly from his teenage looks and partly from his extraordinary gift for expressing the torment of adolescent sexuality, the struggle between childish fantasizing and adult longings, that generally was the subtext of his acting even though he never actually played a teenager (even in *Red River*). All three of his best performances—as George Eastman, the social climber caught in a romantic triangle in *A Place in the Sun;* as Prewitt, the army bugler in *From Here to Eternity;* and as Giovanni Doria, the Italian in love with a married American in *Indiscretion of an American Wife*—are basically explorations of juvenile passions, though the characters are men in their twenties. They mark the first efforts of American actors to touch the tender center of an experience which moviemakers had previously exploited only for comedy and sentimentality. Teenagers, who made up the fastest-growing movie market in the 1950s, responded enthusiastically to Clift in *From Here to Eternity* in 1953, as they would in the years that followed to other performances dealing more overtly with the hurdles of adolescence (Marlon Brando in *The Wild One;* James Dean in *East of Eden* and *Rebel Without a Cause*).

None of Clift's early performances carries the troubled sexual charge of a picture like *A Place in the Sun.* In *Red River* and *The Heiress*, his sexiness is entertaining, even funny. As Matthew Garth in Hawks's *Red River*—a young man whose Oedipal conflict with his surrogate father, Tom Dunson (John Wayne), is resolved easily in a harmless tussle at the end of the picture—he throws out his hip, leans on one leg, and sucks a blade of tall grass. Both muscular and relaxed, he holds his sexual energy in repose behind a languid smile. A modern variant on the western archetype, the strong, silent hero, he speaks as slowly as Wayne does—there's always a slight retardation in Montgomery Clift's speech—but we can sense the sexual force that's curbed by that verbal leisureliness, and we wait patiently through the movie for it to flood through. But it never does: The strongest exchange between Matthew and the woman who loves him (Joanne Dru) is a moment when he cups her face in one hand and places the other on her mouth to stop her wailing. Hawks knows exactly what he's doing; this frustration of our expectations is part of the witty erotic tension that informs the picture.

Clift displays tremendous charm in the role of the adventurer, Morris Townsend, in William Wyler's *The Heiress* (an adaptation of Henry James's *Washington Square*), even though he has a little trouble with Ruth and Augustus Goetz's overwritten dialogue and looks slightly incongruous in period costume. The willful blindness of the heroine, Catherine Sloper (Olivia De Havilland), to Townsend's wiles, and ultimately her obsession with avenging herself on him when he deserts her, are easily traced to Clift's sexual vitality. But Clift seems so contemporary here that at times he threatens to pull us out of the film, especially when he's on screen with Ralph Richardson, who gives a towering performance as Catherine's domineering father.

Clift's gift for conveying childish infatuation gets an early trial in *The Heiress*, where, in his first scenes with Olivia De Havilland, he gives such an unconventional impression of a soul transported by romance that we can't be sure whether he really loves her or is faking grand passion so expertly that he's convinced himself it's sincere. (The movie's ambiguousness about Morris is part of what makes it so memorable; the unexpected force of De Havilland's portrayal of swindled spinsterhood is the other part.) In the ballroom sequence, when Morris returns with a glass of punch for Catherine and finds her dancing with another man, his face falls unashamedly. It's as if her petty betrayal was such a shock to his system that he didn't have enough emotional energy left to look to his dignity. There's one scene, though, where Clift exposes Morris's darkest underlayer. After his first interview with Sloper, he tells Catherine he's afraid her father dislikes him, and for a startling moment he looks like a cornered animal.

By the 1950s Clift's on-screen sexuality had become more complex (as it had off-screen, too), and more than ever the focus of his acting. In *A Place in the Sun, From Here to Eternity*, and *Indiscretion of an American Wife* he's childishly appealing but sexually hungry, almost pathologically reticent and yet incapable of secrecy because all his conflicts are inevitably played out on his brow. There's scarcely a trace of the casual physicality he had as the westerner in *Red River* or the G.I. in *The Search* and *The Big Lift*, even though he's a soldier again in *From Here to Eternity*. Only one scene, where Clift's Prewitt is out on the town with his friend Maggio (Frank Sinatra)—two horny young men in Hawaiian shirts and loose-ass pants—recalls the less tangled roots of this complicated young man.

Vulnerability, the quality that Morris Townsend trades on, is at the core of these later characters; it's what makes them so seductive. Prewitt attracts a woman, Lorene (Donna Reed), as soon as he enters a Pearl Harbor "private club" (a Hays Code euphemism for "whorehouse"), but when she nuzzles up to him he gets a sheepish, virginal look on his face. In *Indiscretion*, when Giovanni arrives at the train station to try to persuade Mary (Jennifer Jones) to stay in Rome with him, his desperation melts her, as a hurt child's might. The scenes where he clings to her are tainted *Pietàs*. When he grows furious and slaps her across the face you're shocked, as if you'd seen a young boy beating up on his mother. Of course Mary's adoring nephew, who has brought her suitcase to the station, immediately dislikes and distrusts Giovanni—they're competitors. When Mary boards the train to go home to her husband at the end of the picture, we feel ambivalent: unsatisfied, because Giovanni represents a commitment to passion Mary can never find at home, yet cognizant of the danger she's escaped, because Giovanni's youth is terribly disturbing in this romantic context. And the director, Vittorio De Sica, acknowledges our mixed emotions by ending the film not on a close-up of Jennifer Jones but on a shot of Montgomery Clift walking away from the station alone.

"Tell Mama all," Angela Vickers (Elizabeth Taylor) whispers to George Eastman in *A Place in the Sun*. Once again Clift is a child–man, sweetly modest when he gives his name to the gateman at his rich uncle's factory, charmingly awkward when a secretary invites him to step into the magnate's office to phone him at home, comically ill-at-ease at his uncle's home for the first time in a brand-new tweed jacket, half-slumped in a chair because he's unsure of how he's expected to hold himself. When Angela, a debutante he's met at his uncle's, makes her presence known while he's talking on long distance to his straight-laced Christian mother (Anne Revere), he has an endearingly embarrassed moment, half-whispering into the receiver, "Mama! I just met her!" Angela adopts the affectionate term "Mama" for herself; she steals this baby away from his real mother. When she phones him at home for the first time, his excitement and pleasure make him restless, and his voice turns very light. Physically and vocally, he seems to be trying to make himself smaller.

The love scenes in *A Place in the Sun* are justly famous. When Angela wanders into the pool room and discovers George, retreating from a party where he knows no one and feels out of place, he relaxes his face and accepts the stronger force of her extraordinary beauty like a happily defeated warrior. She's affected, too—by his inability to keep his feelings concealed. (George makes immediate erotic contact with both the women characters in the film: the factory drudge, Alice, played by Shelley Winters, whom he has an affair with and gets pregnant; and the socialite, Angela, who enters his life after he's already become involved with Alice.) Love shatters George. He confesses his love to Angela as if he were confessing murder, running on fast, feverishly, in a desperate, choked voice, his smile pulled in one direction by rapture and in another by agony.

Angela is forever asking what's troubling George, because he always *looks* troubled—clouded. Clift's ability to push his feelings so close to the surface gives him an astonishing emotional clarity in this role; at every moment we know exactly what's churning around inside him. Passing a small boy singing hymns in the company of adults on a street corner, he communicates nostalgia and wonder and discomfort, all at once, and suddenly we understand his confusion about his own childhood. (His mother was active in a mission and kept him out of school until the law stepped in.) In another scene he devotes his complete, stripped-down attention to a radio announcer listing the statistics on local drownings, and we can read his darkest thoughts—of drowning Alice, who he knows can't swim. It's a frightening moment. His face looks like it's under attack from these thoughts; we can see the struggle that's taking place, and George's soul is losing. For Clift, sexual conflict is always bound up with spiritual conflict. The realm of the spirit was the arena where the actors of Clift's generation fought their most feverish battles; following in John Garfield's footsteps but moving beyond him, they also defined themselves by a brooding, unresolvable sexuality. Clift inhabits both these areas simultaneously, heralding the arrival of a new breed of actor.

A Place in the Sun had its origins in Theodore Dreiser's *An American Tragedy.* Dreiser picketed the first film version of his novel, in 1931, and he surely would have hated the second, too, if he'd lived to see it. His protagonist, Clyde Griffiths, is a shrewd climber on the order of Stendhal's Julien Sorel. The point of Dreiser's social criticism (which is leveled at the society that shaped Clyde) is skewed in *A Place in the Sun* by the casting of Clift, who makes George Eastman soft instead of shrewd, and attractive because of his vulnerability rather than his charm. When George takes Alice out on the deserted lake, Clift chronicles every mental and emotional shift. We see that he originally intends to drown her, but then he wriggles out of the grasp of his private demon and for a moment he flails about—he's lost his bearings. When he begins to brood again he's sad and troubled, no longer menacing; half-turning away from Alice, he bends in on himself, his fist clenched to his cheek, and we see he *can't* kill her.

But Alice drowns anyway after their boat capsizes, and he goes on trial for her murder. When he takes the stand to plead his innocence, the prosecutor (Raymond Burr) berates him and persuades the jury he's guilty, because George isn't able to verbalize the sequence of thoughts and emotions that led to his first taking Alice out in the boat and then retreating from the idea of drowning her. But Clift's *acting* exposes George's feelings so powerfully that we want to shake the jury: Can't they *see* he's telling the truth? In this extraordinary scene, for the first time we watch a Method actor using his emotions to provide a voice for an inarticulate character. This poetic tension between verbal inexpressiveness and emotional revelation became the signature of the Actors Studio generation, as first Clift and then Brando and Dean turned into a Method emblem the troubled boy who can declare himself only in overpowering bursts of emotion.

A Place in the Sun has a very peculiar script (by Michael Wilson and Harry Brown) that ends up at odds with the other elements in the film. The prosecutor's trump card is that he's able to provide proof that once the boat overturned, George could have saved Alice but didn't. And the priest who speaks to George hours before his execution confirms this bizarre interpretation of his actions, telling him that if he even *thought* of Angela while Alice was drowning, then he murdered Alice in his heart. It's difficult enough to accept this hazy moral stand as justification for George's electrocution, but as it happens, the performances of Clift and Elizabeth Taylor—and George Stevens's direction—have already instructed us where to place our sympathies.

The George–Angela romance usurps the center of this movie, and in the movie's terms it's the *real* morality, the *real* religion; it transcends everything else. The picture begins and ends with a close-up of Clift. As he walks to his death in the final scene, a flashback to one of his love scenes with Taylor is superimposed upon his face—the face that, from the outset, has told us everything we know about George Eastman, has claimed our loyalty, and has taught us the romantic ethic we take away from the movie.

From Here to Eternity (1953) is Clift's Method union card. In it he plays a sensitive boxer. Robert E. Lee Prewitt is a fresh transferee to an American garrison at Pearl Harbor (some months before the Japanese attack). He has had a winner's reputation in the ring, but his blinding of an opponent has caused him to swear that he'll never fight again. When his new commanding officer (Philip Ober), who has his heart set on winning the division championship prize, can't talk Prewitt into taking up his gloves once more for the glory of the outfit, he institutes "the treatment"—excessive and unfair physical punishment—to beat down Prewitt's resistance.

Fred Zinnemann's film, an adaptation of the James Jones best seller, is about different kinds of integrity, and Prewitt's consists not only of adhering to his oath but also of being a good soldier—which means receiving as much "treatment" as he's dealt without flinching or complaining. Prewitt has had little education, and his dialogue is correspondingly straightforward and unadorned, but the pared-down, muscular intensity that Clift brings to the role—it's his best performance—gives the lines that define him a taut urgency. "I can soldier with any man," he tells his Captain. "I'm a thirty-year man," he declares to Lorene. "I'm on for the whole ride." When she points out angrily that the army he loves so much has treated him cruelly, he answers, "A man loves a thing, that don't mean it's got to love him back. . . . You love a thing, you got to be grateful." The army, he explains simply, taught him how to bugle. "I bugle well," he adds, narrowing down his pride to these three words. We know the pride is justified when we hear him play: When he does a hot variation on "Chattanooga Choo-Choo," his body tenses like a well-trained animal's in immediate response to the task of making music. Clift is one of the few actors who have ever played a musician with accuracy—that is, with the understanding that making music is hard work.

Prewitt looks cleanly handsome in his Private's uniform, a four-square military man. But despite his loyalty to the army, he won't box, insisting, "A man don't go his own way, he's nothin' " and (almost incoherently, in a drunken moment), "A man should do what he can do." Delivered in the midst of an interchange between two inebriated servicemen (Burt Lancaster plays the other), this last line is almost comic, but as Clift reads it, it gives the scene a surprise burst of poignancy. These lines direct us to the crux of Clift's performance. Prewitt is torn apart by his refusal to either buckle under to the Captain's wishes or desert the army; badly wounded in a fight with the stockade bully (Ernest Borgnine) who murdered Maggio, he crawls back toward his outfit when the Japanese bomb the island. A decent, dedicated soldier, Prewitt is also a rebel because he won't compromise his principles under the pressure of either his superiors or his peers. You can see the renegade line running from John Garfield and his Joe Bonaparte incarnations to Clift's Robert E. Lee Prewitt.

Part of the poetry in Clift's performance in *From Here to Eternity* is in the subtle interplay between hard and soft elements. Prewitt takes one hard stand after another, but he speaks softly and (typically, for a Clift character) slowly, as if the grip of his emotions has retarded him slightly. When he tells the story about how he blinded his boxing opponent, his voice is fuzzy, the truth about his past residing in a tender place. In *A Place in the Sun*, everything George feels is immediately accessible to us, but here, Hinson's description of Clift's "way of nestling a character within himself as if it were a secret, something to be hidden away, or so delicate that it would be bruised by the light"[3] seems absolutely accurate. The common ground in these two performances is that the center of both men lies very close to the surface. (That's why Prewitt's "secret" is in constant danger of being "bruised by the light.")

When the Captain orders Prewitt to apologize to the bully who abused him (at the Captain's behest), his refusal is quiet and soft, too, so when the Captain says of him a moment later, "You can't treat a man like that decently. You have to treat him like an animal," the injustice of that appraisal strikes us roughly. What he means, of course, is that he can't manipulate this man, because wherever Prewitt is dealt a blow his stony defenses deflect it. Clift's way of showing us Prewitt's softness in constant tension with his hard resistance draws our full sympathy. It's a constant surprise, and it lends his work here a poetic resonance.

The scene that best expresses the tension is probably the most famous of Clift's career. Maggio escapes from the stockade, where his own rebellion against the sadistic Sergeant in charge has brought him a series of savage beatings. Reaching his outfit, he dies in Prewitt's arms. That night, Prewitt plays "Taps" in honor of his dead friend. Holding his body taut, giving himself over to the demands of the music, Clift still manages to reveal Prewitt's grief, his soft part; that is, his body does one thing while his face does another. And because he presents this complex piece of acting so directly, devoid of flourishes, it's the most powerfully affecting moment in the movie.

With the single exception of the 1952 *I Confess*, directed by Alfred Hitchcock, where he was atypically inexpressive as a priest who hears a murderer's confession (director and star were a bad match),

Clift gave consistently terrific performances until his accident in 1956. *Indiscretion of An American Wife*, in 1954, contains some of his most unusual line readings. Sometimes he adds an impassioned subtext to a simple punch line by pausing just before it and then dropping it unceremoniously—throwing it away without relinquishing any of the intensity of the buildup. The movie also contains some of his most instinctual acting: He seems to hold nothing back. In the scene where he slaps Mary, Giovanni touches his own face afterwards, as if he'd inflicted the pain on himself. He stalks outside to the parking lot, then suddenly stops dead, his anguish cutting across his cheek like the imprint of his hand on his lover's face.

The automobile accident not only robbed Clift of his handsome appearance but also had the more horrifying effect of diminishing his powers as an actor. The center of his acting had always been that extraordinarily expressive face. Now he no longer had control of it, so in the big emotional set pieces in movies like *Raintree County*, *Lonelyhearts*, and *Judgment at Nuremberg*, he just melted. His range of facial reactions was reduced to one—the strained look of a man about to weep. Watching him, your impulse is to turn away in embarrassment. And his directors weren't much help. In *Judgment at Nuremberg*, where he played a Nazi victim testifying at the postwar trails, Stanley Kramer deliberately overexposed him, encouraging him to hold up his pain as an acting virtue. (*Judgment at Nuremberg* is the kind of aching liberal film that offers pain as proof of nobility.)

Clift often seems shaky on screen in this period. His diction in *Lonelyhearts* is much worse than usual—woolly—and in *Wild River*, though he's working under Elia Kazan, he seems to have difficulty pulling lines out of his mouth. If you've seen *A Place in the Sun*, it's agonizing to watch him play love scenes with Elizabeth Taylor in *Raintree County*: His passion now has a nervous inexactness, the desperation no longer of a soulful, misunderstood lover but of a man impaired by life, physically and psychically—a man who bears no resemblance to the character Clift is supposed to be playing. And the neurasthenic quality in his performances makes him an inappropriate target for even the most harmless jokes. When he drags himself through the swamp in *Raintree County*, in search of the legendary golden raintree (the movie's most insistent and exasperating symbol), and when he gets drunk or thrown in the river in *Wild River*, we don't feel like laughing. And oh, God, how he's aged! Three years after playing Jennifer Jones's immature lover in *Indiscretion of an American Wife*, he now looks far too old for the undergraduate scenes that open *Raintree County*, and he's hopeless at the country-bumpkin boyishness he tries for in his first encounter with Taylor. In *Lonelyhearts* he courts a pretty starlet (Dolores Hart), but he looks older than Frank Overton, who plays her father.

Even more distressing is the fact that he's lost his sexual potency on screen. In *Lonelyhearts* he's cast as Nathanael West's sharp-eyed, ironic young idealist, a journalist who is crucified by the pathetic souls whose agony he seeks to share (though in this defused version of the West story, Miss Lonelyhearts is saved at the eleventh hour by the love of a good woman). As Clift plays him, the reporter's integrity translates unintentionally into sexual repression: His long confessional speech to his cynical editor, Shrike (Robert Ryan), about how he can't laugh at the troubles of the people who write to him, but can't help them either, comes across as old-maidish. In *Wild River*, Clift—as Chuck Glover, a representative of the Tennessee Valley Authority sent to coax a stubborn old matriarch (Jo Van Fleet) off her land—begins an affair with a beautiful young woman (Lee Remick). But even after Kazan has given us every indication that they've slept together we still don't believe it, because Clift seems markedly nonsexual. (He blows Remick a kiss, but the gesture is halfhearted—you can't be sure afterwards that you actually saw it.) In *Judgment at Nuremberg*, this impotence seems deliberate. Wearing a crew cut that makes him look squareheaded, Clift speaks very softly and exposes a flabby, feminine underside. In his pre-accident performances this softness (with its whisper of femininity) was trailed by a sexual fuse, but here it's a confirmation that this man, sterilized by the Nazis, has been unsexed. Consciously or unconsciously, Clift makes it shockingly clear that in this film "sterilization" is a euphemism for "castration."

Too mature-looking for the kind of roles he'd specialized in before his accident, Clift now played a series of liberal intellectuals: a schoolmaster in *Raintree County*, a columnist in *Lonelyhearts*, a neurosurgeon in *Suddenly, Last Summer*, a T.V.A. man in *Wild River*, a physicist turned spy in *The Defector* (his final film, and a woeful swan song), even Sigmund Freud (in *Freud*, his next-to-last film). And since his gift had always been for giving expression to the emotions of inarticulate men, he couldn't make a single one of these well-spoken characters convincing. Never a witty line reader, he stumbles through his character's wisecracks in *Wild River*, obviously not quite comprehending this out-of-his-element, east-coast liberal whose chief weapon of survival is a hip, self-mocking sense of humor. He's a dead spot in the center of the movie. In *Lonelyhearts*, he looks genuinely puzzled by stop-you-in-your-tracks Dore Schary lines like "Is it a sin to feel? Is 'do-gooder' a dirty name? Why should it be?" In *Raintree County* and *Suddenly, Last Summer*, he stands around helplessly while Elizabeth Taylor has nervous breakdowns. He looks permanently stupefied.

Painful as it is to see Clift miscast and out of control in movie after movie, most of them at least contain a bright moment or two, a single right impulse. The beginning of his drunk scene in *Raintree County* is well-timed and funny. His displaced gloom at least seems perfectly in period for the Depression-set *Wild River*, and he has one touching scene with Lee Remick where she asks his advice about whether she should marry the boy friend she doesn't love, and he answers her with the anguished wisdom of someone who's gone through hell. Playing a possibly retarded man in *Judgment at Nuremberg*, he picks up slowly on the lawyers' questions but responds with a full emotional battery to every torturous memory. His trademark sign of agony comes into play here: He opens his eyes very, very wide, as if internalizing a shock. And he's quite appealing in *The Young Lions*, playing a Jew scapegoated by the other men in his outfit during basic training, even though the army scenes are a virtual replay of *From Here to Eternity*, and one detail the filmmakers supply about this character—that he reads James Joyce—seems utterly implausible.

Only once in this final phase of his career did Clift get to give a full-fledged performance, and that was under John Huston's direction. Arthur Miller wrote *The Misfits* for Marilyn Monroe, and it turned out to be Clark Gable's farewell, so Clift's contribution is often overlooked. But as Perce, the unemployed cowboy Gable and Eli Wallach hire to mustang with them, he does far and away the best acting in the picture. The role gives him his first taste of broad comedy and he performs it simply, skillfully—you might almost say with relief. Perce is not a liberal, not an intellectual, not even very articulate, and not much of a sexual creature (though he has a rather sweet, childlike attachment to Monroe's Roslyn Faber). And except for one expertly controlled telephone conversation with his mother, he doesn't share with us whatever solitary pain he may feel. (We learn during the phone call that Perce suffered some kind of injury to his face, and this plain acknowledgment, at last, of the change in Clift's features takes a great deal of pressure off both the actor and the audience.) Clift and Huston have the good sense to emphasize Perce's amiability and charm, rather than his grief, and that's why we're drawn to this character—as a respite from the angst-ridden figures played by Gable and Monroe.

In a sense Clift's performance, one of his last, brings his career full circle. The first glimpse movie audiences had of him was in *The Search*. He sat in an army jeep, happily enjoying a sandwich, and when a hungry child crept down to the road, he offered this boy both the sandwich and his friendship, without fuss. After *The Misfits*, this image of Clift lingers: a cowboy, recovering from a tumble off a rodeo steer, wearing a ten-gallon hat with self-parodic jauntiness over his bandage (he looks like Carmen Miranda in a cowboy get-up), howling drunkenly that he wants to go out and have some fun. After all the agony we've seen pouring from his post-accident performances, it's a delight to see Montgomery Clift acting natural—and relaxed—once again.

Marlon Brando: Expressing the Inexpressible

In one sense, Marlon Brando established a link with the Method tradition just by chance: The original casting choice for the stage role that made him a star was John Garfield. Garfield rejected Elia Kazan's offer to play Stanley Kowalski in *A Streetcar Named Desire* in 1947 because he felt it was Blanche DuBois's play and no one would be especially interested in Stanley. Famous last words.

The most eloquent report on Brando's performance in his first Broadway play, Maxwell Anderson's *Truckline Café*, comes from Pauline Kael, who more than twenty-five years later recalled her first look at Marlon Brando:

> We all know that movie actors often merge with their roles in a way that stage actors don't, quite, but Brando did it even on the stage. I was in New York when he played his famous small role in *Truckline Cafe* in 1946; arriving late at a performance, and seated in the center of the second row, I looked up and saw what I thought was an actor having a seizure onstage. Embarrassed for him, I lowered my eyes, and it wasn't until the young man who'd brought me grabbed

my arm and said, "Watch this guy!" that I realized he was *acting*.[4]

It wasn't just Brando's uncanny absorption in the role that first confused and then overwhelmed Kael and others in the audience: To an ear accustomed to the trained patterns of stage voices, he couldn't have sounded much like an actor. In movies (which he entered in 1950, never to return to the theater) he took Montgomery Clift's natural speech rhythms radically farther. He tore apart the conventional music of a line of dialogue, discovering a way for scripted words to express the tension in an inarticulate man between what flies out of his mouth and what he can't find words for. Playing a subtext at odds with the text is a strategy at least as old as Chekhov, but Brando gave it a new vitality. He created characters who were forced to settle for the text because they were inadequately equipped to get out the subtext.

In Brando's first screen role, Bud Wilochek, the paraplegic World War II veteran in Fred Zinnemann's *The Men*, he attacked his lines in remarkable ways that were to become his trademarks, drawing hundreds of imitators. Sometimes, searching for words, he fills in the spaces between them with a battery of half-formed interjections, stuttered syllables, and expressive grunts, as when he tells his doctor (Everett Sloane) about his disastrous wedding night with Ellie (Teresa Wright): "I don't have nothing. . . . She looked at me like I was a bug." Sometimes he implies another, stronger sentiment in the way he phrases a fairly harmless one: His wilting, spat-out, twisted-mouth "Forget it!" to Ellie is unmistakably a euphemism for "Fuck you!" Sometimes he dives into the middle of the traditional rhythm of a line and grapples with it as if he were swinging a snake around by its middle. When he yells at another man in the hospital ward whose radio is on too loud, "You're very funny—now turn it *down!*" he races for the last word, throwing the rest of the sentence off balance. Here he's using a simple, not especially revealing line to reflect the sharp, destructive shape Bud's depression has taken. What's implied is the inability of these lines to convey the mountain of emotions warring inside Bud, who seems to be trying to vomit all of them out every time he opens his mouth. And it creates a clumsy force in the character that's perfectly suited to the dilemma of a physically dynamic man who finds himself tied to a hospital bed.

Paradoxically—and brilliantly—the key to Brando's performance is Bud's physical strength. If the film were a tragedy, this quality would be part of the tragic premise; here, it represents his hope of triumphing over his situation. Struggling to pull himself up into a sitting position in his hospital bed with the aid of a bar suspended above him, Bud presses his eyes shut and quivers with the pain of the exertion; if Zinnemann had wanted to shoot the scene with nothing but a close-up on Brando's face, we could measure Bud's progress exactly by the gradations in that quiver. It's a fully accomplished acting moment, constructed conventionally—and it was just about the last conventional scene we'd ever see from Marlon Brando. By the coda he's already trying something unexpected. The traditional Hollywood way of ending this scene would be to sentimentalize it: Following his completion of this strenuous task, he ought to accept the cigar the ward clown tosses him as a prize, and bask in well-deserved glory. What Brando offers instead is a strained smile and a simple, accepting nod, his face averted; he doesn't let us forget the pain the effort has cost Bud.

This kind of honesty, which refuses to be undercut by an easy resolution, is something new in American movies. The contrast between the weak image of Bud confined to a hospital bed or a wheelchair, and the strength indicated by his every physical act, is the keynote of Brando's performance. We see it when he grabs Ellie's arm, demanding to know if she's sorry she married him, or when, returning from the wedding night fiasco, he smashes the windows of the recreation room on the ward.

"You'd be surprised how much you can do, doing nothing"[5] is a Strasberg dictum, and Brando's emotionally rich, highly varied performance in mostly a fixed position illustrates it. The young actor carries an enormous weight in his face that threatens to pull him down. It sinks him in Bud's moments of defeat—when the doctor tests his delusion that he's begun to have sensations in his legs by jabbing a needle into his calves that he can't feel, and in the horrifying wedding scene, where he falls down during the ceremony. And the still tension in his face at the end of the picture, when he arrives outside Ellie's door and asks her if he can take her to the movies, shows us that the emotional tide in Bud is changing.

There are points in Brando's performance when he anticipates his own upcoming rebel roles and those of his contemporary, James Dean. His face can register a disgusted protest against the implicit demands or inadequate responses of other people. His frustration at Ellie's maternal reassurances is so strong it's like a blow suffered at her hands. What he does here is well beyond the limits of the script, and that cries out for a new approach to directing a confrontation scene: An actor like Brando, who spills over the boundaries of dialogue, makes the conventional shot/reaction shot technique obsolete.

We don't pay much attention to Teresa Wright in this scene; we never do when Brando is on screen. The contemporary excitement of his performance makes it difficult to watch her wrinkle up her nose and show anxiety and devotion in the manner of a Hollywood wartime ingenue, difficult to listen to the elocution-class cadence of her line readings. Nothing demonstrates the breakthrough nature of Brando's acting more sharply than the old-fashioned acting of his costar (who, to be fair, comes off much better in movies like *The Best Years of Our Lives* and *Shadow of a Doubt*). Wright has such an acceptable, patented nice-girl gentility that we can't believe, even at the end when Ellie has grown courageous enough to accept the implications of living with Bud, that she can ever contain the dark elements we've seen inside him. For Brando is always dangerous; he keeps us on edge. In his review of *The Best Years of Our Lives*, Robert Warshow complained that "the choice of subject is itself an evasion of politics, for the 'veterans' problem' is not an issue, or at any rate it is a false issue, since nobody is against the veterans. . . ."[6] And it's true that in *The Best Years*, everyone treats Homer, the young paraplegic, with love and respect; the movie refuses to hint at the possibility of prejudice against him. But Brando's Bud, accosted by a condescending bigmouth at a bar who commends him showily for his war wound, answers, "God bless you, mister. Can I marry your daughter?" It is such an abrasive line (in a generally optimistic screenplay by Carl Foreman), and Brando's quiet delivery is so menacing, that you wonder if he improvised it.

Brando's Stanley Kowalski in *A Streetcar Named Desire* is dangerous, too—but unlike Bud, he finally acts in a way that justifies our uneasiness. Elia Kazan, who directed both the stage and the screen versions of Williams's play, calls Stanley "the hoodlum aristocrat,"[7] emphasizing both the high and low aspects of his behavior: his monarchical arrogance, the air of *noblesse oblige* in the way he runs his house (he reminds his wife, Stella, of Huey Long's motto, "Every man a king"), as well as his mean survivor's strategies and his vulgarity. As Brando plays Stanley, he does have a gallantry of a kind, but it's inseparable from the undisguised sexual appreciation of women that

Williams asks for in his stage directions. His vulgarity informs his gallantry in an extremely funny manner. In fact, Brando's performance as a whole is so funny that the danger lurking inside Stanley always catches you off guard, even though our very first glimpse of him—a burst of aggressive energy in an argument at a bowling alley—tells you it's there.

Some of the humor is physical. He flicks his fingers to remove the grease before settling down to do business with Blanche and call her on her lies; he bends over her to laugh in her face; he purses his lips, making a big joke out of Stanley's efforts at deep thought, while he calculates the value of Blanche's flamboyant wardrobe. But most of it is vocal. Brando rushes through his words, chopping the tops off, when he recreates a dialogue he had with a former girl friend ("I once went out with a doll who said to me, 'I am the glamorous type, I am the glamorous type!' I said, 'So what?' "). He makes his panoply of "acquaintances" (the jeweler who will appraise Blanche's jewels, the lawyer who will read the Belle Reve papers, the salesman who will check on her reputation in Laurel) into a running gag, and turns the lines about the Napoleonic Code into a parody of legal jargon. He capitalizes on the long-windedness of Stanley's lines. And his timing is outrageous: Hair suddenly wild, Stanley, who feels his wife has insulted him at dinner, shoves his dishes off the table, smashes a plate against the wall, and then addresses Stella (Kim Hunter) and Blanche (Vivien Leigh) quietly, with somber concentration: "My place is cleared! You want me to clear your places?"

Brando plays Stanley as a little-boy sensualist; like Montgomery Clift, his sexuality is adolescent (or, alarmingly, even younger—Kazan suggests that Stanley's mania for thrusting food, drink, and cigars into his mouth is a substitute for suckling[8]). Devouring chicken, he concentrates *really* hard, working his way meticulously up one side and down the other, and then he continues to attack it with small, precise bites, even though he hasn't yet swallowed what he's already packed in his mouth. He spritzes beer all over himself after he's told Blanche the story about his cousin who opened beer bottles with his teeth. Like his story about the doll who thought she was the glamorous type—like all his stories—this anecdote may have no structure, but it certainly has a point: Stanley Kowalski, king of the hill.

Every move of Brando's indicates that though Stanley is not quite, as Blanche insists, primordial, he certainly hasn't progressed beyond the early adolescent phase. Hands thrust tightly down into his pockets, he stalks into Blanche's room during the poker party to turn down the radio in a juvenile semiparodic imitation of adult anger. Waiting for Blanche to emerge from her bath so he can interrogate her about the loss of Belle Reve, he lights one cigarette and slips another behind his ear (extra ammunition), shifting his weight, delighted with his own superior strength and cleverness—a bully lying in readiness for the weakling he swore to beat up after school. Overhearing the two women discussing him, he strolls in with a cat-that-ate-the-canary grin on his face, with no more skill or desire than a child for concealing the fact that he's been eavesdropping. He can't resist imitating the yowling cat in the alley outside, because he knows it rasps on Blanche's nerves; and when he and his friend Mitch (Karl Malden) quarrel about her at the plant, he hurls the line that ends the argument with the fatuous finality of a little boy who has to have the last word. In his climactic confrontation with Blanche, she demands that he step aside and let her pass, and he takes her hysterical outburst as a dare. His reply—"Oh! So you want some roughhouse! All right, let's have some roughhouse!"—is already the cry of Johnny, the teenage motorcycle gang leader he would play in *The Wild One* three years later.

Approaching the role from the opposite end of the technique he used for *The Men*, Brando emphasizes Stanley's amusingly puerile and clownish qualities, and only occasionally reminds us of how dangerous he can be. When he doesn't understand what someone is saying to him, and so isn't sure whether or not he's been insulted (for example, when Blanche asks him his astrological sign), the set look of his jaw swallows up his sense of humor. When he *knows* he's been insulted (the birthday dinner scene), he turns himself into a solid force plowing through his lines, scattering bits of words and phrases to both sides.

But to characterize Brando's Stanley Kowalski merely as funny on the outside and dangerous on the inside would be to leave out the element that makes it a great performance, and an emblematic one in the history of American Method acting: its poetry. Curled up tight inside this character whenever he flies into a fury is the inarticulate child who cannot express himself in any other way, "the silenced, frustrated part" that Kazan asserts we only see "in a burst of lightning."[9] Harold Clurman, reviewing the Broadway production of *Streetcar*, talks about the "Dostoevskian aspect" of Brando's performance arising from "the combination of an intense, introspective, and almost lyric

159

personality under the mask of a bully [which] endows the character with something almost touchingly painful."[10]

Of course there's no filmed record of Brando's performance on Broadway in 1947, but what we see in Kazan's screen version bears out Clurman's words—most memorably in the famous cry "Stella!" which brings his wife (whom he's just beaten) downstairs from a neighbor's apartment and back into his arms. It starts out as a confused whine, but then, as Brando ranges back and forth, it becomes the weeping of a terrified child. When he can't persuade Eunice to send Stella back to him, he stands outside and yells her name, and as he repeats it again and again it grows both more powerful and less defined, a rainstorm in the hot New Orleans night. Kim Hunter walks slowly down the stairs and he crashes to his knees, head buried, as if he was taking a ritual punishment. Then he begins to make love to her (animal-like, as Williams indicates), and carries her, pressed to his chest, into the house. This scene, which inspired Anthony Quinn's last moments in Fellini's La Strada (Quinn replaced Brando in the road company of Streetcar, under Clurman's direction) is brutal but agonized. Brando makes Stanley's brutality poetic.

After Streetcar, Brando had his chance at Steinbeck (Viva Zapata!, directed by Elia Kazan) and Shakespeare (the Joseph Mankiewicz all-star Julius Caesar). This is the only time he's ever tried his hand at Shakespeare, and he's remarkably good; he takes the challenge very seriously. He's a sleek, ultramasculine, soldierly Marc Antony, as well as intelligent and watchful; he stalks the streets and the Senate slowly, in a way that implies strength in repose. There's always something unpredictable about a Brando performance, and what you don't expect here are the solid-force approach (it's not an especially subtle piece of acting) and how long he checks his impulse to turn ironic.

In fact Brando's whole performance is built on an irony—but we don't get the payoff until quite late in the film. The play is about the power of oratory, and when Brando's Antony speaks over Caesar's bier, he rouses the citizens of Rome to anger over the conspirators' unjust condemnation of his friend's alleged ambition. (As an example of American Shakespearean technique, his oration speech is first-rate.) But we don't see his motive until, once he's moved with Octavius onto the top level of the Roman hierarchy, he does a striking, Brando-like thing: He stretches himself before Caesar's bust—a mock genuflection—and,

160

with a little private smile, turns it to face away from him. So, after all, Caesar's death does give a lift to Marc Antony's ambition.

It wasn't until 1954, though, that Brando once again captured the imagination of the American moviegoing audience—especially the teenage audience—by embodying the new, restless force in the youth of the Eisenhower era. It's no overstatement to say that, as Johnny in *The Wild One* and Terry Malloy in *On the Waterfront*, he gave voice to the tentative, intuitive emotional gropings of all the young men in America who felt betrayed or misunderstood by the adult world. (Technically, Terry isn't an adolescent, but his relationship to Charley, his brother, and to Johnny Friendly, the union gangster Charley provides legal counsel to, really is that of a slowly maturing child—eager at first, then rebellious—to the grownups in charge of him.)

In *The Wild One*, Brando defined "cool" and "hot" for an entire generation. The young actors who played toughs in every film from *The Blackboard Jungle* to *West Side Story* owed a debt to his manner of staring his adversaries down, of wiping dust off his sunglasses with a black-gloved hand (more *noblesse oblige*), and of tossing off a non-line like "No, man, that's nowhere," lending all these flourishes an air of supreme authenticity by underplaying them. "Cool" is a combination of undisguised sexuality (the image of Brando in leather and shades; the amazing stillness in the way he holds himself); hip jargon, delivered in a lightly mocking style (a prototype for the put-ons of the 1960s); and the taunting expertise that keeps you just out of reach of adult authority. "Hot" is the tension always present beneath the cool surface. These two temperamental states are in precarious balance when Brando, pushed by an attacker, grabs his jacket, waves his finger in his face, and then talks softly to him. But when he says "I don't like cops," his cool dissipates entirely and every muscle in his face becomes energized.

According to John Paxton's screenplay (based on a story by Frank Rooney called "The Motorcyclists' Raid"), an overwritten piece of 1950s moralizing, Johnny isn't a dangerous rebel at all, just a classically misunderstood teenager, a good boy at heart—like Jim Stark in the following year's *Rebel Without a Cause*. But Brando's dark, complex portrayal undermines the script's conclusion: that, having barely escaped a murder charge, Johnny has learned his lesson, and having responded to the love of a decent woman, Kathie (Mary Murphy), he's been redeemed. The movie never resolves the contradiction that Johnny won Kathie's love by taking her for a ride on his motorcycle, giving her a taste of the wild life of the road, and that therefore her presumed desire to tame him is a denial of what attracted her to him in the first place. Actually, the fact that Brando loses none of his brooding renegade energy (his last act—making a smiling presentation of his trophie to Kathie—is a small concession) undermines the pat solution, acceptable to Hays Code standards of moral conduct, that Paxton and the director, Laslo Benedek, came up with.

Brando's performance has two especially inventive moments: the way he turns a kiss for Kathie into an attack, the result of his fear and frustration because he sees her softness as a threat to him; and the distasteful look on his face when she weeps on his shoulder, as if she'd spilled something sticky on his jacket. A third moment, Johnny's confrontation with the rival gang leader, Chino (Lee Marvin), might be background research for Brando's next film, *On the Waterfront*. Johnny approaches his opponent like a prize fighter—prowling, warning him away with small, sharp, precise moments, then shoving him off his motorbike with one well-aimed thrust.

On the Waterfront, written by Budd Schulberg and directed by Elia Kazan, is the quintessential social-conscience film of its era. The issue is the corruption of labor as seen through the personal conflict of one man, Terry Malloy. On one side is his desire for security—in the form of protection (Terry's brother "watches out" for him), anonymity (Terry has the option of remaining just one among many longshoremen), and approval (of his brother, of the crooked union boss Johnny Friendly, and of his peers). On the other side is his impulse to come clean and lead the decent, honest life held out to him by Edie (Eva Marie Saint), the sister of the old friend he unwittingly helped Friendly's stooges murder. At the end of the movie, having testified in court against Friendly, he stands up to the hostility of his fellow workers, who feel he's betrayed them, endures a savage beating from Friendly's boys, and then drags himself along the docks, calling Friendly out, censuring him publicly, and leading the other dock workers in defiance against Friendly's edict that they don't work.

Terry's triumph transposed the optimism of the old theater of the Left to the social and political milieu of the fifties, and it still held—and continues to hold—surprising power. "He have his goodness now. God forbid I take it from him!" Elizabeth Proctor says of her husband in

Arthur Miller's *The Crucible*, as he is taken to the scaffold. The final moments of Kazan's movie make the same statement about Terry Malloy. (Ironically, whereas Miller meant *The Crucible* as an indictment of McCarthyism, *On the Waterfront* can be read on one level as Kazan's defense of his agreement to turn friendly witness before HUAC.)[11]

On the Waterfront has a noble heritage. Cinematically, it comes down from the Warner Brothers urban pictures of the thirties, the gangster movies that Kazan affirms were "the first breakthrough into working-class life. . . . the first view from underneath,"[12] and their twin, the "problem" films from the same studio, like *I Am a Fugitive from a Chain Gang*, and *Dead End*. Its theatrical parent is Clifford Odets's ubiquitous *Golden Boy*, with its sensitive boxer hero and his temper, the gangster (Lee J. Cobb plays a variation on Odets's Eddie Fuseli, a role Kazan himself had played in New York)—via *Body and Soul*. (Thomas Pauly points out that the pigeon coop Terry cares for parallels Joe Bonaparte's violin.[13]) When John Garfield, having defied his underworld boss and refused to throw the fight, is pronounced champion at the end of *Body and Soul*, his sunken look—the visible proof of his struggle up through the mire into the clean air—prefigures Brando's in a similar moment at the end of *On the Waterfront*. For Terry, the young man who could have been a contender, who reenacts his last prizefight for the man from the crime commission (in a scene that would crop up again two years later in Rod Serling's television play "Requiem for a Heavyweight"), the slow, difficult walk to the pier is the proud statement of a boxer who won't stay down for the count.

Brando's performance has been imitated so widely and parodied so often that it's a shock to return to it and rediscover how tight and economical, how free of affectation and self-indulgence, it really is. Brando's clarity is overwhelming: He lets us see everything Terry sees, lets us feel everything he feels, and he even finds a way of showing us what he's thinking. In the opening scene, when Terry calls Joey (the pal he inadvertently—semiconsciously, at least—sets up for Friendly), he narrows his eyes, taking in the men on top of the tenement roof waiting for their victim. When Joey tumbles off the roof Brando responds slowly, leaning over, sheltering one arm deep in his jacket and muttering, "He wasn't a bad kid, that Joey." We can already spot the glimmerings of conscience, the need to know why Joey deserved this punishment, and the urge to get clean, to assuage his inchoate feelings of guilt at his own involvement in the murder.

Parodies of this performance always isolate Brando's verbal idio-syncrasies, but heard in context they aren't self-conscious; they're wed-ded to the character. He burrows inside his words, reshaping them so they emerge both from the character and from himself. It's impossible to distinguish the actor from the role here. When he speaks, he often raises his eyebrows and addresses a spot in the air, just an inch or two above the face of the person he's talking to, showing us Terry's diffi-culty in moving from thoughts to words, physicalizing the entire ob-stacle course for us. And sometimes the words come out sounding strange or funny. In his first conversation with Edie, when he de-scribes her appearance when they were in school together—"You were a mess"—he pounces hard on the last word, so it hits the air with a splat. Nothing he says sounds prepared. Brando is famous for refusing to memorize his lines, insisting on hanging cue cards all over the set, and in a 1979 *Playboy* inteview he revealed his motive: "If you watch people's faces when they're talking, they don't know what kind of expressions they're going to have. You can see people search for words, for ideas, reaching for a concept, a feeling, whatever."[14] The result is mesmerizing. Superbly overstating the case, Norman Mailer has called Brando "the only player alive who knew how to suggest that he was about to say something more valuable than what he did say."[15]

On the Waterfront chronicles the awakening of Terry Malloy's conscience, which is inseparable from the development of his love for Edie. In other words, it's the story of how a man presumed lost is found, touched by finer feelings. Brando delineates each phase of Ter-ry's progress, keeping us vividly aware of how he responds to Edie, to reminders of Joey, to the priest (Karl Malden) who preaches against the dock workers' "deaf and dumb" attitude about the corruption in Johnny Friendly's union (and about the facts of Joey's death). And because Brando always seems so fervently in touch with his emotions—and keeps *us* in touch with them—there are no dead spaces in his acting. Any moment you might choose to examine is emotionally and psychologically loaded: his gentle invitation to Edie to join him for her first beer; his childlike directness when, after telling her he can't help her find her brother's murderers, he begs for her approval; his awk-wardness in pushing away the district attorney's thanks (he uses his hands to do it) after his case-breaking testimony; the struggle between defeat and defiance when his friends reject him after the trial. At every moment Brando's acting cuts us a cross-section of the character.

There are two related scenes that deserve to be singled out for their unusual power. The first is the most celebrated two-character exchange in the history of American movies: the taxicab scene between Brando and Rod Steiger (Charley), culminating in the "contender" speech. From the start of this sequence, Brando heightens the exasperation of a man who has lived so long with a corruption in his blood that nothing—unkind words from his brother, physical danger—seems worse to him than what he's already suffered from his own feelings of guilt. We've witnessed the development of Terry's awareness, and now we see where it has led him: He's put so much distance between himself and the values Johnny Friendly stands for (and Charley assents to) that he can be ironic with his brother. (Brando conveys irony in Terry's characteristic blocked-expressive style.)

And there's much, much more. When he sees a gun in his brother's hand, Terry's eyes brighten as his thoughts speed up, and he waves the weapon away from a mixture of disgust, incredulity, and deep sadness. The only syllable he speaks is "Wow!" but the emotional range of that word makes sense of all the Method "nonsense" exercises, in which actors work to communicate their objectives in dialogues consisting only of gibberish. Then he gets to the "contender" speech, in which he accuses his brother of wrecking his career as a boxer:

> You don't understand! I coulda been a contender. I coulda
> had class, I coulda been somebody. Instead of a bum, which
> is what I am, let's face it, Charley. It was you, Charley.

Saying these lines, Terry seems to locate his old ambitions at a specific point in space. And the phrase "I coulda had class, I coulda been somebody" has a strange aura to it. It seems almost mannered, until you realize that, to Terry, being a "somebody" is so extraordinary, so poignantly beyond his experience, that the word necessarily distorts his speech and makes him sound a little ridiculous. The most imaginative part of this speech, though, is the moment that follows the last line, when he falls silent and a slight spasm passes through his body. You can believe that admitting the truth has rid him of the disgust he's felt for his brother. It will take him the rest of the movie to complete the process of cleansing himself.

The other scene occurs when, summoned into the street by Friendly's stooges, Terry finds Charley's corpse hanging on a longshoreman's hook in an alley. Before lifting him into his strong prize-fighter's arms and down off the hook, he reaches out and touches his brother's breast. This "psychological gesture," which tells us both that Terry has forgiven his brother and that he himself is asking for forgiveness, has primal power.

Among American actors, Brando has certainly had the most formidable influence on his peers, and his portrayal of Terry Malloy spawned a raft of imitations and tributes. Both Jack Palance and Anthony Quinn were affiliated with Brando early in their careers; Palance understudied him on stage in *Streetcar* and Quinn took over the role of Stanley in the road company, and then won his first Oscar in 1952 for playing Brando's brother in *Viva Zapata!* And both played variations on his performance in *On the Waterfront* when they took the role of the fading boxer in Rod Serling's *Requiem for a Heavyweight*—Palance on television in 1957, Quinn in the 1962 movie adaptation. As late as the seventies and eighties, American actors were still commenting on Terry Malloy. Sylvester Stallone's performance in *Rocky* is a composite of Brando's, Quinn's, and Ernest Borgnine's in *Marty;* and Robert De Niro, playing real-life fighter Jake La Motta in *Raging Bull*, goes so far as to rehearse the "contender" speech in front of a mirror.

Brando's inspiration appears to have had a liberating effect on both Jack Palance and Anthony Quinn. Palance, often an affected actor, is absolutely authentic as Mountain McClintock. (It's practically the only work he's done, aside from the movie version of Clifford Odets's *The Big Knife* and his spirited cameo in *Batman*, that's worth talking about.) He lightens his voice—his head seems to be floating—and, strongly influenced by Brando's diction, he reels around the lines like a punch-drunk fighter instead of hitting them straight on. Surprisingly gentle and sweet-souled, Palance is out in space, a little remote from everyone else; he has to fight his way through invisible obstacles to get his words out, and when he does the words are blocks that he can't move around to form the shapes he wants. He has no difficulty pushing his emotions through, though. When he learns that his manager, Maish (Keenan Wynn), has betrayed him, his kindly bruiser's face falls. Forced to humiliate himself as a show wrestler to make money, he looks at himself in the mirror and speaks one word, "Clown," and that's all we need to undestand the entire pathetic situation. And Quinn gives one of his few uninflated performances in the movie version of *Requiem*. Not normally a Method actor, he certainly behaves like one in this role, abandoning the strong Quinn persona and immersing himself in the role of the barely coherent boxer with the high, hoarse voice.

One of the popular clichés about Brando is that he sold out after *On the Waterfront*, but that's an inaccuracy based on a naive view of how the American film industry operates. In retrospect, his career between 1954 and 1972 seems like an unparalleled example of triumph in the face of adversity. After his work in *Waterfront* won him the official approval of the Hollywood community in the form of an Academy Award he was churned through the system, handed mostly stupid, two-dimensional roles in standard (that is, standardly bad) or substandard big-studio pictures, and punished for his independent-mindedness (both artistic and political) by being publicly jeered at by producers, studio heads, publicists, and gossip columnists. When you read "The Duke in His Domain," Truman Capote's notorious commentary on Brando written during the filming of *Sayonara* in 1957, you wonder how any performing artist could have survived the kind of hostility leveled against him. (Capote participates in the stone-throwing: His article, allegedly an interview with annotations, is an insidious piece of gossip-mongering pockmarked with his own high-handed remarks about a profession he appears to have no understanding of.)

Of the seventeen movies Brando made between *Waterfront* and *The Godfather*, only a handful—*The Fugitive Kind*, based on Tennessee Williams's *Orpheus Descending; One Eyed Jacks*, the western he directed himself; *The Ugly American;* Charlie Chaplin's *A Countess from Hong Kong* (which contained, ironically, Brando's most disastrous performance); and John Huston's *Reflections in a Golden Eye*, out of Carson McCullers's novel—were projects he had any genuine interest in. The others were mere employment. The list is a dispiriting one: *Desirée, Guys and Dolls, The Teahouse of the August Moon, Sayonara, The Young Lions, Mutiny on the Bounty, Bedtime Story, Morituri, The Chase, The Appaloosa, Candy,* and *The Night of the Following Day*. But remarkably, though this arsenal of paltry material sank Brando's reputation (until *The Godfather* revived it), it rarely defeated him as an actor. Something extraordinary emerged in at least a few moments in almost every one of these films. With the possible exception of *The Appaloosa*, where he really seemed burned out (or blocked), he never walked through one of these roles, even when he couldn't disguise his contempt for it.

Few of Brando's female costars (until Maria Schneider in *Last Tango in Paris*) had anything like the kind of emotional/sexual connection with him that Eva Marie Saint had in *On the Waterfront*. The most striking match, perhaps, was Brando and the deep-voiced young actress Pina Pellicer, making her debut in *One Eyed Jacks* (and dead a few years later). But Brando often focused a performance on a character's sexuality, and that choice could keep an entire film breathing. His total masculine control in *Viva Zapata!* provides a center for a role that's mostly made up of John Steinbeck noble-liberal platitudes. God knows Brando's not a believable Mexican; anyway, his glistening make-up and drooping moustache make him look more like a Chinese sage. But he does make Emiliano Zapata a believable sexual creature, leaping past the script's most ludicrous proposition—that Zapata asked his wife (Jean Peters) to teach him how to read on their wedding night. As the fatuously blond German officer who stages a silent rebellion in *The Young Lions*, he employs his full reserve of romantic charm. And, hair silver-tinted, curled, and slicked back, he's a far more sensuous and sly western hero in *One Eyed Jacks* than audiences were used to. There's also an audacious moment in *The Fugitive Kind* when he tells Anna Magnani that if she suffers from insomnia, he knows "how to make little adjustments in the neck and spine that give you sound, natural sleep."

Sometimes what we respond to in a Brando performance is a trademark moment—his restlessness, or his habit of directing a speech above the head of the person he is speaking to (as if conversation were too difficult a proposition to traffic in loosely), or the way he presses his eyes shut, seeming to carry the weight of the world on his forehead. Sometimes it's his panache at wearing a costume: a brightly colored ascot in *One Eyed Jacks*, a snakeskin jacket in *The Fugitive Kind*, an ambassador's garb (top hat, pin-stripe suit, pipe, and natty moustache) in *The Ugly American*. Sometimes it's an amusing flourish, a grace note, like the moment in *The Young Lions* when he drunkenly pours May Britt a glass of her own vodka and then, deciding he's given her too much, trickles a few drops back into the bottle. Or the ironic flat tone in the whooping cry "Hot dog!" in *Sayonara* when he spots his future in-laws at an airport and has to pretend surprise—or the unfolding of the crumpled letter he carries in his pocket in *The Fugitive Kind*, which he turns into a miniature musical number. In *The Teahouse of the August Moon*, his entire performance is a flourish. Cast hilariously as the philosophical Okinawan interpreter Sakini, he does a wry vaudeville turn with an attempt at something like distanced delicacy. It doesn't come off the way he must have intended, but the movie is such a broad, embarrassing mess that you're grateful for the elements of outrageous parody and the self-amusement in Brando's performance.

Occasionally he manages to crack the expensive veneer of these movies and fill the hollow underneath with a suggestion of character depth, as he does in *Viva Zapata!* when Zapata learns that the tyrant Diaz has left Mexico and the fighting is over. And there's a similar moment in *The Young Lions:* his speech about how the horrors of war have altered him, which he delivers with his hands shading his eyes. *Sayonara*, which Brando justly dismissed as "this wondrous hearts-and-flowers nonsense that was supposed to be a serious picture about Japan,"[16] rises above melodrama only when Brando finds occasion to probe the slowly awakening conscience of the easygoing young bomber pilot who astonishes himself by falling in love with a Japanese dancer. A little of his own passion comes through in a scene, late in *The Ugly American*, where he convinces Eiji Okada, who plays a popular leader in a small Far Eastern country, that his revolution is in the hands of the Communists and he's marked for assassination. *The Fugitive Kind* begins with Brando's story about his attempt to retrieve his hocked guitar, a gift from Leadbelly, and it sounds improvised; he cuts through the colorful excesses of Williams's dialogue by reading it in a straightforward manner. This casual introduction is a daring choice both on Brando's part and on the part of the director, Sidney Lumet, who emphasizes it by leaving it unadorned by soundtrack music.

Unfortunately, *The Fugitive Kind* fails to live up to this crackling opening. Brando and the great Italian actress Anna Magnani, who plays opposite him, don't bring out much in each other, and not even the combination of their talents and the young, energetic Lumet's can make sense of the script. But if Brando doesn't illuminate Val Xavier's psyche, at least he retains his integrity, refusing to use the role as a medium for self-indulgence. He preserves the character's mystery, giving a hushed performance that rises to occasional lyric heights during the superbly modulated off-the-beat monologues. (The one about birds that sleep on the wind is extraordinary.)

If it's true that, as Hal Hinson says, "Mystery and ambiguity are the Method actors' stock in trade,"[17] then Brando, in this as in all other things, leads the pack. As early as *On the Waterfront* we see him holding a part of himself back—in this case, when the two investigators from the crime commission try to coax him into talking to them. Seemingly distracted, he barely glances in their direction most of the time, and when he does he appears to be looking at them through a long corridor, from some remote place. In the bizarre Freudian–existentialist western *One Eyed Jacks*, he plays the Rio Kid as a fascinating enigma: Since it's hard to know how much of the film was intended as a parody—you can hear the wit, but the jokes are so submerged you're not sure when to laugh—Brando's inscrutable performance isn't at odds with the rest of the goings-on. And his almost silent presence in the early scenes has considerable power. In fact, when he's stuck in bad movies without any subtext, he's always at his worst when the script forces him to become too explicit (*Desirée*, where he plays Napoleon, and *Guys and Dolls* weigh him down with preposterously overwritten lines) or when he takes the role too seriously (*The Chase*, and the second half of *Mutiny on the Bounty*—though the second may simply be a case of an actor in a lost cause running out of invention).

Long after Brando stopped playing rebels on screen he was still engaged in his own private rebellion against the stupid movies that were for many years the only ones he was offered. "You direct yourself in most films," he's said,[18] and in his case that means inventing humor where the script provides none, adding a dimension of flamboyant theatricality to a drab project, turning a solemn turkey like the 1962 remake of *Mutiny on the Bounty* into a farce by punctuating it with his own self-mockery. And, as Pauline Kael has written, "As with Bette Davis, as with John Barrymore, even when he mocks himself, the self he mocks is more prodigious than anybody else around."[19]

Brando claims he has no gift for comedy, and it's true that his two official comedies, *Bedtime Story* (1964) and *A Countess from Hong Kong*, are embarrassments. (*Bedtime Story* does have one prize sequence, in which he impersonate an idiot prince with an immense, vacant grin.) And he's stiff in the musical comedy *Guys and Dolls*, twisting his mouth around to overenunciate in a Damon Runyon accent; only when he bursts into song is he fun to watch—endearingly incongruous, like an actor on a lark in a TV variety-show guest spot. It's in *serious* bad movies that his renegade sense of humor really breaks loose—in his timing, his way of rolling his eyes up toward the ceiling, his conscious invocation of the Brando trademarks.

The decay of gifted actors and actresses into self-mockery is the way of all flesh in this country, but while most are unaware of the process as it's going on (Katharine Hepburn is a particularly disturbing example), Brando, still so young when he began to make movies pathetically unworthy of him, chose to keep himself artistically alive by turning the *idea* of himself as an actor into a grand joke. No other American film star, for example, has ever used so many delightfully silly foreign accents. They're music-hall dialects that work (in collaboration with extravagant costumes) to draw our attention to the folly of casting an actor so utterly American in roles like Napoleon, Lieutenant Diestl (in *The Young Lions*), and Fletcher Christian. In his ponytail in *Desirée* he looks like a costume-shop mannequin; and, speaking in deliberate, half-whispered tones, he sends up lines like "Did you ever hear of destiny, Desirée? Desirée—desired one?" by pounding lightly on the repeated consonant sound. Similarly, his southern-gentleman Major in *Sayonara* is a game to delight himself with; his German accent in *The Young Lions* is absurdly *haute;* his Asian accent in *The Teahouse of the August Moon* is preposterous; and he devises a riotous western drawl for *One Eyed Jacks*, with "r's" as hard as a brick wall.

Brando's comic *pièce de résistance* is the first half of his performance as Fletcher Christian in *Mutiny on the Bounty*. On his initial appearance he wears a ponytail once again, under a buckled pilgrim hat, and he shoulders a scarlet cape. Pursing his lips into a constipated smile as he introduces his two overdressed lady friends to Captain Bligh (Trevor Howard), he speaks in a fop's accent outrageous enough to dismantle the entire stuffed spectacle of a movie—"like a Dead End Kid playing Congreve" is Kael's phrase.[20] He turns his famous mumble into an aristocratic joke, and half his lines sound like improvised put-ons. After a particularly loathsome demonstration of Bligh's sadism, when one of the sailors hangs around hoping for an antiauthoritarian word from Christian, Brando quips, "Something else you want to discuss? Early Renaissance painting, perhaps?" When Bligh orders him to ready the ship to set sail, he pulls on his gloves as if preparing to serve tea, and in one scene, dressed in a frilly white shirt and an aqua-

171

colored ascot, he stands on deck with easel and palette as the men swab around him. (There's no doubt he's having a subversive high time in this movie. In one shot he lies on the couch in his cabin, a nightcap on his head, a thick robe with a wide ruby collar wrapped luxuriously around him, and a long, curled pipe in his mouth—a Dickens figure of fun in a Hollywood adventure movie.)

Elia Kazan has said of Marlon Brando, "He's very, very underground—you don't know *how* he gets to what he gets."[21] Brando's late performances, in *The Godfather* (1972) and *Last Tango in Paris* (1973), constitute the most astounding comeback of any American actor. Suddenly, rounding fifty, he became once again the most exciting presence in movies—because he was finally playing roles that allowed him to demonstrate the depth and range he'd never lost. These performances bear the same relation to his work in *A Streetcar Named Desire* and *On the Waterfront* that Michelangelo's *Moses* bears to his *David:* They offer a glimpse of a prodigy in maturity. The wonder is not that Brando could give them, but that he ever got the chance.

An earlier performance, unjustly neglected, proved that Brando in his mid-forties had become an even more audacious actor than he was in his late twenties. In John Huston's 1967 *Reflections in a Golden Eye* he plays Major Pendleton, who conceives an infatuation for a young Private at a southern peacetime army post. This may be the most complex and disturbing portrait any American film star has attempted of sexual repression, and possibly only a great actor whose overt heterosexuality has always been such a vital performance factor could delve so deeply into it (just as only an actor of Olivier's stature could play the hell out of a third-rate vaudevillian like Archie Rice in *The Entertainer*). Brando uses a heavy accent here, but unlike his other vocal extravagances, Pendleton's southern drawl—tight, suffocated, with a genteelly effeminate lisp, gilding a frightened voice always in danger of flying into a higher register—isn't just for fun; it exposes an emotionally and sexually straitjacketed personality. (It also sounds uncannily, hilariously like Tennessee Williams.)

Brando centers his performance on the discrepancy between Pendleton's vision of himself and the way he appears to others. He holds himself with absurd, spinsterish care; he rides high in the saddle like a fat dowager, bouncing up and down, his oversized buttocks spread awkwardly. But alone in his study he lifts weights, as if engaged in single combat, pounding his chest to show he's still all muscle, and saluting himself smilingly in the mirror. He's mastered the rules of conduct of an old-school soldier, but not the style: He doesn't realize how comical he looks to the stable boys who watch him ride from behind; how eccentric and out-of-sync he seems to the recruits he lectures in the classroom. And whenever he does worry about how others might perceive him, he makes himself look even more foolish. There's a painfully funny interlude in which Pendleton hears his wife, Leonora (Elizabeth Taylor), giggling with one of the servants in the kitchen, assumes they must be laughing at him, and marches purposefully into the room. Then, realizing he has no good reason for being there, he meticulously sets the clock back one minute before marching out again. He looks just like Malvolio stalking in to break up the party.

What's so alarming about that salute in the mirror is that it's Pendleton's warmest moment. In the company of others he can't release emotion; we see it begin to form in his face, but then he pushes it into his lower lip and seals up his mouth. Whenever his eyes reveal fear or anger, he has to cross so many awkward barriers before he can communicate his state of mind to others that he always ends up blubbering incoherently. In the most unconventional role you could imagine for a man who played Stanley Kowalski in his youth, Brando dares to appear grotesque. When he musters up enough courage to follow Private Williams (Robert Forster), the unconscious object of his infatuation, in the street, his seducer's smile freezes on his lips, and he gets an abstracted look on his face. Then he picks up the empty chewing-gum package Williams has dropped, and suddenly we see the recognition in Pendleton's eyes that he's behaving in a ludicrous fashion.

The tension between Pendleton's outer and inner layers is so taut that we wait through the whole movie for his mind to shatter—and it does, in the final moment of the film, when he discovers Williams in his wife's room and shoots him. Just before this explosion we see Pendleton sequestered in his study, staring at photographs of muscle men, applying cold cream to his face, and—under the sad misapprehension that Williams has entered the house to visit *him*—fixing his hair before he turns off the light. These activities are so intensely private that we feel like invaders when we watch them; we want to look away in embarrassment. Brando's acting here validates the controversial "private moment" exercise in Strasberg's classes, when an actor engages in some activity he would normally perform only in private. In public, the struggle that Pendleton wages between his homoerotic

173

impulses and his image of himself as a paragon of masculine military virtues results in a prim, shocked response to his wife's easy, graceless sexuality (when he finds her leaning over the fireplace in an undignified pose, he hisses, "You disgust me"), and to the sight of Williams, the sensualist, riding nude through the forest.

As Pendleton becomes more obsessed with Williams, his remoteness from others around him becomes chronic. In the two classroom sequences he makes no contact with the men he is lecturing to, asking questions from such a strange distance that they sound rhetorical and no one answers them. When he dismisses the class it's as if he'd just awakened from a long dream and found everything a little unfamiliar. One of his lectures is about the importance of concentration, but Williams rides by the classroom window in the middle of it, and Pendleton loses his own concentration completely. In another scene, a fellow officer (Brian Keith) passes on the news of a neighbor's death, but Pendleton, noticing suddenly that Williams has disappeared, becomes so distracted that he can only repeat odd phrases of Keith's conversation, jigsaw puzzle pieces that he can't fit together.

Brando's performance in *Reflections in a Golden Eye*—easily his best since *On the Waterfront*—was a harbinger of astonishing things to come. And for Francis Ford Coppola's *The Godfather* (1972), he had an audience to register them. In *The Godfather* he plays a man more than twenty years his senior, an Italian emigré who personifies a kind of old-world elegance. He accomplishes this feat, in the Brando style, mostly with gestures. We first see Don Corleone from the back, holding court on the day of his daughter's wedding, an occasion when, according to Sicilian tradition, he can refuse no one's request. As he listens to the sad story of the undertaker whose daughter has been raped and beaten by thugs, his hand is extended and, like an orchestra conductor, he waves it gently to encourage the petitioner to continue. Speaking to an assembly—a conference of the five Mafia families of whom he asks an end to the gang war that has taken his son Sonny's life—he prefaces his first line with that same wave: "Allora," it says, "So let us begin." The way he raises his brow, wrinkling his forehead, or brushes his hand against his cheek comments on what he's just heard; the way he sips wine, absorbing the excess drops on his upper lip by a tiny feat of his facial muscles, reflects his origins and his breeding.

Brando's repertory of gestures, which he's drawn on throughout his career, has always had the air of ritual about it. Our recognition of his trademark movements is part of the drama of the performance; we want to see how he'll modify them to fit a new character or play them against material that has no dramatic energy of its own. In *Last Tango in Paris* they comment on both Brando the man and Brando the actor. In *The Godfather* he employs them in the service of a role that is itself vitally concerned with ritual. When the conference is concluded and the families have agreed on peace, Don Corleone embraces Tattaglia (Richard Conte), a man he despises, for the purpose of the ritual; when he grants the undertaker's request, he allows the poor man to kiss his ring, as if he were a pope.

Except for two brief moments of fatherly force, when he slaps his godson, the pop singer Johnny Fontaine (Al Martino), across the face for "crying like a woman," and when he reads Sonny (James Caan) a lecture for letting someone outside the family know what he's thinking, Don Corleone doesn't display anger. And in every physical aspect he seems ancient and weary (the old man's expression of permanent distaste; the strained voice, as if he had no larynx; the aging businessman's exhaustion in his tone when he says, after hearing the last petitioner, "Now if there's nothing else, I'd like to go to my daughter's wedding"). But there's no mistaking his right to extend his ring to his godchildren: He drips power like a monarch. He takes his time; it's an expansive performance. And Coppola's leisurely, wide, Renoiresque direction—relying on the long shot to tell the story, to juxtapose layers of activity, and to permit the audience the freedom to decide where to look first—encourages Brando and the other actors to explore their roles without the pressure of having to produce dramatic effects on cue.

And explore he does, discovering new ways of expressing emotion. In the recuperative scenes (after an attempt on his life), Don Corleone can barely move his head and whisper, but when Tom Hayden (Robert Duvall), the adopted son who's become the family lawyer, tells him that Michael has entered the family business by avenging him, we understand how he feels by the way he closes his eyes, shakes his head very slightly, and waves Tom out of the room. He expects Sonny's death hours before he receives official news of it, but when Tom confirms his suspicions, we see that anticipation hasn't softened the blow. When he looks up, tears just behind his eyes, and announces to Tom, "This war stops now," and when he shows Sonny's corpse to the undertaker and cries, "Look how they murdered my boy!"—the

175

sorrow spreading from his eyes and mouth through his high cheek-bones to the corners of his face—it's not inappropriate to recall Webster's description of grief in *The Duchess of Malfi*:

> *Th' heaven o'er my head seems made of molten brass,*
> *The earth of flaming sulphur, yet I am not mad.*
> *I am acquainted with sad misery*
> *As the tanned galley-slave is with his oar;*
> *Necessity makes me suffer constantly,*
> *And custom makes it easy.*

If *On the Waterfront* is Brando's *Hamlet* and *Last Tango in Paris* his *King Lear*, then *The Godfather* is his *Tempest*. In his portrayal, Don Corleone is Prospero, a monarch on the verge of giving up his throne, a romantic figure whose final moment of splendor comes at the beginning of the movie, when he dances with his daughter at her wedding. (The only other American actor who has ever carried off this kind of European elegance is Burt Lancaster, as the don whose world comes to an end in Visconti's *The Leopard*. He too plays a Sicilian, and he too kisses off his reign in the courtly style, dancing at a ball.) Tumbled by bullets in a street where he's stopped to buy fruit, Don Corleone resembles a fallen nobleman, his fedora tossed aside, his grey hair awry. Later, as he counsels Michael, to whom he's passed on his scepter, his mind wanders. Stopping in midsentence, he suddenly mentions he's been drinking more wine in his old age, and he repeats advice he's already offered. This distraction is so uncharacteristic of Don Corleone that Brando has only to suggest it to unsettle us. Then we learn that his mind has been on his former ambitions for his son: "I never wanted this for you. . . . Senator Corleone, Governor Corleone, something. . . . There wasn't enough time, Michael. There wasn't enough time." This is the way the old don's world ends: not with an imperial bang, but with the whimper of an old Sicilian whose son did not turn out as he had hoped. At the time he dies of a heart attack in his garden, in a scene that calls on Brando's improvisational skills, he's entertaining his grandson by playing a monster with an orange peel in his mouth—a comic Caliban.

The Godfather cropped up again in Brando's career in an unexpected manner eighteen years later, when he spoofed his own performance in it for Andrew Bergman's *The Freshman*—the movie the actor swears will be his swan song. Brando's always said he can't carry off a real comedy, but that's exactly what *The Freshman* is, and he's sublimely funny and touching in it. The film has the loose-screw charm and spontaneity of a Paramount programmer from the 1930s or early 1940s—one of those cheerfully rambling escapades starring the Marx Brothers or W.C. Fields, Burns and Allen or Hope and Crosby. Matthew Broderick plays Clark Kellogg, a naive kid from Vermont enrolled in his first semester at N.Y.U. Film School who ends up working part-time as a messenger for one Carmine Sabatini (Brando, looking and sounding exactly like Don Corleone).

The movie's loaded with *Godfather* jokes, like the elaborate wedding Carmine imagines for his daughter Tina (played by the dexterous *farceuse* Penelope Ann Miller) and Clark. But Brando's burlesque of his own celebrated 1972 performance isn't just a tossed-off variety-show bit, something a semi-retired star phones in after he's lost interest in acting. He's in top comic form here: Introducing Clark to his first espresso, warning his bad-news stockbroker ("Charlie"—like Terry Malloy's brother in *On the Waterfront*), "I don't like 'em when they go down," making a sweet little number out of the way his tongue rolls around his mouth (scouting for stray *amaretti* crumbs) as he holds court over coffee and biscuits, he's a master parodist.

Bergman takes his cue from Brando's improvisations while staying in control of the material, and you can feel Brando's pleasure in appearing in this charming little movie. He's generous to the other performers, too, especially Matthew Broderick. *The Freshman* has a not-too-convincing subtext about fathers and sons (Clark has lost his father, and his stepfather is a prize jerk) that suddenly comes to life when Broderick and Brando play a scene together in Clark's dorm room and Broderick looks over at Brando, the spiritual father of a generation and a half of American actors, with a mixture of awe and delight. Later, Brando returns the favor: Coming across Clark and Tina dancing together, he breaks into one of the warmest smiles any camera ever recorded. (He also gets to do a little cheek-to-cheeking of his own, on ice skates.) If Brando actually carries out his threat this time and never makes another picture, you couldn't ask for a lovelier keepsake than that smile and this performance.

In the wake of *The Godfather*'s spectacular success, both Coppola and Brando incurred some criticism for romanticizing the aging Mafioso, whose actions might easily have been portrayed as singlemindedly evil. Here's Brando, speaking to *Playboy* interviewer Lawrence Grobel:

> Everybody ought not to turn his back on the phenomenon of hatred in whatever form it takes. We have to find out what the anatomy of hatred is before we can understand it. . . . I don't see anybody as evil. When you start seeing people as evil, you're in trouble. The thing that's going to save us is understanding. The inspection of the mind of Eichmann or Himmler. . . . Just to dispense with them as evil is not enough, because it doesn't bring you understanding.[22]

As early as *Burn!* (two years before *The Godfather*), Brando had attempted to penetrate the mind and heart of a man whose actions could be called evil. Sir William Walker is a nineteenth-century Englishman sent by his government to engineer an insurrection among the slaves on a Caribbean island. Ten years later, after the slave (Evaristo Marquez) he trained and installed as the rebel leader has proven to be intractable, Walker returns to plot his downfall. Gillo Pontecorvo's film, which indirectly addresses the issue of American involvement in Vietnam, furnishes Sir William with a self-defining speech in which he claims he can't explain why he does the sort of work he does, but that he feels a compulsion to perform it well and see it through to the end. He also says that he's not "the author of this small masterpiece" but only the instrument.

Walker's cynicism and detachment don't bring out the best in Brando. He's intellectually absorbed in the role, but his emotions are engaged in only a few scenes, the ones where Walker observes the fire in the young slave's eyes and we can see his excitement at the prospect of shaping him into a political force. Brando has a dissolute gentleman's look here—greyish-sandy hair, scruffy at the edges, scraggly beard— and one of his fop accents, with a trace of Yorkshire in it. But he clearly believes in the movie too strongly to send it up (and his instincts are right: With all its flaws, it's a marvelous picture). So he stops short of the flamboyance that make his other exotic roles so entertaining. What's more, the script has to make Walker look foolish at the end, weak and defeated, in order to send home the point that it's impossible to extinguish a true revolutionary spark. And Brando foolish, when he's not mocking *himself* (or caught in the grip of a complex role like Major

Pendleton in *Reflections in a Golden Eye*), is, inevitably, Brando diminished. (This, incidentally, may explain why he goes stiff in *The Ugly American* when his character starts behaving stupidly.)

On the other side of the fence (he plays a good guy), Brando's commitment to Euzhan Palcy's anti-apartheid melodrama *A Dry White Season*—his comeback film after nearly a decade off the screen, released in 1989—is the only thing that redeems it. Brando is extraordinary as McKenzie, a celebrated race lawyer engaged by an Afrikaaner teacher (Donald Sutherland), roused by the prison murder of his gardener, to bring the brutal police force to justice. McKenzie's face has been scarred by years of shadow boxing in the courts of South Africa; there are pockets of disgust in it, and his natural expression is heartsickened scorn. But he uses his humor and irony as a shield against the poisons of his great adversary—the scared, backed-against-the-wall, self-protecting white society he came out of—and it works as a burnout preventative, too. Watching Brando's McKenzie in court is a thrill: He's like Charles Laughton in *Witness for the Prosecution*, plus depth.

Other pictures let Brando examine the unconscionable behavior of human beings in greater depth. In *The Nightcomers* (1971), an ill-fated "prequel" to Henry James's *The Turn of the Screw*, he gives a provocative performance as the malevolent Peter Quint, whose actions— feeding a cigar to a toad for the pleasure of watching the creature explode, mocking the children at their prayers, tying his lover (Stephanie Beacham) to a bedpost for a bit of sadistic foreplay—have a creepier cast because they're perpetrated with such unabashed playfulness. (The sexual savagery looks ahead to *Last Tango in Paris*, where it's lost the element of play.)

In Arthur Penn's *The Missouri Breaks* (1975), written by novelist Thomas McGuane, Brando plays Lee Clayton, a "regulator" hired by a rancher named Braxton (John McLiam) to track down a crew of cattle rustlers. Despite his employer's efforts to rein in Clayton's enthusiasm for the chase, Clayton insists on hounding each of the rustlers to his death. (This movie's not content to be just a period western. Clayton's disinterested passion for trapping and murdering these men with a collection of weapons awesome in their precision is supposed to symbolize the impersonal deadlines of modern warfare.) The performance begins as a deluxe Brando put-on: He enters swinging upside down from a horse, hair flying out at the sides, wrapped in a fringe-covered jacket and a ridiculous Irish brogue (roughly the same one he used for

The Nightcomers). Like a comic evangelist he strides into the middle
of the funeral of Braxton's foreman (supposedly murdered by rustlers),
censures the rancher publicly for "pampering" thieves, and hauls the
corpse out of its coffin by the collar to underscore his point. Then he
tells Braxton's daughter (Kathleen Lloyd) what he'd like for dinner,
and, pressing a hanky to his cheek, turns prissy, begging leave to
withdraw because of a toothache. He wears preposterous clothes
throughout the movie—headbands over his white aging-hippie hair
(the entire film strives for a post–Vietnam flavor), floppy carmine-
colored velvet hats, something that looks like a paper sailor's cap, even
drag. He leaps from accent to accent, pretending to be a tobacco-
chewing, guitar-picking itinerant in one scene and bursting playfully
into his Fletcher Christian voice in another.

At first you can't match this grandstanding clown with his lethal
occupation, but when he interviews Logan (Jack Nicholson), whom he
suspects of stealing Braxton's cattle, his eyes grow dangerous and
you're suddenly conscious of the wheels turning inside his head as he
conducts what is essentially a cross-examination. That's our earliest
indication that, though Clayton may occupy a separate world within
this movie, he's not as benign as he appears. Before the film is over he
has killed off nearly every likable character on screen (strategically,
McGuane and Penn make all the rustlers sympathetic), and made Lee
Clayton recognizable as a sort of walking evil delighting in its own
deadly cleverness—a killer in motley.

Unfortunately, McGuane has written Clayton as a symbol rather
than a human being. The most Brando can accomplish by way of an
explanation for his relentlessness, his callousness, and his contempt for
everybody and everything is to suggest a hidden agenda that we're
never allowed to read. In other words, he preserves Clayton's mystery.
But the way he uses his imaginative theatricality as both a screen for
Clayton's malevolence and a comically distorted manifestation of it is
truly remarkable. We don't understand this man, but he scares the hell
out of us.

Not all of the late performances rate high in the Brando canon. As
Kurtz in Francis Ford Coppola's lost-in-the-jungle epic, *Apocalypse
Now*, a variation on the trader swallowed up by the "heart of darkness"
in Conrad's novella, he's meant to stand in for the tainted spirit of
America in Vietnam. His obliqueness in this role, exacerbated by Cop-
pola's peculiar decision to shoot him entirely in shadow and record his

voice so we can barely hear him, may represent the nadir of his post–
Godfather years (along with his ridiculous walk-on in *Superman* the
previous year, which isn't acting at all). And though he has an amusing
midwestern accent in *The Formula* (he looks and sounds as if he
stepped right out of a Sinclair Lewis novel), the movie itself is a pallid,
mechanical retread of *The Godfather*'s ideas about business and crime,
and he fades along with it.

He's extraordinary, though, in the final episode of the 1979 TV
miniseries "Roots: The Next Generations," where he appears in a single five-minute scene as George Lincoln Rockwell, head of the American Nazi Party. The amazing true-life context is that Rockwell allowed
Alex Haley (James Earl Jones in the series) to interview him at home
for *Playboy* without asking whether Haley was black. So what we see
is a face-off between these two men, one struggling to suppress his
growing anger while the other explicates and demonstrates his racism.
It's a daring turn for Brando, a real *Heart of Darkness* vignette. As
Rockwell grows more amused by the situation—he keeps a pistol on his
desk throughout the interview, and sprays the air merrily with deodor-
ant as he addresses his black guest—he becomes more crazily self-
assured, at one point singing the lyrics of a mocking song about blacks
and Jews that he calls a "hate-enanny." Brando skillfully underplays
the entire scene, but because Rockwell makes no attempt to minimize
his hatred for the man on the other side of his desk, this encounter
between two legendary American actors has an almost unbearable tension. It may be the best-acted five minutes in the history of American
television.

No more trenchant exploration of the darkest reaches of human
emotion ever came from Brando—or any other American actor—than
his greatest performance, in Bernardo Bertolucci's *Last Tango in Paris*
(1972). It located the last great frontier of the Method: the realm of
sexuality. Having walked the avenues of repressed homosexuality in
Reflections in a Golden Eye, Brando now played a profoundly troubled
heterosexual in the first major film to address the topic of sexual relationships in the direct—even relentless—manner in which D. H. Lawrence and Henry Miller had plumbed it in their novels.

Last Tango is the tragedy of Paul, a transplanted American whose
wife has killed herself. Under the burden of his grief he's come to
believe that the only way to avoid damage in a relationship is to restrict
it to its sexual component. So he begins a crazy romance with a young

French *bourgeoise*, Jeanne (Maria Schneider) in which "[You] don't have a name, and I don't have a name either. No names here. Not one name." Like Sol Nazerman, the character Rod Steiger plays in *The Pawnbroker* who closes himself off from human contact because he's afraid to expose the layers of pain he acquired at Auschwitz, Paul is already destroyed when we first see him. But he's not hard-shelled like Nazerman (who's a kind of walking corpse). Paul is incapable of *not* feeling, and so the sexual experiment is fraught with contradictions from the outset.

Brando looks ravaged in the opening shot. This time the eyes, folded thoughtfully beneath the creased brow (his code for expressing hesitation and indecision), have passed through the period of artifice and self-parody and into a new era of psychological realism, marked by an anguish so private that nothing we've seen before—even from Marlon Brando—prepares us for it. When he speaks his voice is low and small, with a tiny hint of desperation at the far end of it.

Paul plays out his emotional turmoil when he makes love to Jeanne: After their first sexual encounter he lies on his stomach, holding his head, as if he were recovering from a binge, and she rolls away from him and across the floor of the apartment. This is the kind of sexual desire that vomits itself out of men and women after depositing the seeds of their destruction inside them. Brando conducts such an exhaustive investigation into the dark, poisonous side of sex that the romantic fatalism of John Garfield's characters seems almost childlike and naive by comparison. In one horrifying scene Paul buggers Jeanne, forcing her to repeat his words like a litany while she writhes underneath him. Later in the picture, when Jeanne, narcotized by their lovemaking, begins to fall in love with him, envisioning him as a cracked contemporary version of her girlish dream of a knight in shining armor, he breaks into her fantasy by demanding that she shove her fingers up his ass. Even during this act, though, he remains, as always, the sexual controller, subjugating her will to his power: He forces her to "prove" her love by agreeing to participate in a series of hypothetical acts, each of them revolting, excessive, preposterous.

If the sex in *Last Tango* reeks of Strindberg, it's also the neurotic, addictive sex of Tennessee Williams. Paul inevitably recalls Stanley Kowalski: He carries Jeanne in his arms, before they begin their lovemaking, in the same perversion of gallantry that Brando's Stanley called upon when he lifted Blanche to the bed before raping her (a witty

grace note on a caveman rite). In one scene he even wears the Kowalski emblem: a white T-shirt. In Norman Mailer's words, "Brando
cashes the check Stanley Kowalski wrote for us twenty-five years ago—
he fucks the heroine standing up."[23] But the case is far more complicated. According to Pauline Kael, "Paul carries a yoke of masculine
pride and aggression across his broad back; he's weighed down by it
and hung on it."[24] He's a Stanley laden with guilt, a Stanley whose
sexual power has crippled him, a Stanley with a measure of Blanche
DuBois inside him. The agonized release of the sexual connection he
forges with Jeanne—his attempt to retreat from the nightmare of his
wife's suicide—evokes one of Blanche's most potent lines:

> Death—I used to sit here and she used to sit over there and
> death was as close as you are. . . . The opposite is desire. So
> do you wonder? How could you possibly wonder? [Scene 9]

For Blanche the path of desire leads to madness. For Paul—who
finally can't separate desire from love; who walks out on Jeanne, only
to return, dressed politely, to woo her in a semiobscene parodic variation on that most stylized of courtship rites, the tango; who finally tells
her his name as a pledge of his emotional bond to her—desire and
death turn out to be the same thing. Doffing his cap to her, touching
her hair tenderly and smiling a beautiful half-smile (it's the most purely
romantic moment of Brando's career), Paul plays Benedick to Jeanne,
and then finds death lurking at the bottom of his desire: She shoots
him.

In a sense, Brando's entire career is in this performance. Stanley
Kowalski is here, and Paul's final gesture (taking the gum out of his
mouth and sticking it on the balcony railing of Jeanne's apartment) is
a comic tribute to the tough-guy rebel tradition that brought us characters like Stanley, Terry Malloy, and Johnny (in *The Wild One*).
Catherine (Catherine Allegret), the chambermaid who discovered his
wife Rosa's body, quotes the Paris *gendarmes*' description of Paul:

> They said "Nervous type, your boss. You know he was a
> boxer?" So? "That didn't work . . . so he became an actor,
> then a racketeer on the waterfront in New York." So? "It
> didn't last long . . . played the bongo drums . . . revolution-
> ary in South America . . . journalist in Japan . . . One day he

183

lands in Tahiti, hangs around, learns French . . . comes to
Paris and then meets a young woman with money . . . he
marries her . . . and since then . . . what does he do, your
boss?"

Some of the experiences attributed to Paul in this speech are obvious
references to Brando's roles: Terry Malloy in *On the Waterfront;* Sir
William Walker, the *agent provocateur* who instigates a revolution in
Burn! (1970); Fletcher Christian in *Mutiny on the Bounty.* Others
allude to Brando's own life: "he became an actor"; "he lands in Tahiti,
hangs around, learns French." (Brando lived with his *Bounty* costar,
Tarita, who bore him a child; and his home is in the Tetiaroa Islands,
ten miles north of Tahiti.)

This remarkable mélange of real and fictive facts, memories of
Brando's past life and of his past characters' lives, carries right into his
performance. In one scene, ignoring the rules that he himself set up,
Paul breaks into a long, revealing monologue about growing up on a
farm in Nebraska. Some, if not all, of this story actually derives from
Brando's childhood experiences, and his description of his parents
("My father was a . . . a drunk, whore-fucker, bar fighter, super-
masculine, and he was tough. . . . My mother was . . . very poetic,
also a drunk . . .") is a revelation to us: It begins to explain the powerful dichotomy between machismo and poetry in Brando's acting, as
far back as *Streetcar.* "My soul is a private place,"[25] Brando claimed in
his *Playboy* interview, but he bares it for us in *Last Tango.*

The best acting often seems like an invasion: Julie Harris once told
an interviewer that when she saw Laurette Taylor in *The Glass Menagerie,* "Her performance shattered me. . . . It was so personal I
couldn't believe I was seeing it."[26] But Brando's acting in *Last Tango*
takes us inside him in a way that few actors have ever allowed, and
possibly no one else but Jason Robards in his O'Neill roles has ever
brought off. And no matter how close he comes to his own core,
Brando never stops being Paul; this is acting, not self-indulgence.
(That's what distinguishes the improvisation in this film from the inflated, fakey improvisational acting in the movies of John Cassavetes.)
The effect is to shock us into recognition, in the same way that a great
production of *King Lear* does. As Kael writes, "If Brando knows this
hell, why should we pretend we don't?"[27]

Brando's improvisations in this picture have the rhythm of actual conversation without its tonelessness. They're the dramatic equivalent of stream of consciousness—poetic representations of actual shifts of thoughts. They extend the feat of the opening scene of *The Fugitive Kind* (the guitar story), and one of them, the monologue to Rosa's corpse in her bower, is practically an aria. (Of course, there's no way of knowing how much of this scene really was improvised. The language often has a lyrical quality—he calls her a "fake Ophelia drowned in a bathtub"—which suggests scripted dialogue, but there are eruptions that you can't believe anyone could have planned.) The monologue is a variation on the Requiem scene from *Death of a Salesman*, in which Linda Loman confides to her dead husband that she can't understand why he killed himself. Paul's unanswerable question is phrased more explosively: "Even if the husband lives two hundred fucking years, he's never going to be able to discover his wife's real nature. I mean, I might be able to comprehend the universe but I'll never discover the truth about you, never. I mean, who the hell were you?" Brando and Bertolucci allow Paul the natural human response that Miller is too tasteful to give Linda: Furious at what Rosa's suicide has done to him, he screams abuse at her, then dissolves in tears.

This monologue is the most searing exposure of Brando in the movie, including the moment when Paul weeps mysteriously in a corner of the apartment. And it elucidates Paul's lunatic insistence that he and Jeanne explore each other in no other way but carnally. "All the mysteries you're ever going to know in life are right here," he tells Jeanne. When she's dissatisfied, longing to discover more about him, he says, "Well, if you look real close, you'll see me hiding behind my zipper." His complaint about women is that "[They] always pretend to know who I am." But he *does* reveal himself to Jeanne, just as Brando reveals himself to us—and so her final speech, after she's shot him, is the ultimate betrayal. Preparing a story for the police, she repeats, "I don't know who he is. He followed me on the street. He tried to rape me. He's a madman. I don't know his name." But we do. If ever an actor scrawled his name across the history of American acting, it was Marlon Brando.

7

MYSTICAL COMMUNION: JAMES DEAN AND JULIE HARRIS

♦ ♦ ♦

I felt that Dean's body was very graphic; it was almost writhing in pain sometimes. He was very twisted, almost like a cripple or a spastic of some kind. He couldn't do anything straight. He even walked like a crab, as if he were cringing all the time. . . . But I also think there was a value in Dean's face. His face is so desolate and lonely and strange. And there are moments in it when you say, "Oh, God, he's handsome—what's being lost here! What goodness is being lost here!"

—Elia Kazan[1]

The exquisite pain of feeling too much—that's what the gifted youngsters of the Method, James Dean and Julie Harris, brought to acting in the 1950s. They meet in Elia Kazan's 1955 adaptation of *East of Eden*, which encompasses only the last part of John Steinbeck's epic novel, the Cain and Abel section, where Dean (in his movie debut) plays a bursting, neurotic Cain to Raymond Massey's stolid, declamatory Adam. (Kazan says that he tacitly encouraged the temperamental gap between these two actors because it underscored the tensions between the characters, but for once his approach backfired: You can't believe these men come from the same family.) Dean is Cal Trask, who feels a desperate rivalry with his brother (Richard Davalos) for their father's love. He punishes him by confronting him with the long-buried fact that their mother (Jo Van Fleet) is a whore. This is Genesis, Freudian style. Julie Harris plays Abra, who adores Cal. (Dean was twenty-four when the picture was released, Harris thirty, but they both read as much younger.)

East of Eden isn't very well crafted; it's misshapen in spots, and only semiformed in others. Kazan botches the narrative, and the movie lopes and bounds and jerks from scene to scene instead of building

186

gracefully to its conclusion (Adam Trask's acceptance of Cal). It's clear that Kazan's energies lie in the direction of Dean's and Harris's performances, and because he encourages them to reach for some unusual lyrical effects in their scenes, the film has an intense vitality. No other relationship in the picture is like Cal and Abra's; they inhabit their own secret world, and what's more, they seem to be creating it together as we watch. Seeing these two completely intuitive actors in mutual response, you still have the sense of being present at the creation of a new acting technique, the invention of a new set of rules. They play off each other with the fervor of great jazz musicians, throwing out the traditional, reverent approach to text and improvising the dialogue. Lines dart out when you least expect them and then retreat abruptly, often overlapping, in a kind of sprung rhythm. Half the time the subtext and mood so overpower the words that the conventional use of language to shape thought and feeling seems to be an outmoded form the actors have to clamber over in their search for new musical phrases. Dean—agonized, desolate—specializes in low notes while Harris, with her silvery half-laugh, plays in the high register.

Dean is the most inward of actors: His performances are always about the beautiful chaos in his own soul. Harris extends herself to the human life around her; she takes on the pain of others. What they share is a touching combination—a capacity for extreme emotional states and a frightening, Puccini-esque fragility, so you're always afraid for them, afraid the strain of their emotional baggage will sink them. Their relationship to the world is purely instinctual; they seem to move entirely on an invisible plane of vibrations, which gives them a haunted, poetic presence. When they're together, you feel you're watching two spirits in mystical communion.

James Dean

Some actors appear to be the embodiment of the ideas and style of certain writers. Lillian Gish, who can transform sentimentality into art by the suffusion of feeling, might be Charles Dickens; Greta Garbo, who presents a new identity to the camera with each close-up, Pirandello; on a pop-literary level the gleaming, ingenious, unsinkable Harold Lloyd of the 1920s is Horatio Alger. And James Dean is Sigmund Freud—or rather a postwar American reading of Freud which says each of us is a mass of neuroses that pierce our all-too-transparent skin at every angle. Dean was a wonderful actor, but he's always a little embarrassing to watch, because his control switch was permanently on "off"; his complexes were always leaking through the holes in his delicate sensitivities. He was a phenomenon of his time, as much because of his Freudian bent as because he had a Method style; as much because he dropped the reins of his own life and flickered out so fast (he was dead before his twenty-fifth birthday) as because his screen persona jibed with the frustrations of a nation full of teenagers champing at the bit.

"It is one of the larger ironies of the history of the Actors Studio," writes David Garfield, "that James Dean, the young actor whose name comes so readily to mind whenever the Studio is mentioned and whose style of acting the world has taken as a definitive creation of that institution, was very inhibited there and worked very little in class."[2] Ironic, yes; surprising, no. Dean was certainly influenced by Marlon Brando, and probably by Montgomery Clift, but unlike them, there's little craft in him; he grooves on the impulse that's supposed to be at the heart of the Method: to get at the truth by putting yourself at risk, by exposing the most private corners of your psyche. Stanislavsky would never have picked him as a model for his students, because his performances are lived in the expectation of inspiration—which, fortunately, served him well for the extent of his brief career. He never got much beyond that youthful, waiting-for-the-muse phase, though there's some indication in his last performance, in the posthumously released *Giant*, that he might have developed a craft if he'd lived. In any case, though Dean could have arrived at his style of acting (the tremulous expression of trammelled-up feelings in conflict with each other; the renegade bursts of emotional energy) even if Lee Strasberg and the Actors Studio had never existed, his presence in those classes, however erratic, tells us he felt an affinity with Strasberg and not with other acting teachers. It's significant, too, that the project he chose to work on at the Studio was Chekhov's *The Sea Gull*, in which he played the classic misunderstood youth, Konstantin Treplev.

Before Dean ever made it to Hollywood he had a series of TV roles, and played a homosexual opposite Louis Jourdan and Geraldine Page in *The Immoralist* on Broadway. (He received excellent reviews but left the cast before the end of the run.) He began performing on television as early as 1949, though some of his very early appearances, which have survived in bits and pieces, are more amusing in retrospect than they probably were at the time. The compilation–bio film *James Dean: The First American Teenager* contains a scene from one un- named drama in which he plays the Apostle John in an absurd deep voice. An undated traffic safety short with Gig Young shows him in a cowboy outfit, so withdrawn he barely seems to be on camera at all. He refused to look at Young, as if he were there merely on a whim, entertaining himself. But he makes a striking impression in three TV dramas from 1953—"Harvest" (on "Robert Montgomery Presents"), and "Keep Our Honor Bright" and "A Long Time Till Dawn" (both for "Kraft Television Theatre").

In "Harvest" he's the son of a farmer (Ed Begley) who expects him to take over the family land. Instead the young man falls in love with a city girl, a summer visitor, and though her interest in him flags as soon as the season is over, he lights out to find the world beyond the farm that she's tantalized him with. It's a stock fable (guess how long it takes this kid to make it back to the old homestead), and except for Dean, the actors give stock performances. He's the only one who tries to reproduce natural speech rhythms or—the Actors Studio trademark—to stuff the pauses between words and phrases with im- provised sounds. The undistinguished young actress who plays oppo- site him enunciates in an elocution-class manner popular in television dramas of this period, and the better-known actors (Begley, Dorothy Gish, Vaughn Taylor) play to the balcony. Dean alone seems to be aware of the proximity of the camera; he contains much of his perfor- mance in his eyes, holding back while the others are thrusting every- thing they have toward the camera and past it. And his consciousness of sensory detail is more acute than theirs. When hail falls, bringing destruction to his father's crops, only Dean's face registers the sound. What the other actors offer is an artificial response, a kind of theatrical approximation.

Dean is excessively intense. When he finds it difficult to express his frustration at his father's expectations (anticipating Cal in *East of Eden*), he's all nerves, spilling out in five directions at once. God knows it's an inexact piece of acting, but it is an affecting one: While the rest of the actors content themselves with a standardized repre- sentation of emotion, even Dean's most florid displays (when he finds no letters have arrived from his girl friend, he rests his chin lightly on the mailbox, in a demonstration of romantic ardor) are assurances, at

189

least, of some emotional life welling up inside him. And when the banal script doesn't provide a tension between opposite emotional impulses, Dean invents one to keep himself going—throughout his performance anger battles with loyalty, love with shyness, hurt with embarrassment. His best scene, maybe because its comic tone exercises an automatic control on his acting, is the one where he eats dinner with his girl friend's family for the first time. Stooping slightly and holding his head low so he seems too small for the clothes he wears, he gives the impression of being painfully unused to the tie and jacket slung on him. He improvises a few awkward gestures, like holding the chair for his host as well as his girl and attacking his food enthusiastically before anyone else has started. (Judging from the rest of the direction, I'd *guess* these moments were Dean's own improvisations.)

He portrays his first tortured young man in "Keep Our Honor Bright": Jim, a student who's caught cheating on an exam and tries to kill himself. His final scene, played from a hospital bed, prefigures his roles in *East of Eden* and *Rebel Without a Cause*—he agonizes, diving recklessly from laughter to tears—but it's also completely unrestrained and lacking in originality. His earlier scenes give us a better idea of how imaginative he could be. When he admits to the other shocked students that he's cheated, he breaks into a disarming, sweet smile; his terror of what they'll do to him makes him overly accommodating, and while they argue about his fate, he ducks his head as if terrified they'll resort to corporal punishment. Again he makes himself look very small by crouching and holding his chest in. When his classmates recommend expulsion, he bargains with one of the student leaders (Michael Higgins), warning him that his girl friend was involved, too. He leans in very close when he passes on this information, his hands almost on the boy's lapel; we see this blackmail scheme is less a power play than a fierce plea for mercy. Dean depicts this trapped weasel as a sympathetic weakling, and since once more he's the only real actor in the cast, his situation is the only one we respond to—which skews the meaning of the script.

In "A Long Time Till Dawn" Dean plays Joe, a young man fresh from six months in prison who returns home to find his wife has left him. One of the other characters offers this description of Joe: "He's a poet and he's a gangster; he's a sensitive kid. . . . He's got brains, but he has the logic of a little boy." These lines could be a thumbnail analysis of the Dean persona. Indeed, Joe is a prototype for Jim Stark, the hero of *Rebel Without a Cause*, though with a more pronounced capacity for violence—Jim attacks his father in rage, but Joe beats a harmless old man to death. Joe is one of the tragic–demented–young-man roles that enjoyed some popularity on TV during this era (Paul Newman did one in Tad Mosel's "Guilty Is the Stranger"), and it doesn't make much sense. The writer, Rod Serling, seems to want us to feel sympathy for this boy even as we're condemning him for his lack of remorse. Dean doesn't succeed in unraveling it before it falls apart completely in the impossibly extravagant climax where, cornered by cops in his bedroom, he falls backwards into childhood and hears the voice of his best friend. (This anatomy-of-a-tough-guy's-collapse scene comes to TV via *Dead End, Angels with Dirty Faces*, and *White Heat*.)

Bad as much of it is, though, Dean's performance is fascinating, partly because so much of it anticipates *Rebel Without a Cause* and partly because of the surprises Dean plants in it: the underplayed line readings in his confrontations with his long-suffering father, the breaks in the prescribed rhythm of scenes, the insistence on improvising and experimenting. He yells or cries when you least expect it, then suddenly withdraws, or tosses away a punch line after building carefully up to it. When his father tries to grab him, Joe hurls his arm into the air as if he were winding up for a pitch; abruptly, in the middle of an argument, he rushes at the door. Messy and overwrought he certainly is, and in dire need of a director's control: You wish he wouldn't throw in such obvious Actors Studio touches as chewing his lapel or fingering the top button on his wife's blouse (a tribute, probably, to Brando in *Streetcar*). But he does inhabit his environment in a way that no one else in the show does. When he enters his father's house he flops onto the sofa, slaps a cushion alongside his head, and all of a sudden this studio set feels like somebody's home. Shifting restlessly around his old bedroom, fiddling with a football, sacked out on his bed, Dean shows us Joe's need to reclaim his childhood space. The importance of childhood as a symbol of escape and freedom will resurface in *Rebel Without a Cause*, which begins with a shot of Jim Stark drunkenly holding onto a toy monkey, and contains an abbreviated idyll in which the three troubled teenage protagonists take refuge in an abandoned mansion and play "house." A decade later a new generation, rediscovering the seductive appeal of childlike behavior, would reinstate James Dean as a culture hero.

There's a great anecdote about Dean. It seems he was walking down the street one day in 1954 with his pal Arthur Kennedy, who was praising the work of Elia Kazan. Dean was skeptical: "What's Kazan ever done for me?" A year later, after *East of Eden* had been released, Dean ran into Kennedy again and finished the sentence: "Except make me a star?" *East of Eden* begins with a close-up of Cal Trask sitting on a curb, waiting for his mother (who doesn't know who he is) to pass by. His face is smashed in with pain, and we immediately understand that this picture is going to be a chronicle of Cal's emotional life. The caved-in face, the palm that holds up the permanently clouded brow, the skulking walk with hands thrust straight down in the pockets; the constricted voice, which sounds as if he had an obstruction in his windpipe, the stutter, the rambling filler added at the beginnings of lines, the mumbled drifting-off at the butt-ends of speeches; the steady, quizzical gaze, as if he were trying to pierce the fog that other people carry around in front of their eyes, the paranoid 180-degree whirl to check on activity behind his back, the abrupt explosions of violence; the penchant for pumping a line too full of emotion, the unconscious seductiveness—in short, all the Dean emblems—emerge from the character here, so these tendencies come across as Cal's and not Dean's. (The character sometimes seems like an anchronism in the California of the 1910s, but even so it's not just a random collection of James Deanisms. It's all of a piece.)

The tragedy of Cal's young life is his inability to express his love for his father and receive love from him in return. When he talks to Adam, his words come out in banal spurts. So the feelings he can't frame in his father's presence release themselves in aggressive physical acts like throwing stones at his mother's house, or shoving down a chute the ice Adam's been storing, or knocking his brother Aaron to the ground. Only at some remove from Adam can he smile in admiration at him; the first sign of happiness we see on Cal's face comes when, standing out of Adam's sight, he silently shares his father's joy as Adam experiments with calculating the practical potential of ice as a preservative. When the summer heat melts the ice and threatens to ruin Adam (who's invested in it), Cal hatches a plan to restore the lost money: He grows beans to take advantage of the wartime shortage. Kazan says that, directing Dean, he "realized there was a great value in his body. His body was more expressive, actually, in free movement, than Brando's."[3] So he gave Dean a scene where Cal lies on his stomach in the fields, gazing at the newly sprouted beans, and then breaks into a kind of rain dance. This moment is a small epiphany.

Dean's Cal pours so much emotional energy into his plan to surprise his father that we just know it can't work, and that when it fails Cal will have some sort of breakdown. The debacle comes at the birthday party he and Abra give in Adam's honor, and it gives Dean an opportunity to physicalize the depth of Cal's despair. When Adam discovers how his son earned the money, and accuses him of war profiteering, all Cal can do at first is whine and stutter and wave the money feebly at him. Then he bends over the table and shrinks, weeping, into his father's arms, letting the money flutter down his chest. But Adam responds unfeelingly, rebuking him again—so Cal slides out of the room, bumping into the table, his feet scarcely able to control his movements. This is anguish as emotional drunkenness. The scene lends dramatic credibility to another moment, when Cal confronts Adam with the lies he's told him about his mother, and Adam says he lied in order to spare Cal the pain of knowing what his mother was. "Pain?" Cal replies, half astonished, half mocking. The subtext of the line is that his father is a goddamn fool—Cal's never felt anything in his life *but* pain.

Rebel Without a Cause, released later the same year, is the James Dean myth movie. It has conscientiously overstated direction (by Nicholas Ray) and dark, heavy, neurotic cinematography (by Ernest Haller). It's no work of art; Stewart Stern's screenplay hammers its messages home like twelve-inch nails. (It's a perfectly Hollywood irony that in a movie called *Rebel Without a Cause* the cause of the hero's rebellion is explained with perfect clarity.) But, like *The Wild One*, it was a key film for the teen audiences of the mid–1950s, articulating their complaint that adults did not understand them, indulging their romantic longing to be at the center of a tragedy (one of the three protagonists, Plato, is killed by cops in the final reel), and affirming the belief—the credo of hundreds of youth-market pictures since—that all adolescents are decent human beings at heart whose lives have been wrecked by self-centered, unstable grown-ups. That isn't to say that *Rebel* is a cynical piece of commercial filmmaking; it's melodramatic as hell, but (in the parlance of its teen characters) it's "sincere." And it provides an effective vehicle for Dean to make powerful contact with his audience. Brando's performance in *The Wild One* had focused the private struggles of American adolescents in 1954, and James Dean's portrayal of

193

Jim Stark in *Rebel*—drenched, florid, yet imaginatively phrased and intensely concentrated—had the same effect in 1955. (Not so coincidentally, '54 and '55 were also the birth-of-rock-'n'-roll years.)

The three main characters in *Rebel* come from Freudian monster families. Jim Stark's weakling father (Jim Backus) is a slave to the wishes of his wife (Ann Doran): Whenever Jim gets in trouble, she grows anxious about what the neighbors will think, and Mr. Stark dutifully finds a new job and moves them to another town. Judy (Natalie Wood) adores her father (William Hopper, in his pre–"Perry Mason" days), but he views her demonstrations of affection as childish habits she should have outgrown by now; in one scene he responds to her display of warmth by slapping her across the face. Plato (Sal Mineo) has been abandoned by a wealthy mother to the care of a black housekeeper (Marietta Canty), the only sympathetic adult in the film besides Ray (Edward Platt), the policeman who calms Jim down when he's brought in on a "D & D." Significantly, though, both the housekeeper and the policeman are ineffectual, and always arrive too late upon the scene. Naturally, the absence of responsible adults forces the teenagers to make their own decisions.

In the role of Jim Stark, Dean gets to show off his Method actor's equipment—that is, his gift for conveying conflicting emotions at the same time. We see Jim's love for his father, and his rage at the man's ineptitude; his determination to please his parents by keeping out of trouble, and his sensitivity to the taunts of other teenagers (which always drags him right into it); the manly urge to take charge when his friends are in trouble (his kindly treatment of Plato, whose crypto-homosexual attachment to Jim takes the form of filial trust), and the childish desire to escape from the adult-dominated world. He's fully committed to all these emotions.

Judy's complaint about her other friends is "Nobody acts sincere"; when Plato describes Jim to her, he tells her, "He doesn't say much, but when he does, he means it—you know he's sincere." Dean's acting is the apotheosis of adolescent "sincerity": it's absolutely unrestrained. His whole body responds to the weight of each episode in Jim's story. In the police station he sits crumpled in a chair, his arms thrown over the sides and his head tipped, imitating the sound of a siren outside as if his body were a medium for the activity out on the street. In Ray's office he vents his anger at his chronically bickering parents by smashing his knuckles against a desk. When Buzz (Corey Allen), Judy's tough boy friend, challenges him to a knife fight, his terror of being labeled a "chicken" energizes his taut, heavy movements. Buzz is more agile, but Jim is propelled by a more potent emotional force (Corey Allen moves like an athlete, but Dean moves like an actor). He sees his father dressed in an apron, preparing his mother's breakfast, and his rage at Stark's willingness to be emasculated can find no words, so he grabs the dish towel his father is holding and hurls it to the ground, all in a single stroke. In an older-brother gesture he lets Plato wear his leather jacket. Reaching down to zip it up on the younger boy's diminutive frame he has a dangling, awkward grace that seems to be the form of his youthful restlessness—he looks about to fall over, or at least fumble with the zipper, but somehow he maintains a precarious balance. Even the simple act of drinking milk focuses so much of his energy that it becomes emblematic: He swigs it from the bottle as if he needed to slake a thirst too deep to be merely physical. (In his lecture on "poetic" theater in *Method—or Madness?* Robert Lewis mentions a moment in William Saroyan's *My Heart's in the Highlands* when a character drinks a glass of water after walking five thousand miles. For a moment in *Rebel*, Dean recalls that parched wanderer.)

Dean expresses Jim's fury at his parents mostly in physical actions and in the powerful vocal releases that most people think of when they remember the picture: his scream at his parents, "You're tearing me apart!," in the cop-station scene; and (perhaps the most famous moment) when he exhorts his father, "Stand up for me!" and then spins around, hoists his father up by the collar, and starts to choke him. Other times he expresses it in the form of a put-on. (No wonder Dean was even more beloved by the sixties generation—he was doing put-ons long before *Bonnie and Clyde* or Jack Nicholson.) When his father enters the station in dress clothes to bail him out, Jim sends him up, touching his shirt lightly as if he meant to dust it off. The gesture looks tender and admiring at first, but there's a chilling undertone of menace in the way he asks Stark if he had a "ball" at the club that evening. Later, when he and his new friends are hiding out in an abandoned house, playing at being a family, Jim breaks into a genuinely funny parody of a suburban husband, using it to discharge his fury at his parents' lifestyle. He speaks haltingly, as if he were stoned, in a deep squeak that distorts Jim Backus's voice in a weirdly familiar way: It's the stylized voice Backus adopted for Mr. Magoo.

According to George Stevens, who directed him in *Giant*, Dean "had the ability to take a scene—sometimes he broke it down into so many bits and pieces that I couldn't see the scene for the trees, so to speak. . . . [He] was always pulling and hauling, and he had developed this cultivated, designed irresponsibility."[4] It works: Dean's is the only performance in this immense, rambling, preposterous (but entertaining) epic that hangs together from beginning to end. The film spans two generations of a wealthy Texas family, it's set almost entirely on their spread, Reata, and it clocks in at 198 minutes. Dean plays Jett Rink, a shiftless hired hand fired by Bick Benedict (Rock Hudson) who ends up an oil millionaire, and it's easily the most controlled piece of acting he ever did.

Rink begins with an amused, detached response to Benedict, who dislikes him; he saves his anger for much later in the film, after he's struck it rich and has something to hold over Bick's head. When we first see him, leaning over a jalopy, a ten-gallon hat shades his eyes and a cigarette hangs from his mouth. When he is forced to take to his feet he ambles, shifting uneasily from side to side as if this kind of physical exertion were something new to him. Dean's trademark muttering and verbal meandering are appropriate for Jett, and he uses them for comic effect when he tells Bick's bride Leslie (Elizabeth Taylor) how beautiful she is, so uncomfortable handing out compliments that he keeps sputtering and backtracking and starting over. The way he slips his hand forward to shake hers, and slides into his car, slung low in the driver's seat, when Bick dismisses him, are amusingly sheepish. When Bick's sister Luz (Mercedes McCambridge) dies and leaves Jett a small parcel of land in her will, Bick and his lawyers try to buy him out, but Jett sits deep in an expensive chair in Bick's study, playing absently with a lasso. He grins at Bick and quietly refuses all offers; he'll "gamble along" with the land, he says with a little *frisson* of irony, and maybe one day he'll name it "Little Reata." Then he leaves Bick with a small parting gesture: a wave of his hand signifying "No sale." Later, when he's hit oil, he gives Bick that wave again; but this time he's riding past the Benedicts in a limousine, at the grand opening of the Jett Rink Airport, and his wave says he's entered the aristocracy.

The appealing bad boy of the film, Jett is another James Dean rebel figure, of course, but unlike Cal Trask and Jim Stark, he meets up with an extraordinary stroke of luck that brings him material success and changes his character. This twist harkens back to the prototypical rebel figure, Joe Bonaparte. In *Golden Boy* Joe and his gangster–manager, Eddie Fuseli, have the following exchange:

> **EDDIE:** A year ago Bonaparte was a rookie with a two-pants suit. Now he wears the best, eats the best, sleeps the best. He walks down the street respected—the golden boy! They howl their heads off when Bonaparte steps in the ring . . . and I done it for him!
>
> **JOE:** There are other things . . .
>
> **EDDIE:** There's no other things! . . . You're in this up to your neck. [Act III, Scene 1]

Odets argues that success goes against the rebel grain, and though Jett Rink lacks the sensitivity and youthful buoyancy of a Joe Bonaparte, he does have something to lose once he becomes rich: his unassuming charm. He begins to sport a gigolo's moustache and Damon Runyon clothes; he drives fancy cars (Joe Bonaparte's passion), and he springs the sexual power that we saw coiled up in his early scenes, making passes first at Leslie and then at her naive teenage daughter (Carroll Baker). The movie goes too far in turning him into a villain in the second half, but Dean makes the transformation psychologically believable by showing us all along how he's storing up his justified resentment against Bick Benedict for treating him so meanly. Technically, this is his best acting. His detractors say that, if he'd lived, he'd have been lost after he outgrew his sensitive–neurasthenic–youth phase. But they're ignoring the contrary evidence of his swan-song performance.

Julie Harris

By the time Julie Harris played Abra in *East of Eden* she was a three-year veteran of movies, and before that she'd appeared on the New York stage, in Carson McCullers's *The Member of the Wedding*, under Harold Clurman's direction.

> I was twenty-four, at that time, and Frankie Addams is supposed to be twelve and three quarters years old, so I was

twice her age. He never said anything about acting childish or acting like a child. He said, "Your age doesn't matter. You could be fifty-two and still play that part. If you put yourself in the circumstances and properly feel her pain people are bound to think you're the right age."[5]

When adult actors—even very good ones—are cast as children, they have a tendency to play down to their roles, unconsciously. Julie Harris's performance, preserved in Fred Zinnemann's 1952 film version (her movie debut), contains not a hint of condescension. McCullers poises Frankie midway between childish longing and adult perception, and Harris acts with one foot in each camp, claiming her prerogatives in one and gingerly testing out the waters in the other.

She makes her first appearance in knee-length short pants that emphasize Frankie's ungainly height (her *bête noire*—she's afraid she'll grow into a circus freak). She wears her hair in an eccentric tomboy cut that accentuates her clear, dark brown eyes. Harris presents such an amazing contrast to the conventionally pretty actress who plays Janice, her brother's fiancée, that they might belong to different species; but the one who captures our attention immediately is Frankie. Zinnemann makes Harris's face, where the psychological battles of the drama are played out, the focus of much of the film, keeping her in close-up as much as possible. (His secondary focus is the face of Ethel Waters, the incomparable singer–actress who plays Berenice Sadie Brown.) As Janice consoles Frankie, calming her fears about her height, we see Frankie's desperate intimacy with her new sister-in-law and the way her admiration melts into a schoolgirl crush; she wears her feelings for Janice on her face like a telltale stain. A few moments later a snobbish girl taking a shortcut across the Addams yard tells Frankie she hasn't been elected to the neighborhood club, and that face becomes a new canvas, with shock, fury, grief painted boldly across it.

For McCullers, adolescence is a constant workout, a testing of new feelings, and the journey to the end of each day is exhausting because there's so much emotional ground to be covered. That's what Harris shows us, in scene after scene. Frankie hasn't yet worked out how to cushion the passage from one feeling to another. Each one still has the power of a thunderbolt, so her responses are always extreme, and the transitions between them uncontrolled and exaggerated— more likes leaps and plunges than shifts. Pulling at her spare, scraggly hair, she moans that she wants to wash it and try to "stretch" it; then she turns gentle and vulnerable, pleading that all she wants is to look pretty for the wedding; and a moment later she's on her high horse, demanding that Berenice clean and iron all her best clothes because she's planning to leave town after the ceremony.

Often these responses have a self-reflexive quality. Caught up in the urgency of the moment, Frankie enjoys the feeling of giving herself over to it, and that free abandon isn't just an actress's flourish: It comments on the character's emotional state. These theatrical flights of fancy are therapeutic for Frankie, too. When she cries, her tears shake her frame; the force of her weeping operates as a purge, washing away her anger and the pain embedded in it. "They were the two prettiest people I ever saw," she says of Janice and Jarvis. "Yet it was like I couldn't see all of them I wanted to see. My brains couldn't gather together quick enough to take it all in"—and she cradles her fingers and tries to press the image into her brain. The dissonant sound of the piano tuner next door drives her crazy; she throws her head back and swipes violently at her brow—Frankie Addams as Camille. Sitting at the kitchen table (her usual haunt), she buries her head in her arms, mourning her distance from her brother and his fiancée ("They came and went away, and left me with this feeling"). But then she segues into anger, hurling a knife at the door. When it sticks in the wood, she turns into a circus showgirl, spitting proudly on her hands. She's continually reaching dead ends—she insists that Berenice and her little cousin John Henry don't understand a thing she tells them—but she never remains cornered for long. She always follows a moment of hopeless despair with a burst of incredible energy, like the way she races around the room, kicking over chairs, when she acts out her preposterous fantasy about going off with Janice and Jarvis and becoming "members of the whole world." (When her energy shuts down, she ends up collapsed in Berenice's arms.) She lives in constant anguish, and she can't cope with it quietly; it makes her restless. The transformation of emotional into physical energy in Harris's performance makes it obvious that, for Frankie, the two are inseparable: She is trapped by her rapidly changing body, and at the same time feelings she never grappled with before assault her, overwhelm her.

What makes Frankie a unique case, of course, is her poetic sensibility; and the special distinction of Harris's performance is the tremulous warmth of her line readings, her feverish attention to the color of a phrase, her instinctive understanding that language is Frankie's emotional medium. We can actually see the emotions rising up inside Frankie and metamorphosing into the poetry that spills out of her mouth like flood water from a weakened dam. The *physical* poetry in her acting—the way she whips around the kitchen, tilting at invisible windmills, or the emblematic moment when, refused passage in the honeymoon car after the wedding, she holds herself rigid on the curb, her head tipped over, her upper body bent like a broken piece of metal—anticipates and parallels the verbal poetry.

This isn't a somber performance, though. We recognize the accuracy of Harris's portrayal of adolescence and we can't help laughing, like Mrs. Soames in *Our Town*, remembering how awful and wonderful life was. Sometimes the humor comes from the juxtaposition of Frankie's reactions, extreme and melodramatic, with the banality of the circumstances: In one scene she uses a kitchen knife to remove a splinter from her foot—a dramatic object fitted preposterously to a trivial task. Often the humor comes from the way Harris keeps us conscious of the interplay between the child and the adult in Frankie. She examines her small suitcase, discussing the difficulty of fitting everything into it as though she were a society matron packing for a cruise, while at the same time she slips a fist into a baseball glove.

One of Harris's best (and least seen) movie performances is entirely in a comic vein. In 1955 (the year of *East of Eden*) she played Sally Bowles, a role she'd created on Broadway, in the British picture *I Am a Camera*, the earliest screen version of Christopher Isherwood's *Berlin Stories*. Her Sally is mock-feline and sexy, in a flirtatious schoolgirl way. Much is made of Sally's devotion to promiscuity, but she always seems so conscious of the absurdity of her behavior that we can't take it seriously—it's so obvious she's getting high off her own excessiveness, her own ridiculousness. Harris's vision of Sally couldn't be farther away from the one that's stamped on most people's memories, Liza Minnelli's in *Cabaret*, the musical version of this material (which came seventeen years later). Harris is more controlled, less flamboyant, and there's no edge of desperation in her. (That's not a value judgment; I think Minnelli is marvelous.)

Harris hasn't had a role since that has allowed her so much self-amusement and has so blissfully ignored her neurotic range. She slurps eagerly when she speaks, like a cat lapping up milk, or else she tears into her lines, famished, tossing away moderation. In one particularly satisfying scene she persuades uptight, frugal Chris (Laurence Harvey) to buy her a drink in an expensive restaurant, then gorges on caviar and champagne that neither of them can afford. "Oh, look, Chris!" she cries as the cigarette girl approaches their table. "Little yellow cigarettes with *tubes!*" In this blithe, enjoyable film, Harris makes hedonism a great comic subject.

Between 1955 and 1962 Julie Harris didn't make any movies in this country (she appeared in *The Truth About Women* in England and *Sally's Irish Rogue* in Ireland, both in 1958), but she managed to maintain her reputation as the most gifted young actress in America almost entirely on the basis of her work on TV. The so-called "golden age of television drama" has long been assumed to be the heyday of a gifted crop of playwrights, but in fact it was a golden age of actors. The teleplays that Rod Serling, Paddy Chayefsky, Reginald Rose, Tad Mosel, Horton Foote, James Costigan, and others supplied were seldom more than economically constructed melodramas, long on theme and short on characterization, with conflicts presented unambiguously, in the honored tradition of the "problem" plays of the thirties. But what made even some of the most obvious and unsophisticated TV drama memorable was the crackling immediacy of the performances, a first-night aura that often resulted from the tension of performing live or, if not, from the heat of having to assemble a role fast and furiously. You wouldn't say that the work of Rod Steiger in "Marty" or Mickey Rooney in "The Comedian" or Sterling Hayden in "Old Man" was polished, but it's exciting to watch; reviewing kinescopes of that era, it's still possible to catch the spirit of those hectic, summer-stock days. And you can see Method actors like Steiger, Harris, Eva Marie Saint, Paul Newman, James Dean, Kim Hunter, Maureen Stapleton, Geraldine Page, and Kim Stanley working at full steam under the hand of a new generation of directors (Arthur Penn, John Frankenheimer, Sidney Lumet, Franklin Schaffner). The best of these directors carried with them their sensitivity to actors, as well as their love of the visceral pleasures of working in close, when they left TV for the movies in the second half of the decade.

Mostly ignored by Hollywood (*The Member of the Wedding* flopped at the box office), Harris turned to television for the opportunity to play challenging new roles. She continued to do stage work, too: Through the 1950s and early 1960s she appeared on Broadway almost every season, and she repeated a couple of her stage roles (*The Lark* and *Little Moon of Alban*) on George Schaefer's "Hallmark Hall of Fame," the TV anthology series she's most closely associated with. She also appeared on "The U. S. Steel Hour," "DuPont Show of the Month," and others.

One of her earliest television appearances was in "A Wind from the South" in 1955. A variation on *The Sea Gull*, but written by James Costigan in a style obviously borrowed from John Millington Synge, it tells the story of the romance between Siobhan, a fanciful young woman who runs an Irish country inn, and an unhappily married American (Donald Woods) on vacation. Costigan's Gaelic platitudes block Harris in a few scenes, where she seems blurry and mushmouthed, but the performance also contains moments of high romantic flight—her specialty. She makes her first appearance running, out of breath, bringing the bloom of the Irish countryside with her. The most sensual of actresses, she physicalizes the character's awakened romantic feelings. Her best scenes come in the third act, when Siobhan has flung herself heedlessly into her passion for Robert. As Harris plays her, Siobhan really seems like a dry run for Chekhov's Nina (a role she never got to try).

She's better known for playing another Costigan heroine, Brigid Mary, in "Little Moon of Alban" (originally televised in 1958). If "A Wind from the South" is Costigan imitating Synge, then "Little Moon," set during the Irish "troubles," is plainly derived from Sean O'Casey. Brigid Mary's fiancé (George Peppard, in a surprisingly effective early performance) is killed by English soldiers; in a fury she rejects God. But she recovers her faith with the help of the Sisters of Charity, and in gratitude joins their order. Upon receiving her vows she finds herself assigned to an English hospital, where her rage at the enemies she's obliged to care for dissipates when she falls in love with a badly wounded soldier (Christopher Plummer) whose bitterness eclipses hers. It's a clumsily structured, unsatisfying play: The most interesting dramatic material is in the first act, and then there's a slow decline once Brigid Mary joins the Sisters. And Harris and Plummer (who acts with a cold efficiency) are stylistically mismatched. Still, she gives one of her most feverish, driven performances—perhaps her most compelling one after *The Member of the Wedding*.

The scene where Peppard dies in her arms is a case of a great actress not merely transcending her material but transforming it. Up till now we've seen this impassioned young woman in a summer mood, chiding her lover girlishly for his lack of attention to her; now her former words of complaint sting her, and she whips herself for them. "I wish I'd the pain on my tongue for every cruel or wicked thing I've ever said to you," she tells him, her voice scalded, and she drives her clenched fished into her chest over and over, reciting the Catholic penance. When her fiancé dies, she blocks the priest's path to his body and renounces "your deaf God, your little God of death and grief"; then she crushes out the light of the altar candles with her hands. It's a shocking gesture, comparable to the amazing scene in *The Lonely Passion of Judith Hearne* where Maggie Smith breaks into the altar in her church, searching for the God who has eluded her all her life. Suddenly you feel you *are* watching Sean O'Casey. (Harris played Brigid Mary once more, in a remounted version in 1964, with Dirk Bogarde replacing Christopher Plummer. But her performance was tired by then—the high emotional moments in the first act had lost some of their color, her pace was more sluggish, and overall there was less control in the acting.)

In a stiff, musty, Classics Illustrated version of *A Doll's House* on "Hallmark Hall of Fame" in 1959, surrounded by a comically ill-matched collection of actors (Christopher Plummer as Torvald, Jason Robards as Dr. Rank, Eileen Heckart as Christina, Hume Cronyn as Krogstad), Harris gave a fascinating interpretation of Ibsen's Nora. She's the most nakedly emotional of the contemporary Noras: She hurls herself with furious speed from one feeling to the next, displaying a childish joy at seeing Christina again after so many years, and shrieking at Torvald when he interrupts her frantic confidence to Christina about the blackmail note she's received from Krogstad. Her out-of-control emotionalism makes Nora more sympathetic than she often is (certainly more than in the resolute, protofeminist readings of the play that have proliferated in the last twenty-five years). It also clarifies a great deal in the character—those appalling moments of seductiveness (Harris sits in Plummer's lap when she begs him for extra Christmas money), and even her thoughtlessness. When she dismisses Christina's problems in the first act, for example, we see she's preoccupied with herself because she can't help it: She's always vulnerable to the wave of her own passions.

In her article "The Will and Testament of Ibsen" (the finest analysis of the playwright I know) Mary McCarthy says:

> Ibsen is not very good at making big events happen; he is
> better at the small shocking event, the psychopathology of
> everyday life: Hedda and her husband's aunt's hat, Nora,
> when she nonchalantly pushes off the sewing on her poor
> widowed friend, Christine, Hjalmar, when he talks himself
> into letting Hedwig with her half-blind eyes do his retouch-
> ing for him . . . These are the things one knows oneself to be
> capable of.[6]

Julie Harris's performance is strong in these "small shocking events"
and weak in the larger ones. She's charmingly loose-limbed and flirtatious as she dances around the parlor, humming and eating forbidden
macaroons, sincerely distressed by Rank's forwardness when he confesses his love for her (this is a remarkable representation of that
outmoded state, outraged gentility). But in the tarantella scene she
goes over the top—though with Schaefer's obtrusive camera sitting on
her face, distorting her expression, it's hard to know how much of this
is her fault. And she plays the entire "doll's house" scene—Ibsen's
anti-dénouement—on one slightly hysterical note, with tears in her
voice, undermining whatever dramatic surprise this once-familiar sequence might have left.

In an unusually resonant 1960 dramatization of Edith Wharton's
Ethan Frome, Julie Harris plays Mattie, the poor relation taken in by
the Fromes, a hypochrondriac shrew (Clarice Blackburn) and her unhappy husband (Sterling Hayden), as a servant. Mattie is less expansive and imaginative in Wharton's novel than she is in Harris's
interpretation, and a lot less likable. As Harris plays her, we can see
how Mattie's desperate anxiety to please, and to believe the best of her
willful cousin, Zeena, motivates her to fling herself into her work with
far more zeal than skill, and glom onto the smallest kindness as a proof
of Zeena's good will (in this case, a red ribbon Zeena gives her to wear
at a church sociable). She's at sea when her cousin insults her; in her
naiveté, she doesn't understand the impulse to injure another human
being. And in his scenes with Harris, Hayden, whose intensity is very
different from hers, responds feelingly to her penchant for empathy
and compassion, as well as to the breathless romanticism and the finely
tuned ear for the poetry in dialogue—Harris trademarks from this era.

Harris's performance is about emotional generosity, and finally
about how it gets twisted by circumstances: A failed love affair with

Zeena's husband Ethan. What makes the transition in Mattie's character work is the potential for hysteria that keeps the whole performance on the edge. We see it in the scene where Mattie, on the brink of getting her first illicit kiss from Ethan, shatters Zeena's prized pickle dish and screams as if she'd burned her fingers. In the chilling coda, when we see Mattie for the last time, disfigured by the sledding accident that was intended to be her *Liebestod* with Ethan and emotionally shrunken by years of bitterness, the scratchy high pitch of her voice and the paranoid look frozen in her eyes are more horrifying than her gargoyle face. This is all that's left of Mattie. Creepily, she has metamorphosed into Zeena Frome.

These four plays are definitely the highlights among Harris's TV appearances—at least, the ones I've been able to look at. She's generally competent in the others (except when she plays Joan of Arc in Anouilh's *The Lark* as an overage tomboy, a kind of holy Peter Pan); and I've seen a scene from a 1963 production of *Pygmalion* in which she uses the Julie Harris grimace (the twisted mouth, the expression of distrustful befuddlement) for comic purposes, creating a hilarious symphony out of Eliza Dolittle's Cockney discharges. Probably she shouldn't have played so many great-lady roles for George Schaefer (Queen Victoria in *Victoria Regina, Anastasia*); these days, she doesn't do much else, and there's something dispiriting about seeing an actress of Julie Harris's invention and emotional range impersonating an institution like the Emily Dickinson of the one-woman show *The Belle of Amherst*.

Harris has made a number of movies since 1962, but none of them suggests the poetic fervor of her early work. For years the only roles she got were the desiccated–neurotic kind (though she could be pretty effective in them). The best of the lot are the elegantly made supernatural thriller *The Haunting*, where she and Claire Bloom have some lively scenes together, and *Reflections in a Golden Eye*, where she plays Brian Keith's wife, a psychological invalid. By this time her pain-crossed eyes have taken on a crotchety air, and her breathy voice has become scorched. In her final scene in *Reflections* she dines with Keith at the psychiatric institution he's put her in, and her grand, gentlewomanly manner of holding her cigarette, meant to distinguish her from the other patients, who sit at neighboring tables, is funny and charming and terribly sad. It's a terrific, character-defining moment. A few scenes later, when we hear that this woman is dead, we don't even have to ask. We know she died of shame.

8

THE NEUROSIS KIDS
♦ ♦ ♦

Clearly it's no accident that the Method won an unprecedented popularity around the time Americans were giving more credence to Freud than ever before. The very nature of the Stanislavskian approach to acting, with its emphasis on psychological realism and its validation of the most private corners of the soul as resources for meaningful theatrical expression, links it up with Freudian therapy; in a certain way, the two processes are analogous. So you might have expected to find, among the actors who worked at Actors Studio in the 1950s and 1960s, a conspicuous group that specialized in portraying neurotics. This was the most actorish, "Methody" wing of the Studio—the tic-tockers. It was largely these actors who tended to prompt attacks on the Method: Not everyone wanted to watch performers who seemed to wave their compulsions and insecurities like banners, even though some of them were (and are) freakishly talented. The three I'd place at the forefront of this group are all actresses: Geraldine Page, Kim Stanley, and Sandy Dennis.

Geraldine Page

Sinewy, combative, fiercely eccentric, Geraldine Page was for years (until her death in 1987) the *grande dame* of the Method. She first attracted notice in 1953, the year she starred in the famous off-Broadway production of *Summer and Smoke* and made her movie debut in *Hondo*, with John Wayne, winning an Oscar nomination for Best Supporting Actress. The earliest of her performances I've seen is in a 1958 kinescope of Faulkner's *Old Man*, an episode on "Playhouse 90" where she plays a pregnant woman rescued from a Mississippi flood by a convict (Sterling Hayden). She's way over the top in this role—all jagged edges and acting flourishes. Her face is frozen in a distortion of a smile, underscoring the puffiest apple cheeks in show business. She moves her mouth a little before she speaks, and twists up her face; she blinks a lot; her right arm flies about as if it were disconnected from the rest of her body; her voice is high and whiny, and trails off unexpectedly; she slathers a huge southern accent over her dialogue like ketchup. She appears to be on the verge of nervous collapse, and though you're meant to be sympathetic to her plight, you want to tell Hayden to shoot the poor, crazy bitch and put her out of her misery. Yet somehow, from the weird first look she throws him—it's somewhere between loony pride and indignation—she's mesmerizing. Watching this display nearly thirty years after John Frankenheimer directed it, I kept thinking, "What the hell did a TV audience in 1958 make out of *that*?"

Whatever you may think of Page, it's not appropriate to speak of her acting in terms of range. She's defined by a series of immediately recognizable trademarks: the comic obstinacy; the little-girl snits; the parody of aristocracy; the lacerating, whiplash outbursts. Vocally: the thin, braying, mimicky voice; the snarl; the breathless delivery; the mocking way she stretches one-syllable words into two ("sow-urr" for "sour" in *The Pope of Greenwich Village*) or breaks up two-syllable words for sarcastic emphasis ("Is she pret-ty?" In *You're a Big Boy Now*); the moments of exaggerated quiet. Physically: the grimace, the curdled smile, the overbroad grin, the creased chin, the sagging jaw, the wrinkled nose (which seems to ask, "What am I supposed to do now?"), the cheeks like stuffed pockets; the tendency to crinkle up her face and pull down one corner of her mouth; the half-walk, half-run that sinks her weight awkwardly onto her knees as she moves. The eyes: bleary and crossed to show bewilderment or disdain; sometimes rolled up toward the ceiling as if someone had hit her over the head with a mallet (like a clown in a slapstick skit); then suddenly bright, popping half out of their sockets like Joan Crawford's used to, or fake-coy, in a parody of seduction. And her appearance! After years of seeing her impaled on idiotically severe hairstyles (like the braided egg bread creation she sports in *Interiors* to show how uptight the character is) or made shapeless by ill-fitting wigs, melting under cobra-woman make-up, her frumpy dresses dripping off her (in the stage play *A Lie of the Mind*), I started to assume these atrocities were in her contract—that she was luxuriating in the physical peculiarities of women who've changed into monsters or simply let themselves go. (It's a shock to return to *Summer and Smoke*, made in 1961, and remember how lovely she could be, or to see her in decent clothes for once, in the bit role of Baryshnikov's agent in *White Nights*.)

Page certainly had a proclivity for flamboyant masochism, and she leaned toward roles that brought it out, like the neurasthenic Tennessee Williams heroines she was associated with all her professional life—she created several on stage, recreated two (*Summer and Smoke* and *Sweet Bird of Youth*) in early–1960s movie versions, and played several others in revival (including, inevitably, Amanda in *The Glass Menagerie*). But she wasn't the great Williams interpreter that, say, Blythe Danner is today. Perhaps in the theater she did something magical that didn't translate onto the screen: With a dullard like Peter Glenville directly *Summer and Smoke* for the movies, and the irritatingly overheated Richard Brooks in charge of *Sweet Bird of Youth*, we can't dismiss that possibility. After all, her performance as the spinster Alma Winemiller in *Summer and Smoke* seems tamed down, even dried up, on film.

When Danner played this role in Williams's rewritten version, *The Eccentricities of a Nightingale*, she revealed the passion trembling just underneath the repression. But there's no passion in what Page does—nothing but musty theatricality. Possibly, after nearly a decade of playing the part, she'd worked out all the life in it; it's a highly conscious performance, with carefully rounded line readings and elegantly shaped eruptions of hysteria. Her responses to the big moments—like the scene where John Buchanan (Laurence Harvey), the man she's loved all her life, accuses her of being responsible for his father's death—are strangely passive, and even a little mistimed; and, oddly enough, she doesn't appear to get the jokes. After she's mooned languidly over John for months, her father demands to know what he's supposed to tell people is wrong with her. "Tell them I've changed," she snaps back, "and you're waiting to see in what way." It's one of those glorious moments in Williams when a character in the advanced stages of breakdown suddenly shows enough wit to comment on her own situation—but Page doesn't play it that way.

It isn't much fun to watch her outsize eccentricities in movies like

Sweet Bird of Youth and *You're a Big Boy Now;* as the hard-shelled semi-invalid grieving over her dead-cop son in *The Pope of Greenwich Village;* in the picture for which, predictably, she won her Academy Award, *The Trip to Bountiful;* or even on stage in Sam Shepard's *A Lie of the Mind.* These performances are mostly a series of jags, and they're pretty shameless. She does come up with a couple of amusing readings in *Sweet Bird:* When Alexandra Del Lago, the post–Norma Desmond fading star she's playing, begs her young lover (played by Paul Newman) for a hit of oxygen, she adds, "Will you hurry? I'm dying"—and the last word sounds as if she'd hurled it down a canyon. And she at least makes an unnerving entrance in *Interiors:* She seems to be walking a tightrope, and you're afraid the slightest disturbance, even a noise from the street, will cause her to topple.

In the 1966 film of the notorious Actors Studio production of *The Three Sisters* (directed on stage by Lee Strasberg), one of the great theatrical follies of our time, Page is a cut or two above disgraceful—unlike almost everyone else in the cast (Kim Stanley as Masha, Sandy Dennis as Irina, Kevin McCarthy as Vershinin, Gerald Hiken as Andrei, James Olson as Tuzenbach, and Robert Loggia as Solyony). At least she's cast right (she plays Olga). She shares their habit of not talking to anyone else: All the performers in this picture are so concerned with their own idiosyncrasies, so busy "acting," they barely notice there's anyone else in the room. (Self-important, self-indulgent, this *Three Sisters* is a nightmare to sit through; you can see why it became the focus for so much anti-Studio babble.) And she does some ridiculously dramatic bits, such as peering at Kim Stanley from behind a screen like a madwoman when Masha tells her she's in love with Vershinin, and a goggle-eyed reading of the last speech in the play (she gives it a real nineteenth-century hysterical tang). She's relatively calm in the role, though—not as bad as you might fear.

What's ironic about Page is that, though she was drawn to crazies, she had an earthbound humor and sanity that could provide a safe harbor, and sometimes in surprising places—like the Broadway production of the ghastly *Agnes of God,* where her rousing portrayal of the Mother Superior brought down the house. She's a more riotous Prioress in the too-little-seen Muriel Spark comedy *Nasty Habits* (Watergate set in a convent, with Page as Haldeman). Basically she's camping up her own mannerisms (as she does in the best parts of *Sweet Bird of Youth*), and it is a tremendous relief—like watching Kathleen

Turner in *The Man with Two Brains*, sending up all that *femme fatale* nonsense she took seriously in *Body Heat*. And in her last performance, as the unreasonably hearty psychic Madame Arcati in a New York revival of Noel Coward's *Blithe Spirit*, Page was richly enjoyable, playing games with her English accent all evening. (She died during the run, in June 1987).

Perhaps it's that undercurrent of humor that makes even the worst of Page watchable—that and her courage in taking her roles all the way, far past the borders of pristine good taste. She's a little like a relative who insists on showing up at family parties and scandalizing everyone by wearing an antique feather boa or tossing back too many glasses of punch. She can be terribly embarrassing, but you have to admire her propensity for kicking up a fuss—and for never being anything less than herself.

Kim Stanley

"Normal" emotional states—relative calm, an uncomplicated connection to others, a logically sequenced drinking-in of the stimuli of people and situations—are completely out of Kim Stanley's range. She's the embodiment of the actress as neurotic. When you watch the performances she gave in the flush of her career, the early 1950s through the mid–1960s, you can't separate out the instability of the characters she's playing from her personal traumas; and for many people, apparently (including Lee Strasberg, who was also drawn to Marilyn Monroe's extravagant fragility), there was a perilous excitement in the spectacle of an actress who seemed constantly about to break down. An unmatchable honesty, too: After all, this wasn't acting, it was the real stuff—tender nerves fraying to the jangling percussiveness of Paddy Chayefsky's prose (*The Goddess*, inspired by Monroe's career), or the more musical tones of Chekhov (*The Three Sisters*). Stanley played Masha, in New York and London and in the 1966 film of the Strasberg production, as a woman tottering on the brink of collapse who receives temporary respite from her affair with Vershinin, then falls off the precipice when he leaves. Shortly afterwards, the actress had a real nervous breakdown and retired from acting for almost two decades.

The problem is, when you see *The Goddess* or the *Three Sisters* movie or the 1964 *Séance on a Wet Afternoon*, you don't believe in the hysteria and the fragmented emotions, even if they *are* genuine. Even Method teachers who favor emotion memory generally advise actors to allow a distance of five or ten years from the event they're using as a spur to their feelings; otherwise it's difficult to exercise the kind of control that clarifies a piece of acting and makes it not merely an explosion of emotions but a coherent, comprehensible one. Stanley's acting is all "private moment" exercises, so close to the surface that you see nothing else. In these early roles she's like a pouty, attention-getting teenager who keeps telling you she's going to kill herself. You can't tell if she means it because the threat, serious or not, is buried in a garbage heap of scenes and acted-out impulses and feints and passes that just make you tired. After a while the whole performance begins to seem like a fake.

It's possible that, on stage, the spectacle of Stanley's unraveling psyche was everything her fans have said it was—or that she was sufficiently in command of what she did to shape her performances. There *is* some skill in her portrayal of Myra Savage, the medium in *Séance*, a quiet tyrant whose willfulness and delusions dominate her soft-spoken, sensitive husband (Richard Attenborough). (He carries through her crazy plan to kidnap a little girl so that Myra, employing her expertise, can "find" her and become famous—become, as she puts it, "recognized for what I am.") She's certainly tensely in tune with the role. And she has a handful of moments in *The Three Sisters* when you recognize the *contours* of a character (especially her farewell to Kevin McCarthy's Vershinin). But then she spoils it all, negates it, by flying off into her usual theatricality, breaking off contact with the other actors and taking her focus into outer space, hyperventilating, pressing her fist to her forehead and leaking tears into her breathy voice—and the character just blurs out again. At times like these you think, it's not that she's unskilled; it's that she doesn't *care* about skill. She rides roughshod over it because she's giving in to the demands of private (or theatrical) demons.

In a 1954 telecast of "The Scarlet Letter" on "Kraft Television Theater," Stanley trembles with Hester Prynne's pain. Her face is thick with emotion. Far from trying to look glamorous, she makes her own features—the chubby face, the armored neck, the squat body—her actress's self-declaration. And she takes this ethic to a shocking extreme in the opening minutes of *The Three Sisters*, when, turned away from the others, staring into the air, she uses her weight to give

Masha a careless, gone-to-seed shapelessness: She's a monster statue, a Sphinx, set lumpily in the midst of her sisters' lives, disconnected from them but impossible to ignore.

The center of these performances is a heavy, unrefined self-indulgence. In *The Goddess* she plays Rita Shawn, a sort of stock-company Blanche DuBois, as an almost unbroken series of gargantuan effects: the scene in which she falls to her knees and weeps at her mother's breast, the one where she tells her mother she hates her and wants her to die, the one at her mother's grave. Though presumably she wrung each of these displays from her very soul, none of them actually contains a spontaneous impulse. And she's all push, sending Rita's shivering emotions out to the balcony. In the big séance set-piece in *Séance on a Wet Afternoon*, Stanley gives everything away, all at once. This sequence is a catalogue of weird Stanley mannerisms—the insistent distractedness; the ritualistic singsong dissociations; the cry of release on a sharp intake of breath; and the buzzing, closed-off tantrum (as if she heard some inner hum and was pulling in all her energies to track it down).

In her early performances, like "The Scarlet Letter" and *The Goddess*, Stanley's stock-in-trade is her ability to project youthful innocence and the decay of agony at the same time. In other words, her acting is all about how the pain of feeling too much ravages the young. Her jumping-off point for these tempests of splayed emotion is a soft-spoken gentility, a childlike meekness that turns breathless and haunted when her characters grow desperate. Someone has trained these women to be perfect young ladies; their coming-apart is more of a rebellion against the tyranny of decorum (and all that implies) than anything else. Once again the Actors Studio approach appears to be aimed at depicting arrested adolescence. On a Freudian level, Stanley's reading of these characters makes sense, and they might be interesting if you could believe in the child at the base of her performances. But it's pure affectation, like the three-note silvery laugh she does in *Three Sisters* when Masha tells Vershinin he makes her laugh; or the Amanda Wingfield coquette number she glides into when she's courting his attentions. It's amazing: Here is an actress trained in the American Method, the favorite of the Actors Studio guru, and at moments in this movie she falls blithely into the artificial style of the Romantic era—only without the careful music of that antiquated mode of acting.

The real failure of Stanley's acting, however, isn't that it's excessive or self-indulgent or rhythmless, but that it doesn't illuminate the characters or explain the texts. She's too preoccupied with her own feelings to pay attention to the relationships between dialogue and action, action and motivation, character and context (of all kinds—setting, situation, the other characters). You could argue that in *The Three Sisters*, when her responses seem unmoored to the lines that preceded them, what she's *trying* to do is suggest Masha's alienation from her surroundings—to imply that this woman is dangerously close to collapse. But the separation between cause and effect is too much a constant in her acting. You can see it just as clearly in "The Scarlet Letter," where, in a scene in which Hester is delirious with fever, Stanley's eyes blink shut, her mouth hangs open, her head rocks from side to side, and she can barely get her words out. These demonstrations are as inauthentic in their way as the "standard American" she substitutes for an English accent in *Séance*. They tell us nothing about the character, and they go against the grain of the script. We don't ever learn what makes Rita a star; we don't understand how Billy Savage, weak as he is, can stand living with a nagging, nutsy bore like Myra. These performances violate the basic trust an audience invests in an actor: They make it impossible for us to believe in the character on an essential human level, although that's exactly what Method acting is supposed to achieve above all else.

Stanley's more recent work—as the child-eating monster–mother in *Frances*, the gruff-and-tough barkeep in *The Right Stuff*, and Big Mama in the calamitous TV revival of *Cat on a Hot Tin Roof* (with Jessica Lange and Tommy Lee Jones)—has lost the mannered *politesse* of her younger performances. It's in the sashaying-old-bitch category many American actresses enter when they reach a certain age (often because they're suffering from the limited sensitivities of male screen-writers). She hasn't become any subtler with the years, and she's even harder to watch: She's lost all sense of shame. In *Frances*, the worst of the three, she looks appalling. The hollows under her eyes are as big as the eyes themselves, and her wig, plopped unceremoniously on her head, suggests the long-planned revenge of an embittered coiffeur. She rips into the part of Lillian Farmer as if it were a pie-eating contest with bonus points awarded for slurping. She seems to be saying, "This may be ugly, folks, but it's life, and I'm here to show you that a real

213

actress isn't afraid to rub her nose in it." It's the kind of misplaced zeal that gives Method acting a bad name.

Sandy Dennis

If there's one actress who has a larger repertoire of tics than even Kim Stanley, it's Sandy Dennis, and in her worst movies (like *Up the Down Staircase* and *The Fox*) they're a Method nightmare. She grins her toothy, rabbitty grin, but her face goes slack, pasty, as if not all the nerves were functioning; she shakes her head stiffly, erasing some invisible blackboard inside; and her focus is unreadable—her eyes don't open very wide, and she often appears to be looking at nothing. When she's worn out, psychic exhaustion forces her mouth to gape open. At times we catch just a glimpse of a private smile, but it materializes and vanishes in a moment. There are odd, abrupt little motions she seems not to realize she's making, like tickling herself under the nose, biting her lip, or caressing her upper lip with the back of her hand. She almost transforms herself into a marionette, manipulated by an unseen puppeteer. Her walk has a certain purposefulness, but she hoists herself around by her shoulders. The rest of her body, as far down as her legs, sags with bag-lady dispiritedness, loose and shapeless.

Pauline Kael once wrote that Dennis had made an acting style out of postnasal drip.[1] Her voice sounds like it's shooting out from a small, dark, narrow room (technically, it's coming straight from the throat rather than the diaphragm), and it carries all sorts of excess baggage with it—little "mmm" sounds that zoom into the beginnings of sentences; swallowed "ums" and "uhs" and "ahs" grafted onto words; involuntary repetition of some phrases, like a rickety typewriter that's developed repeating keys. There are weird, blocked pauses in her lines that seem to denote tiny anxiety attacks around certain words. Then her breath gets ahead of her and she has to work to catch up. She has an irregular stutter, or else she breaks into sudden, inappropriate giggles or makes a childish, mocking descent into basso profundo. Then there are the explosions of laughter we're meant to read as a displacement for tears.

Dennis's career is full of mannered jags, as in *Who's Afraid of Virginia Woolf?* (for which she took the 1966 Best Supporting Actress

Oscar). She plays Honey, the eager-to-please wife of a biology prof (George Segal) newly hired at a small New England college. As the drunken night wears on, Honey is revealed to be slightly unhinged, prone to hysterical pregnancies, and easily deceived by her ambitious, sexually adventurous husband, Nick. Dennis moves so rapidly through her collection of tics on her initial entrance that you wonder what she's going to do for the *rest* of the movie. The performance is basically an extended (bad) sloshed routine aimed somewhere above the heads of her costars, who include Richard Burton and Elizabeth Taylor. It's made up entirely of ridiculous, uncontrolled flourishes like dancing around in circles, waving a handkerchief in the air—like a camp version of Isadora Duncan—or cutesy, little-kid pleading when Burton's shrewdly manipulative George gets her to admit she's never wanted children.

The same year, she played Irina in *The Three Sisters*, and here her approximations of emotional states are utterly bizarre. When in the final minutes she receives the news of her fiancé Tuzenbach's death, she's like a possessed Raggedy Ann doll, whipping around in a frenzy— the kind that has no reference to anything beyond the walls of the theater. This Irina is a spinster schoolmarm long before Chekhov peters out her youthful energies. It's a measure of how poor an understanding Strasberg had of *Three Sisters* that he chose as his Irina an actress whose most distinctive trait is the burden of neurosis that cripples and ages almost every character she plays.

But Dennis isn't quite in the Kim Stanley category. There have been memorable occasions when she's harnessed her mannerisms to a character—worked out a role completely in terms of her vocal and physical idiosyncrasies so they emerge from the character rather than just existing for their own sake. Obviously her peculiarities restrict her: It doesn't make sense to cast her as Irina, or even as the earnest schoolteacher in *Up the Down Staircase*. But she's given stunning demonstrations of extreme states of repression in two Robert Altman pictures, *That Cold Day in the Park* and *Come Back to the 5 & Dime, Jimmy Dean, Jimmy Dean*. And she has a jagged, self-reflexive wit. In comedies like Neil Simon's *The Out of Towners* and Muriel Spark's *Nasty Habits*, she turns her trademark weirdnesses in on themselves, making herself into the movies' best-sustained gag—in the first as a jangled Ohio tourist besieged by all the horrors of New York City (her nasal outcry "Oh my GOD!," charting her increasing panic and dismay, is what most people remember best), and in the second as a hilariously dense John Dean figure, unconsciously spilling privileged information whenever she opens her mouth to let out that high-decibel whine.

No one else has a comic style or timing remotely like Sandy Dennis's; she's a verbal Harpo Marx strung out on downers. In a bit as an unforgiving former friend of the heroine (Gena Rowlands) in *Another Woman*, Woody Allen's New Yorkese retread of *Wild Strawberries*, she brings a spiky, sour-grapes quality to a dull, dull party and at least enlivens it for a few minutes. And she's a delight in Bob Balaban's spooky, high-flying black comedy, *Parents*, as an elementary-school social worker who dresses like a *distrait* gypsy but manages to get on the same wavelength as the little boy (Bryan Madorsky) she tries to help. (The movie takes a bit of a nose dive after it unwisely kills her off.)

Nothing else I've seen from Dennis is as impressive as her two Altman films. She's one of those actors (like Karen Black or Keith Carradine or Elliott Gould) who reveal infinitely more interesting dimensions under his direction than they've shown elsewhere. As a movie, *That Cold Day in the Park*, one of Altman's earliest features (it came out in 1969, the year before *M*A*S*H*), is a dank, unpleasant, and rather academic exercise in creating and extending suspense. Dennis plays Frances, a spinster who picks up a young man (Michael Parks) in the park across from her apartment and tries to keep him. It's *The Collector* in drag, though this relationship is even more Gothic and has even creepier implications: When Frances's bottled-up sexual energies explode, they suddenly turn violent. (She hires a whore to service the boy, thinking that's what he must want when he refuses her own advances; then she interrupts them in bed and murders the whore.)

There's a chilly efficiency to Dennis's acting here, but it emanates from the character and the enclosed narrative—this isn't a typical, expansive Altman. And Dennis is absolutely in character straight through. The trademark lip-biting, for example, shows up when Frances, terrified that this visitor will abandon her, gives him new clothes to wear. It helps us to understand the whole gesture (she might be a high-school wallflower who tries to bribe a boy into taking her out on a date). Her acting has marvelous concentration and uninterrupted tension. And focusing, as she often fails to do, on other actors (this is Altman's contribution), she creates a false sense of normalcy in the first scenes that makes the movie's deeper and deeper exploration of Frances's craziness shocking.

After you've seen Dennis in the half-dozen or so performances that preceded this one, her rigorous control over the character in *That Cold Day* is startling. She's splendid at defining this woman's fastidiousness and her peculiar, constrained brand of generosity, and she works an arid, knotted humor out of scenes like the one where she tells the boy about a course she once took in music appreciation—her idea of participating in the world outside her fantasies. (Naturally, the class does nothing but feed her already gnarled inwardness.) Since the boy, for reasons that aren't too clear, opts to present himself as mute for most of the story, Frances's interaction with him is a nonstop monologue; he's the perfect "guest" for her—up to the point where he fails to fulfill the hidden sexual agenda she hasn't even allowed herself to be conscious of. He's like her music appreciation course—something from the outside she wants to add to her reclusive existence without making any actual alterations. At the end of the first day she puts him to bed and tells him, with unsmiling matter-of-factness, "It's been a lovely day for me. I'm glad you're here."

Dennis's sagging face, puffed up with moldy emotion, is the emblem of *Come Back to the 5 & Dime, Jimmy Dean, Jimmy Dean*. Mona, a woman irrevocably lost in a past half real, half made-up, is the archetypal Sandy Dennis role, and she climbs so far inside it that, even more than in *That Cold Day*, the same flourishes that translate into annoying mannerisms in other films strengthen her performance here—they define the character. We may start out by recognizing individual pieces of business from the Dennis repertoire, but each one seems to expose a corner of Mona's personality, which is deeply disturbed, though in a winged, dreamy, completely unsettling way (like Alma's in Tennessee Williams's *The Eccentricities of a Nightingale*, as Blythe Danner played her; or like Piper Laurie's evangelical mother in Brian DePalma's *Carrie*). Dennis portrays Mona as a series of displaced parts—girlish, pain-wracked, autocratic, matter-of-fact, old-maid-schoolteacher indignant—each phase disconnecting as she gropes for the next, as if she were playing emotional hopscotch on the shards of half a dozen shattered personalities.

The film is something of a miracle. Ed Graczyk's play, which is about the reunion of the members of a James Dean fan club in a cobwebby Texas town, twenty years after Dean's death and various unrelated personal crises broke it up for good, is a thick stew in which you can taste large chucks of O'Neill, William Inge, Edward Albee, and (especially) Tennessee Williams. (Even the rhythm of the dialogue, with its distaste for contractions and its fanciful, overloaded sentences, is imitative of Williams.) But with Robert Altman directing Dennis, Cher (as the one-time cheerleader, Cissy) and Karen Black (as the transsexual, Joanne, who in her earlier incarnation, as Joe, fathered Mona's baby), the movie has an emotional potency and believability that belie the banality and stagy hokum of the script. At first you can separate in your head the bad play from the magnificent performers and direction. Then you begin to hear the lines solely through the filter of the production, and suddenly you're no longer sure you're not listening to Chekhov or Ibsen (the original sources of this tragedy of ghosts and unfulfilled dreams).

The instrument Altman uses to work much of his magic is a wall-size mirror that divides the action into present-day scenes and flashbacks to these women's teenage years, in the mid–1950s. At that time life was centered in the five and dime, at meetings of the Disciples of James Dean. It reached its apex when Dean arrived in nearby Marfa to film *Giant*, and seemed to stop with his demise. The cuts between eighteen-year-old Mona and Mona in her late thirties are shocking because in the young scenes only Dennis's eyes betray the cloudy burden of her fantasizing, while in the older sequences, her whole face seems to be sinking, her chin droops so low that her mouth looks like an immense open wound, and her voice becomes cracked and breathy when Mona feels exhausted—as she often seems to. (How Dennis manages to register decay in her face without the crutch of make-up is a true acting mystery.)

The first time we see Mona is in a flashback to 1955. Dennis's characters have often come across as overage adolescents (the one she plays in *Another Woman* has never forgiven her best friend for an alleged offense thirty years earlier), but here she's more convincingly young than she was as Irina in the *real Three Sisters*. Sailing into the store on the wind of her own breathless energies, she asks Joe (Mark Patton) for the new *Photoplay* with a maidenly reticence and nervousness, pooh-poohing his gossip that her idol, James Dean, is in love. Her youth is in her movements—especially in the way she shifts, with a funny blend of slovenliness and cautious self-consciousness, into the

McGuire Sisters moves she and Joe and Cissy like to mimic while "Sincerely" plays on the jukebox. It's hard to tell, for a long time, how deeply out of sync this girl is, how close to the schizophrenic edge, because you might think she's just a hypersensitive version of a typical small-town teen fan. When she hears Dean is coming to Texas, her entire body freezes except her head, which dips and rises as if she had no control over it; she can't speak—she internalizes everything—and she has to work hard to control her breathing. She looks lightning-struck. You can hear the actress's inner monologue ("I'm going to take this news slowly and ingest every syllable") as distinctly as if her pulse were tapping it out in Morse code.

It's really the combination of her manner and her actions that reveal Mona's craziness—that and the juxtaposition of the flashbacks, which lay the ground for her to take up permanent residence in the fantastic past, with the present-day scenes, where we see her creepily at home in that past. There's a scene where she shows up at the five and dime only weeks after she's left for college and explains to her employer, Juanita (Sudie Bond), that her asthma got so bad that she was sent home. Her melodramatic spiel, delivered on one breath, has a childlike intensity and sweetness—but suddenly we register the asthma as psychosomatic and see she's given up her life to return to these four walls, where she feels safe. In another scene, where she opposes Juanita's firing of Joe for showing signs of homosexuality, she flaunts a very adolescent fugitive bravado, but she's on the brink of running away. She's present and absent at the same moment—and though the pull between them has a kind of charm, it's disturbing, too.

When Mona talks about James Dean the loony extreme of her feelings for him shivers her voice and catches in her throat. She says she can't express them, but she's pregnant with them—it's just a small step to her declaration that it's his child she's carrying and not Joe's. The farthest she can extend herself to Joe, to any boy, is to see him in James Dean's image. When she tells Joe she's sure he could be just like Dean, she seems to be floating: She knows this is special magic, and she has to use it carefully, delicately, on tiptoe. But it's Dean's death that seals her into her fantasy forever. Her eyes retreat (like those of Katharine Hepburn, anesthetized by morphine, in the final scene of Long Day's Journey into Night)—it's almost imperceptible at first, but then we realize that Mona has placed herself irretrievably at a remove from both Joe and the rest of the world.

Walking into the store with her suitcase, after her yearly pilgrimage to Marfa (where the facade of *Giant*'s Reata was constructed so many years ago), Mona seems far older than thirty-eight or thirty-nine. We hear years of strained patience in her voice when she bosses Juanita around, insisting on her undivided attention while she invokes her hero's name (respect for the dead). Her hypochondria has grown chronic: She complains of her back and her heart as well as her asthma. When she talks about how Marfa has deteriorated, she tips her head and her focus passes inside so suddenly and so completely that it's truly alarming. She moves heavily, and there's something—a ghost?—just over her shoulder, in the corner of her eye. When she looks at an old photo of the Disciples and glances into the mirror, she's drawn in, as if under a spell. The past is all around her, and it narcotizes her.

Dennis's Mona can drag herself through the commonplaces of her day-to-day existence, but they're ordeals for her; it's clear her energy is leaking away. She does have a social manner for customers (she assumes that Joanne, when she enters the store, is nothing more than that), but it's a little rushed, unsteady, pushed in all the wrong places. Actually, what she's waiting for—what she *lives* for—is an excuse to break into her treasure chest of James Dean memorabilia and indulge her own recollections (both real and imagined) of the filming of *Giant*. Mona has elected herself chief custodian of the Dean myth, and she's always ready to play tour guide. She smiles with childish pride as she boasts to Joanne that she appeared in the picture, and when she admits that it was she who brought Dean's son into the world, that her celebrity "put McCarthy, Texas on the map for a brief but glorious period of time," she sounds like a schoolgirl, gleaming with patriotic fervor, at a Fourth of July pageant. Later, when the reunion gets under way, Stella Mae (Kathy Bates) mentions that in all the times she's seen *Giant*, she's never managed to catch Mona on camera. Mona considers the issue and gives a serious, measured reply. This is her business, after all, and she approaches the question as if it were a business problem to be clucked over and surveyed from all angles.

Mona is a cockeyed madonna, sheltering her reverie of sex with Hollywood's sublime young god. Dennis really soars in the scenes where she breaks out her divine mystery; they have a terrifying, vertiginous excitement, as the most reckless heights of other great movie madwomen do—Vivien Leigh in *A Streetcar Named Desire*, Isabelle Adjani in *The Story of Adele H*. At the reunion, some of the others press her to tell the story of her encounter with Dean. She takes a long pause—waiting for the inspiration, settling on the perfect moment—and then she giggles nervously and begins. Her recitation has the quality of ritual, thoroughly rehearsed but full of the joy of anticipation. It might also be the retelling of some beloved legend: Every patch of it is well-worn, everyone in the room has heard it a thousand times but can't help sharing in her mesmeric delight in repeating it. And she's built in pauses for reflection and for audience approval. When she approaches the crazy centerpiece section about making love to Dean, it has a mystical hush and a sudden, private withdrawal. She protects it with all her strength, with her whole consciousness, shutting it off from the others so they can't soil it with their doubts. This speech has a breathtaking internal poetry—but Mona hasn't enough energy to keep her balance all the way to the end: In the last moments of the story she's wobbly, and she stutters a little. She collapses into home plate as she winds up the tale, and Joanne (who by now has revealed herself as Joe) says the whole thing is a lie.

Joanne is Mona's nemesis, of course; her presence throws the whole fantasy into doubt. Mona's way of dealing with this truth-telling ghost is to hide behind her shrine (a cardboard miniature of Reata) and stare back with a weird, unbalanced look in her eyes. (Dennis does incredible things with those wavering eyes of hers in this picture.) And Mona isn't a benign madwoman. She's capable of surprise attacks: When Cissy censures her for pretending all his life that her son, whom she calls Jimmy Dean, is a moron, Mona laughs and then nearly shakes Cissy off the stepladder she's standing on. (The idiot-child-of-James-Dean idea is Graczyk's big symbol, and it *really* creaks.) When it comes to her son (whom we never see), Mona has a fierce, twisted protectiveness. All of the disappointments she can't face are projected onto the boy. They've transformed him, in her eyes, into something damaged, defective, and when she talks about him her face gets flabby and grotesque—she turns into a gargoyle, a monster that eats its young.

At the end of the movie, when Joanne has exposed Mona's lie, and Juanita and Cissy confess they've known for years who Jimmy Dean's real father is, Mona's small brown eyes dart softly, seeking refuge. She's balanced so precariously on her inventions of the past (James Dean) and the present (Jimmy Dean) that you can hardly bear to watch her. She admits she's lied—and then, as the other women vow to reunite again in twenty years, she retreats behind the cut-out of Reata, and you have the feeling she'll never venture forth again. Who could have expected a performance of this depth from Sandy Dennis—a performance whose emotions are so close to the surface that you have the sense you could reach out and touch them; where every recogniz-able mannerism turns out to be a signpost pointing to layers and layers of revelations? It's a performance that reminds you of the capacity of American Method acting to astonish.

9

METHOD SANITY

♦ ♦ ♦

I'll tell you how the Method helps you. According to the Method, you see, you have to give yourself. The Method is to be true, to be real, to be true to the part in the play, not for . . . your own self-indulgence; it's never meant for that, never has been. It's to be as true and real, and alive and fresh in the part each time. That's your job.

—Maureen Stapleton[1]

Not all the actors to emerge from the Actors Studio have worn their neuroses on their sleeves. We tend to remember the self-perpetuating fires of James Dean's psychic struggles, or the unhinged ferocity of a Sandy Dennis, and forget that some of our sanest performers share those actors' schooling and approach. Think of the unflamboyant, normal-range work of actresses like Maureen Stapleton, Eva Marie Saint, and Kim Hunter. Think of two of the Method's wittiest practitioners, Rod Steiger and Rip Torn, who have made careers out of playing characters with a shrewd, unclouded eye and common, all-too-recognizable desires—money, power, sex. This group of five actors represents the way the Method can ground performance in the realistic, the familiar, the earthy.

Maureen Stapleton

Like Geraldine Page, Kim Stanley, and Sandy Dennis, Maureen Stapleton has always relied on her own unglamorous physicality to center her acting; she's always been an antistar, in the Hollywood sense, though there are few character actresses who command more general respect. In her early movies, like *Lonelyhearts* (where she's an unhappily married woman who drags the columnist, played by Montgomery Clift, into an affair) and *The Fugitive Kind* (where she has a tiny role as the sheriff's wife), she has a bristling, theatrical presence—an Actors

Studio hallmark in the 1950s and early 1960s—and a quavering, neurotic edge. But it's her directness above all that makes an impression. In *Lonelyhearts*, Stapleton is practically the only person on screen who seems to be playing a character rather than an attitude, and though you wish there had been a real director behind the camera to clamp down on her movie-debut excesses (the shocked crying in her big confession scene with Clift goes on too long), she makes this woman's dumpy hopelessness touching. She even carries off the Pinteresque shift in the character—the sharpness and dissonance that come out of nowhere after she's slept with the columnist. In *The Fugitive Kind* she's all nerves, but her bright-eyed fatuousness is charming, and she knows how to mine a few laughs out of her overwritten lines.

What distinguishes Stapleton from Page, Stanley, and Dennis, even in these early flighty roles, is that she doesn't put the accent on the characters' craziness, but on the area in their emotional spectrum we can best identify with: their normality. And, as her career continues, she leaves the company of the neurotics to play ordinary women in distress (*Airport*) or ordinary women with extraordinary powers of understanding and warmth (*Interiors*, the 1974 Mark Taper Forum production of *Juno and the Paycock*). Even when she plays an extraordinary woman, like Emma Goldman in *Reds*, there's an essential modesty to her acting that sits side-by-side with a penetrating, unsentimental intelligence. You can spot this combination even in a throwaway drama like "No License to Kill," a 1958 "Alcoa Hour" episode where she's cast as an auto accident victim.

In *Airport* Stapleton plays Inez Guerrero, Van Heflin's long-suffering wife—he's a dreamer who can't hold on to a job, and she keeps them (barely) solvent by working in a hash joint. These two are the only traces of humanity in the whole dumb, assembly-line picture, and they have a lovely, unaffected rapport in their one brief scene together before he boards a plane, armed with a bomb. (He has a nutsy scheme to blow up the aircraft so Inez can get the flight insurance.) Stapleton is terrific as a woman who's used to a hard life but not bothering anyone about it. There's a core of low-key sanity to her performance, and a soft-spoken intensity that refuses to draw attention to itself.

She can't have more than half a dozen scenes in the movie, but each is a small gem of genuinely felt, beautifully controlled acting—like the moment when Heflin tells her he loves her and, impulsively, she leans across the counter of the diner and tenderly holds her hand against his cheek; and the one where she has to invent a reason for insisting the airlines tell her whether he's boarded the flight; and the one where she gives Burt Lancaster (as the airport's chief of staff) humiliating personal information about her husband. At the end, when the bomb's gone off, Guerrero is dead, and the pilot (Dean Martin) has landed the plane successfully, Inez wanders dizzily among the injured passengers being brought in on stretchers and in wheelchairs, apologizing to them. It's one of those touches (like Melinda Dillon, in *Absence of Malice*, stealing the morning papers from her neighbors' lawns so they can't read the story that alludes to her abortion) that are simultaneously hokey and inspired when a fine actress imbues them with a sense of desperation and grief.

Stapleton has a knack for getting into the heads of practical, down-to-earth women like Emma Goldman in *Reds* and Juno Boyle in *Juno and the Paycock*, Sean O'Casey's tragicomedy set during the Irish troubles, where she maintains a tender tension between emotional fullness and no-nonsense pragmatism, hard-knocks realism and endearing softness. Her best moments in the two performances are similar: the rational calm in her readings of the speech in *Juno* where she cuts through her wounded son Johnny's political bravado ("You lost your best principle when you lost your arm"), and her disenchanted explanation in *Reds* to Warren Beatty's John Reed that she's decided to leave Russia because this land of revolutionary promise suppresses the human rights she so fervently believes in. Her Juno is a steady, watchful piece of acting. We read Juno's character through the attention Stapleton pays to the other actors, and since she's playing a woman whose life is defined by her children, her refusal to take center stage— a personal quality we always respond to in this actress—seems especially appropriate here.

She does maybe her best work in *Reds*, though, illuminating— always without self-consciousness, without clamor—the fabled revolutionary's warmth and the grip of her intelligence as well as her dogmatic, obstinate side. Stapleton has less than ten minutes on screen in Warren Beatty's epic, but she fills in this sketch of Goldman with a fully worked-out character. She's like a figure in the corner of an Impressionist painting: The closer you look, the more you see. A few seconds of a ferocious soapbox speech, delivered in a powerfully scratchy underlayer of her voice Stapleton doesn't often get to use in her performances, is so rousing and gutsy you want to hear more. In a brief scene between Goldman and Reed in Petrograd, the driven speed of her dialogue tells us how much there is to be done in this new old land. When they speak of Louise Bryant (Diane Keaton), the wife Reed left in America, Stapleton's Emma moves gently from bafflement at his sexual jealousy to maternal warmth that's filtered through her usual reasoned disinterestedness. (Sexual jealousy is an emotion Emma is legitimately incapable of understanding; that's an intriguing psychological touch, and a tribute to Goldman's instinctively democratic way of moving through a complex world.) Beatty's achievement as a director is in the way he keeps his celebrated characters scaled down to human dimensions; they're never dwarfed by either their own fame or the size of the movie. In one direction he's aided by Jack Nicholson's wry, comedy-sketch Eugene O'Neill, in another by Stapleton's wonderfully realistic Emma Goldman.

Stapleton's performance in Woody Allen's *Interiors* is fascinating in terms of her development as an actress. She plays Pearl, the loud, passionate (and implicitly Jewish) Florida widow Arthur (E. G. Marshall) is drawn to after he leaves his stiff-necked, fiendishly tasteful WASP wife, Eve (Geraldine Page). Pearl enters wearing a red dress, a fur stole, and a slightly vulgar hairstyle, and she brings some much-needed life to the movie; she softens its careful, severe, imitation Bergman contours. Allen clearly intends Pearl as a contrast to the rest of the characters (the members of Arthur's repressed family), and he ends up using her shamelessly as a life force symbol—she even tries to save Eve's life by artificial respiration after Eve has thrown herself into the ocean. Pearl is the unfortunate instrument of Allen's attack on these frigid, self-loathing WASPs. But she does manage to say some of the things we've been thinking about the other characters and their environment ("This house is so *pale*" is her immediate reaction to Eve's pristine decorative scheme); and Stapleton's sloppy straightforwardness in the role is almost the only infusion of vibrance the film has. Thanks to Stapleton, Pearl functions as Allen's good conscience, the genuine human being who splashes through the east-coast intellectual sauce he's smeared over everything. It's wonderful to see how this actress, who came as much out of the neurotic-acting-out wing of the Actors Studio as Geraldine Page, is now cast as her foil—as the voice of blessed sanity.

Eva Marie Saint

In "The Anatomy of Falsehood," Robert Warshow's provocative attack on *The Best Years of Our Lives*, he claims that the craftsmanship of the director, William Wyler, serves a brand of realism that ends up subverting his intentions:

> The actors . . . are so manipulated as to become embodiments of the physical reality of human beings. More clearly than the important events of the plot, one remembers how the actors hold their bodies: Teresa Wright slouched over a stove, so much like a real woman over a real stove that the scene can become almost unpleasant, as it was certainly not intended to be.[2]

Warshow's central point (that Wyler didn't realize what he was getting) is arguable. And there's an underlying assumption about naturalism in film which Warshow himself may not have intended, and which also is debatable: that there's something basically unattractive about the faithful replication of a banal activity like cooking soup. Warshow is working off a pre–Marlon Brando prejudice: He expects people in movies to have a certain glamor (though he doesn't say so), and, not understanding why a director would be tempted to follow another path, he assumes the effect Wyler gets is a mistake.

Actually, when you look back at *The Best Years of Our Lives* after the experience of *On the Waterfront*, it's hard to see the hard-working, resolutely not-bad actress Teresa Wright as the embodiment of dull domesticity. She looks pretty damn good—nicely made up and immaculately coiffed—stirring that soup. What would Warshow have thought of Eva Marie Saint in *A Hatful of Rain*, bent over the kitchen table to hand a cup of coffee to her sloshed brother-in-law (Anthony Franciosa), holding herself with the heavy awkwardness of an extremely pregnant woman?

For all its virtues, *A Hatful of Rain* doesn't translate well to the screen (even with Fred Zinnemann at the helm); the camera, which you might expect to pay tribute to the accuracy of Michael V. Gazzo's depiction of lower middle-class life, instead exposes the triteness of his dramaturgy. And then it's badly cast: Franciosa, Don Murray as the junkie war vet, Lloyd Nolan as their mostly absent father aren't deft or believable enough actors to confirm the layers of experience Gazzo hints at, or test the strength of his built-from-improv, lifelike dialogue. Only Eva Marie Saint as Celia Pope, the role Shelley Winters played on Broadway, is both self-effacing and skillful enough to make her character's ordinariness dramatic. Celia is, to put it mildly, a modest role—a woman with little imagination and few words to describe her feelings of discomfort at her husband's unexplained restlessness and frequent truancy, a woman who takes an almost childish pleasure in small satisfactions (like making a special dinner for her father-in-law when she meets him for the first time). Saint, a superb actress far too subtle and unostentatious ever to gain the stardom she deserved when she was young, imbues the part with a glowing saneness and reason-ableness. The imaginative precision of her real-life observations about Celia is actually thrilling: the way she hangs onto the door when she sees Nolan off; the way she bends one leg back and rubs it while she argues with Murray, tipping her head as she reminds him of the all-night talks they used to have; the way she bounces out of his arms when he doesn't respond to her embrace, ricocheting around the room to express her character's emotional and sexual hunger. (Her whole demeanor changes when he won't hug her back; her temperature seems to sink.)

In one scene, Polo (Franciosa) confesses he loves Celia, and she asks him why he doesn't just take her away. But then she adds, "I might be a little heavy; I'm carrying your brother's baby." It's a killer line, meant to slay Polo and the audience, the kind of line that rarely works. Saint reads it calmly, rationally, as a plain statement of fact—and it kills you. In another scene Celia arrives home from work, set to tell Johnny (Murray) the marriage is finished, and finds him already there, the apartment cleaned, a gift for the coming baby in his hands. Immediately we see her confusion because his sweetness and con-scientiousness—the new leaf he's turned over—make it difficult for her to carry through her plan. They muddy the issue: They remind her of how much she still loves him, and she doesn't want to slide back into her softness for him now that she's reasoned the whole thing out and reached the logical decision to leave him. When he hands her the gift, a dress for the baby, she weeps with exasperation at what he's making her feel.

In her first movie, *On the Waterfront*, Saint got to play almost every scene opposite Marlon Brando, and held her own beautifully. Saint manages something extremely difficult in this role: She plays a good Catholic girl, brought up in a convent school outside the city, incapable of deceit, without desexing her or making her incorruptible ethics seem unbearably superior. You sense that for Edie Doyle there's never been a choice between right and wrong; she acts out of instinct, and when someone blocks the path she knows is the right one, she doesn't hesitate to fight like hell. It's not that she isn't afraid; Saint betrays Edie's fears in tiny tremors, in the way her eyes dart back and forth like those of a child who suddenly finds herself in an unexpectedly dark room. What's remarkable about Edie is that she pushes ahead regardless—it doesn't seem to occur to her that she might give in to those fears and back off.

Early on in the picture, the waterfront priest (Karl Malden) sizes up her attitude toward him in the wake of her brother's murder. "You think I'm a gravy train rider with a turned-around collar, don't you?" he offers. And when she responds with an uneasy silence, he adds, "I see the sisters taught you not to lie." He's right. She can't lie—about what she thinks is right (probing for the truth about who killed Joey), about her anger at Brando's Terry Malloy when he confesses his part in Joey's death, or about her love for him despite his involvement. When he breaks into her father's apartment to see her she screams at him to stay away, she tries to fend him off with a hairbrush, but she never denies she loves him. She unleashes her rage at him for setting Joey up and (this is the child part of her struggling irrationally against a situation she can't control) for turning out to be guilty after she'd fallen in love with him. But once she's given in to his kisses, she stands by her decision to forgive him. And that's the last time in the movie she tries to pull away from him.

Though *On the Waterfront* is first and foremost the story of Terry Malloy's moral coming of age, Edie experiences an ascension to adulthood, too: We understand without being told that Terry is the first man she's had serious feelings for. It is touching and funny to see her sample new sensations the nuns didn't prepare her for, as Terry introduces her to them. When she visits him on the rooftop, where he raises pigeons, he invites her out for a beer. Saint has a lovely, unspoken moment of hesitation before accepting, when we can read Edie's thoughts as she weighs his offer against her notion of what's right and wrong, struggling to come up with something in her experience she can compare it to. Then, awkward in the unfamiliar milieu of the saloon, she watches Terry gabbing comfortably with the barkeep; you can tell she's not sure whether she should go (which would be a lot easier) or stay. But Edie has made up her mind to enter the world, over her father's pleas to return to the convent where she'd be protected from "things not fit for a decent girl to see" (the brutality of life on the waterfront). So she stays. She downs the liquor Terry orders for her, sips the beer, and experiences her first drunkenness (more on romance than on alcohol).

Edie does try to run away when he refuses to help her find Joey's murderers, but she gets caught up in the midst of a wedding celebration in another part of the bar and has to rely on Terry to escort her out. Here we see her uncertainty about how to deal with her feelings for this man she's not sure she should be attracted to: The liquor has rushed her emotions to the front of her head, and she's overwhelmed. This scene is never mentioned in discussions of the way movies of the fifties depict adolescent confusion and sexuality, but though Edie is probably around twenty-one, in experiential terms she might as well be fourteen, and her dance with Terry—during which she tells him, "I feel like I'm just floating, just floating"—is the equivalent of a teenager's dream date.

What's amazing about Edie, as Saint plays her, is that she retains her childlike straightforwardness in her encounters with the adult world (which is another way of explaining her courage). Having opted to learn a little of life on the streets, she acquires something akin to, but not quite the same as, jauntiness (e.g., on the rooftop with Terry and his teen disciple, who helps him tend the pigeons and mock-boxes with him). It's an expression of her willingness to come to terms with the world she knows she's been carefully sheltered from, and it's the quality that pushes her through moments that unnerve her initially, like her first glimpse of the bar Terry takes her to. Sitting opposite him, she doesn't hesitate to tell him what her impressions of him are—to ask him about what she reads as his lack of "sentiment or romance or human kindness." And when the Feds arrive in the middle of their dance to subpoena him, she forces him to face her, pirouetting around him until he can't look away, and calls him a bum. Then, before running off, she answers his question "What do you want me to do?" with an insistent "Much, much, much more." This line has the simplicity of a child's demand; as complicated as her own feelings become, her sense of right and wrong never wavers. And the movie, with its problem-play morality, doesn't present her with a choice that forces her to confront actual shades of grey. Terry, moved by his love for her and by his brother's death, turns into the man of conscience she would have wanted all along.

This dramatic convenience doesn't lessen the emotional impact of the relationship, or of either performance. Terry and Edie are a fascinating couple, forever shifting parent and child roles. She looks to him, worldly as he is, to show her how to act and where to step in an atmosphere he's at ease in (like the bar), and when he leaves her with Charlie's body, she looks like a little girl abandoned by her playmates in unfamiliar territory. But she also sees through his tough act to the innocence inside him, and his tentative grasping at the world *she* knows—the world of values, of definite moral choices—brings out the mother in her. It may be this interplay that makes the scenes between Saint and Brando so incredibly sexy—this and the fact that, as Saint plays her, Edie is, miraculously, as straightforward about her sexuality as she is about everything else. You can see the turned-on gleam in her eyes when she first speaks to Terry; and when he breaks into her apartment she's huddled on her bed, wearing a slip, but she isn't modest or retiring about the way she's dressed. Obviously that's less important to her than what she feels for Terry (both love and anger). This scene still stirs audiences.

Saint's performance in *On the Waterfront* is sensational, and you'd imagine it would have started her off on an exciting career. But once she'd won her Best Supporting Actress Oscar for it, she faded quickly into dull ingenue roles in movies like *That Certain Feeling* and the blighted *Raintree Country* and *Exodus*, and eventually into dull enduring-wife-and-mother roles in even duller movies like *Nothing in Common*. Aside from *Waterfront*, the only picture she's made that most filmgoers can identify quickly is Hitchcock's *North by Northwest*, where she shows a sexy dry wit as the secret agent Cary Grant falls in love with. (It's not much of a role; Grace Kelly could have played it. Hitchcock may not have realized how good an actress he was getting.)

But though Saint's work hasn't attracted much notice, she's often been terrific. *A Hatful of Rain* (1957) was only her third movie; five years later, in *All Fall Down*, as a woman doomed by her love for a shallow, self-absorbed man (Warren Beatty), she has an unusual mixture of sexually assured worldliness and an almost masochistic romantic commitment. It's hard to forget her first appearance—her unaffected beauty; the bounce in her voice when she tells Beatty's kid brother (Brandon de Wilde) she's the "old maid from Toledo" he and his family have been expecting; the way she flirts with the boy in a lazy, rolling midwestern style that turns him into an instant basket case. You can believe her origins (that she grew up bowling and tinkering with cars) just as you can believe her Catholic working-class heritage in *On the Waterfront*. You can believe her past, too, when she describes the alcoholism and eventual suicide of a one-time boy friend, and you fear for this woman, whose ebullience and assertiveness mask a real emotional recklessness. Few American actresses have ever been as good as Eva Marie Saint at conveying tacit sexual longings and tensions, and (in this case) their capacity for turning self-destructive in some women. (Anne Bancroft in *The Pumpkin Eater* comes to mind.)

Saint did a fair amount of television work in the 1950s, including "The Trip to Bountiful" with Lillian Gish (they'd both played these roles on stage the same year, 1953) and "Wish on the Moon" with Phyllis Kirk, both on "Philco–Goodyear Playhouse," and a fairly stupefying musical version of "Our Town" on "Producer's Showcase," with Paul Newman as George and Frank Sinatra as the Stage Manager, singing that love and marriage go together like a horse and carriage. Only a five-minute segment of "The Trip to Bountiful" is still extant, and it's mostly a testimony to the peerless Gish; Saint just sits next to her on a bus and listens attentively. But she's charming as Emily in "Our Town"—convincingly petulant and wonderstruck in the adolescent scenes (and when she confesses her love to George—"I am now, George. I always have been"—you can feel her rise magically to adulthood, the way teenagers suddenly do), poignant in her last-act farewell to earth. She approaches Emily's famous departing speech in a way I've never seen other actresses try it: She makes it clear that what Emily is saying goodbye to isn't so much the world she's known as her *feelings* about it. You can hear her pulling away from emotion as she prepares to join the dead.

And in "Wish on the Moon," she gives an intriguing performance as a woman without ambition who falls into celebrity as a model and ends up unhappy and alcoholic. Saint has a natural radiance in this role, and a relaxed, midcountry rhythm. But she has an unsuspected edge, too—spirit in unthought-of places—and, while it prevents the character from being blanded out by the commercials she makes her living in, it also makes her too tough for the expert manipulators who get their paws on her and pronounce her "temperamental." Watching her in the last act of this otherwise uninteresting drama, you can't help thinking what a great Frances Farmer she would have made in those days. (Saint even has some of Jessica Lange's sexy sparkle.)

Her best performance after *On the Waterfront* was on the big screen, opposite an astonishingly expressive George Segal in the 1970 *Loving*. Irvin Kershner's sharp, painful, Saul Bellowesque drama (written by Don Devlin) about the wreck of a marriage anticipates *Shoot the Moon*. Segal plays Brooks Wilson, a commercial illustrator who's no longer nourished by either his work or his family. Saint is his wife, Selma, who takes care of him, feeds him, takes his phone messages, serves him coffee, cleans it up when he carelessly spills the cup down the stairs—and tries vainly to supply the energy he no longer appears to have to keep the family in some semblance of happy motion. In a telling scene early on, he poses Selma and himself as Civil War lovers for a photograph he needs for one of his illustrations. Setting her upright in bed in an embrace, he runs back to the camera, abandoning her with empty arms while he rigs it, and you can see Selma's fear that she's stuck in a pose emblematic of their marriage, that she's powerless to stop him from slipping away from her. She doesn't know he's promised Grace (Janis Young), the secretary he's been sleeping with, that he'll get a divorce as soon as he's won the big account his firm is wooing. *He* doesn't know himself whether he'll really go through with it, but keeps pulling away from Selma. And as the movie goes on, Saint shows us how his aloofness and on-again, off-again sensitivity toward her wears holes in her humor and patience, and how she alternates between growing anger and futile attempts to draw him back to her.

Saint, her voice scratchier, more broken-up than in the glory days of *On the Waterfront*, uses that lovely balance of glamor and self-effacement to suggest both Selma's dependence on Brooks to define her existence, and her increasing acknowledgment that she deserves better than he's giving her. Like Beth, the young wife Ellen Barkin plays in *Diner*, Selma is caught in the last gasps of the prefeminist era: The movie may be set in 1970 (as opposed to *Diner*'s 1959), but Selma began raising her family before consciousnesses were raised (and no doubt she went about it the way her mother taught her). She senses there's something wrong with the way her life is going, but she doesn't have the experience of self-confidence to give her suspicions expression, so she keeps banging her head against the wall.

And unfortunately she's in love with her husband. When he comes home drunk from the city, won't confide in her the latest developments at work, and then walks away from the dinner she's kept warm for him (to throw up), Saint swoops down on the plate and swoops it up in hands bent like claws. A few moments later she struggles to glide them both over this ragged patch by trying to lure him into bed, but he opts to stay up and work—and *now* he wants to know if there's anything to eat. Yes, this is domestic comedy, but it's laced with the pain of people who have lost touch with each other. And the two actors, often with just a few lines or in silence, sketch in the thousand tiny disappointments that constitute the Wilsons' marriage.

Saint has her best scenes in the second half of the picture. In one, set in a department store, Selma models a dress for her husband, and her childish insistence on his approval—"Shall I keep it?" she asks, adding a heartbreaking, involuntary little nod—shows us how desperate Selma is for a lover's appreciation of her appearance. Making up for a party, she questions him about the house they looked at that afternoon, and when he calls it "a thirty-year trap," she (rightly) interprets his remark as a comment on their marriage, slams the medicine cabinet shut, and finally locks her anger into place. In the car, she roars into an argument that only stops when he declares a cease-fire for the duration of the party. Later, she has second thoughts and, relying on the sexual compatibility that's clearly been a cornerstone of their relationship, she tries to get him to take her home. But he's too screwed up to know how to respond to her advances: He *thinks* he wants Grace, who is leaving for Europe, and when she puts him off he ends up making love to a neighbor (Nancie Phillips) in the nursery.

Saint is phenomenal in the scene where one of the party guests inadvertently switches on the host's camera in the den to record the activity in the nursery and within minutes the surprise real-life sex show has become the evening's prime entertainment. Another actress would do something conventional here—cry or turn away or look around frantically for a hiding place. Saint's choice is to fling one arm onto her neck, as if she'd suddenly noticed her dress was too tight; she's frozen in place, her face creased with acute physical distress. When she and Brooks are alone on the street at the end, she begins to

234

whip him with her purse. Then she stops, still shaking, half bent over. Saint turns Selma's emotions into actions; she physicalizes them. Watching her in these last couple of scenes is a lesson in how Method technique can transform a potential soap opera moment into a small, bloody stretch of real life.

Kim Hunter

Despite all the praise she received in the stage and film versions of *A Streetcar Named Desire* (she won the Best Supporting Actress Oscar in 1951), Kim Hunter usually gets passed over in discussions of the members of the Actors Studio generation; if you mention her, people often assume you're talking about Kim Stanley. But Hunter's credible, understated style is actually the opposite of Stanley's. Over the years she's shown up in surprising places—notably as one of the simian scientists in *Planet of the Apes* (where she gave a spry performance under pounds of make-up)—but she hasn't had many good roles. The best medium for examining how she puts the Method to work is still her portrayal of Stella Kowalski in *Streetcar*.

In his director's notebook on the play, Elia Kazan says that Stella's "spine" is to keep Stanley at all costs.[3] But though Hunter makes it clear that she'll eventually choose him over Blanche, the most interesting element in her performance is the suggestion that it's not such an easy choice. Most actresses who have played Stella since—including some fine ones, like Frances McDormand in the 1988 revival at New York's Circle in the Square—have emphasized Stella's languid, sassy side, concentrating on the qualities in this woman that make her a match for Stanley. Hunter's approach, a mixture of light humor, maternal warmth, and sensitivity (which balances both Brando's little-boy Stanley and Vivien Leigh's coming-apart, feverishly needy Blanche), and reserves of toughness, is to occupy a space somewhere between the two protagonists.

In the disastrous birthday party scene, where she vents her rage at Stanley for his cruelty to Blanche by criticizing his table manners, Hunter shows traces of the aristocratic temperament that drew him to her—so he could satisfy his urge to, as he puts it, pull her down off the pillars of her privileged southern upbringing. She's patient with Blanche's outbursts, which she recognizes from their childhood relationship ("Go on, Blanche, say it all," she assents, like a little sister who knows she's in for a lecture). And she's instinctively sympathetic to Blanche's needs: Hunter has a lovely moment when, hearing her sister wish for a future with Mitch, she pushes loyally past the implausibility that those two could ever sustain a romance and assures her, "It *will* happen, honey!"

But Stella has to align herself, finally, with her husband, and Williams specifies that she does so out of a deep satisfaction with him as a lover. Kazan says she's "narcotized" by Stanley's lovemaking.[4] The most enjoyable part of Hunter's performance is the tender and unmistakable suggestion that Stella is breathlessly appreciative of Stanley's sexual raucousness—the way she points him out to Blanche in the bowling alley ("He's the one making all the rhubarb," laughing to herself over his cock-of-the-walk noisiness); the intensity in her voice when she talks about how much she misses him when he's away overnight. And the scene where Blanche finds her lolling happily in bed the morning after Stanley hit her, boasting of his strength when, in a drunken temper, he hurled her radio out the window, is as funny a bit of postcoital coziness as Vivien Leigh's in *Gone with the Wind* after Clark Gable's left *her* bed.

In some of her work from this era, Hunter suffers at the hands of weak directors. As the fed-up wife of a weakling (Mel Tormé) in "The Comedian," a celebrated 1957 entry in the "Playhouse 90" anthology series, she has a certain fiery energy, but the camera seems to catch her at all the wrong moments. It's the one time I've seen her overwrought, excessive, and neurotic in the Methody style of some of her contemporaries. John Frankenheimer, the director of "The Comedian," also uses her awkwardly in his motion picture debut, *The Young Stranger* (a remake of a TV drama). She brings her trademark softness to the role of rebellious teen James MacArthur's glamorous mother (she's the only sympathetic grown-up in the movie), but her performance lacks the rhythm a more experienced director would help her get.

Hunter is seen to better advantage in another television drama, "Requiem for a Heavyweight" (1956), with Jack Palance, Keenan Wynn, and Ed Wynn. She plays Grace, the employment counselor who becomes involved with Palance's Mountain McClintock, a has-been heavyweight fighter. Here, as in *Streetcar*, you see how she can use her empathic gifts (her ability to extend herself emotionally to other actors) dramatically, and the realistic grounding of Method

236

acting—the close, intent listening that's part of the training—to make a quiet statement about her character. In her first scene with Mc-Clintock she focuses vividly on his words but retains a cool distance from him. It turns out to be a function of her professionalism: As the scene goes on she climbs over the invisible line she's drawn between them, after he slams his hand down on her desk to underscore the urgency of his situation, and she becomes consoling, maternal, concerned that he's hurt himself. When Julie Harris took over this role in the 1962 movie version (opposite Anthony Quinn) she came off as drab; you could tell she was burying a part of herself to play this kind, limited woman. You missed the neurotic spark in Harris, the poetry. Kim Hunter isn't a great actress like Harris at her best, but she has a gift for giving characters like Stella and Grace—unspectacular women, women who are complacent (Stella) or even a little dull (Grace)—a sympathetic glow.

Rod Steiger

Along with Brando and James Dean, Rod Steiger has the most instantly recognizable style of any of the Actors Studio performers. He tends to speak in a honey-coated, weirdly energized whine punctuated by heavy sighs (meant to suggest worlds of sorrowful experience, as well as an obvious superiority to the person he's talking to) and occasional stutters. In a fit the stutter may even be staccato, and he can suggest tremendous destructive power behind it. He often concludes a line with a melodramatic tremolo—a hand-me-down from turn-of-the-century Yiddish theater. He has incredible vocal control: One of his trademarks is to build to a blasting crescendo, talking a mile a minute all the while, and then skillfully undercut it, letting the wind out of his own sails without sacrificing an inch of the menace underneath. He acts with his big, sagging frame and his mouth muscles; no one has ever made disgust (Steiger's favorite emotional response) as hilariously palpable. Fiercely excitable, even frenzied, he's like a superanimated, outsize leprechaun. An overstated sardonic sense of humor colors almost every role he's ever played. And he's an incorrigible ham, a terrifically gifted one, with a penchant for indulging his own delight in Method trickery. (He makes superb comic use of this hamminess, especially in *The Big Knife* and *In the Heat of the Night*.) Clownishly

237

overheated in movies like *The Harder They Fall*, where he plays a fight promoter, he camps outrageously for the camera, like Brando in his costume parts: When he gives a pep talk to a boxer he's handling (Mike Lane), there's so much heavy breathing he sounds as if he were jogging at the same time.

It would be inaccurate to say Steiger's always a clown, though. In fact, there are few categorical statements you can make about Steiger that hold true for all the work he's done, because he's had a more bizarrely checkered career than any other Method actor. In the early 1950s it was said that the toughest task facing a director who worked with him was to keep him from bursting into tears, and if you watch something like "Other People's Houses," a 1953 "Goodyear Playhouse" segment, you can believe it: He weeps just about every two minutes. But it's his dry-eyed sweetness, as well as his good-humored beefiness, that makes "Marty," televised the same year, as enjoyable as it is— God knows it isn't the Paddy Chayefsky script. And that was the role that made his reputation. (Chayefsky wrote it for Martin Ritt, but Ritt was blacklisted at the time and NBC couldn't get a clearance for him.)

Steiger is entertainingly emphatic in both *On the Waterfront*, as Terry Malloy's brother, Charlie the Gent (personal lawyer to gangster Johnny Friendly—a smoothly up-to-date version of that stereotype, the brains of the gang, who wears specs as well as a vicuña coat and a handsome fedora) and *The Big Knife* (where he appears in short platinum hair and shades, playing with his manicured fingers), as Hoff, the vicious, intractable, megalomaniac studio head. *The Big Knife*, with its Clifford Odets script, is a nifty medium for Steiger's *shtick;* he has line readings that are as funny and memorable as Tony Curtis's in Odets's other wonderfully overwrought fifties tale of corruption, *Sweet Smell of Success*. When Hoff tells his current victim, actor Charlie Castle, played by Jack Palance, to ask his wife to leave—"Why does the woman have to be here?"—he makes "woman" sound vaguely like "whore." And he cracks you up when he blinks his eyes, twists his mouth around, and hisses, "Psychoanalysis! Psychoanalysis!" and when he tells the rebelling Castle, "Charles, Charles, I am going to have to take this very much amiss." But he's loose and relaxed in a movie like *The Mark* (1961), where he plays an unconventional shrink who's treating Stuart Whitman. And he's capable of giving a completely straight performance that never leaks beyond the boundaries of character and period (*The Pawnbroker, Doctor Zhivago*).

In the late 1960s, Steiger fell into a decline. His mannerisms had become so familiar, and he'd begun to use them so predictably, that he lost the element of surprise that powered his best work in the 1950s and the mid–1960s, and the hugeness of his presence became tiresome. However, when you least expected it, he'd suddenly turn around and hand in a trim, restrained piece of acting, as he did as the lawman in Lamont Johnson's (almost unknown) 1980 comedy–western charmer, *Cattle Annie and Little Britches*.

One thing is certain, however: Steiger hit his peak between 1965 and 1967, when he played—back-to-back—concentration camp survivor Sol Nazerman, adrift in New York, in *The Pawnbroker;* the deft seducer Victor Komarovsky in David Lean's Russian Revolution epic *Doctor Zhivago;* and the redneck southern sheriff in *In the Heat of the Night*—three superb performances in roles that couldn't be less alike. *The Pawnbroker* is Steiger's fiercest moment. Sidney Lumet's film, with a script by David Friedkin and Morton Fine (based on a novel by Edward Lewis Wallant), is far from subtle; every scene in it feels like it was worked over long before the actors got hold of it. And, with its intercutting between Nazerman's experiences in the pawnshop and on the streets of the city, and the memories of Auschwitz he's using all his energy to suppress, it sure works *you* over. Lumet places Nazerman behind a counter, with bars on either side to protect the merchandise— and to protect Nazerman from the wrecks who come into his shop every day. His profession is awfully symbolic. He takes the shreds of people's lives they offer him and pays them the bare minimum, ignoring the personal value they attach to them, just as he, as destitute as any of them, refuses to acknowledge his own humanity.

But there's no use pretending this picture doesn't have power. I was all set to see it on its release, when I was fourteen; but my mother got to it first, and I'd never seen her so unmoored by a movie. She was upset for days. And when I finally watched it myself, many years later, I understood why: Between its bull's attack on the extremely volatile subject matter, and Steiger's amazing acting, it scrapes you raw. And in some way, everything that's wrong with it—its obviousness, Lumet's close-in technique, the mid-sixties visual jazziness (to match the jazz score), the symbolism—works for it in terms of emotional force.

Steiger uses his bulk as insulation in this role—against the world and, in vain, against what's inside him. His flabby face is like dead cells, and when he speaks he has a fastidious, chilled-out evenness that's terrifying. The concentration camp has tortured him into this state of nonfeeling, this walking death; even in sex (he sleeps with the widow of an old friend) he's numb, automatic. We want Nazerman to plunge into himself and dredge up some human response to the horrors he sees around him (the violence outside, the desperation of his clients inside), but the spaces between his lines are so ominous that we're scared of what might be in him. And we're right to be. When his assistant, Jesus (Jaime Sanchez), asks him to explain the Jewish gift for business, Saul reveals a blinding, poisonous anger. And there's a thick lining of pain behind everything we see in him—his distractedness (when he tells one client, a strung-out, anemic girl, that the diamond ring she's trying to pawn is only glass), his exhaustion (sitting on a couch, his head thrown back, eyes closed under his glasses)—that we know implies much more. When something outside him triggers a memory—when a whore who bares her breasts (hoping to seduce him into paying her more for her goods) reminds him of his wife, whom he saw forced into the humiliation of servicing a Nazi officer—scalding tears pour out of him. He clenches his fist and points it at his own face, furious at himself for letting her penetrate the barrier he's put up inside.

At the end, Nazerman lets his guard down and reacts emotionally to Jesus's death during a robbery at the shop (unfortunately, the assistant is a Christ figure who dies to liberate Saul's humanity). He's like a man who has nearly died from third-degree burns: He's covered with dead tissue, but once something gets through it all and connects to the living nerves underneath, the pain is more than it seems any human could bear.

Steiger gives a magnificently controlled performance with almost no false notes. Perhaps only one: the cry of horror, when he remembers his son's death, has a hollow theatricality. On the other hand, when his face contorts into a silent scream at Jesus's death, the fact that we can see how Steiger creates this moment dramatically doesn't diminish it, because he takes it so much farther than we could have imagined. (There's a similar effect in *The Trojan Women*—Vanessa Redgrave's scream when her child is torn from her by soldiers—that loses none of its power even though we've seen the actress prepare it.)

Steiger exudes intelligence in the role of Komarovsky in *Doctor Zhivago*. It's that shrewd kind of intelligence that takes everything in; you're sharply aware of this man's brain ticking behind his darting eyes. According to the program notes for the movie, the character is "an opportunist who survives all regimes"; he's also a master seducer who discovers the sexual possibilities of Lara (Julie Christie), his mistress's daughter. As Steiger plays him, his pervasive sexuality is his great motivating force—you see it especially in the scene where he appraises Lara's looks in her mother's shop and throws a veil over her, recognizing she's grown into dazzling adulthood; and in the scene where he takes her out in her first long gown (an episode the filmmakers, David Lean and Robert Bolt, borrowed from both *War and Peace* and *Gigi*).

But Komarovsky's sexuality isn't all there is; he's full of surprises. Steiger shows his complex panic when Lara's mother attempts suicide: He's concerned for her *and* afraid of the scandalous consequences. There's a tense, scary, superbly played scene in which, warning Lara that a marriage to the revolutionary Pasha (Tom Courtenay) would be a disaster because he's a virgin and she's a whore, he tries to prove his point by raping her. And when, late in the picture, he shows up after a long absence to offer her sugar for the child she bore him, he makes something forceful and memorable out of a reprobate's fury: His anger at her for refusing his help has an undercurrent of desperation. The movie suffers when he's off screen; he and Christie are its lifelines.

Steiger deserved the Academy Award he won in 1967 for his portrayal of Sheriff Gillespie in Norman Jewison's comic detective thriller *In the Heat of the Night*. In this deeply satisfying good-liberal picture, he does his most graceful and at-ease acting in the role of the arrogant lawman in a small southern town who fumbles a murder case but blunders into an authentic moral education. Sidney Poitier plays Virgil Tibbs, the northerner Gillespie's men arrest at the train station on a murder charge because he's black and a stranger. Tibbs turns out to be a confident big-city homicide detective who (at first reluctantly, then out of anger and pride, and finally out of professional excitement) becomes Gillespie's special guest partner and solves the crime.

Steiger and Poitier, actors whose individual timing can be nearly miraculous, are superb together. But Steiger's performance is the mechanism that makes the movie run. He plays a man who's inured himself to all the inadequacies and incompetence in the crummy town of Sparta, yet yells routinely at those around and under him for screwing up (though he doesn't really expect anything better)—it gives him a grousing kind of pleasure that he's superior to the rest of them. What makes us care about him is that, though he makes the dumbest mistakes himself and keeps jumping to conclusions, he's capable of learning, and decent enough to shift perspective, however grumblingly, when he sees he's been wrong. The awkward friendship that grows up between him and Tibbs, which the movie has the good sense to treat comically, is the fruit of his altered point of view. The filmmakers (the script is by Stirling Silliphant) go out of their way to show us that he's also a lonely man, eking out a miserable solo existence, but that's melodrama—an attempt to wring sympathy out of us. Steiger does it legitimately.

This performance is the best example of Steiger's penchant for distilling comedy from his Method training—from his deep focus when he listens, the way he allows things to dawn on him *really* gradually. Even his relaxation is funny: He sits back in his office chair, spreads his legs, and throws one up on his desk, using his size without embarrassment as part of his comic equipment. He's a Deputy Dawg kind of sheriff, with a smoking southern accent that's purest ham. He chews gum chronically and manically. His slow, broad grin is a caution. And he has sudden eruptions of emotion, like a popgun going off. The moments you tend to remember most vividly years after seeing the picture are the way he yells, "Yeah! Oh, yeah!" when his moronic deputy (Warren Oates) sees Virgil's badge for the first time; his sarcasm on a phrase like "Fine!" or "Thank *you*!"; and his salutation when he picks up the phone—"Yeah, talk to me"—which my moviegoing high-school friends quoted for months after the film came out. Or his exaggerated patience when he asks the receptionist what he knows is an unlikely request: "Courtney, would you *try* and get me long distance?" And Steiger transforms Gillespie's defensiveness into an aggressive put-on style.

It's a triumphant performance, the pinnacle of Steiger's great period. Unfortunately, it was also the end of it. Though he worked constantly over the next couple of years, his choice of film projects (*No Way to Treat a Lady, The Illustrated Man, Three into Two Won't Go, The Sergeant*, etc.) didn't help him, and he ended up unbankable in Hollywood, working abroad much of the time in second-rate French and Italian pictures. He's shown up intermittently in the last decade and a half, but only once to advantage—in *Cattle Annie*. And no one went to see him in it.

Rip Torn

The name "Rip Torn" sounds like something out of the Andy Warhol factory, but it belongs to one of the most fiercely gifted and exasperatingly underrated actors in the country—and the man who was married to Geraldine Page, in what must have been the most intense Method marriage since Harold Clurman and Stella Adler. Both are seasoned comedians with a lively, unorthodox sense of humor. But if Page's specialty was uncorseted, neurotic spinster roles, Torn's is playing amoral bastards with a shrewd appreciation of how to gain power in a corrupt world, and a blissful enjoyment of the pleasures that power can get you. Torn may not be a household word, but he's the character actor you always remember—in movies like *The Seduction of Joe Tynan*, where he plays a senator—because he's got sex in his eyes and a permanent erection. When we first see him in *Joe Tynan*, he's telling fellow politico Alan Alda an outrageous story about having sex in an airplane. He's got a deep, very clean vocal delivery—he thrusts his lines out like a bass singing an aria—and he's incredibly high-spirited, a wild, screaming party animal who always boogies with the most obviously available woman in the room and gets cheerfully laid in his office during coffee breaks. (In one scene his aide walks in while a young woman under Torn's desk is attending to that erection.)

Like Page, Torn has done his share of Tennessee Williams. His early movies include *Baby Doll*, where he has one ticklish scene as a fresh-faced young dentist, sporting a smile that manages to be both bashful and sexually explicit, flirting with Carroll Baker while her husband (Karl Malden) is in the office across the hall; and *Sweet Bird of Youth*, where he looks slim and feral and uses the first of many burnt-to-a-crisp southern accents. In the 1985 TV revival of *Cat on a Hot Tin Roof*, looking like a magpie with his funny hooked nose, his mouth turned way down, and his chin pulled out, he plays Big Daddy as Burl Ives never played him—as a mean son-of-a-bitch who chomps on a black runt of a cigar (it could be his emblem) and carries his brutishness and commonness around like medals. It's a terrible production, but Torn grabs hold of the character and plays the hell out of him; sinfully showy, with his sneaky ironies and sour little grin, he manages to breathe a little life into at least his first scenes.

We can believe this rich planter didn't get an education: He's practically semiarticulate. Torn leaves Williams's long speeches like unplowed fields, tracking through the mud of the language without bothering to clarify or define it, twisting the lines out of shape, rushing up to odd pauses in the middle and then abruptly spitting the ends out, stretching one of his words taut and then snapping the next one like a slingshot. (I love the way he asks his son Brick, played by Tommy Lee Jones, "Were you cuttin' yourself a piece o' poontang?"—pausing before "poontang" and savoring it, sucking all the dirty juice he can out of the first consonant.) Mostly what's wrong with the play is that the characters are so unappealing that we don't give a damn what happens to any of them. Torn is honest enough to cut through the Burl Ives ingratiating-crude-bulk-of-a-man bull and play Big Daddy as the most unattractive of them all, but that means we get fed up with him a lot sooner. Besides, there's no one behind the camera exerting any control over Torn, who finally slobbers over so much scenery that we can't watch him any more.

Torn is usually great fun to look at, even in very small roles, and he's given a couple of brilliant film performances. He's ferociously good in Daryl Duke's 1973 *Payday*, playing country singer Maury Dann, whose last few days are the film's focus. The combination of Duke's carefully distanced approach and sharp, documentarian's eye, and screenwriter Don Carpenter's ear for revealing details of diction and vocal style, brings us close enough to Torn's morally repellent Maury to see how he works, but not close enough to inhabit his skin; the filmmakers want us to stay outside him, examining him as if he's an extraordinary contemporary specimen. The movie is definitely a cool experience, but a memorable one. The filmmakers aren't moralists (they're not pulling back to make a judgment on Maury) but rather fascinated observers. (Viewed again after all these years, *Payday*— which went almost unnoticed on its release—forms a telling comparison with another country-singer tale, the overrated 1983 *Tender Mercies*. In the latter picture the central character, played by Robert Duvall, is inexpressive, and there's nothing underneath the film's gritty naturalistic surface.)

As Torn plays him, Dann is an impossible, spoiled child. He thrives on life on the road because it satisfies his restlessness and his greed (he knows there's money to be made that way), but also because he's a sensual creature who grooves on temporary satisfactions. ("We only pass this way once. Might as well pass by in a Cadillac" is his motto.) And he knows he can pick up everything that gives him that kind of pleasure on the road—booze, dope, the sort of sex he can dive into and then discard at his whim. (He throws one mistress, played by Ahna Capri, out of his limo in the middle of the highway.) He's the performer as master consumer: He throws everything away, even his loyal driver Ted (Cliff Emmich), whom he allows to be murdered without a second thought to save his own ass. That's the chilling underside to the smiling, sexy Maury Dann appeal.

And Dann *is* appealing, on stage *and* off. On stage, he's got a fouled-up talk–singing style that gruffly refuses to sit on the actual notes (or to admit how much fun singing is), sort of like Leonard Cohen's or Neil Young's. It's a style that announces, "Music doesn't have to be pretty to be good." Maury adds languor; he makes debased art out of his own enervation. Off stage his boundless delight at the very idea of sex is a turn-on to the people around him. He loves to screw, but he gets almost as much fun out of the thought of other people engaged in sex or of other people's voyeurism. In one scene, getting off in the back of the limo, he comes up for air like a champion swimmer who's done his laps, his hair mischievously awry, sees a pair of teenage girls in a passing car, and grins at them. He even enjoys watching other people *thinking* about sex: He catches one of the members of his band ogling his current hick girl friend (Elayne Heilveil), and you can see his mind conjuring up what's bound to go on between these two. (The next morning he gets a kick out of marching in on them and rousing the musician out of bed so they can go bird shooting.) And though he's cold and cynical, there's a mock gallantry to his sexual approach which drags women under (that and his bottomless enjoyment of sex): When he touches Capri's thigh and tells her, "Time to go courtin', lady," you can see her melt. "I love you, sweet man," she tells him after they've made love; and his enigmatic, cooled-out reply is "Thank you, dear."

Maury's used to getting what he wants right away. He throws tantrums when he's denied. On a whim, he makes Ted drive him to the house of the wife he rarely visits, and when he sees her in bed with another man, he heaves a rock through her bedroom window and yahoos like a wild bird. When he throws a fit he twists his face into weird contortions, trying to exorcise his anger by stylizing it, giving it a grotesque shape and then detaching himself from it. And he's capable of extremely ugly, almost sociopathic behavior: When he wants to remove someone from his life (like a musician friend who insists on keeping a dog Maury can't stand), he gets an antisocial look on his face—half-irritated, half-furious—and we know we're seeing the blunt end of something.

Maury can get any woman into bed, but he can't make the simplest human connections with people; there's a dead circuit somewhere inside him. And his loneliness and boredom are unstoppable, unfathomable, scary. In one haunting scene, unable to sleep or even calm down, hating his own company but too mean and blue to want anyone else around him either, he gets up in the middle of the night, swigs bourbon, and writes a song. He works very hard at staying unconscious (the sex, the drugs, the drinking, the whirlwind of the road, the childish games), but there's always something bothering him that he can't get at, and all the anesthetics do for him is keep him from figuring out what the hell it is.

As an actor, Torn is as devious as Maury Dann is elusive; he has a way with a line that seems to hit it squarely but really ducks under it and smashes it on the rebound. (His timing is weird and wonderful.) A good example is the moment when a club manager tells Maury that the next time he appears there, the owner will want a piece of the gate, and Maury replies, "People in hell want ice water, too." And as Marsh Turner, the backwoods farmer in Martin Ritt's 1983 *Cross Creek*, Torn's readings (which are always a little sodden) have a rhythm all their own. Nobody else could say "Somebody shot my pig" with the same ripped, rolling glide he gives it; it tumbles out of his mouth and sits in the air, curiously lopsided, balanced precariously on its own eccentric shape.

Nothing could be farther from the malevolent-Pan showboating Torn specializes in than this performance, which has a comic nobility and a passionate expansiveness that surpass anything he's shown before. At first he seems to be doing a variation on the country fool type who's more wised up than his sophisticated city neighbor (Marjorie Rawlings—the author who comes to live and write at Cross Creek—played by an oddly prim, certainly miscast Mary Steenburgen). But he takes it so much farther that you can barely see the bones of the stereotype underneath. Shooting a snake at Marjorie's dock and hurling it into the woods, he goes off like firecrackers. He whoops hoarsely and challenges her with light banter and one eyebrow cocked; when she beats him (by shooting his hog), he's red-faced, his brow creased, but he admits defeat and lets it roll off him. Constantly knocking back moonshine, he's a sloshed cavalier; astride his horse, swinging back in his merry drunkenness, grasping the reins like the bar of a roller coaster to keep himself from sliding off (he leans back so far he's really tempting gravity—you're not sure just how the hell he stays on that horse), he's a hick Don Quixote, transported smilingly.

But we get to see the reality that makes him drink: land that's stubborn to yield; children to feed; a crazy wife with delusions of grandeur whom he adores and treats with a delicate gallantry that could break your heart. (When he kisses her, he reaches behind her head as he leans over her, as if he were afraid she'd fall over.) Marsh has a deep patience born of grief and poverty, and a wisdom born of a sense of balance with his difficult, hand-to-mouth, rural world. Underneath these qualities is a profound sorrow we see when he gently escorts Marjorie away from his farm as soon as his wife's peculiarities start to pop out; and when he speaks of her to Marjorie ("She's slippin' away from us—she's found a more peaceful world").

Marsh's lifeblood is his relationship with his daughter Ellie (the fine young actress Dana Hill). He loves her too much to deny her the one thing he can give her and knows she shouldn't have—the right to keep a yearling, Flag, as a pet. The scenes between Torn and Hill are so good they even overtake your memory of Clarence Brown's 1946 treatment of this material, *The Yearling* (which is in every other way a far superior movie); the actors infuse them with some of the complexity and painfully unresolvable knottedness that Hill and Albert Finney gave to the father–daughter scenes in the previous year's *Shoot the Moon*. Marsh knows that making a pet out of the animal is unfair to it, and that it takes food out of the family's mouths (Ellie sacrifices her own portions for Flag). But he can't bear to see his daughter unhappy. He accedes to her requests, though you can see how the decision tears him apart.

When Flag gets loose and does some damage, he lets her persuade him to keep the animal one last time, venting his anger in the only way he can (by smashing a chair against a table); his face is puffed up with his love for her and his understanding that he's going to end up shooting the animal. (It's Ellie's birthday. That's symbolic: As Marjorie tells us repeatedly, the yearling represents the childhood Ellie doesn't want to leave behind quite yet.) Torn turns this section of *Cross Creek* into Marsh Turner's tragedy. When, inevitably, Flag breaks out of its pen again, he marches out to kill it while Ellie grabs hold of his leg, trying to stop him. He knows he's killing their relationship, too, and later he tells Marjorie, "It'll never be the same again." His own useless death shortly afterwards, at the hands of the sheriff, is a virtual suicide.

Hardly anyone has seen Torn's work in *Payday* or *Cross Creek*, even though the first is remarkable and the second touches greatness. The terrible character roles he does to keep solvent (he's forever showing up on some dreary TV movie of the week as a psycho or a Nazi) don't provide a clue to his gift for comedy or—as his Marsh Turner demonstrates—for tragedy. Rip Torn remains one of American acting's best-kept secrets.

10

JASON ROBARDS: THE METHOD AS INSTINCT

◆ ◆ ◆

The basic elements of Method, really, are just horsesense. They humanize acting. You know that you've just been somewhere which makes you come into a scene in a certain way. You know you want something of the people you're playing the scene with. You know that want can be achieved only under certain conditions. So, the director has to set the conditions under which that want can be achieved. . . . Any good director uses them. You have to use them with an actor like Jason Robards who says, "Method? Shit! Just tell me what button you want me to push! The angry button? The sad button?"

—Elia Kazan[1]

Method acting isn't necessarily just a matter of getting the right training—working with the right teachers. If it were, what Barbara Stanwyck and Sylvia Sidney did instinctively in their 1930s movies would be much different from what John Garfield did after a few years in the Group Theatre, and the evidence of our eyes and ears tell us it's not. Similarly, there's no good reason for including David Wayne or John Forsythe, who took classes at the Actors Studio, in a list of Method actors and excluding Robert Ryan, who never walked in the door. No performance I've ever seen from John Forsythe suggests Method drive and conviction, but Ryan's work in movies like *Caught, Clash by Night, The Wild Bunch*, and *The Iceman Cometh* explodes with it. The same might be said about the best performances by Jason Robards.

Jason Robards isn't famous for making wisecracks about the Method (like Laurence Olivier), or for sneering at Lee Strasberg (like George C. Scott), but it's clear from his remark above that he's never considered himself a Method actor. And in a way his stentorian cracked bass, his glowering, Lincolnesque face, and his gift for caricature, which lies midway between Dickens and vaudeville, can be seen as a link to the most glorious of the pre–Method matinee idols, Walter Huston and John Barrymore. But the Robards movie and TV audiences are most familiar with—the playful character actor from pictures like *All the President's Men* and *Julia,* the scene-stealing guest who drops by in a celebrity role like Ben Bradlee or Dashiell Hammett to lend the party a little class—doesn't bear much resemblance to the Robards who is the world's greatest interpreter of Eugene O'Neill. And it's the latter Robards, who feels a mystical connection to O'Neill's protagonists and sounds the depths of his soul (and his own alcoholism) to find the roles of Jamie Tyrone in *Long Day's Journey into Night* and Hickey in *The Iceman Cometh* and Jim Tyrone in *A Moon for the Misbegotten* in himself, who's the true Method actor. The process he undergoes to discover these characters may be a subconscious—instinctive— application of the Method, but there's no more powerful example, this side of Marlon Brando, of how the process works.

Eugene O'Neill wasn't intimately involved in the development of the American Method, as Odets and Miller and Tennessee Williams were; his plays don't readily present themselves as texts for actors trained at the Group Theatre or the Actors Studio. But the three masterpieces that climaxed his career—*The Iceman Cometh, Long Day's Journey into Night,* and *A Moon for the Misbegotten*—are still the most rigorous emotional workouts any playwright has ever devised for American performers, and they arrived (one of them posthumously) during that decade after the war when the Method was altering the shape of the American theater. (*Iceman,* written in 1939, was first performed in 1946; *Misbegotten,* written between 1941 and 1943, received its first production in 1947; *Long Day's Journey,* completed in 1941, finally made it to the stage in 1956.) And *Iceman* really deserves to be thought of as O'Neill's tribute to the American actor. It's the most democratic of plays: Everyone who crosses the stage, except for the cops who hear Hickey's confession in the final act, has a motivating force and ten minutes (at least) in the limelight to display it. *Iceman* isn't an ensemble piece like *Awake and Sing!* or *Camino Real;* it's more of a vaudeville show, with the actors making their contributions in turns. (William Saroyan's barroom tragicomedy, *The Time of Your Life,* also written in 1939, falls into this category too.) And what a magnificent vaudeville show—with Death and Destiny booked to perform the final numbers.

250

O'Neill's career was astounding. When he entered the theater in the 1910s, writing one-acts for the fledgling Provincetown Players, his impressionistic *S. S. Glencairn* cycle reflected the commitment of his predecessors (playwrights like James Herne and William Gillette, and producers like David Belasco) to reproduce real life as accurately as possible on the stage. During the 1920s and early 1930s, having gulped down the influences of the Symbolists and the Expressionists, the Freudians and the Primitives, O'Neill conducted a series of experiments with masks and interior monologues, with characters who dramatized the fragmentation of personality and scenes that stood for way stations in the inner journeys of his protagonists, with enormous casts and oversized plays. Other American dramatists were testing the same European waters, but while Elmer Rice and Irwin Shaw were content to stick a foot in, O'Neill tried the most fantastic high dives: *The Emperor Jones, The Hairy Ape, The Great God Brown, Marco Millions, Strange Interlude, Lazarus Laughed, Mourning Becomes Electra.* Some of these plays weren't very good, but they were all the kind of lunatic endeavors that make theater history. And all this time O'Neill was developing his themes—the necessity of illusion, the mother and the whore, the inescapability of the family, the division between the social and private selves—and slowly acquiring a steely control of craft that no American writing for the stage, before or since, has equalled. He had that control by the time he returned to naturalism with *The Iceman Cometh.* The play wasn't produced until 1946 because O'Neill sensed that wartime audiences would want no part of anything so relentless and bleak. And at that time it was sufficiently advanced to forefront the new psychological realism in vogue in those Freudian days.

In *Iceman*, O'Neill hasn't yet attained the sublime transcendence of craft we find in *Journey* and *Moon for the Misbegotten;* his dramatic strategies keep calling attention to themselves. There are the perfect-square, four-act structure, and the parallel patterns of disillusionment and resurrection in the sodden baker's dozen buried in the back room of Harry Hope's bar. There's the solemn presentation, complete with evangelical flourishes, of the Gospel According to Saint Hickey, the fast-talking salesman who claims to be handing his buddies their souls by forcing them to confront the impossibility of their booze-fed dreams of the future but who, we realize as O'Neill's immense dramatic machinery makes one last quarter-turn, is in fact selling them the same death that's infected his own home.

251

It's easy to find fault with this play. Mary McCarthy, writing of the original (and, by most accounts, inadequate) New York production directed by Eddie Dowling, compared it to the hardware Hickey flogs from day to day: "Ugly, durable, mysteriously utilitarian, this work gives the assurance that it has been manufactured by a reliable company; it is guaranteed to last two-and-a-half hours longer than any other play, with the exception of the uncut *Hamlet*."[2] She called O'Neill "a tone-deaf musician" and (along with James Farrell and Theodore Dreiser) "among the few contemporary American writers who know how to exhaust a subject. . . . Their logical graceless works can find no reason for stopping, but go on and on, like elephants pacing in a zoo."[3]

But McCarthy's witty dissection of *Iceman*, like all the other attacks leveled at O'Neill because of the length of his plays or their repetitive nature or their banal dialogue, misses the point. It's really the point of all American naturalism: that its thoroughness, its familiarity, its obsessive recreation of American life in all its commonplace detail, are the very elements that give it its power. In the most rewarding productions of his best plays, O'Neill's private agonies and those of his family, whose pain and conflict fueled all of his late work, spill into the audience and illuminate our voyages into our own private hells. And when Jason Robards plays Hickey, or Jamie or Jim Tyrone, he has so absorbed and personalized those agonies that he becomes the medium through which we link ourselves to the play. The fact that we can't distinguish between Robards and these characters makes our own identification with O'Neill's truths—about lives lived out desperately in the shelter of illusion, about the way family ties function as addictions, about death-in-life and the meager and miraculous chances for salvation—more immediate and binding.

O'Neill's early plays are crammed with stage directions that might very well baffle a naturalistic actor. A student of Yeats and Craig, an avid reader of Charles Sheeler on African sculpture, he was obsessed with masks, and even when he didn't call for them outright in performance (as he did in *Marco Millions*, *The Great God Brown*, and *Lazarus Laughed*), *Beyond the Horizon*, *The Hairy Ape*, and *Mourning Becomes Electra* often demand (in stage directions) that the actors hold their faces in mask-like poses. These masks are meant to abstract and dramatize the concept of social façades that protect our vulnerabilities, keeping them under wraps from the wounding glances of others. This idea is explored in a fiendishly complicated way in *The Great God*

Brown, where the leading female character fails to recognize her own husband when his mask is off, and where one of the two male protagonists (alter egos) wears his dead friend's mask and succeeds for a while in usurping his identity. (Under the influence of—you might almost say mesmerized by—Freud, O'Neill also wrote the oddball, one-of-a-kind 1928 melodrama *Strange Interlude*, substituting interior monologues for masks: The characters have two sets of lines, one spoken out loud and one addressed to the audience that indicates their unspeakable private thoughts.)

In his late naturalistic plays, O'Neill took the logical next step: He made the masks psychological and absorbed the shifts between interior monologue and dramatic interaction into the dialogue process. In *The Iceman Cometh*, characters often contradict themselves; they reveal too much and then pull back, making a sloppy attempt to unsay what they should never have blurted out in the first place. The most sensational example comes at the play's high point, the conclusion of Hickey's spellbinding fourth-act confession speech, when he lets slip that he hated his wife Evelyn, whom he supposedly killed out of pity. He admits the last words he said to her were "you damned bitch," and then he tries feebly to shove the words back into his mouth. And, because the unofficial drunkards' club at Harry Hope's bar is founded on the tacit principle of mutual support for the members' life-lies (what today's substance-abuse counselors would call "enabling"), these men are only too glad to pretend they don't notice when their buddies reveal themselves inadvertently. Whiskey is the great loosener of tongues in this play, of course, the great relaxer of masks, and in *Long Day's Journey* it's joined by morphine (for Mary Tyrone). As Travis Bogard points out in his fine examination of O'Neill's plays, *Contour in Time*, these are also the naturalistic devices the playwright relies on to move from the Expressionist style of a *Great God Brown* to the profound realism of the monumental late tragedies.

When O'Neill took this step he was actually redefining the central problem for the actor in his plays—to articulate both the mask and what lies beneath it—in basic Method terms. An actor playing Jamie Tyrone in *Long Day's Journey* has to layer his performance so the wounded child, damaged irreparably by catching his mother in the act of shooting-up heroin, is clearly visible when liquor dislodges the cynical, I-don't-give-a-damn mask he wears for protection against yet another disillusionment. It's the same tension you find in Brando's

Stanley Kowalski between the little boy and the bully, the poetic pull of opposites that's at the root of all Method acting.

Jason Robards's breakthrough as an actor came in 1956, when he played Hickey in José Quintero's legendary revival of *The Iceman Cometh* at Circle in the Square in May (the production that finally won the play the recognition it deserved) and Jamie in the first American *Long Day's Journey into Night* in November. He repeated these two performances, respectively, on television in 1960 and on film in 1962, both under the direction of Sidney Lumet. (When John Frankenheimer brought *Iceman* to the screen in 1973 he cast Lee Marvin rather than Robards, for reasons that remain elusive: He claimed that Robards had Hickey so much in his blood that directing him in the role would be as futile as directing him to go to the bathroom. Even in the service of stroking Frankenheimer's ego, this seems like peculiar logic.) Quintero later resurrected the reputation of *A Moon for the Misbegotten* in much the same way as he had for *Iceman* when he directed Robards and Colleen Dewhurst in it on Broadway in 1973, and that version was televised in 1975. In addition, Robards starred as the elder James Tyrone in two productions of *Journey*, the second under Quintero and opposite Dewhurst, in New Haven and New York in 1988; he had a fling at O'Neill's late one-act, *Hughie*, as "Erie" Smith, both on stage (in 1964) and on TV; he appeared on Broadway as Con Melody, the pride-blinded hero of *A Touch of the Poet* (the only one of these roles I haven't seen him play), in 1977; and—in repertory with the 1988 *Long Day's Journey*—he attempted the flip side of James Tyrone, Sr.: the benevolent Nat Miller in O'Neill's lone comedy, *Ah, Wilderness!* It's well known that Robards feels a mystical connection to O'Neill, and specifically to Jamie O'Neill, the playwright's brother (who appears in various forms throughout the plays, and transparently as Jamie in *Long Day's Journey* and Jim in *A Moon for the Misbegotten*). In a *New York Times Magazine* article called "Jason Jamie Robards Tyrone," written during the Broadway run of *Misbegotten*, O'Neill biographer Barbara Gelb lays out the amazing set of coincidences that links the two men:

> Like Jamie O'Neill, Robards was the older of two sons born to a popular, handsome, hard-drinking, touring actor; like Jamie, he chose to rival his father by adopting an acting

career; also like Jamie, he never recovered from a childhood
sense of rejection by an absent mother, and he grew up, like
Jamie, with ghosts in his eyes.[4]

Furthermore, Robards joined the navy at seventeen (Eugene was a
sailor at a young age), coming across his first O'Neill play—*Strange
Interlude*—in the ship's library. (The first one he saw performed, appropriately, was *Iceman*, in its original New York production, when he
emerged from the service after the war, set on an acting career.)
Robards was thirty-four when he played the thirty-three-year-old Jamie
Tyrone on Broadway. And though we can dismiss these parallels as
mere chance, it's obvious that Robards doesn't; his identification with
the O'Neill characters he plays has brought him close to the edge on
several occasions. Gelb reports that one night during the New York
run of *Iceman*, he substituted his own wife's name, "Eleanore," for
"Evelyn" during the confession speech. (Their marriage had run
aground.) And when he lost the part of Hickey in the *Iceman* film to
Lee Marvin, Robards embarked upon a "suicidal rage" culminating in
a car accident that nearly succeeded in killing him.

In *Contour in Time*, Bogard explains at great length how the
alter-ego relationship of the twin protagonists in O'Neill's early plays,
Beyond the Horizon and *The Great God Brown*, is another form of
the way he split his heroes into the haunted-but-not-yet-doomed
young poet (Edmund Tyrone) and the darker-souled brother, already
bound on a wheel of fire (Jamie Tyrone). It's a very complicated,
sometimes fascinating psychoanalytic process by which Bogard seeks
to prove that O'Neill was really splitting *himself* into two. What's
helpful in understanding Jason Robards is to see that he identifies
with the "dark" O'Neill hero, the one who is clearly lost from the
moment he walks on the stage, who arrives with a touch of the grave
upon his face. And Hickey (though he isn't one of Bogard's examples)
is such a figure.

Robards's Hickey—the performance that put the actor and the
play on the map—has astonishing range and invention. He rides it on
a single extended burst of whirling energy, whipping down the coils of
a live wire buried deep inside him, and not reaching the bottom of his
reserve until the two cops haul him off to jail after his confession in the
final act. Robards brings Hickey in (late in Act I) with dollar bills stuck
in his boater, singing at the top of his lungs. It's a phenomenal show-

man's entrance that prepares us for the theatricality underscoring everything this Hickey does in the next three acts.

You can't believe the number of different hats he puts on: life of the party, evangelizing son of a preacher man, hard-sell hardware drummer, compassionate bosom buddy to every man and woman in Harry Hope's bar. He even plays a nineteenth-century stage villain once or twice, when he thinks he's got the upper hand—when he's sure the boys in the saloon are responding to his program to turn their heads around—and that's when he gets a sly, superior look, one eyebrow raised, a Snidely Whiplash smile slapped across his mug. One of the whores says that despite his tireless hounding, as he struggles to convert everyone to his newly-won philosophy of freedom from illusion, you can't help liking the bastard. And Robards's strategy is to center Hickey's appeal in his bottomless bag of show-biz tricks, his sleight of hand, his clever shifting of masks.

Hickey is a grand master of the old school of salesmanship, all right; and he's got so many tracks running at once that you don't know which one you're responding to at any given moment, or which one he's *really* trying to put you on. His initial talk of salvation is tinged with just a hint of mockery, so you can't be sure he isn't kidding. Then, when he starts to preach the Gospel According to Hickey to the inmates of Hope's bar, he falls into a glorious, singsong Elmer Gantry voice, referring to them as "brothers and sisters." And soon you feel like one of them. At first you resist this evangelical grandstanding, but it catches you up, and at one point you realize that even your resistance is part of Hickey's scheme (or Robards's). You're drawn in and repelled at the same time, as by a carnival sideshow.

Robards's Hickey is a whizbang drummer with astounding timing and an unerring instinct for spotting the tiniest opening: When Larry (Myron McCormick) sees him go after pathetic little Hugo (Sorrell Booke), the would-be anarchist with aristocratic leanings, and tries to pry him loose, Hickey zooms in on this bit of compassion from a man who styles himself a cynic, and, leaning over, tipping his hat over his forehead, launches into a brand-new sermon especially for Larry's benefit. He sizes up Don Parritt (the amazingly young, callow-looking Robert Redford) so cannily that we're as unsettled by his scrutinizing once-over as Parritt is himself. Later, Hickey explains that what makes him such a good salesman is his skill at psyching out a prospective client. That's exactly what he's doing with Parritt, and it's creepy as hell.

This Hickey has such a vivid and volatile presence that when he suddenly trips on a chair and keels over from fatigue before the party even gets going, the play suddenly turns ominous and frightening— you can't figure out who switched the power off. Hickey grows scared, too; he doesn't understand how he lost control. What Robards does that's so amazing here is to set up this complex structure of quasi-religious salesmanship and then double back and slash through it, puncturing it here and there, programming Hickey to hit a sagging pocket where he expected to find a fresh reserve of energy, as he always has before, that would pump him up and keep his brilliantly rehearsed act riding high. That's when the character begins to fall apart—when he reveals his bewilderment as Harry (Farrell Pelly) fails to return from his bout with the world outside the bar with a happy smile, or as the gentle-voiced one-time journalist Jimmy Tomorrow (Harrison Dowd) flings a drink in his face before heading out the door for his own date with reality, and you catch the fury in Hickey's eyes for a moment before he gets hold of the reins again. Robards keeps showing us Hickey's impatience that the show he's putting on isn't moving as fast as he'd anticipated. Sometimes he even gets confused or scared, and these emotions translate into a sudden scarlet rage. At one point he turns into a tantrummy kid, bawling the gang out for not responding to him: When they won't join him in a chorus of "Sweet Adeline," he pounds on the piano with his fist, and you can feel yourself wondering, like Harry Hope and the others, if he's actually gone crazy.

Robards's Hickey is defined by his theatricality. He plays deftly, potently against it in his most grandiloquent moments, and at other times he seems to be possessed by his own dramatic creation—like Michael Redgrave in thrall to his ventriloquist's dummy in *Dead of Night*. In the fourth-act, half-hour confessional, all of Hickey's contradictory impulses and all of Robards's intricately devised opposing strategies operate simultaneously. This scene is both a mesmerizing stripping-away of façade upon façade and the most stupendous and horrifying show piece of them all, the number where the performer— Hickey the Great—stops being able to control how much of himself he's drawing on to fuel his act, and ends up at empty by the final curtain (like Laurence Olivier's Archie Rice at the end of *The Entertainer*). And since Hickey and Robards cross-reference each other—Robards seems to be dragging Hickey's emotions up out of his own memory bank—this scene has something of the tightrope walker about it: You can barely stand to look, but you can't look away; you're not entirely sure the performer's going to make it to the end this time.

Here are some of the highlights of the confession scene, where we learn Hickey's killed his wife, Evelyn, and (more shockingly) we learn why. Early on, Robards does a transition, from a tears-in-the-voice plea to his friends to listen to his story, to a sharp, authoritative full stop: "That is plain/damned/foolishness," rapping out the beat of the words with the knuckles of one hand across the palm of the other. He's back in command now. (Salesman and actor both: We know Robards hasn't leaped for the climax of the scene too early, as we'd feared.) A little later he gets riled again—"She was a sucker for a pipe dream"—and this time the transition is faster and tenser, and the desperation underneath it more visible. In close-up he describes his date with Evelyn the night before he left town to go on the road for the first time, and Robards softens his voice, turning almost unbearably personal: Hickey's youthful yearning for Evelyn is more intimate than the details of his sex life could ever be, because sex is something Hickey can finesse, like selling, and certainly something he can talk about in a barroom with his drinking buddies. He can't stay in this private corner for long, though; almost immediately he snaps into his salesman routine, describing how he plies his trade.

When he tells us, "I never could learn to withstand temptation!" he stretches out his arms—he's making a declaration, a self-defining statement. When he talks about feeling free on the road (free of Evelyn's unspoken but ever-present moral rectitude), he sounds anything *but* free; he's tensely pulled from inside. Anger and self-disgust fight for the upper hand as he admits he picked up a case of VD ("a nail") on one of his trips; but while he flagellates himself, part of him remains detached, viewing his situation with a sad irony. As the speech goes on, his trumpeted love for Evelyn roller-coasters into a hatred for her he can't control, and so his little theatrical flourishes—the tight little jig when he alludes to himself as "a happy-go-lucky guy," the tap-dance finger-snapping—grow more and more unnerving. (He actually does the finger-snapping bit just before he confesses to Evelyn's murder!) Crescendoing on "You damned bitch!" he slams his fist into the piano, and then, terrified of what he's said, tries to take it back—"No, I never said that—it was a lie!" The phrase, high and intense and piercing, sounds like keening.

And *still* there's more. When Harry Hope, for reasons of his own, seizes on his claim that the salesman must have been insane when he offed Evelyn, Robards's Hickey recovers: He peers around, crafty as ever, and confirms Harry's comment. We can't tell if he's really gone over the edge and then come to himself enough to recognize it, or if, since his program for converting them all has failed miserably (for reasons he now understands, as he finally understands his own previously hidden motives), he's making a gallant last stand for Hope and the others, so they can at least return to the mercy of their life-lies.

Robards was forty when he played Hickey on television; when he recreated the role in José Quintero's 1985 Broadway revival he was sixty-five, and indeed he seemed bowed down by age from his initial entrance. (This was in keeping with, or more likely the reason for, Quintero's Decemberish reading of the play, where *everyone* seemed over the hill—even young Paul McCrane, with his thinning pate, as Don Parritt.) In this version Robards plays toward Hickey's physical collapse at the end of Act I from the moment he appears. Entering the bar, moving among the gang in a well-worn route of handshakes and hugs, he's an old-time sport, a Shriner who's made it, heart pounding and short of breath, to his last convention, dragging himself through the beloved rituals with the mysterious energy of the exhausted. His voice is deep and thick; he's swimming in it, barely able to keep his head above water to get his long speeches out, and he cracks or winds down before a line is finished.

It would be inaccurate to say that Robards has no power in this reconceived *Iceman,* but it's certainly a different *kind* of power, a sour, spectral power, like the smell of a corpse that has begun to turn. Larry Slade says of Hickey that he's brought the touch of death with him, but O'Neill takes four acts to prove that it's literally true, and the revelation is usually a shock for the audience. This time Robards makes it clear from the outset that Hickey is dying a slow death; he seems to be playing this salesman, who must have inspired Arthur Miller's, as if he were *already* Willy Loman.

This older Hickey is just about out of tricks, and he's such an instant wet blanket that his very appearance in Act II, at the height of the preparations for Harry Hope's birthday party, douses the celebratory mood. He's turned from Elmer Gantry to a crusty schoolmaster smiling in exaggerated tolerance at the inexperienced behavior of his charges. When he does evoke the preacher, the ghost of Hickey's papa, his imitation is threadbare, breathless, and he presents it as a little show for the momentary amusement of the others before cutting back—as if to say, "There's a bit of the old evangelist routine, but that's as much as I can manage these days." The same spirit of self-defeat carries into his declaration that he feels no grief over Evelyn's death. He seems to be almost past grief, and past joy, too.

Everything about Robards's performance seems heftier than before. His grey pinstripe suit and boater appear to weigh him down; he removes the hat, but still his movements are much more inhibited than they used to be. I found myself focusing not on his snapping fingers or his twinkling eyes, but on his shiny bald spot as he stomped around the room trying to pummel some energy into his congregation while he himself had so little. Robards obviously knows exactly what he's doing; he's made a choice to play Hickey this way at sixty-five, and you can't blame him, especially when you begin to sense as early as Act I that he has to be conserving himself for the killer confession scene in Act IV. It isn't a false piece of acting, or a stupid one, and there's something emotionally satisfying in his intelligence and his consistency, as well as in the moments when he rises to something like his old power (the first meeting of Hickey and Parritt, Hickey's furious response to Larry's accusation that he's brought death with him). But somehow his decision to make Hickey lethargic and transparent, practical as it is, deflates the theatrical experience of *The Iceman Cometh*.

God, he works like a slave in the last act, though. The confession scene has its flashes of brilliance, especially when he digs into his bowels and touches the same pain he reached the last time he played Hickey. I suspect he found different lines on different nights to pierce that agony: When I saw the show, he gave splendid renderings of "She'd look into my eyes and then she'd know" (Hickey's recollection that Evelyn always sensed when he'd been unfaithful to her) and of Hickey's disgust at himself for lugging his drunken carcass "into her home, which she kept so spotless and clean." And he hit the climactic note of the scene so hard that for a moment the stage seemed to explode. At that moment, I felt the play's greatness in a way I hadn't all evening—in the way his 1960 Hickey harnessed it. In between, though, he pushed and pulled at the confession, struggling like hell to make it come alive again, drumming on the tables, banging on the piano, working like a comeback heavyweight to rev up the requisite energy and strength. One moment would be ragged, the next one a clever approximation, and then suddenly he'd tap into the emotion and it would pour out with a purity and clarity that made you gasp—and then, a second or two later, he'd lose the connection. By the end of the show I wanted to give him the Croix de Guerre. But I still had to admit that his Hickey had been less than a triumph—this time, anyway.

Sidney Lumet's movie version of *Long Day's Journey into Night*, released in 1962, is a high point in the history of theater on film. And Robards, the only one of the four stars who created his role on the stage six years earlier, gives a towering performance as Jamie Tyrone, whose cynicism and nightly binges and forays to whorehouses conceal the depth of his disillusionment about his mother's morphine addiction and his own failure to get his life in hand. The actors play O'Neill's text as a chamber opera for four voices. Robards's gravel-scooping *basso profundo* counters Ralph Richardson's classically trained, superbly modulated Shakespearean baritone and Dean Stockwell's naturalistic light tenor, while the breathtaking Katharine Hepburn dances through the whole scale, sometimes settling tremulously in the lower register and then, without warning, taking off on a coloratura flight for Mary Tyrone's dope-induced variations on the mad scene from *Lucia di Lammermoor*. Robards has range, too. He'll suddenly break out of his whiskey gruffness, the voice of hard-bitten experience ("Love your guts, kid," as he tries to keep a bottle away from his brother Edmund, who's suffering from an extended "summer cold" they both suspect will turn out to be T.B.), and fly up on an agonized high note, revealing the hysteria that drives him to liquor, but which—anticipating the fate of the older, half-dead Jim Tyrone of *A Moon for the Misbegotten*—liquor can't always anesthetize.

Since the end of the last century, drama in this country has aspired to the heights Ibsen scaled. *Long Day's Journey* is the moment in theatrical history when it finally attains them, and in a distinctly American style. Ibsen's great theme—the past that eternally haunts the present—allows him to indict Norwegian (and generally European) society in the late 1800s for its blindness and repressiveness, and the root corruption of its values. Other playwrights have tried to move this ethic into American drama (notably Arthur Miller, who even adapted Ibsen's *An Enemy of the People* for Broadway) with mixed success.

Translated into our idiom, this kind of exposé tends to thin out, become awfully high-minded and finger-wagging and civics-classy.

By the time he produced *Long Day's Journey*, O'Neill had worked through his own attacks on American values, in his Expressionistic one-acts *The Emperor Jones* and *The Hairy Ape*, in *The Great God Brown* and *Marco Millions*, and in his depiction of the rock-hard, materialistic Mannons in *Mourning Becomes Electra*. And he'd come to see that, for Americans, the richest source of tragedy is found at the source of greatest strength: the family, where nothing is forgotten or forgiven, where guilt and forgiveness and recrimination are bound together in a crazy, back-and-forth dance and every word is a step, conscious or semiconscious or unconscious, into the perilous territory of wounds that have never healed and feelings that won't stay buried. It's the territory, in other words, where the past and the present are irrevocably intertwined. None of the characters can loose the painful ties of the past, finally; liquor and dope and the fog won't drown it—they only isolate the characters from the rest of the world, and, ironically, bring into sharper focus all the bitter truths they're struggling to evade. Even Mary Tyrone's descent into girlhood at the end of the play is finally unsuccessful. Her last words are a reminder to herself that her youth vanished when she "fell in love with James Tyrone and was so happy for a time."

Into this emotional morass walks Robards, who is a genius at showing two conflicting layers of emotion at the same time—the ideal tool for playing this drama of unresolvable tensions and mixed motives. When he swears to his father that he loves Edmund, that they're "not like the usual brothers," his troubled expression actually reveals that they're the *prototype* of "the usual brothers," tied to each other as much by hatred and jealousy as by love. Sharp-eyed and suspicious of his mother's actions from the beginning, brutal with Edmund for ignoring the symptoms that she's gone back on dope, Robards's Jamie lets us know that his whiplash attack on his brother merely covers his own pain at having gambled emotionally on Mary so many times and lost—and at the implications her defeat has for his own battle with alcohol ("I'd begun to hope, if she'd beaten the game, I could, too").

There's a fine, ominous exchange between Robards and Hepburn when, on entering the parlor, she finds his scrutiny (as he checks for signs that she's injected herself) unsettling: Her hand flies up to her head, and she asks nervously if her hair is coming down. On her next appearance the narcotized sweetness in her voice, and her languid rambling, confirm his suspicions, and we get the flip side of Jamie—his "Take a look at your eyes in the mirror!" is the strangled cry of a heartbroken youngster. It locates the childish hurt beneath his fury at Mary's addiction; he was the one, remember, who first caught her shooting-up. That first memory is regenerated every time he looks at Mary or hears her shuffling across the floor of the upstairs spare room, and he can't help translating it into horrible, stinging remarks that, hard as they are on the other Tyrones, harm him the most; they're a kind of penance he has to serve for what she and he have both become. When he refers to the hell of having a dope fiend for a mother (a comment that rouses Edmund to slug him), Robards shows us Jamie's self-inflicted punishment even before Edmund can get at him, in the way he pulls away instinctively, repulsed by his own words.

At one point James, Sr., remarks that Jamie does nothing but sneer, and Jamie, unguarded for a moment, replies, "That's not true, Papa. You can't hear me talking to myself, that's all." The way O'Neill has structured Jamie's fourth-act drunk scene (another of his final-act confessionals), we *do* hear him talking to himself—we're privy to thoughts and feelings so private they make for tough listening. His entrance is a drunken clown's: He executes a deft pratfall, cursing the front steps and the lack of light (i.e., his father's miserliness in refusing to leave one burning), stalking across the floor to brazenly switch on the lamp, slurring lines of poetry in a loud, declarative style and then fading out like faraway music. Spotting the whiskey bottle his father has left out and open, he tips it with mock courtliness and dabs a little behind his ears. There are many layers to Jamie's drunkenness, and during this confession sequence ("in vino veritas stuff," Jamie calls it) Robards peels each one off like the skins of a onion to reveal the one beneath: burlesque raucousness, sentimentality, resentment and fury at his father's niggardliness, self-contempt, rage at Mary for going back on the morphine, desperate pain and self-pity, sloppy love for Edmund, and the jealousy and hatred struggling tooth-and-jowl with that love.

It's a hypnotic piece of acting. As Robards gets closer and closer to Jamie's knotted core we can't look away, not even when we're faced with the gall that lines Jamie's inside, which no one in the family is safe from. So we're confronted with his sarcastic recitation of "Mother o' Mine" and the crude question that follows it, "Where's the hophead?";

with his allusions to his father as a miser, "Old Gaspard," and a bastard; with the horrifying revelation that he's never been able to forgive Edmund for being born, because it was the pain of his labor that started Mary on dope. When he tells this to Edmund—Robards soars into one of his marvelous, keening vocal flights here—we can feel his personal demon clutching at his throat, battling with the deep love for his brother that's prompted him to bare himself before him. His statement of the bond between them—"I made you"—is an eruption of sodden grand passion, wrenched from Robards's gut. He ends with a fine flourish: He intones quietly, "Don't die on me. You're all I've got left," and then blows Edmund a cavalier's kiss before falling asleep.

The need to confess is the impulse that unites Hickey, Jamie, and Jim Tyrone in A Moon for the Misbegotten, the play in which Jamie, older now and veering toward the death he so fervently wants, finally finds peace. For O'Neill, whose plays are deep-dyed, chapter and verse, in Catholic ritual, both accepting of and pulling against the Catholic mind-set, it's a primal need, like the desire for cool water to soothe a parched throat. The critic Michael O'Neill points out that the confession ritual is specifically invoked both in Iceman, when Larry pronounces absolution first on Parritt and then on Hickey before they move off into the wings, and in Long Day's Journey, where each of the male characters—especially Jamie—serves as both penitent and confessor for the others:

> He says colloquially what a priest says at the end of the confessional rite. The confessor reinforces the penitent's humanity and reminds him he is good because God created him; Jamie says, "You're a damned fine kid. Ought to be. I made you" (167). The confessor tells the penitent to go and sin no more; Jamie says, "So go and get well. Don't die on me. You're all I got left" (167). Lastly, the confessor gives Christ's blessing; Jamie says in closing, "God bless you, Kid" (167).[5]

In José Quintero's revival of Misbegotten, playing opposite a superb Colleen Dewhurst as Josie Hogan, Robards is at the height of his powers. By the time he's climbed past Hickey and Jamie to the role of Jim Tyrone, perhaps the most challenging of all O'Neill's heroes, there's clearly no one in the country with a better understanding of

the strip-down-to-the-soul way the confessional works in these plays—
or a more impressive range in depicting alcoholic behavior, or a purer
naturalistic approach. It's a majestic performance, and there's not a
trace in it of theatrical self-consciousness. Robards's readings have
fallen into a casual rhythm; through the haze of Jim's profound world-
weariness, we can still hear hints of the character's exalted diction (a
holdover from *Long Day's Journey*), but it's a habit he's lost his youthful delight in. For Robards, all technique seems to have been swallowed up in the lived-out authenticity of the acting, just as O'Neill
himself gives the impression of having flung away technique in this late
drama and flown directly to the hearts of his two protagonists. The play
is structured, of course, but you have to stare hard through the extraordinary fluid two- and three-character scenes to see just how he
builds on a classical farce outline to set up the long third-act *pas de
deux* between Jim and Josie, then dissolves it gracefully to allow the
real drama—the exorcism of Jim's ghost, and the coming about of
Josie's beautiful sacrifice—to take over. O'Neill has moved as far away
from the heavy dramatic apparatus of *The Iceman Cometh* as a playwright can. Speaking solely in terms of dramaturgical skill, *A Moon for
the Misbegotten* is an even more sophisticated and limpid piece of
naturalistic drama than *Long Day's Journey into Night*.

Robards appears frighteningly old as Jim Tyrone. Josie says he
looks like he's walking behind his own coffin, and we can see the mark
of death on his sallow skin, his sunken eyes, his dry lips. One of the
ironies of his performance in the 1960 *Iceman* was that Hickey, the
messenger of death, had such a compulsive, clattering energy. Here
Robards is prone to pauses, moments so still they're like tiny black
holes in the air. He trails off on the ends of his sentences as if he were
lost in the skies somewhere, and at times he's weirdly becalmed, as if
death had already stolen him away. But this walking corpse still has the
capacity to feel remorse, and that's the most horrible thing of all. He's
pain-wracked, his guilt clanking behind him like a rusty chain. When
he keens (the Robards vocal trademark) we seem to be hearing the cry
of the undead.

Robards is practically the *emblem* of pain in this role; all trifling
feelings have been pared away. When Josie, forgiving him for his late
arrival at their moonlight tryst in Act III, reminds him lightly, roman-
tically, that they still have the whole night ahead of them, he looks up
at her as if she were speaking some foreign language—the language of

those who can still hope. Robards's Jim Tyrone is a man whose ghosts live so deep inside him he's no longer capable of deluding himself that he can stop their torment and find his way back to the land of the living. "We can kid the world, but we can't kid ourselves—nor run away from ourselves," he tells Josie. (He's right about Josie, too, but her lack of self-delusion connects her to life, not death. And it's her life-affirming quality, her earthmother-ness, that he finds he can cleave to at the last.) This inability to hide from the horrible truth distinguishes Jim Tyrone from O'Neill's other agonized heroes. His honesty's his penance; he wears his guilt like a brand for all to see, even though we don't find out until the great confession scene what exactly he's guilty *of*.

Robards gives Jim a stiffened gentility, and he's drunk from the moment he appears. Not flamboyantly, falling-down drunk, like the Jamie of Act IV of *Journey*, but constantly oiled. It's part of his constitution, so now Robards's line readings have a slight, soused retard and a wavering distractedness. And, since the booze long ago ceased to do anything for him short of blurring him into eventual unconsciousness, when he's awake he walks around in a constant state of self-disgust, a creature half crusted over with the slime spawned by his own evil thoughts, his own self-hatred. (His "I've slept with drunken tramps too many nights" is the cry of a man suddenly stirred to shake off the accumulated crud of his dissolute years who finds, once again, that it's too hard a task for him.) He's poisoned with it; there's something in him that automatically curdles whatever he comes in contact with— even Josie, whose romantic spirit is deflated when she encourages him to make love to her in Act III and he responds by treating her like a whore. Here's a man who stalks the earth in a graveyard darkness, watching others with a spectral detachment, scarcely able to feel anything but pain and horror and nausea at what he knows himself to be capable of: sex with a prostitute, night after night, while his mother's corpse, bound home from her burial, lies in its coffin in the next train car.

In this play the confessional comes in the third act rather than the fourth. The twin motives for Jim's behavior on that train (he wanted to forget his sorrow at his mother's passing/he wanted to punish her for abandoning him), twisted together into the whip he uses to flog himself, link the scene to both of the earlier plays—to Hickey's love/hate for Evelyn and Jamie's protective/destructive instincts toward Edmund. And Jim's obsession with his mother's face in death links it to Brando's monologue to his wife's corpse in *Last Tango in Paris.* Like Brando, Robards keeps churning up emotions, brought smoking to the screen from some private place in his soul, way past the point where we're sure an actor would have nothing left to offer. There's a kind of fearlessness in these men's acting that leaves you speechless, grateful— even altered, in some not easily defined way. By the time Jim begins to sing a line from the bathetic ballad "In the Baggage Car Ahead," the nettling mockery of the song in this context is inseparable from the outpouring of his sorrow; the grief and the poison are a single festering wound that gnaws at what's left of Jim's life. Then, without warning, Robards pulls away from the full-out emotional battery of this moment to the shocking detachment of the line that ends Jim's confession: "That's all—except I was too drunk to go to her funeral."

It's necessary that Robards drag us into the fetid depths of Jim's horror in order for us to emerge, as he does, to the grace of the fourth act, which is unlike anything else O'Neill ever wrote. Act III ends in a *Pietà:* Jim weeps at Josie's breast, and she says she forgives him in the name of his dead mother. When he wakes in her arms in Act IV, with a strange sense of calm displacement after his first unblighted sleep in all the years since Mary's death, he doesn't remember Josie's words of comfort at first, or the scene that provoked them. But just as he's about to leave, the recollection of his confession hits him, and Robards looks as if he'd misstepped, sprung a trap, and plummeted back into last night's agony. Then Josie reaffirms her maternal forgiveness, and suddenly Robards is Lear waking to Cordelia's tears, Leontes seeing the statue of his perished wife Hermione come to life and slip into his arms, Peer Gynt saved from the Button Molder's grasp by Solveig's faith, hope, and love. O'Neill gives us the magic of affirmation at the point beyond despair, and Robards makes us understand and embrace it: When we look at him we see the face of a man rescued from the jaws of hell. In this production, the final act of *A Moon for the Misbegotten* has the infinite tenderness of a blessing.

Not all of Robards's O'Neill portrayals have been so brilliantly successful. As Erie Smith in the one-act *Hughie,* he cuts a dazzling, old-style figure in a Panama hat and an ice-cream suit, a gaudy hand-kerchief dangling from his breast pocket, showing a full set of nicotine-stained choppers whenever he grins. And he has a couple of nice, understated moments. (When he stops short on his way up to his hotel bed, mops his brow, and confesses, "Christ, it's lonely!" he's a poignant reminder of the drunks in *Iceman* who would do anything to avoid going up to their ghost-ridden rooms.) But he plays solidly for the house, and though he gets his effects, we recognize them from other performances: *Hughie* is "Jason Robards's Greatest Hits."

Similarly, in the 1988 revival of *Ah, Wilderness!* at Yale Repertory Theater, Robards's effortless, crack timing and laid-back, old-pro leisureliness, pleasing as they are, can't compensate for the production's essential blandness. Director Arvin Brown fails to suggest the real tensions beneath the affectionate, salt water taffy veneer of O'Neill's only comedy, so the play melts into a sitcommy mush only temporarily relieved by George Hearn's Uncle Sid and Elizabeth Wilson's spinster Aunt Lily. Robards and Colleen Dewhurst are the ostensible stars, but neither is well served by this complacent reading of the play; as the loving parents, Nat and Essie Miller, they're about as lively as Walter Pidgeon and Spring Byington. When he's not working at full tilt, Robards isn't about mugging, and during the man-to-man talk with his son Richard (Raphael Sbarge), his way of pulling a long face—to telegraph Nat's lack of conviction in the stern-father role he feels he's got to fill—becomes awfully tiresome. But it's fun to see him play a lighthearted drunk scene for once: On his entrance in Act I, Scene 2, fresh from a Fourth of July celebration with the boys, he's gruffly charming, helpless to wipe the grin off his gin-warmed face.

The production was half of a repertory project, in honor of the O'Neill centennial, to stage O'Neill's two family plays, the comedy *Ah, Wilderness!* and the tragedy *Long Day's Journey into Night*, on the same set with (some of) the same actors. The idea was to underscore the fact that the plays are mirror images of each other—the same autobiographical material viewed two ways. (This plan didn't originate with Yale Rep; the first such pairing was tried in Milwaukee in 1977.) José Quintero directed the *Long Day's Journey*, with Robards as James Tyrone, Sr. and Dewhurst as Mary, and when his production reached New York following its New Haven run, it received merely respectful reviews (or worse). There may be a good reason for the disappointment: The producers threw it into a Broadway house far too large for the intimate, hushed style of the performance, and from what New York friends have told me, it sounds as if Quintero didn't have a chance to rework his ideas for a larger space (if indeed he could have, which seems doubtful), and the actors, never adjusting to it, lost the delicate energy that had fueled the show at Yale. That's a dismaying fate for a production that stirred me as powerfully as anything I've ever seen on a stage. The following impressions of Robards's performance are based on what I witnessed in the relatively small Yale campus theater in the first stage of this show's run.

The opening scene, an exchange between Tyrone and Mary, has a lighter, more bantering tone than in other versions, and Dewhurst's appearance has a nostalgic effect you wouldn't expect: The pallor of her face and the powdery grey hair framing it suggest the fragile, faraway beauty of a Victorian matron in a cameo. You might almost think you were about to watch *Ah, Wilderness!* except for Tyrone's obsessive, trying-to-convince-himself allusions to her healthy looks, and his ill-spirited crack about Jamie's gambling. Quintero and the actors root this domestic tragedy completely in the recognizable, unalarming (and sometimes funny) dissonances of everyday familial chatter. What they understand by O'Neill's naturalism is that the pattern of guilt and defense and recrimination that makes up the texture of the play is less a cycle than strata, built up through the years, where father and son, brother and brother, husband and wife aren't on safe ground for long: The slightest fissure in the top layer exposes wounds that still throb beneath. That's why the first-act family gathering around the living-room table of the Tyrones' Connecticut summer home can be so relaxed and enjoyable, until Robards's James, Sr., makes a casual remark that upsets Edmund (Campbell Scott), and Jamie (Jamey Sheridan), rushing into an old alliance of brothers against their father, snaps at him, "The kid is damned sick," shifting the tone and tarnishing the breakfast good humor that covers so many toothed, unresolvable issues—Mary's morphine addiction, Tyrone's miserliness, Jamie's drinking and whoring, Edmund's consumption.

Naturalistic drama traditionally records the cries of despair of women and men trapped by who they are and where they are and by their reflex reactions to the impulses of the moment. "None of us can help the things life has done to us," Mary tells her sons, and, as the revival makes clear, none of the Tyrones can help picking at each other's scabs and salting each other's wounds; awful words pass before the speaker half-realizes what's tumbled out. Tyrone censures Jamie unceremoniously for his vices, his cynicism, his career failures, his corruption of his kid brother, his literary tastes; as Robards reads them, the lines often have a rote quality, because he knows, and Jamie knows, that he's voiced the same complaints a thousand times before. You can't miss the love he has for his son—Robards pulses with warmth toward him. But it doesn't save them; it can't prevent them from clawing at each other. It even facilitates their battles: It's brought them close enough to memorize each other's weaknesses and be able to puncture them, time and time again, with unerring precision. In the last act, when Edmund's accusations trigger the cruelest remark Tyrone could possibly counter with—a reminder that it was Edmund's birth that started his mother on morphine—Robards buries his head in his hands as soon as the words are out of his mouth, as if he'd like to hammer his head against the wall for what he's just said to his son. Out of remorse, he uncharacteristically promises Edmund he can go to any sanitarium he likes, regardless of the expense—though you know he'll slide back into his tightfistedness in a little while. He even confesses, a moment later, that he can't help himself.

Robards is wonderful in this show, and the qualities he brings to the role are completely different from other memorable Tyrones: Ralph Richardson's exuberantly witty theatricality in the 1962 movie version; Robert Ryan's iconic black Irish agony in the last major New York stage revival, in 1971; Laurence Olivier's operatic grandeur in the National Theatre of Britain production, which was televised in 1973. If Robards's performance isn't quite on a par with his three classic O'Neill turns, it may be because the role doesn't lend itself to that kind of *tour de force;* until Act IV, James, Sr., is less a presence on stage than either Jamie or Mary. (Olivier, the great exception, was a mesmerizing Tyrone who dominated the play—but he was playing opposite an inferior Mary and a painfully inadequate Jamie.) And in the final act, from the moment he staggers onto the stage sloshed, Robards is as much a marvel as ever. His white hair askew, his mouth puckered, his diction flannelly and dropsical, he's a wavering, unable-to-focus drunk, fuzzy with age. His speech about his childhood poverty (which drove him to his grasping love of money and land) is yet another towering O'Neill confessional, as clear and exposed and lashing as a great passage in Dostoevsky. When he reaches the climactic line, "It was in those days that I learned to be a miser," he opens his outstretched hand (a clever bit of visual irony) while the jagged edge of his collapsed baritone slices into you. He stylizes the line—he's playing Gaspard, the tightwad whom Jamie (in his most uncharitable moments) compares him to. But alcohol has eroded the nineteenth-century grace and fluidity of Tyrone's impersonation, so what we get is a Gaspard turned in on himself, all sour breath and twisted bone.

How the hell does Robards get so much color into that hoarse voice of his, and how does he manage to touch all those levels of pain when he talks about how his mother worked herself to death? At this point in his life he's conveying grief through so many accumulated layers of bitter experience that when we hear him read these lines we can detect overlapping echoes from each of those layers *at the same time*. He's matured far past any kind of self-consciousness now; when he's at his best, he's simply indistinguishable from his roles. And he's capable of a more profound humor than ever before. Jason Robards reaches down fearlessly into the most tortured recesses of his soul— and comes up with something *funny*? You can scarcely believe what this actor is capable of.

The final moments of this *Journey* are astonishing. When Dewhurst's Mary comes down the stairs holding her wedding gown, Robards lifts it from her hands with exquisite gentleness, as if it were gossamer; then he drapes it over his wrists. In an ingenious article called "O'Neill's Shakespeare" (part of a forthcoming book), Normand Berlin points out that the portrait of Shakespeare hanging on the wall of Ben Edwards's set in this production underscores the frequency of allusions to Shakespeare in the play, both explicit and implicit, and he compares the devastating conclusion to the end of *King Lear*.[6] That's obviously what Quintero had in mind: Robards looks like Lear holding Cordelia's corpse, Dewhurst might be her spirit wandering upstage of him, and the way Jamey Sheridan reads Swinburne's "A Leave-taking," it's a eulogy for his mother. Few moments have so overwhelmed me in the theater. I felt chilled to the bone by the awful power of O'Neill's tragedy.

Not all of Robards's best work has been in O'Neill, but much of it does connect in some way with his O'Neill explorations. In the 1968 movie *The Night They Raided Minsky's*, executing a marvelously assured turn as a burlesque comedian, he draws on the emphatic comic force, the foghorn-piercing bellow with the slightly rancid punch at line's end, that mark Hickey's routines. And there's a hint of the Hickey–Evelyn tensions in the relationship between Robards's Thompson and his wife Ellie (Olivia De Havilland) in Sam Peckinpah's superb 1967 TV transciption of the Katharine Anne Porter story "Noon Wine":

Ellie is so "decent" (abstemious) that Thompson needs to get drunk in town, away from her watchful gaze. Thompson is a garrulous farmer whose life is destroyed when he kills a stranger while defending his hired hand (Per Oscarsson). "Noon Wine" is the tale of a man who loses his bearings and drifts toward suicide, and Robards's impassioned performance brings an O'Neillian sense of the tragic interplay of character and fate to bear on Porter's narrative.

Best of all Robards's film performances after *Long Day's Journey* is his appearance in the 1980 comedy *Melvin and Howard*, written by Bo Goldman and directed by Jonathan Demme. This is a sweet fantasia built on an amazing human-interest anecdote: the story surrounding the much-contested "Mormon will" that left a sizable chunk of Howard Hughes's estate to one Melvin Dummar. Dummar claimed he once picked up an old man who'd suffered a dirt-biking accident in the Nevada desert and said he was Hughes. It's this encounter that makes up the first quarter of Demme's movie, with Paul Le Mat as Melvin, and Robards—his face longer and more gaunt than ever, his eyes more sunken and sad, his hair flying out at every angle like the rays of a star—as Howard. (Behind his goggles in the opening scene, yelping with delight and grinning at the air as he skips over the desert on his motorcycle, he looks amusingly like John Huston.) Robards leaves the picture when Melvin deposits Howard in Vegas, and doesn't return until the very end (when the filmmakers are smart enough to bring him back in a brief flashback). But he's the spirit of the movie, hovering over the scenes he's absent from just as Brando does in *The Godfather* and Vanessa Redgrave does in *Julia*. These are *star* supporting performances.

It's hard to think of an actor who's managed to look so eccentric and so tragic at the same time. Robards's eyes are very, very bright, almost white, burning out of an ancient, leathery face, and his wild hair—muddied white—seems, with his beard and moustache, a finger extended staunchly against respectability. Maybe you have to have played Hickey and Jamie and Jim Tyrone as magnificently as Robards to know how to play Howard Hughes. O'Neill would have understood the bitter failure in Hughes's success; Robards's imaginative trope on one of America's mythic figures is a comic twist on an O'Neillian tragic life, an extended grace note. Decades of pain shape this man's terror when Melvin helps him into his car: terror of the cold, of his injury and the thought of a doctor's examination, of his vulnerability out there on the early-morning desert, and of this stranger who's intruded on his life. And later, when Howard is moved to confide in Melvin, decades of pain support his reminiscence of his father, which is a moment of remarkable purity and simplicity. But though *Melvin and Howard* is implicitly a criticism of the American dream, it isn't a study in pain and disenchantment. It's about working through your illusions and coming out on the other side, and the Hughes section that opens the picture is about rediscovering your humanity. This old wreck of a billionaire sits in Melvin's car, blood drying on his ear, and he finds his way back to life—by forging a bond with a simple-souled ne'er-do-well who gets him to while away the time in a singsong.

Robards's *a cappella* rendition of "Bye Bye Blackbird" is sheer magic. "Don't be crazy," he chides gently when Melvin coaxes him to perform this, his favorite song; then he pauses, clears his throat, and starts to hum, low and private, afraid his toneless crooning might embarrass him. When Melvin urges him to sing full out, his cracked, muted bass tells us about Hughes's loneliness, about the mournful distances he's traveled from the childhood the song recalls. On "No one here can love or understand me / Oh, what hard luck stories they all hand me," the soft, hoarse touch of his voice on the sad mess of his rich life is inexpressibly moving. But there's a loony humor to his singing, too. He's back in the great existential vaudeville show once again. For a moment you think you might be watching one of Samuel Beckett's clowns, kicking up his heels to entertain the silent cosmos. From *The Iceman Cometh* to *Waiting for Godot* isn't such a large step after all.

11

SUBMERGING TECHNIQUE AND OTHER OPTIONS

◆ ◆ ◆

Every young and revolutionary group of actors in the history of the theatre, and I think this applies with equal force in the shorter history of the movies, has seemed more natural than its predecessors.

—Alexander Knox[1]

In the late sixties and early seventies, American movies experienced an unexpected renaissance—a period when directors like Robert Altman, Sam Peckinpah, Arthur Penn, Francis Coppola, Martin Scorsese, Bob Fosse, Paul Mazursky, and Irvin Kershner made daring, often elliptical films, upending the conventions of different genres in an attempt to challenge the assumptions beneath them. It was the most exciting time for movies in this country since the height of the silent era. And, appropriately, a new generation of actors helped to establish its distinctive tone of hip disenchantment. Some brought unique, not easily classifiable approaches: the Method-trained Jack Nicholson, Barbra Streisand, Elliott Gould, Liza Minnelli, Joel Grey, Lily Tomlin, Goldie Hawn, Charles Grodin, Mia Farrow, Keith Carradine, Shelley Duvall, and the now-forgotten Renée Taylor (of *Made for Each Other*). But many others represented the newest breed of Method actors. This second group included Dustin Hoffman (*The Graduate, Midnight Cowboy, Straw Dogs*), Warren Beatty (*Bonnie and Clyde, McCabe and Mrs. Miller, Shampoo*), Jane Fonda (*They Shoot Horses, Don't They?, Klute*), Gene Hackman (*I Never Sang for My Father, The French Connection, Scarecrow, The Conversation*), Al Pacino (*The Godfather* pictures, *Scarecrow, Dog Day Afternoon*), Robert De Niro (*Mean Streets, The Godfather, Part II, Taxi Driver*), Cicely Tyson (*Sounder,* TV's "The Autobiography of Miss Jane Pittman"), George Segal (*Loving, Born to Win, Blume in Love, California Split*), Ellen Burstyn (*Alex in Wonderland, The Last Picture Show,*

Alice Doesn't Live Here Anymore), Harvey Keitel (*Mean Streets, Alice Doesn't Live Here Anymore, Taxi Driver*), Donald Sutherland (*M*A*S*H, Klute, Don't Look Now*), Robert Duvall (*The Godfather* pictures), James Caan (*The Godfather, Slither*), Jon Voight (*Midnight Cowboy, Deliverance, Conrack*), Jeff Bridges (*The Last Picture Show, The Last American Hero, The Iceman Cometh*), and Blythe Danner (*Lovin' Molly, Hearts of the West*).

If you went to the movies in the early seventies, it was fascinating to see these young actors side-by-side with their spiritual parents—to watch Brando and Pacino as father and son in *The Godfather* and then, two years later, De Niro playing the young Vito Corleone in *The Godfather, Part II*, a movie that also featured Lee Strasberg and the author of *A Hatful of Rain*, Michael V. Gazzo. (The first two parts of *The Godfather* are a Method history lesson in themselves.)

The third generation of the Method was marked by a more devoted—almost fanatical—application of Stanislavskian principles. Like the Moscow Art Theatre actress who played the whore in Gorki's *Lower Depths*, Jane Fonda spent weeks interviewing prostitutes before she began to shoot *Klute;* Jon Voight lived in a wheelchair for hours each day and hung out with paraplegics during *Coming Home*. Improvisation became a significant part of the filmmaking process in Scorsese's *Mean Streets*, in Bertolucci's international production *Last Tango in Paris*, and in all of Altman's movies, where the Method met the new revue style of comedy (which grew up in the wake of Nichols and May and had its first huge popular success on television's "Laugh-In"). Method-trained performers brought an even greater concentration than past generations on accuracy of detail, both physical and vocal, and strove more fervently to submerge actorly technique; the greatest compliment you could pay Gene Hackman and Jane Fonda (in her prime) was to say you couldn't catch them acting. Sometimes the determination of the actors in this group to bring real life onto the screen led to misguided efforts: When, in 1980, Robert De Niro put on fifty pounds to play boxer Jake La Motta in Scorsese's *Raging Bull*, literally making himself into what earlier actors had simulated by the use of creative imagination, he was confusing actual physical transformation with acting. (In "Some Notes on Method Actors," Hal Hinson calls De Niro "the Method's Dead End Kid."[2])

There are far too many representatives of this third generation to explore here. They would require another book, which would also include such relative latecomers as Nick Nolte, Gary Busey, Sean Penn, Sissy Spacek, William Hurt, the controversial Meryl Streep, and Diane Keaton (extraordinary in the eighties). But one actor seems to me to bridge the gap between the Actors Studio era and its heirs: Paul Newman, whose work has undergone tremendous change since he started out in the early 1950s. And one performance, perhaps more than any other, indicates how far and in what direction the American Method has traveled since the thirties: Dustin Hoffman's in the 1984 Broadway revival of *Death of a Salesman*, in a role originated by Group alumnus Lee J. Cobb. Finally, the careers of Blythe Danner (mostly in stage and television productions of the classics) and wild-card performer Jack Nicholson suggest other alternatives some members of the third generation of Method actors have pursued.

Paul Newman

Paul Newman is the Method actor that got away. Though he was trained at the Actors Studio in the early 1950s, and his early performances in movies (*Somebody Up There Likes Me; The Left Handed Gun*) and on television ("Guilty Is the Stranger," "The Battler") had a distinctly Method flavor, the qualities that made him a star in the 1960s had little to do with acting. They were his superb athlete's body (Patricia Neal, playing the knowing housekeeper with the burnt-almond Texas drawl in *Hud*, tells him that the sight of him with his shirt off has made her put down her dish towel more than once), those melting electric blue eyes, the cool presence dancing confidently right on the edge of insolence, and the worlds of sensual experience and bedroom prowess that all these promised. The movies audiences have loved him most in, like *Cool Hand Luke* and his two slow-canter rides with Robert Redford, *Butch Cassidy and the Sundance Kid* and *The Sting*, contain nothing like his best work; with Redford, he doesn't really act at all. But they furnished him with the kind of role his public has always responded to most happily: the sleek, laid-back antihero, the con with charm. And so when, in the mid–1970s, he finally broke out of that commercially secure mold and began to bring a new emotional expansiveness and authenticity to his acting, audiences (and critics) ignored him for the most part. They didn't notice that he was finally making good on his Method training, delving inward to locate the reality of the kind of characters he'd faked as a young man.

Many of Newman's early roles were Method types. Under Arthur Penn's direction in Tad Mosel's "Guilty Is the Stranger" (on "Goodyear Television Playhouse," 1954), he plays a veteran driven half crazy by his responsibility in another soldier's death. He's a shattered innocent, a child–man seeking shelter and salvation; it's a proto–James Dean part. Newman displays the Actors Studio trademark concern with finding the right street sounds for this character, but his efforts to come off as untutored, by breaking down language (as Brando does in *Streetcar* and *On the Waterfront*) and emitting occasional semiarticulate noises, look self-conscious. You can sense the Yale Drama School (which he attended before taking classes at the Studio) and Broadway (where he played the rich fraternity boy in *Picnic* in 1953) lurking uncomfortably beneath every line; he hasn't yet learned to rely on his modest origins—Cleveland, where his father ran a sporting goods store; the navy, where he served as a radioman during the war—to make a true connection with the part. But there's an openness in his face that gives you something to believe in, a suggestion that he and the character he's playing do at least inhabit the same world. He's cast right, at least. And no one seems more cruelly abused when he's miscast than Newman— as Plato in "The Death of Socrates," a 1955 "You Are There" (which Sidney Lumet directed), where, his face set in actorish commitment, he looks callow and foolish; or even in one scene in *The Young Philadelphians* where the director, Vincent Sherman, unwisely has him smoking a pipe. (In this picture he plays the bastard son of a lower middle-class Irishman, Brian Keith, who slips the bonds of his birth by joining a prestigious law firm.)

In "The Battler" ("Playwrights '56," 1955) and again the next year in the film *Somebody Up There Likes Me*, Newman has his whirl at the archetypal Method role, the tough boxer with the tender, aching heart. His performance, again under Arthur Penn's direction, as Ad Francis in "The Battler" (an adaptation of one of Hemingway's Nick Adams stories) is a failed experiment with the sort of acting Jack Palance would succeed at the following year in "Requiem for a Heavyweight." Buried under a mound of scars that make him unrecognizable for the first and only time in his career (his ears look as if an opponent had chewed on them), Newman reads his lines in a fuzzy, deep voice, his tongue stuck between his teeth, knotting up his eyes and throwing free passes at the air to show how punch-drunk he is. You have to admire his concentration—he does establish an inner rhythm for Francis—but there's so much pausing and puzzling and searching in his acting that you can't believe in the *external* reality of the situation.

As Rocky Graziano in the biopic *Somebody Up There Likes Me*, he wears a fleshy face and an inflated nose that must have influenced De Niro's make-up in Scorsese's *Raging Bull*. But the movie, written by Ernest Lehman and directed by Robert Wise, is a glossy, sentimental Hollywood melodrama with a New York ghetto setting, urban–ethnic dialogue, and a combination of theme and dramatic structure (a tough kid from the wrong side of the tracks learns how to channel his destructive energies in a positive direction, and discovers the love of a good woman) that throw you right back to the Depression heyday of Warner Brothers. Newman's Italian–American accent is far from convincing; it's an indication of how hilariously fraudulent this film is on all levels that the only *genuine* Italian in the cast, Pier Angeli, plays Rocky's Jewish wife. (Their courtship, which begins in goofy mutual embarrassment, is the obvious source of the Stallone–Talia Shire romance in *Rocky*.) Besides, Newman's not John Garfield, and he's not De Niro: He doesn't give the impression of violence about to erupt inside him. So when the Sergeant in the forces who trains him to box points out the quality that will make him a champion—hate (for his bitter, has-been father)—it's impossible to take him seriously.

The other Method archetype Newman played during this early period was the adolescent who refuses to grow up, a variation on the vulnerable-youth roles Brando and James Dean made famous. Twice in 1958, in Richard Brooks's sanitized film version of Tennessee Williams's *Cat on a Hot Tin Roof* and in Irwin Shaw's "The Eighty-Yard Run" on "Playhouse 90," he appeared as a young adult trying to relive his glory as a college football hero. (Just as *Golden Boy* is the source of the emotionally torn boxer portrayed by so many famous Method actors, so these once-great sports figures probably derive from another Odets character, Ben Gordon in *Paradise Lost*, via Biff Loman in *Death of a Salesman*.) Both of these performances have their moments. Newman is undeniably well cast as an athlete; it's convincing that the disappointment of both these characters at not being able to sustain the visceral excitement of their university days leads them to liquor and dissatisfaction in marriage.

Newman brings just the right dissolute sexiness to the role of Brick Pollitt in *Cat*, who keeps turning his wife (Elizabeth Taylor) on long after he's stopped sleeping with her. And he does a few neat takes—like his deft, pointed avoidance of the glass she's sipped from when he gets up to freshen his drink. (Only a man who looks like Paul Newman could kick Elizabeth Taylor out of bed and not risk losing audience sympathy.) And though there's not a great deal of substance to fill out the performance, Brick's involvement with his own misery does come through in some of his early scenes, in a masochistic/narcissistic way that's romantic and appealing, in the style of Dean or of the young Warren Beatty who starred in *Splendor in the Grass*. In "The Eighty-Yard Run" Newman has a good, pained scene in which, trading in on his fame as a campus ball player, he tries to sell a suit to an undergraduate and then, realizing he can't stand to see his status reduced in the kid's eyes, edges out of the room. These aren't terrific pieces of acting (Brick is basically a cold-fish part), but they do provide intimations of depth that not all his work in this era suggests.

Most of the big set pieces in Newman's early movies and television appearances come across as Methody flourishes. Reliving the night his buddy died in "Guilty Is the Stranger" (Mosel recycles Arthur Laurents's hit play *Home of the Brave*), he's overwrought, out of control; you can see him reaching for the emotions. When Rocky Graziano, serving time in a reformatory in *Somebody Up There Likes Me*, is visited by his hysterical mother (Eileen Heckart, in a glum, self-flagellating performance that's practically camp), his weepy penitence is all surface—he's switching the faucet on and off. There are similar scenes in *The Young Philadelphians* (when he learns that a friend has lost an arm in a car accident), and even as late as the 1962 *Sweet Bird of Youth*: Told his mother has died, he pivots around slowly, landing on his hotel bed, head bowed, one hand clutching the other arm. As Billy the Kid in Arthur Penn's 1958 existential/Method western, *The Left Handed Gun*, Newman has a moment when he finds his beloved boss's corpse, falls on his knees, and rocks back and forth with his eyes closed and an agonized expression on his face. It's emblematic acting, Method style—purely synthetic, as Method acting became in these years whenever it turned fancy and showpiece—yet its hothouse intensity seems fascinatingly old-fashioned to us now. It suddenly makes 1958 seem light years away.

Newman was fantastically appealing in those years, though, even when his performances fell through, as in the misbegotten musical adaptation of *Our Town* on "Producer's Showcase," where he played George opposite Eva Marie Saint's Emily. He was hopeless in a teenage role, and he strained at the gee-gosh rural reg'lar-folks routine. He was so full of bad ideas about what to do with his mouth before speaking that by the time he got the line out, you'd stopped listening to him. But when, puzzling over his math homework with his baseball glove on, he broke into that thick-lipped grin, you couldn't help liking him. If Newman's most obvious problem as a young actor was his tendency to overscale his reactions, that was also part of what audiences were responding to: All that boyish energy pouring out of him was hard to resist, even if his freewheeling style and his little-kid boastfulness ("Boy, am I gonna break training!" he exclaims proudly to his bride in a flashback in "The Battler") did seem forced. You could be touched by something ingenuous at the heart of all this playful exhibitionism. It was in the way his Chris Darling gulped his scotch down and complained about the modern art his wife (Joanne Woodward) had put up on the walls in "The Eighty-Yard Run," or the way his Billy the Kid took the Bible offered by his employer, promising solemnly to "look over some words," or the way his Anthony Lawrence (in *The Young Philadelphians*) handed his ex–girl friend (Barbara Rush) a drink at the party, adding quietly, "It's all right. I haven't touched it."

It's difficult to overrate the effect of Newman's amazingly handsome appearance on these performances. His eyes were really the center of his acting: As he gets drunker in *Cat on a Hot Tin Roof*, they begin to sparkle and blur like diamonds glimpsed through tears. This picture, mostly a huge pseudo-southern talkfest, gets a lift from the moments when Newman and Elizabeth Taylor are alone on screen because they're such a gorgeous couple; when Brick finally throws Maggie a look of pure sexual desire at the end, you feel the time you've spent has been justified. King of the close-ups, Newman is most potent when he's shot straight on, and his eyes always seem to be asking for sex. (When Joanne Woodward refuses him in "The Eighty-Yard Run," *she* loses audience sympathy—and never gets it back.) Add that country-boy grin, already turning insubordinate in the reformatory scenes in *Somebody Up There Likes Me* (a warm-up for *Cool Hand Luke*), and the ease and relaxation Newman starts to illustrate on camera in the late 1950s in flirtatious moments, or when he's tickled by his own hijinks, and you no longer have the earnest young Strasberg graduate plying his trade, but a full-fledged movie star.

It's the combination of his unruffled assurance and his dazzling good looks that make him such a pleasure to watch in early–1960s movies like *The Hustler, Paris Blues*, the first few scenes of *Sweet Bird of Youth*, and *Hud*. In all four he plays young men whose cool is a vital part of their calling—or, in Hud's case, of his avocation. In Robert Rossen's famous film, Eddie Felson hustles pool. In the opening sequence he fakes a charming, cozy drunkenness, messing up his first few games as a lure for possible opponents. When one (Vincent Gardenia) bites, Newman's confident smile rounds the corner almost into cockiness as he shoots, suddenly perfectly sober, and takes the sucker's money from him. When he jumps into a car where his partner, Charlie (Myron McCormick), is waiting for him, Eddie seems entirely unconscious of the potential danger for him in this scam; his face glows with self-approval.

Newman still has traces of the Actors Studio polish on him here: His big moments, like the shaking voice and hysterical laugh when he demands money from Charlie (who wants them to quit this game), are far from his best. And the dialogue (by Rossen and Sidney Carroll) has an imitation-poetic ring that tends to work against him. But when Eddie is hustling, Newman's delight with his own finesse is infectious. As they enter the pool hall where he's set to face off with the legendary Minnesota Fats (Jackie Gleason), Charlie's unsettled by the eerie quiet of the place and makes a comment about stiffs being laid out on the tables. "I'm going to be alive when I leave this place," Eddie insists. He thinks of himself strictly as a champ; when Fats's bankroller (George C. Scott) calls him a loser, Newman looks startled, dazed, as if he'd been cracked over the head with a pool cue.

Ram Bowen in *Paris Blues* (directed by Martin Ritt) is a gifted jazz musician who aspires to compose "serious" music; Chance Wayne in Tennessee Williams's *Sweet Bird of Youth* is a go-getter who plays stud to a neurotic movie star (Geraldine Page) with a taste for marijuana, in the hope that she'll promote his acting career. The screenplays provide both these young men with reserves of moodiness and insecurity, but we don't care about any of that: What's supposed to pass for depth here comes off looking like existential window dressing. (Everybody talks about what a has-been Chance Wayne is, but with his spiffy shades on and that broad toothpaste grin, Newman must be the freshest wash-out in town.)

Newman plays a cattle rancher's son and partner in *Hud*, but he spends more time raising hell in bars and in the beds of his married neighbors than he does with the cows. The director, Martin Ritt, and the screenwriters, Irving Ravetch and Harriet Frank, Jr., set up his first entrance with wry skill. His nephew Lon (Brandon de Wilde), sent to fetch his wayward uncle home, follows a trail of clues leading him to Hud's pink Cadillac boldly parked outside a house whose owner is conspicuously absent. (His wife is not.) The gentleman of the house returns just as Hud is taking off with Lon, and Hud, blithely unflappable, manages to pin the seduction on his virgin nephew and to get them both out of there in one piece. The filmmakers cleverly build large portions of the movie around Newman's cool world-weariness—the way he advises Lon to live all he can at seventeen because "It sure wears down after that"; his spare physical actions, like tipping his ten-gallon hat over his eyes, or lounging against the counter in a local coffee shop, sticking his hand out behind his back so his girl friend can drop cigarette money into it. Best of all is the repartee between Newman and Patricia Neal, cast as Alma—a contemporary–western variation on that classic role, the earthy servant. These two tease each other right to the edge of her narrow bed, gaily upstaging the sexy dialogue (the best the Ravetches have ever written) by playing an even funnier scene with their eyes and their smiles.

There's an old-fashioned Hollywood moralism at work in both the touchingly well played *The Hustler* and the vastly entertaining *Hud* that keeps threatening to dampen the proceedings. This is the stage in Newman's career when he's expected to pay for his good looks and easy charm—for making everyone fall in love with him when he flashes those bedroom eyes. *The Hustler* is a variation on the soured-American-dream plays of the thirties and forties (most famously *Death of a Salesman*), and on Rossen's own best-known script, for the John Garfield picture *Body and Soul*. When Eddie complains that Charlie dreams on too small a scale, we know he's headed for spiritual bankruptcy, dragging a woman of obvious value (Piper Laurie, who is given an emblematic limp) down with him. In *Body and Soul* the tainted fighter rejoins the land of the living at the end, flipping off the gangster who pressed him to fix the title bout and marching proudly out of the arena with his wife on his arm. In *The Hustler*, Piper Laurie has to kill herself in order for Newman's Eddie Felson to gain salvation; *then* he can walk out on Bert Gordon (George C. Scott), who symbolizes the corruption he's fallen into. The ending, a mixed triumph for Eddie, makes it possible for us to live with the fact that the movie has used the very qualities we love Newman for to score points against him.

Hud is a different matter. Here it's Newman who stands for the moral dangers of the easy life; his humorless, sermonizing father (Melvyn Douglas) who represents goodness; and Lon who walks the narrow line between the two. If Hud weren't so appealing, the line wouldn't be so narrow: The filmmakers don't seem to believe in hazy shades of grey in moral issues. Old Man Bannon learns that his cattle might be stricken with foot and mouth disease, and Hud's response is instantaneous: Sell them before the lab sends the test results back. "If you separate the saints from the sinners, you're lucky if you're left with Abraham Lincoln," he tells his father, but Homer, who is (dull) living proof that the Lincolns haven't died off yet, opposes his son's dishonest scheme. Newman can't bring off Hud's nasty side, however; his voice grows raspy and grating when he's called on to read lines like "This world is so full of crap that a man's gonna get into it whether he wants to or not!" And when, agitated by a particularly rough lecture from Homer, Hud stalks into Alma's room and almost succeeds in raping her before Lon can pull him off, the movie curdles. Part of the problem is that, as Brandon de Wilde plays him, Lon seems withered with virtue. The chief concern in the movie—as it is in another memorable film of a Larry McMurtry novel, *The Last Picture Show*—is the kind of models young men pick for themselves in the arid, boring towns of the new west. But in this case, despite what filmmakers strive to tell us, we can't help thinking that contact with Paul Newman could only improve Brandon de Wilde.

Largely because *Hud* is so expertly directed, it's hard to tell how much Newman's performance is crisp underplaying and how much of it is cool, dry-under-the-arms nonacting. For nearly a decade and a half following, Newman, now the most popular male star in the country, did far more of the second. As Ross Macdonald's detective in *Harper*, he blinks his baby blues and makes a motion with his mouth that looks vaguely like gum-chewing. And as the strong-and-silent hero of Martin Ritt's incredibly bad *Hombre*—a white man raised by Indians who scorns his own race—he's so inexpressive he barely seems to be on camera at all.

He's much more energetic in *Cool Hand Luke* (in 1967, the same year as *Hombre*), playing a version of a Method archetype, the Rebel Without a Cause, that's purest sixties. Luke, an antiestablishment figure down to his soul, carries a heroic war record but no promotions. Pitched onto a chain gang for decapitating a few parking meters while

in his cups, he refuses to be demoralized by the sadistic prison authorities, choosing instead to stage a full-scale rebellion against them by
infecting the other convicts with his indomitable high spirits. When
the jail bosses respond with inhuman treatment, he turns his energies
to devising an escape. Stuart Rosenberg's movie could be called *A
Fugitive from a Chain Gang Flew Over the Cuckoo's Nest*. Wearing his
smile as a badge of honor, Newman is fine as long as the picture
maintains a comic tone. But when it turns serious his performance
thins out, and in the climactic scene where he learns of his mother's
death, his eyes glaze over as he picks up his banjo and starts to sing
"Plastic Jesus." (The selection of this tune is the worst idea Rosenberg
and the writers, Donn Pearce and Frank Pierson, dreamed up for this
movie—and it prepares us for more Christ imagery to come.)

As an actor, Newman reached his nadir in his greatest commercial
triumphs—two George Roy Hill comedies, the hip-nihilistic *Butch
Cassidy and the Sundance Kid* in 1969, and the inexplicably popular
Oscar winner *The Sting* in 1973. Both times he played opposite Robert
Redford, a newer pinup who'd become a star without having bothered
to become an actor first. And it seemed to be Redford who was influ-
encing Newman in this film, instead of the other way around. By now
Newman's handsomeness had acquired a worn-leather sheen, lending
it more character and making him a grander camera subject than ever.
But in these movies he merely trades off his looks, playing supercool
while he and Redford (in his slicker, slightly sharper manner) behave
like superannuated brats. *Butch Cassidy* displays the most tiresome
kind of sixties sensibility: The heroes' dopey childish games are supposed to be justified by their renegade status—renegades being people
who refuse to graduate to the adult world. It's like a cartoon version of
a Godard comedy, made without sensibility. *The Sting* doesn't even
have that much distinction: Take away the contemporary presences of
Newman and Redford and you've got nothing but a Damon Runyon
retread, full of cutesy con men hatching schemes like practical jokes.

Two seldom-seen Newman performances from the early 1970s
show off a skill for comedy that neither *Butch Cassidy* nor *The Sting*
taps. In a few off-the-cuff moments in *Somebody Up There Likes Me*,
his neat timing and unfussy manner in promoting a gag suggest he
could have made a satisfying light comedian. Unfortunately, most of
the comedy scripts he's chosen (*Rally 'Round the Flag, Boys!*, *A New
Kind of Love*, *What a Way to Go!*, *Lady L*, *The Secret War of Harry*

Frigg, the George Roy Hill pictures) have done nothing for him. But as the legendary hanging judge in John Huston's otherwise undistinguished *The Life and Times of Judge Roy Bean* (1972), Newman sports a trim beard and a flat-brimmed hat and digs up his lowest growl. In one scene he serenades his daughter with "The Yellow Rose of Texas" in a toneless croak that's very funny, and he has an even better interlude, a drunk scene with a bear. The brand of comedy he engages in here is broad and caricatural, but he plays it in a surprisingly low key, a choice that also marks his work in Robert Altman's *Buffalo Bill and the Indians*. There's a peculiarity about both these performances that may be tied as much to Newman's reluctance to throw himself into a comic role as it is to the unusually ambiguous quality of the material. These movies present us with a Newman we haven't seen before—often imaginative but less relaxed, controlled but more tentative. You get the feeling he's searching for a new style.

In 1975 Newman told interviewer Leonard Probst, "I'm falling back on successful things that you can get away with. I duplicate things now. I don't work as compactly as I used to work, simply because the demands aren't asked of me anymore."[3] Beginning with the 1977 *Slap Shot*, Newman's acting underwent a startling metamorphosis: Through some invisible combination of will, age, restlessness, and fate that we can only guess at, he succeeded in halting the duplication process and turning himself into one of the best actors in the country.

Slap Shot isn't a good movie. It's a screamy, self-consciously boisterous comedy about a hockey team that finds itself on the verge of being disbanded through the whims of its detached, self-absorbed owner (Anita McCambridge). Neither the script (by Nancy Dowd) nor the direction (by Newman's old buddy George Roy Hill) does anything to raise it above the level of, say, *The Longest Yard*. But Newman's performance, as player–coach Reggie Dunlap, is a marvel of completely lived-in acting. Everything about his work here, from the way he wears Reggie's loud outfits (fur-collared leather coats and insistent orange jackets; sporty striped pants and shirts with the kinds of prints on them you might see on the walls of an eight-year-old boy's bedroom) to the way he reads the dumb, obvious, obscene lines, has a rock-bottom authenticity. You've never seen Newman so completely engaged in a movie before: When he watches his teammate and best friend (Michael Ontkean) quarreling with his wife (Lindsay Crouse) in a bar, Reggie's rapt interest in the spectacle is so vivid that even the dull domestic tiff he's hooked into starts to sound funnier and more suspenseful than it is.

There's a slightly-larger-than-life quality in Newman's enthusiasm in this movie, but it's not artificial; it's built right into the character. Newman plays Reggie as an overgrown adolescent jock—old territory, sure, but he's never given it this kind of energy before. He isn't just nursing an injury, as he did in *Cat on a Hot Tin Roof* and "The Eighty-Yard Run," and his childishness is an acting choice, not a strategy for winning a popularity contest—as it was in his other George Roy Hill pictures. As a result, even Reggie's stupid practical jokes (like his way of taunting members of a rival team) and his misguided outbursts of aggressiveness (like his exhortations to his teammates to beat up their opponents instead of concentrating on their hockey skills) aren't offensive; Newman executes them with an undisguised glee that we can respond to without feeling embarrassed. Anyway, he shows us so many examples of Reggie's open-hearted response to friends and lovers and ex-wives that we aren't in a position to disapprove of his actions. Newman, always responsive to other actors, extends a new, powerful warmth to them in *Slap Shot*. In one scene, learning the woman he's just slept with (Melinda Dillon) is bisexual, he makes Reggie's awkwardness generous rather than judgmental. In Newman's hands, Reggie can even show a strong sexual interest in his best buddy's wife without coming off like a snake, because Reggie's treatment of women is always full of wonder and admiration. In his handbooks, acting teacher Robert Cohen writes about the importance of approaching a role as if you shared the characters' beliefs; Newman's performance in *Slap Shot*, and in the movies he's made since, are an embodiment of that principle.

It's the honesty of the characters Newman's been playing for the last decade and a half that draws us to them—their unabashedness about saying who they are. Michael Gallagher, the liquor wholesaler in *Absence of Malice* (1981) victimized by an newspaper story implicating him in a union chief's disappearance, has no more use for feminists ("Most of them are ugly") than he does for unions (when his outfit suffers a longshoremen's strike as a result of the article, he quips, "I didn't know those guys could read"). But as Newman portrays him, both Gallagher's conservatism and his traditional masculinity are part of his strength, inseparable from his loyalty or his sensitivity or his acute sense of justice. From his first appearance, confronting Megan

(Sally Field), the reporter whose story fingered him, you can see the integrity that propels Gallagher's actions in the quiet concentration, solidity, and succinctness of Newman's movements and delivery.

This modest drama, a collaboration between writer Kurt Luedtke and director Sydney Pollack, is too neatly prearranged; the filmmakers seem sure of how everyone *should* have acted in this situation. But there's nothing pat about Newman's performance (perhaps his most economical and, in terms of sheer craftsmanship, his most impressive). Everything in it claims allegiance to Michael Gallagher. Newman has found a distinctive humor for this man: When he tells the reporter, Megan, he'll pick her up for lunch, adding, "It's a tan wagon. I'll put some stiffs on the hood," the thickness of his reading disguises the joke, so it hits us late, rumbling unexpectedly underneath the tempo of the line until we have to run it back in our heads to realize how funny it is. Gallagher's unapologetic way of making a joke might be a symbol for his method of functioning in the world: solid, straightforward, assertive, with a tenderness—unanticipated in its openness and intensity—for the people he loves (like fragile Teresa, a lifetime friend, played by Melinda Dillon, who ends up suffering the most from the machine that Megan throws into motion). None of Newman's other characters has used the gruff, grunting noise we hear from Gallagher when he wants to apologize for behaving badly. Even the way his voice hesitates in the message on his answering tape, as if he were uneasy with the amount of narcissism it takes to record yourself, reflects something of Michael Gallagher's personality.

The same completely rounded approach to a character secure within himself distinguishes Newman's most astounding performance—in the same year's *Fort Apache, the Bronx*, a deeply affecting, failed movie about cops written by Heywood Gould and directed by Daniel Petrie. Newman plays Murphy, who has ridden out eighteen years in possibly the worst precinct in the greater New York metropolitan area by remaining sane and reasonable and honest. He doesn't mind making a fool of himself in the line of duty: When a crazy street person waves a knife at a frightened crowd, Murphy goes into a loony dance number, distracting the man by being more flamboyantly demented than he is. What makes him angry are the efforts of some of the crooks he encounters to grease him; he responds with fresh fury every time it happens (he bashes the car of one pimp who offers him a bribe), resenting the assumption that he's the kind of guy who can be bought.

Unlike the cops in other movies *(Serpico, Prince of the City)* who demonstrate a repulsion against unethical practices that is incongruous in a brutal urban setting, Murphy make sense to us: Newman opens him up so wide that we see how he can combine a seasoned policeman's comprehension of his beat with a genuine (and un-self-righteous) uncorruptibility.

When Murphy sees another member of his precinct, Corelli (Danny Aiello), throw an innocent Puerto Rican kid off a roof, he can't live with it. It poisons his life. At this point Newman's performance tightens and darkens; everything changes—the way he holds his body as he leans against his locker, the way he stands at a bar, tossing back his drink, indicate layers of shock and disgust. But there's no moody self-reflectiveness here, as there would be if another Method actor, say Pacino or De Niro, were playing this role. Newman doesn't take the information inside and close up; he keeps himself exposed to us, moving through the second half of his performance with a beautiful, piercing simplicity and emotional purity. (The moment when he tells Corelli what he knows—says that every time he looks into Corelli's eyes he sees that teenager falling—is extraordinary.)

Newman was acclaimed for his work in *The Verdict* (1983), where he plays a down-and-out lawyer, Frank Galvin, who sees a malpractice case as a chance to redeem himself and reverse the course of his professional life. It's not really in the same class as what he does in *Slap Shot, Fort Apache,* and *Absence of Malice,* but on and off it's a very good piece of acting. Newman pins Galvin's exhaustion down in the first scenes: He walks slowly, with difficulty, up a flight of stairs, and the effort tells in his hoarse, breathless voice. Polishing himself up for a new client, he squirts Murine in his eyes and dabs them with a handkerchief, showing the grim experience of a man whose livelihood depends on convincing strangers of his respectability. The main problem with the performance is in David Mamet's script, which works in suggestions of dark corners in Galvin's character but then cleans them out before we've had the opportunity to consider their implications. The brother-in-law of the plaintiff in the case accuses Frank of using his clients for his own selfish ends, and the movie might be fascinating if it developed this possibility, or if Frank really had to struggle with himself before refusing the fat sum his opponents offer him for backing off. But Mamet has made him as noble as a Frank Capra hero (he even cures himself of alcoholism), and that decision doesn't give Newman enough to play. Plus the movie has a joyless, self-important self-consciousness, a trait of Sidney Lumet pictures. It leaks from the discreetly remote camerawork, the somber, impressive theme music, and the solid, architectural elegance of the art direction, right through into Newman's performance. Lumet has obviously directed him to make a bid for an Academy Award, so his big scenes seem slowed down, a little overrehearsed, and essentially dried out.

The idea of casting Newman, at this extraordinarily fertile time in his career, as a middle-aged Eddie Felson in a sequel to *The Hustler—The Color of Money*, scripted by Richard Price and directed by Martin Scorsese—is rich enough to make your mouth water. And for the first two-thirds of the film, he's even better than you might have anticipated. Eddie is now a bourbon salesman who gets his kicks managing promising young players; seeing his younger self in a cocky kid named Vincent Lauria (Tom Cruise, a flyspeck next to Newman), he decides to teach him how to hustle, and preps him for the nine-ball classic in Atlantic City. Sporting a dapper moustache, Newman looks like a man in his fifties who's never abandoned the slickness of his younger days and is still fit enough to carry it off. His hipster style has practically turned into an old-world elegance, as gracefully archaic in its way as Burt Lancaster's colorful 1940s panache in *Atlantic City*.

You can tell right away, from the seductive romantic energy he concentrates on his barmaid girl friend, Janelle (Helen Shaver), that Eddie's salvation at the end of *The Hustler* didn't stick, thank God. But other parts of that experience did—the painful parts, which burned deep holes in his reserves of trust and emotional resilience: His flattering attentiveness to women (which suggests how good he must be at his salesman's job, like Hickey in *The Iceman Cometh*) is as close as he can comfortably get to commitment. Eddie's a compulsive freewheeler. There's a terrific scene in which Janelle, hurt that he's decided to take Vincent on the road without consulting her, walks out on him, and he's left standing in a corridor, apologizing to the air. And he's got an even better one in which he calls her long-distance from his hotel room, ostensibly to tell her he wants to live with her, but he's so frightened of what he's saying that he keeps her at a bantering remove even while he admits (sort of) that he loves her.

Newman's portrayal is complex and full of unresolved inner edges, some unshielded (you see them whenever he talks about his past) and some perilous. When Julian (John Turturro), the coked-up pool player he's been handling, learns Eddie's switched his loyalties to Vincent and grows insulting, it's *Julian* you get nervous for, because he's venturing recklessly into Eddie's danger zone. As Newman plays him, Eddie has such a smooth veneer, after decades of different varieties of hustling, that the dynamic of the performance seems to be centered in our response to him—in the constantly shifting balance between the vast enjoyment we derive from watching him hook up his strategies, and our unsettled awareness that even his affection for Vincent is a ploy; that this man is totally self-absorbed.

It's a shock to realize how much of Bert Gordon really rubbed off on Eddie. At first Vincent's not at all sure he wants to quit his department store job and accept Eddie's offer, so Eddie—Iago as a confidence man—plants the seed in the kid's mind that his girl friend, Carmen (Mary Elizabeth Mastrantonio), who's been managing him up to this point, has grown bored with him and is certain to leave him unless he can guarantee her some excitement. Newman's Eddie plays the two "temptation" scenes with just the right devilish blend of friendly concern and cynicism—the one where he makes the suggestion, and the follow-up, where Vincent returns to see him, insisting frantically that Eddie's perceptions must have been wrong.

On the road, Vincent's innocence and his fresh young champ's ego make it difficult for Eddie to teach him the tricks of the game; he'd rather show off his finesse and beat the pants off his opponents than lose and create the illusion (essential if he's to be a money-making proposition) that he's no threat at all to the big boys. He even has scruples about whom he's willing to scam. (He backs off when his competition turns out to be an old, sick player.) So, to protect his investment, Eddie employs a combination of resources. He punishes Vincent by abandoning him to the ire of some townies he's hustled—a trick he learned from Bert Gordon. In one pool-hall scene he eggs Vincent on by really turning on the juice: He incorporates a public pass at Carmen into one of their hustles, taking advantage of her undisguised sexual interest in him to make a piece of acting look a little too real. And—the most effective device of all—he gives Vincent paternal lectures. Vincent is so moved by what he thinks is Eddie's fatherly interest in him that he gives his manager a hug. It's a chilling moment, because we know Eddie's been faking it.

Newman can't keep his acting on this amazing level in the last third of the picture, but it's not his fault. The filmmakers make a bad mistake: setting up a second redemption for Eddie Felson. A large part of Eddie's motivation for dropping Julian and picking up Vincent was that the kid's passion for winning brought back to Eddie the excitement he felt as a young man (in the first half of *The Hustler*). What he wants is to mold Vincent into a young Eddie Felson—to turn back time—and he's too jacked up on the idea to see it can't work. Eddie's seduction by the specter of his own past is the real substance of the movie, the part that makes it worth watching. It's focused, as it should be, in Newman's brilliant performance, and its apex is in the scene where a young black pool player (Forest Whitaker) succeeds in hustling Eddie, sending him into despair when he realizes that, as he says, he missed all the signals.

Unfortunately, Newman's performance bottoms out at the same time: Forty minutes still remain of the movie, and there's nothing it can do except either show us Eddie descending lower and lower, or else reverse his luck and turn him into a hero. The first would kill the film's spirit, and since it would likely kill it at the box office, too, the filmmakers take the second option. Eddie gets a new pair of tinted glasses (hiding Newman's eyes—always a bad idea), dons a spiffy tie and sweater, and shows up in Atlantic City for the competition, straight and honest and just brimming over with what Janelle (who appears to cheer him on) calls "character." To us, though, his metamorphosis is a *reduction* of character. Newman's acting necessarily thins out when his role becomes a repository for the filmmakers' stale notions of how a man behaves when, felled by a combination of cruel circumstance and his own flaws, he rises again.

You might not think of casting Newman as Louisiana's grandstanding surprise-liberal (that is, good-ol'-boy liberal) governor, Earl Long; someone like Randy Quaid, the marvelous LBJ of TV's "LBJ: The Early Years," would be a more logical choice. But Newman is wonderful as Long in Ron Shelton's *Blaze*, an erratic, enjoyable hip burlesque of Louisiana politics. His hair radically white, his nose hawk-like, his cheeks hoisted up, he looks so strikingly un–Newman-like that you need a little time to get used to him—and to the tensions between his submersion approach to acting and the character, who's a showman all the way. The tension works for the performance, finally; it suggests how much goes on underneath Long's show, and in his scenes with the stripper Blaze Starr (Lolita Davidovich) it allows him to play Earl's boyish sweetness against his taste for raucous hijinks. These scenes, among the most unconventional romantic-comedy *tête-à-têtes* in recent movies, linger in the mind.

Even a shallowly self-impressed courtroom drama like *The Verdict* or a maudlin, incoherent mess like the 1984 *Harry and Son* (which he coauthored and directed) or the last third of *The Color of Money* can't disguise the turnaround in Newman's acting over the past decade. He's now capable of giving the kind of performances he couldn't bring off in the 1950s: He's become the great proletarian Method actor. Other major practitioners of the Method have suggested either a bruised poetic nature (Garfield, Clift, Brando) or, in the third generation, a brooding intellectualism (Pacino, De Niro); Newman brings the same depth to characters whose response to the world is more likely congruent with that of most Americans. The relative "normality" of men like Reggie Dunlap, Michael Gallagher, and Murphy may mask the intensity of his commitment to these performances, especially for movie watchers accustomed to associating the idea of great acting with *angst*, and that probably explains the lack of attention that Newman's received, in most quarters, for his work in these movies. Only when he lands a role in an "important" picture like *The Verdict* or *The Color of Money* does he really attract notice.

But a backward glance through Newman's career shows a growth synonymous with a naturalistic ideal. To return to the words Calvin Tomkins used to describe the paintings of the American realist Thomas Eakins, he's "looked so long and so unflinchingly at the surface of things that he has gone right through to the heart of them."[4] That is, he now *lives* the kinds of characters he could only guess at in his early years, when he played the eager, troubled young soldier in "Guilty Is the Stranger," the street-educated boxer in *Somebody Up There Likes Me*, the athlete who despises pretension in "The Eighty-Yard Run." He's married the lessons he learned at the Actors Studio in the 1950s to the qualities that made him so much fun to watch on screen in the 1960s: Now he has a good, relaxed time on camera *in character*, and (the cornerstone of the Method experience) he can articulate pain so sharp and devastating that it can't be shaped into words, and he can do it without histrionics.

What are arguably the two best scenes in Newman's career so far—Michael Gallagher's assault on Megan when her meddling provokes Teresa's suicide; and Murphy's crazy, desperate efforts to resurrect his junkie sweetheart (Rachel Ticotin), dead of an overdose—

show us something undiscovered in an actor we once thought we knew inside out: a psyche grappling naked with the physical fact of death. This is daring, confrontational acting, acting that recalls, once again, Brando facing off his wife's corpse in *Last Tango in Paris*. The usual pattern for gifted actors in this country is that they begin by offering something new—a set of eccentricities, an idiosynratic perception of character, an unconventionally skewed vision of the world—and then end up imitating themselves. Paul Newman has moved in the other direction, and he's done it almost imperceptibly. The actor who once impersonated experience, charmingly, has become the genuine article.

Dustin Hoffman

"If you can't make a part your own, don't play it," Michael Dorsey (Dustin Hoffman) instructs his acting class at the beginning of *Tootsie*. Sydney Pollack's wonderful 1982 comedy is, among other (more obvious) things, a tribute to Method acting. In it, a New York actor–coach follows the advice he regularly hands out to his students, and accepts "the greatest challenge an actor could have"—to turn himself into a woman (named Dorothy Michaels) in order to play a female role on a TV soap (a hospital administrator called Emily Kimberly). And this role-within-a-role taps all of Michael's best impulses. The man who's made himself the most unwanted actor in town because of his relentless insistence on authenticity (against his director's orders he refused to sit down while playing a tomato in a commercial, because tomatoes don't sit) shows what a virtue truth in acting can be. And Hoffman, whose notorious on-the-set temperament is being kidded here, plays all three characters with exemplary comic clarity, so you can see how each is distinctive from the others, and yet how they cross-reference each other. In the most breathtaking high-wire moments, Hoffman lets more than one of Michael's identities come forth in a single scene: When Dorothy's best friend and costar, Julie (Jessica Lange), whom Michael has fallen in love with, confesses that knowing Dorothy has made her feel lonely—as if she wanted something she couldn't have—it's Michael, not Dorothy, who leans forward to kiss her. I've seen Maggie Smith play Rosalind in *As You Like It*, and, great as she was, she was no greater than Hoffman in this scene, where he suggests the tension between his true male self and his created female self with a comic delicacy most actors can only dream of.

De Niro put on weight to play Jake La Motta; what Hoffman does in *Tootsie* isn't body-building, it's pure acting. Hoffman's nasality and his quizzical–intellectual look, his vocal and physical limitations, became such instant trademarks when *The Graduate* made him a star in 1967 that no one expected the kind of versatility from him that's ended up as the constant in his career—even though his second big film role, as Ratso Rizzo in the 1969 *Midnight Cowboy*, required a huge stretch from his first, the virginal college grad Benjamin Braddock. He's taken one challenge after another: impersonating Lenny Bruce in *Lenny;* playing a college kid once again (at the age of thirty-nine) in *Marathon Man;* stepping into the unattractive, offbeat role of an ex-con who can't break out of the recidivist cycle in *Straight Time;* altering his rhythm completely for the part of the workaholic businessman who learns to be a father in *Kramer vs. Kramer.* And though the material has sometimes defeated him (as in *Lenny*), only once has he stopped short of fully inhabiting these characters who exist, many of them, so wide of Hoffman's personal experience.

As the autistic savant Raymond Babbitt in *Rain Man*, his performance is nothing but empty technique—a quirky, right-angled walk, darting eyes that respond to the mass of stimuli he encounters, tipped head and skewed focus, outbursts of uncontrollable anxiety. These choices seem accurate enough, but all they have is the *patina* of reality; you can see Hoffman locking each one in place, but you don't feel him engaging with the character underneath. By taking on the "acting challenge" of playing an autistic man, Hoffman finally outmaneuvered himself: The limitations of Raymond's condition impose limitations on Hoffman's acting that he can't get around, so he ends up caving into them. The Motion Picture Academy dutifully awarded him an Oscar for playing such a difficult role, but didn't seem to realize he had to reduce himself to do it. It's the one time, certainly in recent years, when Hoffman has failed to submerge his technique and, through the force of his imagination, transform himself into the role he's playing. (Even as Shylock in Peter Hall's stage production of *The Merchant of Venice*, surrounded by classically trained English actors, he got at something genuine in the character. His limitations were infinitely more interesting than their range.)

Perhaps the most amazing metamorphosis Hoffman has ever put

himself through occurred in 1984, when he took on the part of Willy Loman in a New York revival of *Death of a Salesman* directed by David Rudman. "I'm a character actor. Age has no effect on me," Michael Dorsey says in *Tootsie*, and Hoffman proved it on the Broadway stage, playing a man two decades his senior. (Lee J. Cobb was even younger when he first played Willy, and Morris Carnovsky was in his thirties when he created the role of Jacob Berger, the grandfather, in *Awake and Sing!*; there's a considerable Method heritage being tapped here.) Unfortunately, when the production was filmed for television the following year, Hoffman didn't scale it down sufficiently for the camera, and it came across as slightly showy and inflated, as it hadn't in the theater—a peculiar error for a movie actor to make, though the director, Volker Schlondorff, may be largely to blame.

Hoffman's stage portrayal of Willy Loman is as significant a milestone in the history of American Method acting as Lee J. Cobb's was in 1949. (In 1966 Cobb preserved his approach to the role by repeating it on television, where his transition was far more successful than Hoffman's.) Two performances in the Method tradition, separated by fewer than four decades, and yet in some way the two actors seem to be emissaries from different theatrical worlds. For though Cobb initiated the run of *Salesman* two years after the opening of the Actors Studio, and recreated it for the TV camera a year before the earliest signal performances of the third Method generation (Hoffman in *The Graduate*, Warren Beatty and Gene Hackman in *Bonnie and Clyde*), he was still a representative of the first group of Method actors, the Group Theatre, where he received his training and his first parts. So when you juxtapose his Willy Loman and Hoffman's, what you actually see (beyond individual differences in style) is how the Method has changed in the more than half-century since American audiences had their first opportunity to watch it in action. (My comments on Cobb are based on the 1966 TV production directed by Alex Segal, my comments on Hoffman on the performance I saw him give on Broadway in 1984.)

The most immediately noticeable difference between these two men in this role is a physical one—Cobb is a large man and Hoffman a small one—and in a sense the entire distance between their performances springs from that basic discrepancy in size. Cobb's always conscious of how he carries his oversized body; he gives an immense, heavyweight performance, playing Willy (in Lloyd Rose's words) "like a huge, wounded animal dying from a bullet he never heard coming. . . ."[5] (In fact, according to Edward Dwight Easty, Cobb's preparation for the role relied heavily on a Method improvisation known as "the animal exercise," and the animal he chose to study for Willy was the elephant.[6]) The famous opening image of Cobb walking through the door upstage center, bowed by the strain of carrying his bags, setting them down and resting bent over the kitchen table as he mutters, "Oh boy, oh boy," suggests an aging, exhausted monarch, his eyes weighed down by mightily creased brows. He has a way of looking down at other people (they're invariably shorter than he is) over his shoulder and shaking his head at their ignorance—at Charley, for instance, who urges him to take a job in his company rather than borrowing money from him every week—that indicates he's always felt a natural superiority to them.

When his excitement speeds up his walk, when he bounds through his back yard crying out that his brother Ben has affirmed (he thinks) the values he's passed on to his sons, Cobb's trademark manner of propelling himself on the balls of his feet gives the impression of a great deal of power balanced carefully on a path strewn with jagged rocks. And he's similarly conscious of his voice—a rich, stage-trained voice with its aristocratic Yankee accent that attains moments of Shakespearean grandeur on lines like his bewildered plea, "Why is he stealing? What did I tell him? I never in my life told him anything but decent things." Cobb reveals Willy's weariness by playing against that physical and vocal enormity, losing control of his muscles, sagging under all that weight (planting seeds in his garden in Act II and talking to the image of Ben in his mind, he finally sinks onto the ground, propping his body up on one arm), experiencing difficulty in getting out entire sentences. He displays Willy's confusion by stretching out words ("under . . . current") and struggling with his gestures, barely able to bring them to completion. There's no doubt he's the tragic hero Miller envisioned: He's Lear on the heath.

Hoffman, on the other hand, is Lear's Fool mimicking Lear. When he enters the house at the beginning of the play, he stumbles under the weight of his suitcases, almost tripping over the doorway, and shoving them into the closet is an ordeal that makes him sigh. Flatfooted, he takes tiny steps when he walks, thrusting his toes into the air like a man on snowshoes. He has a craggy, raw voice; as usual, Hoffman makes no attempt to hide his nasal quality, and here he accentuates his New York accent as if he were playing vaudeville.

Everyone else in the production towers above him: Kate Reid, who plays Linda, looks as if she could carry him into the bedroom; and in one flashback sequence Biff (John Malkovich) actually lifts him and whirls him around. The director, David Rudman, mines comedy out of the image of Willy's boys (Stephen Lang plays Happy) standing several heads taller than their dad, and he uses the difference between Hoffman's and Malkovich's height to get some striking effects. At the end of Act I, Biff tells Willy repeatedly not to yell at Linda, and finally stands up and orders him to stop. Forced to look all the way up his grown-up son's frame, Hoffman's Willy seems to shrink; he rises quietly from his chair and fades out of the room.

In the climactic flashback scene in the hotel room in the middle of the second act, we see precisely when Willy ceased to have any power over his son. Biff, having discovered Willy's infidelity to Linda, begins to run out of the room in tears. Willy blocks his path, but Biff keeps going, and in the process knocks his father down. The sight of Dustin Hoffman shouting, "I gave you an order! Biff, come back here or I'll beat you! Come back here! I'll whip you!" with pitiful insistence from a prone position on the floor of a hotel room is a painful emblem of Willy's ineffectualness. When this Lear rages on the heath, the storm drowns him out. He's certainly Miller's small man, as Lee J. Cobb could never be, but he violates Miller's idea of the play as the modern equivalent of a classic tragedy.

When we watch Lee J. Cobb's performance in this famous role, and then Dustin Hoffman's, we're seeing the progress of Method actors closer and closer to the naturalistic ideal Stanislavski dreamed of. In their day, Group Theatre actors like Morris Carnovsky and Luther Adler made startling amendments to Americans' approach to acting that might seem a lot less startling to a contemporary audience weaned on Method acting. These performers, after all, came out of a tradition of physical and vocal self-consciousness—theatricality—that preceded the Method in this country, and even an actor like Lee J. Cobb, who was a young man when he worked with the Group, never shook off that tradition completely. So occasionally his Willy Loman, compared to Dustin Hoffman's, seems to be a marvel more of technique than of sympathetic reproduction.

That's not to say that he pulls Willy out of reach. When we see how intently he listens to James Farentino's Happy putting forth the idea of the Loman Brothers' sporting-goods line, when we hear the warmth in his voice as he castigates Mildred Dunnock's Linda for mending stockings, we're reminded that it was the actors of the Group Theatre who brought a more vivid humanity to the American stage than had been seen before. But we're conscious of (and applaud) the fluidity of his transitions from one mood to another: from the way he backs down from the high emotion of his response to Happy's idea, to the humility of "Give my best to Bill Oliver—he may remember me," when Biff opposes him; or, answering Bernard's remark that Biff is failing math, his shift from anger at this unpleasant reminder (of a situation he can't cope with) to an amused dismissal of it: "Don't be a pest, Bernard! . . . What an anemic!" We admire Cobb's handling of the eccentricities of the dialogue (the ellipses, the mélange of high-flown language and colloquialism), which he stylizes subtly. We admire, too, the scale on which he recreates Willy's frustration and bewilderment—like that of a man dragging himself home through a fog—when he confesses, after being fired, "The gist of it is that I haven't got a story left in my head, Biff." Dustin Hoffman's Willy delivers the bad news as quickly as possible, anxious to swipe it out of the way so he can hear about Biff's interview with Bill Oliver and (he hopes) feel better.

Especially telling is Cobb's reading of the Dave Singleman anecdote that gives the play its title. He sniffs authoritatively, as if to clear the path to the main artery of his story, and builds the narrative line to a crescendo: "You can't eat the orange and throw the peel away—a man is not a piece of fruit!" Then he proceeds calmly, like a schoolmaster obliged to raise his voice in order to gain the undivided attention of his pupils but now able to continue with the lesson. Throughout this scene we're conscious of watching a solo number, a piece of theater: Cobb's unusual feat here is to absorb into the character the idea of an actor taking center stage—it's *Willy* who takes center stage.

Hoffman has no interest in the beauty of the speech. He keeps running out of breath and even, it seems, out of emotional energy; concerned only with conveying Willy's physical and emotional exhaustion as he fights to meet one more dismal failure (losing his job), he deliberately undercuts the grandeur of this famous monologue. This is the kind of revisionist approach that aims to slice through the accepted doctrine about a role to a new (that is, previously unrecognized) reality underneath, and though not only Method actors practice it, I'd suggest it shows the influence of the Method's concern with psychological realism on all kinds of acting. Here's an example. Actors who must deliver the most beloved passages in Shakespeare's plays often complain that these speeches are a burden because celebrity has distorted them—they sit in the middle of a scene like bars of gold no one can lift. When he played Jaques in *As You Like It* at Stratford, Ontario in 1977, Brian Bedford introduced the "All the world's a stage" speech so casually that it was half over before I realized I was hearing a famous poetic fragment. As a result, for perhaps the first time I could *really* understand what the character was saying. Hoffman's approach to the Dave Singleman monologue has the same effect.

Cobb's performance encompasses Miller's dramatic *idea* brilliantly, but Hoffman breaks through all the pretension to the *crux* of his play, and that—the real human being inside all of Miller's talk—is what he's faithful to. Whereas Cobb plays Willy without any specific ethnic identification (he remains true to Miller's WASP whitewashing), Hoffman is unquestionably Jewish in the role. He recalls sentimental old men, second-generation immigrants, who pinch the cheeks of adults they knew as children, and carry around pictures of their families; who occasionally forget a word or a name and then, self-deprecatingly, parody their own error; who warn listeners of their annoyance at an interruption or a contradiction by commenting sarcastically on it, lending their words the lilt of Yiddish folk music, and then abruptly reach the end of their patience with an explosion out of proportion to the words that provoked it.

Hoffman includes all these details. He seems to have based his portrayal on an uncle or a grandfather; it has the unquestionable authenticity of life experience, without any apparent trace of stylization. When Hoffman says, "I slept like a dead one," the archaic line no longer sounds out of place: By reverting to Willy's Jewishness, he tacitly acknowledges the debt to Odets (who has one of his characters use the same words in *Awake and Sing!*), suggesting that this old-country phrase might have been passed down to Willy by a member of his parents' generation. Miller must have intended Willy and Charley to suggest Lear and Gloucester on some level, but when Louis Zorich appears, a patch of white fuzz stuck incongruously above his forehead while the rest of his hair retreats toward his neck, and sits down to play cards with Dustin Hoffman, these fussy old men bickering (in a production shot through with Jewish domestic humor) are Lear and Gloucester reimagined as The Sunshine Boys.

Death of a Salesman has never been so funny. It's the familiarity with Willy Loman (and his entire family) that prompts us to laugh in recognition. Hoffman plays Willy as a card, a cutup, a Jewish version of Uncle Sid in O'Neill's *Ah, Wilderness!*—though finally sadder, more hopeless. He mock-waltzes with his wife, mimics a Charlie Chaplin exit, recycles antique burlesque routines (he shoves his wife aside with a thrust of his buttocks and his hands fall surreptitiously onto her large breasts), and because Kate Reid is so much larger than Hoffman, they suggest a Laurel and Hardy marriage. And an actual marriage, for once: We *believe* this Willy has been to bed with his wife.

Sometimes, like Laurence Olivier as Archie Rice in *The Entertainer*, Hoffman's Willy depends on music-hall flourishes to pull him through awkward or horrific moments. When Howard fires him, Willy keeps a smile on his face and then, astonishingly, executes a little dance step (and immediately grows dizzy and has to reach his hand out to find his chair). When George C. Scott played Willy Loman (splendidly) in the 1975 Circle in the Square revival of the play, he smiled often, too—the broad, practiced grin of a traveling salesman, but a chilling one, a warning of a coming eruption. Hoffman's is a brave-little-soldier smile. He has it when he tells his wife, in the opening scene, "I couldn't make it. I just couldn't make it, Linda"; when he criticizes Biff; when he recites the Dave Singleman story; and it accompanies the moment when, having lost his job, he sticks his hand out for Howard to shake, to show him there are no hard feelings.

Rudman retains this authenticity throughout the production. Stephen Lang's Happy (true to Miller's obvious intention in creating the character) is a junior version of his father, a clown whose cheerfulness and timing endear you to him on a first meeting and make you wary of him on a second. Both he and John Malkovich are square-looking and terribly ordinary, so lines such as "That's why I thank Almighty God you're both built like Adonises" and "A star like that, magnificent, can never really fade away!" are clearly ironic from the very beginning; we see how deluded Willy is concerning his boys. These casting choices, which underline Biff's struggle to counteract Willy's blindness and see himself for what he is, shift the emphasis from Miller's undigested treatment of the American Dream theme to the relationship between Willy and Biff, which is the play's strong suit—making fresh sense of the climactic recognition scene between father and son, near the end of Act II, in which Biff utters the famous cry, "Pop, I'm a dime a dozen, and so are you!" (When the handsome young George Segal speaks these words in Alex Segal's television production, it's impossible to believe him.)

If it's the business of great acting to make us see something we have never seen before, even in a play that's as much a part of our culture as *Death of a Salesman,* then Dustin Hoffman proves himself (once again) a great actor in this production. In Cobb's performance, Willy's suicide seems somehow noble, a wrong-headed action that redeems him only because it's a sacrifice for his son. When John Malkovich embraces Dustin Hoffman, Hoffman begins to weep silently, and he can scarcely form the words to express his discovery that his son still loves him. And then he clarifies the point that Cobb (as well as George C. Scott, and Fredric March in the 1951 movie version) glossed over: that, not knowing what to make of Biff's demonstration of love, he misinterprets it, in the Willy Loman fashion, as a sign of the boy's greatness: "That boy—that boy is going to be magnificent!" Missing the entire substance of what Biff's been telling him, he rushes to his car, happy to die what we suddenly understand to be a completely valueless death.

Harold Clurman and Lee Strasberg in the 1930s longed to create a theater that was free from compromise, and the approach to acting they advocated, grounded in emotional and psychological reality, was meant as an expression of that uncompromising spirit. Strasberg's fanatical insistence on true emotion, which he carried over to the Actors Studio in the fifties, fostered a modification of the Method that his critics complained undervalued or even distorted the text, while seizing a neurotic and uncouth reality as its focus. But in fact his approach was a logical extension of the spirit of the Group Theatre actors, who strove to find a way to illuminate character through the holes in the text as much as through its strengths. Dustin Hoffman's performance in *Death of a Salesman* represents a dedication to the Method ideal: He serves the text by cutting through to its essence and thus, in a sense, transforming it. This isn't the *Salesman* we know from our highschool English classes, but we recognize a reality at its center that has eluded productions of the play for three and a half decades.

Obviously the American theater could not reach Dustin Hoffman's achievement without building on Lee J. Cobb's. What we see in Cobb's Willy Loman is a crucial step on the way to Hoffman's magical transformation. Juxtaposed, these performances—one by an actor trained in the Group Theatre and one by a member of the third generation, the post–Strasberg generation, of American Method actors—illuminate at least some of the distance covered in half a century of the Method in performance.

Blythe Danner

Perhaps the most gifted contemporary American actress is virtually unknown outside a small circle of east coast theatergoers. Blythe Danner has been in not many more than half a dozen movies, and only one of them, *The Great Santini,* made an even moderate commercial showing. Though she's appeared on television (in episodes of "M*A*S*H" and "St. Elsewhere," as a regular on the short-lived series "Adam's Rib" and "Tattinger's," and in a handful of TV movies), her most extraordinary performances in that medium have been for the PBS "Theater in America" series, which drew limited audiences. Even her appearances on the New York stage have been relatively few, though she won a Tony Award for her first, in *Butterflies Are Free* (1969). The heart of her work, in a dazzling array of roles that includes Masha in *Three Sisters,* Linda in *Holiday,* Candida in *Candida,* Elena in *Uncle Vanya,* Raina in *Arms and the Man,* Rose Trelawny in *Trelawny of the "Wells",* Maggie in *After the Fall,* and most recently Blanche in *A Streetcar Named Desire,* has been in week-long runs at the Williamstown Theatre Festival in the Berkshires, where she did thirteen seasons under the late Nikos Psacharopoulos. It's possible that no actress of her stature—certainly of her generation— has kept such a low profile.

There was a time when Danner could have become a movie star, had the studios and the mainstream press demonstrated any imagination. Her film debut was as Martha Jefferson in the moldy operetta *1776.* Trailing golden curls like unraveling streamers, she had nothing to do but lip-sync a polka with a juvenile-risqué lyric while gamboling around in one of those stiff, structured period gowns that look like they could propel *themselves* around the set. She gave memorable performances in *Lovin' Molly* in 1973 and in the sweet, nostalgic comedy *Hearts of the West* in 1975, but the first was badly distributed and the second was roundly ignored. She'd played a hippie on Broadway in *Butterflies Are Free,* her unaffected charm transcending the dismal script; and in *Lovin' Molly,* an adaptation of a Larry McMurtry novel, she played a western protohippie, a woman who passes her life as the lover of two men. (Anthony Perkins and Beau Bridges were the Texan Jules and Jim.) Radiant in floor-length dresses, and wide-brimmed hats like soft crowns that her hair tumbled down from, she was a magnificent camera subject, and she displayed the kind of full-blown, independent woman's energy that American movies seemed ripe for once again. Though I haven't seen the picture since its release, I can still remember her pride when she told Perkins she was pregnant, and thrust out her belly.

Danner *was* pregnant during the filming of *Lovin' Molly.* She looked slimmer in *Hearts of the West*—more like a romantic comedienne from the period in which the movie was set, the thirties. She'd frizzed her frosted brunette hair so it hung in funny clumps on either side of her hat. You could see her great long legs for the first time as she executed what would become a trademark bouncy stride. And that sexy contralto, building to a throaty squeak to punctuate a zinger, was ideal vocal equipment for the role of Trout, the script girl who courts the wide-eyed hick hero (Jeff Bridges). Suddenly Hollywood had an actress who could do the kind of parts Jean Arthur had played in her Frank Capra movies and in *The Whole Town's Talking,* and even the Philip Barry heroines Katharine Hepburn had brought to the screen in *Holiday* and *The Philadelphia Story.* There was a delicacy behind that gum-chewing, wiseacre feistiness which could suggest both aristocracy and neurasthenia; like Margaret Sullavan (whom she resembled here perhaps even more than Jean Arthur), she would have made an inspired Daisy in *The Great Gatsby.*

And with this seemingly boundless potential, what role did she land next? Tracy Ballard, the TV journalist who becomes investigative reporter Peter Fonda's partner in *Futureworld,* a dim, nonsensical sequel to *Westworld,* Michael Crichton's sci-fi adventure about a robot-hosted fantasy resort. Stuck as a dupe for the first half of the picture, and with all the boastful bum lines about how newspaper reporting is obsolete because no one reads any more, Danner—almost miraculously—still manages to give a performance. And in the second half, when Fonda finally convinces her they're being hoodwinked by the authorities at "Delos" who invited the press to tour the newly re-opened facilities, she finally has a chance to shake off this woman's dopey, sunshiny naiveté and try her hand at a few nifty scenes. There's one in which she tries to seduce a robot, and one where she plays both the flesh-and-blood Tracy and a clever mechanical reproduction, in an armed confrontation: You can tell which is which only by the pitch level of that squeak in her voice and by the tiny traces of fear in her eyes.

To date, Danner's loveliest performance in the comic–romantic vein may have been in the 1979 television production of Kaufman and Hart's *You Can't Take It with You,* directed by Paul Bogart (though she made an enchanting Elvira in a Broadway revival of Noel Coward's *Blithe Spirit* a couple of years ago, too). This production attracted considerably less notice than either the APA–Phoenix staging in the mid–1960s with Helen Hayes, or the more recent New York version (also televised) with Jason Robards and Colleen Dewhurst, but I don't imagine the play has ever been more beautifully acted. (The amazing cast also included Art Carney, Jean Stapleton, Paul Sand, Eugene Roche, Beth Howland, and Barry Bostwick.) Again Danner recalls Hepburn—the way she wears those glorious bonnets, the boyish stalk across a room, and above all the depth of passion, the vibrant sexuality she can bring to an ingénue role—as well as Jean Arthur, who was cast in this part in the 1938 movie adaptation.

Most productions of this play revolve around the amiably loony family; the sane daughter, Alice, and her Madison Avenue beau, Tony, are just the obligatory young couple on whom the plot is conveniently hung. In the film the director (Frank Capra) and the screenwriter (Robert Riskin) expanded this relationship for Jean Arthur and Jimmy Stewart so that it formed the thematic center. Blythe Danner and Barry Bostwick achieve the same effect merely through the warmth and emotional completeness of their performances. Danner roots Alice so firmly in the crazy Vanderhof family that you no longer question how such a reasonable young woman got placed in it. When Tony hands her an engagement ring, her response is an incredulous laugh: You can see she's inherited her family's love of the ridiculous, as well as her grandfather's horse sense (the ability to recognize absurdity when you come across it). Danner's Alice truly is a woman torn between her love for her family and her need to keep herself separate from their lunacy, moored in a world where ordinary human beings interact. (She's the only one in the house who holds down a steady job.) Tony's proposal forces her, she believes, to choose between them, and because Danner's performance is grounded firmly in both camps, because she makes her adoration of Tony so palpable, the crisis it provokes becomes emotionally as well as structurally the dramatic climax of the play. (It's a special gift she has for conveying unguarded emotion; you can see it even in something as small-scale as the episode of "M*A*S*H" in which she shows up as Alan Alda's old flame.)

Almost everything Blythe Danner has done in the realm of popular entertainment has challenged her to locate the beating heart in dead, conventional material. She accomplished this feat in the 1978 made-for-TV bio "A Love Affair: The Eleanor and Lou Gehrig Story" (the unwieldy title is a clue) opposite a charmingly square Edward Herrmann (in one of his better performances), and again in 1980 in *The Great Santini,* which is little more than "Father Knows Best" with a hard-drinking Marine daddy hero who's martyred in the last reel. The lack of development in the Gehrig script prevents Danner from giving the fully realized portrayal you can see she's working toward; it's remarkable that she gets so far, and that she has so many terrific moments. (One is her shrugged confession to a friend after she's met Gehrig that she wants him; another is a childlike admission that, acting on impulse, she called Lou in the middle of the night and he hung up on her.) Her best scene—Eleanor's reaction when the doctor informs her that her husband is terminally ill—works not because she steers away from all the clichés inherent in the dramatic situation, but because she plays straight through them, discovering so much genuine feeling at the core that they cease to be clichés. Similarly, in her big scene in *The Great Santini,* where Lillian Meachum stands up to her pathologically competitive husband (Robert Duvall) when he refuses to accept defeat in a one-on-one basketball game with their son (Michael O'Keefe), she reveals such a complex woman underneath her apron and well-bred southern-hostess manner that the domestic tension, though it has a familiar soap-opera rhythm in the writing, acquires a new keenness.

The keynote in Danner's acting is discovery. She was trained at Bard and Hobart/William Smith, but her method has been to supersede the Method—that is, to internalize her acting training to such an extent that everything she does seems purely intuitive, as if she were experiencing the given circumstances of a text along with the character she's playing. Although this approach to acting is the ultimate aim of the Method, only a handful of performers have actually accomplished it: Brando, Julie Harris, and Robert De Niro in their early performances; Jane Fonda in *Klute;* Jason Robards in his O'Neill roles and in *Melvin and Howard.* If we extend the field across the Atlantic, we might add Vanessa Redgrave and (at her best) Julie Christie. Even the most sublime performance by Dustin Hoffman or Diane Keaton contains the imprint of the actor's intellectual engagement with the role, but when you watch Blythe Danner act you can't tell how much she's thought out. And considering the number of marvelous performances she's given at Williamstown, within notoriously truncated rehearsal periods that can defeat any actor, it's hard to believe that what you're seeing isn't *completely* intuitive, the spark of a Duse or a Lillian Gish.

Not surprisingly, Danner's least satisfying work at Williamstown has usually been in shows that force her to adopt a style, such as (in 1982) the Pinero spoof of nineteenth-century theatrical practices, *Trelawny of the "Wells"* (lovely in the straightforward scenes, she was distracted and off tempo—at half-mast—in the meodramatic bits), and Nikos Psacharopoulos's generally embarrassing *Cherry Orchard* (in 1980), in which she played Dunyasha. Psacharopoulos staged the Chekhov as a broad farce, with the actors rushing around, throwing themselves at the furniture and at each other, faking every response. It was comic-strip Chekhov, and the only members of the cast who managed to acquit themselves well were the ones with strong farce training, Austin Pendleton and Christopher Reeve.

Of all the Blythe Danner performances I've seen, the ones that best illustrate her penchant for "discovering" roles are her Nina in *The Sea Gull,* televised by PBS in 1974 (based on a production at Williamstown); Alma in Tennessee Williams's *The Eccentricities of a Nightingale,* on "Theater in America" in 1976 (based on a production at San Diego's Old Globe); and Blanche DuBois in *A Streetcar Named Desire,* first on Williamstown's stage in 1986 and then (in a revised production) at Circle in the Square two years later. The first thing you might notice about Danner in *The Sea Gull* is how extraordinarily vivid her entrances are. Like Julie Harris in her early television dramas, she bursts in, ecstatic—through the woods, over a bridge, to join Treplev (Frank Langella) at the beginning of Act I, or into the dining room in Act III to engage Trigorin (Kevin McCarthy) in a game of chance to determine whether she should become an actress. (One hand closed and outstretched, she makes him guess how many peas she's holding; when he guesses wrong, she laughs at her own disappointment.) This Nina is vibrantly innocent, rather than timid or reticent; everything we come to know about her in Act IV grows out of what we've seen in Act I. Her reading of Treplev's strained symbolist poetry is childlike and amateurish, but in the occasional cracked-voice delivery of a line there's a suggestion of depth, even though we can't tell whether we're hearing genuine understanding or just Nina's own nervousness piercing through the lifeless dialogue and suffusing it with emotion. When Treplev later alludes to the "moments of talented screaming, talented dying" that glimmer amid the mediocrity of her stage work in the provinces, we know exactly what he's observed. When she's introduced to Trigorin for the first time, she makes immediate eye contact with the legendary novelist, and we can see, all at once, the audacity that will allow her to take up the bohemian life—daring social ostracism for bearing this man's child and then surviving his abandonment of her—as well as the fascination with fame that seduces her into both the theater and the beginnings of her passion for Trigorin.

At first it's impossible to separate the last two. Nina moves with childish logic from infatuation with the tormented young would-be artist Treplev to adulation of his celebrated actress mother: She hovers around Irina Arkadina (Lee Grant), breathing in her greatness, offering her a flower in tribute and kneeling by her hammock in the garden like a lady-in-waiting. Then she develops a crush on Arkadina's equally famous lover, Trigorin. She becomes exasperated with Treplev, grown as tired of him as a little girl can grow of an old playmate. She can barely tolerate his outburst of jealousy and narcissism in the second act, when he gives her the sea gull he's shot down. When he announces Trigorin's arrival in this scene she looks startled, drugged, her hair clinging to her face—caught out, like a masturbating child. When she's alone with Trigorin and questions him about his writing, she appears to be trying to leap up at him, as if she could catch his fame like a happy disease if she got close enough. As he talks about his own dissatisfaction with his work, Nina makes herself part of his monologue, drinking the nectar of his words, feeling whatever he's feeling—sorrowing for him when he talks about "tramping his best flowers" when he writes; laughing when he says he's crazy; reaching out to touch him in sympathy when he says his soul feels rotten and then pulling her hand back as if she fears she's gone too far. After he kisses her at the end of Act III she kisses her own hand, to hold onto his kiss, to taste it again.

The Nina we see in Act IV, which is set two years later, is wracked with adult love—disappointed love, hopeless, unrequited love. In an ugly, dark dress, her eyes black and puffy, she looks closer to forty than twenty-five, and she's exhausted and nerve-exposed. There's a new, harsh quality in her voice when she describes the repulsive attentions of the merchants during her tour. She's traveled so far away from the juvenile amorousness she experienced with Treplev that when he begins to talk to her as if nothing had changed (for him, nothing has), she's too remote even to comprehend him: "Why does he talk like this?" is the only response possible for her. She keeps trying to deny she still loves Trigorin; whenever she wanders, distracted, into the famous phrase "I'm a sea gull" (that is, a victim of his careless sexual destructiveness), the line "No, I'm an actress!" that follows on its heels is a protest against the feelings for him that continue to entrap her. So when she recognizes his laugh in the next room and cries out, "I love him! I love him more than before!" her confession is as painful for us to hear as it is for Treplev. Out of that pain we hear her reminiscences of her youth with Treplev, remembering the Nina of the earlier acts who turned her domestic agony into *joie de vivre*. When she repeats the monologue from his play, which she's never forgotten, we compare this hushed, wraith-like reading of the lines with her original, tremulous recitation, and understand for the first time that this woman is doomed.

The Eccentricities of a Nightingale is a little-known rewritten version of *Summer and Smoke* that in fact ranks among Williams's best works. The earlier play is a rather too schematic contrast between the worlds of poetry (represented by the Mississippi minister's daughter Alma Winemiller) and carnality (represented by the wild, dissolute doctor's son, John Buchanan), which long for connection with each other. In his revision, Williams eliminated the melodramatic elements and solved the dramatic problem of the contrast by shifting the focus to Alma, who contains both worlds—at war—within herself. As a character study of a particular kind of southern feminine gentility, the play's in a class with *The Glass Menagerie* and *Streetcar*, and as Blythe Danner plays the role, Alma is situated midway between Amanda Wingfield, clinging insistently to the antebellum Dixie manner (now faded into absurdity) and Blanche's neuroticism (the south in decay, the south of the American Gothic novelists).

Danner uses a slightly exaggerated, slightly absurd accent which is most humorously pronounced when she tries to speak French ("bête noire" comes out "bett-a nwa"), and there's wit in the way she makes conversation about the weather ("The Gulf Wind has failed us this year"). Alma styles herself as one of the few citizens of Glorious Hill, Mississippi, with any understanding of art; she runs a weekly *kaffee-klatsch* with her friends, the town's misfits. When John (Frank Langella again), considerably tamed down in this version, speaks to her of the poetry of science, her eyes narrow as she grapples with this new intellectual food: Danner gives us a perfect definition of the provincial culture vulture. But Alma has an authentic love of poetry under that provincialism. It moves her deeply when she recites it, and it informs not only her own diction, which is intensely lyrical and entirely fantastic, but also her way of looking at the world. She sees the first snowflakes on her eyelashes as rainbows in her eyes, and the uncontrollable flurry of emotion that's her reaction to every small upset (like dropping the ladle in the punch when John pays a Christmas call at her father's rectory) is a kind of lived romantic poetry.

The play begins with Alma singing publicly at a Fourth of July celebration, her eyes glistening, her hands (as she later describes them) "flying up like wild birds" in dramatic expression. At one point she glances back at the bandleader, panicked over an imagined mistake; she nods when he reassures her, but then she has to close her eyes, as if this crisis, now passed, were more than her heart could stand. When the fireworks demonstration begins, she is so saturated with excitement that her face goes flabby with it, and she blinks tightly, blinded for a few seconds. As Danner plays her, Alma has no calm ground. She can be self-parodying and self-revelatory one moment and transported on a lyrical flight the next, rushing recklessly from one to the other, daubing her sweating face and allowing herself no space for recovery. She pitches herself into attacks of what she calls "palpitations" when she gasps in the middle of a sentence, can't get her breath, waves her handkerchief in terror because she can't swallow or work her fingers right to open her pillbox. This hysterical paralysis is beyond the comprehension of most of the other characters, just as Blanche's scream is when she can't frame the words of an S.O.S. telegram or when Stella spills water on her dress. But *we* can understand it because Danner charts our path to these explosions of invisible nerves. We get to see what John doesn't: the exhausted emotion in Alma's voice—as if her passion for him had nearly drowned her—when he turns off the lamp in his bedroom, across from her own, and she says to the air, "My love, my love, your light is out. Now I can sleep."

The other side of Alma is her sexual longing, which powers the poetry of her devotion to John. Danner throws her head back whenever she emits Alma's odd, high-frequency laugh. A perfect blend of genteel delicacy and raucousness, this display defines the precarious plateau upon which the starved spinster exists. Set off by his analysis of her "palpitations" (he says her real problem is loneliness) and liberated by a glass of brandy and her anger at his behavior toward her, she exposes her feelings for him and then has enough momentum to build her confession into a liaison. We can see her emerging sexuality when, out on a New Year's date with John, she tells him about the stranger who touched her leg in a movie theater, and admits she took the same liberty with John earlier that evening. Her desire for him carries her out of her rectory self into womanhood, and since she approaches him in that uncategorizable poetic style of hers ("All breath is warm, pitifully," she says, touching his face lightly, and "I feel like a water lily on a Chinese lagoon"—an exquisite metaphor for sexual excitement), he allows himself to be seduced, submitting to it as if he were under an enchantment. (A word should be said for Frank Langella, who partners Danner beautifully in both these PBS productions. He seems to respond to her with a modesty and simplicity that belie the theatricality he's famous for. These are his warmest and most human performances.)

Blythe Danner's Blanche DuBois in the Williamstown *A Streetcar Named Desire* also comes equipped with an odd, risible southern accent—overenunciated, schoolmistressy. But it's a very different performance from her Alma: less lyrical, less attentive to the poetry of Williams's dialogue, especially in the first act. From the outset this portrait of the best-known fallen heroine in American drama is a lot funnier than we might have expected. Danner walks precariously into Stella and Stanley's flat on high heels, making a joke out of shoes that force her to move with an eggshell delicacy and give her the impression of a stick figure about to fall over. She holds her cigarette in an aristocratic manner that just skirts the ridiculous; at times she seems to be in a particularly manic production of a Noel Coward farce, and at other times she might be sending up some archaic well-bred notion of *noblesse oblige*, parodying the kind of overcultivated acting Greer Garson used to specialize in. Danner's line readings are inventively witty; she even digs a few laughs out of the beginning of the "Grim Reaper" speech, in which Blanche castigates Stella for leaving her alone to tend their dying relatives. We're never unaware, however, that the physical and vocal tension in her Blanche has a psychological resonance: "about to fall over" translates into "about to fall apart," the death monologue picks up speed like a rollercoaster ride on Blanche's nerve endings (a jag you feel she has no control over), and everywhere underneath her valiant humor you see those nerves like tiny swords piercing the skin.

The dynamic between these two levels in Danner's performance distinguishes it both from Vivien Leigh's exquisite one in the Elia Kazan movie version—Danner's Alma in *Eccentricities*, pitched on the edge of a precipice from the opening moments, is actually much closer in spirit to Leigh's Blanche—and from Ann-Margret's unconvincing fling at the role on television a few years ago, in which Blanche had such a normal emotional range for the first half that her collapse in the second seemed to belong to another play. Like Ann-Margret, though, Danner is much earthier than Vivien Leigh, much more candid about sex. In Kazan's director's notebook on Blanche, he locates the source of her instability in the disjunction between her old-fashioned southern upbringing, which denies the brutal potency of sexuality, and her desires.[7] I don't know how Jessica Tandy made this reading of Blanche work in the original stage production, but on screen Kazan's interpretation may have been aided, ironically, by the Hays Code: Most of the dialogue that suggests Blanche is more straightforward about sex (at least in conversation with her sister) didn't survive into the movie. So in the Williamstown production Danner's undisguised sexual subtext for Blanche's line about the streetcar named Desire that brought her to this place finds confirmation in other lines like "Why, you must have slept with him!" the morning after Stanley beats up Stella, and (again to Stella) "But the only way to live with such a man is to—go to bed with him! And that's your job—not mine!"

Nikos Psacharopoulos's original mounting of *Streetcar* was badly designed, messily staged, and underrehearsed. And considering the cast (Christopher Walken played Stanley and Sigourney Weaver was Stella) it was surprisingly lacking in electricity. For some reason Walken decided to go for a fretting, distracted Stanley with no apparent sexual interest in either of the women, and the direction abetted him. In the dialogue preceding Stanley's rape of Blanche, he seemed, until the last moment, to present nothing more menacing than a physical obstacle to her movement; and although you didn't want a replay of Brando's Stanley, the way Walken sidled up to Danner and kissed

311

her (rather sweetly) on the lips seemed a pathetic substitute for the celebrated image of Brando carrying Vivien Leigh to bed. Even the final lovemaking between Stanley and Stella was cut: He gave her a peck as a quick consolation for the loss of her sister, then went back to his poker game. It was such an internalized performance that there wasn't much Sigourney Weaver could do in response (she came across as unusually colorless), and in the scenes between Stanley and Blanche, Blythe Danner might almost have been acting alone.

Perhaps it was due to all these difficulties that Danner's performance didn't completely take hold until the second act, but from that point on her emotional purity flamed through the insufficient trappings of the production, past even the formidable problem of Walken's wrongheaded performance. Fortunately, she did have a fine Mitch in James Naughton; their scenes together played with a balance lacking in the rest of the show. The way she flirted with him in their first moments together (Scene 3) was charming: She heated her face up, struggling to be serious and sensitive for his benefit, and when he complimented her on her youthfulness and she thanked him for his gallantry, you could see in her eyes a hint of success, as if she were thinking, "Aha! It's working!" In Scene 6, after their failed, dispirited date, she fluttered all over the room, trying hard to play the old role of a woman passionately interested in what her man has to say (trying to do, in other words, what she says is "obeying the law of nature"). At the end of the scene, after confessing her part in the suicide of her young homosexual husband, Alan, her voice became small, thin, and private. You saw how desperate she was when she responded gratefully to Mitch's awkward, bullish groping for an appropriate emotional response ("You need somebody. And I need somebody, too. Could it be—you and me, Blanche?"), especially since we knew that Danner's Blanche didn't desire him. She'd made it clear in the previous scene, in the strange interlude with the newspaper boy, that what she wanted was an image of Alan, a "young, young, young man" who looked like "a young Prince out of the Arabian Nights." Kissing the astounded teenager, she'd conveyed a frightening sexual intensity. The scene was revelatory, dumfounding.

Because there's no way for us to understand how Blythe Danner "gets to what she gets" (to use Elia Kazan's phrase for Brando), it seems somehow inadequate to discuss her work in terms of acting choices. Many moments in her performance in *Streetcar* seem inspired: Sharing with Stella the approach she'd taken to discussing business with Stanley, like a schoolgirl enjoying a post-mortem with a friend after a hot date; clutching the pink Japanese lantern to her face when Mitch, drunk and furious, snatches it off the lightbulb so he can see how old she really is; the wittily self-indulgent, even narcissistic, color she lends to Blanche's madness in the final scene. Hysteria is torn from her, as it is from Lillian Gish in *Broken Blossoms* or *The Wind;* in fact, Danner has never seemed so much in the Gish spirit. Watching the final scenes of the show, I remembered that Tennessee Williams had written Blanche with Gish in mind, and his great tragedy of crushed sensibilities suddenly seemed to come full circle.

The New York reviewers were bafflingly unkind to Psacharopoulos's reconceived production when it opened at Circle in the Square in 1988. You would have thought he'd desecrated the play instead of giving it the thoughtfully understated reading *I* felt it received. Their wan, uncomprehending response didn't prevent the audience from digging into the show the night I attended. They seemed to know they were rediscovering something remarkable, and Danner's Blanche— once again the *raison d'être* of the production—held them in thrall.

Danner's approach to Blanche here is quite different from her first attempt at the role; you might say her Williamstown performance was a stop on the way to this one. She's swept all the delicately shattered colored glass out of the character—there's no Lillian Gish left. Her starting-off point seems to be the most daring part of her earlier reading—the revelation, in the paper-boy seduction scene, that what Blanche really wants in her bed is an adolescent. (The way Vivien Leigh played this exchange, with a kind of enchanted, schizophrenic poetry, it was more a metaphor for Blanche's unhinged psyche than anything truly carnal.) This time around, Danner is more than just flirtatious and frank in her sex talk with Stella; she's sexy in a startling direct way: You realize, before Stanley confirms it, that this woman has gorged herself on the vices the play hints at (in other words, that she's been to all the places Tennessee Williams had before he created the character). Thrown out of Oriole for pedophilia and general promiscuity, she's desperate to ground herself somewhere; when she turns on the refined southern-belle charm for Mitch, it's obviously a routine she's called up before to get what she wants. (It's funny to watch Frank

313

Converse's sad-sack Mitch, a lug with a wayward trace of sensitivity, fall for her bait. He can't believe his luck at having stumbled across this fragile flower and persuaded her to go out with him.)

Here the Blanche–Mitch scenes are firmly back in second place, and the relationship between Blanche and Stanley is once more what the play is about. But it's not the conflict between tender sensibilities and careless brute strength that you typically see when *Streetcar* gets performed; it's not a cat-and-mouse game, with a mischievous, predatory Stanley and a frightened, trapped Blanche. This time around Blanche is the shrewd manipulator, always calculating her next move; Stanley unnerves her because she can't melt him, the way she's always melted men. As Aidan Quinn plays Stanley, there's something flat and blunted about him that doesn't respond to her amazing sleight of hand. He likes his women to be straight with him. Her fancy perfume wafts right past him, but he catches with it a whiff of sex, and when he rapes her, that's what he's going on: He's pinning her down, calling her hand on the desire he knows she's been hiding. The first time they meet, he tests her to see how quickly he can get underneath her flower-of-southern-womanhood act. He cracks a toilet joke and then checks to see its effect on her: "I'm afraid I'll strike you as being the unrefined type." You figure that's the tactic he used on Stella; it was how he began to pull her down off the columns of her plantation girlhood.

Aidan Quinn is a slender, romantic, sleepy-eyed actor with a gift for conveying the tentativeness of a man who holds himself in reserve. There's something not fully formed about him; he's in the Montgomery Clift mold. You'd never think of casting him as Stanley, and, to be honest, he does have trouble with Stanley's two displays of sexual prowess, the "Stella!" scene and the rape scene. They're no more than fair, simply because his build and his recessive quality hold him back. But the intelligence of his performance makes up for this shortcoming. He's worked through the role from the standpoint of Stanley's anger at Blanche—and though that may not be the most creative approach, it is dramatically effective, and it does lay the troublesome ghost of Marlon Brando's Stanley as no other actor has ever managed to.

Brando and Quinn couldn't be farther apart in their approaches to playing Stanley. As Quinn does it, his needling of Blanche in the first scene isn't malicious. It's partly a test, and partly his unsubtle way of reminding her she's in his territory and he intends to watch out for himself (the "Napoleonic code" speech). He doesn't go after her until

314

she begins to put him down in front of Stella. As Psacharopoulos stages the scene in which Blanche confronts Stella about the Neanderthal she considers her sister has married, it's clear that Stanley overhears the entire exchange; Quinn's entire performance is geared to that relatively simple fact. *This* Stanley doesn't instigate the hostilities—but once he believes war's been declared he has no compunction about playing dirty. And once he begins to press Blanche, even dig up information about her past, she has to spend most of the rest of the play madly improvising tactics to keep herself ahead of his persistent attempts to keep her from settling in and making a new life for herself in the French Quarter.

She doesn't win, of course. Trying to catch Mitch, maintain a respectable front so her darker desires don't come peeping through, and stave off Stanley's attacks on both of these fronts turns out to be too much for her, and she begins to fragment. The climax of Danner's interpretation is the moment when Mitch, who now knows the truth about Blanche, paws her drunkenly, hoping for a taste of "what I been missing all summer" (while she's been passing herself off as a virgin) and then tells her, "You're not clean enough to bring in the house with my mother." The way she screams "Fire!" to drive him away is truly frightening: Danner's performance, which drags us into the bowels of this woman's uncontrollable desires, makes it alarmingly clear that it isn't only her head and heart that are going up in flames.

Jack Nicholson

"You are never satisfied," Karen Black complains to Jack Nicholson in *Five Easy Pieces*. That line might be a slogan for some of the best roles Nicholson has played in his thirty years on screen—men who keep themselves from being suffocated by bureaucracy and corruption and deadening boredom by champing constantly at the bit. The characters Nicholson is most famous for are obsessively renegade, and their rebelliousness seems bred in the bone. George Hanson, the wild-man lawyer he plays in *Easy Rider* (1969), pickles himself in alcohol to freeze out the demands of his moneyed father and to maintain a clean distance from the rednecks surrounding him. Bobby Dupea in *Five Easy Pieces* (1970) backs away whenever he sniffs other people's expectations in the air: He walks out on his family, on a concert career,

315

on a pregnant girl friend (Black). He's a bastard, but an honest one—he refuses to tell the woman he lives with that he loves her; to play the role of the caring son; or to accept a compliment on his performance of a Chopin piece when he's certain the words of praise were intended as a covert seduction.

And the beat goes on. Petty Officer Buddusky, in *The Last Detail* (1973), assigned to escort a young sailor (Randy Quaid) to the brig for filching forty bucks, turns the journey into a raucous coming-of-age party for his charge, out of a disgust for military officiousness and out of that most unmilitary of qualities, an irrepressible humanism. He teaches the boy how to rebel, too, in the small but satisfying ways that are open to everyone. J. J. Gittes, the neo–Sam Spade detective of *Chinatown* (1974), has an allergy to lies, and recoils instinctively at the powermongering of the decadent villain (John Huston) who has the rest of L.A. tucked neatly away in his breast pocket; Gittes is more than willing to double-cross a client in order to help a victimized woman escape. In *One Flew Over the Cuckoo's Nest* (1975), Randle McMurphy, surely the part Nicholson was born to play, rouses a ward full of terrified neurotics by giving himself the mandate to unnerve and unravel the tyrannical head nurse (Louise Fletcher). No wonder Nicholson was such a culture hero for the movie-mad Vietnam generation: To the men he played in those years, accepting the status quo meant writing your own epitaph.

Nicholson's career is generally reckoned to have begun with *Easy Rider*, but actually he made sixteen movies prior to that, most of them for Roger Corman's low-budget American International Pictures and almost all of them dreadful. He's absurdly miscast in some of these films—it's hard to stifle a giggle when he turns up in nineteenth-century military costume in a sluggish, incoherent horror picture like *The Terror* (1963)—but his amazingly sleek, primed-for-anything presence is always bracing, especially in the languidly opaque westerns (*The Shooting* and *Ride in the Whirlwind*) he coproduced with his friend, director Monte Hellman, in 1966. He has a weird standout bit in the original *The Little Shop of Horrors* (1960) as a dentist's patient hooked on pain who laughs maniacally, in short, orgasmic breaths, in anticipation of the treats that await him in the chair.

Nicholson already was thirty-two and the veteran of more than a decade of fringe-of-the-industry movies when he caught the imagination of audiences in *Easy Rider*, Dennis Hopper's flower-child American odyssey. The movie's low-grade, trendily repetitive dialogue and heavy romantic depressiveness were fatuous even then (though its naiveté has grown more touching with the years), but Nicholson, who's introduced in a jail cell, awakening from a bender, comes across with a hip finesse and a sardonic, self-amused charm that cut a bristling swath through the sleepy film. He's startling, a high-voltage mixture of W. C. Fields, John Barrymore (he's a handsome devil), and the manic Eddie Bracken of the Preston Sturges comedies. Nicholson manages to make a hangover life-affirming, and in the campfire scene where Peter Fonda teaches him how to smoke a joint (the most famous, most entertaining of all the dope scenes of that era) he grins like a snockered scarecrow as he tastes the unaccustomed pleasures of a new high. Rapping with sly mock-seriousness to his hosts about UFOs, he's pitched right on the edge of a fresh, contemporary brand of burlesque.

Warren Beatty and Faye Dunaway had incorporated the put-on into a basic Method approach to acting two years earlier in *Bonnie and Clyde* (1967); Nicholson elevated it to a style all its own. Physically (the leering grin; the raised eyebrow; the look of slightly pained amazement; the series of moustaches he dons, beginning in *The Last Detail*, that operate like quotation marks around everything he says) and vocally (the gruff, pebbled voice limned with slivers of irony; the withering exactitude of his insults; the bravado in his curses; the way he tramps around in an obscene story like a gleeful child smearing mud all over his church clothes), he's practically the *embodiment* of the put-on.

You can see that Nicholson grew out of the Method (and one post–Method, acting-as-psychotherapy handbook, Eric Morris and Joan Hotchkis's *No Acting Please*, carries his endorsement), but he's sharply different from the internalizing stars of the previous generation, Brando, Dean, and Montgomery Clift. His triumphant flamboyance, his crowing delight in his own stores of wit, suggest an actor who has dug his way out of the Method and is sitting on top of it, proud as a peacock. That's what you see when for instance he dances among the cars in the traffic jam in *Five Easy Pieces*, improvises a full-scale cheering response to an invisible World Series game on a switched-off TV set in *Cuckoo's Nest*, and explodes at a racist bartender or preps himself for a men's-room brawl in *The Last Detail*.

The years between 1969 and 1975 constitute the first great Nicholson epoch—not that every performance he gave in that period was pure gold. He's enervated as the world-weary reporter who takes on a

317

dead man's identity in 1975's *The Passenger* (the director, Antonioni, employs him pretty much as a marionette) and oddly muted in *Chinatown*, in a role he should have been sensational in; Roman Polanski's inflated-apocalyptic direction, which tries to parlay the first-rate Robert Towne script into fatalistic whining about the rot at the top of the American hierarchy, seems to have a sedative effect on Nicholson's acting. And although he's able to energize material he's overpoweringly superior to in both *Easy Rider* and *Five Easy Pieces*, he buckles under to the smugness and superficiality of the 1971 *Carnal Knowledge*. He has a few amiable offhand moments—giggling when his roommate (Art Garfunkel) confides his conviction that women don't enjoy sex; jitterbugging with Candice Bergen—but he's used badly, as a straw man for writer Jules Feiffer and director Mike Nichols's message about the emptiness of American men's sexual lives. Even his famous grandstanding anger has a tinny ring without the context of a character we can identify with; his eruptions play like acting-class exercises.

The way Nicholson's rage works in his best performances is an example of his uncanny ability to let us experience directly what his characters are going through, as if we were living inside his skin. The appeal of the crowd-pleasing restaurant scene in *Five Easy Pieces* is not just that Nicholson acts as the spokesman of his generation when he lacerates the unimaginative waitress who refuses to bend the rules, but that he's tuned us so closely to his responses that we're able to ride the crest of his fury right along with him. The same is true of the climactic sequence in *Cuckoo's Nest* where McMurphy reacts to a fellow patient's suicide by trying to strangle the head nurse, who drove him to it. Not even Nicholson's most gifted contemporaries (Hoffman, De Niro, Pacino, Gene Hackman) have ever had this kind of audience empathy.

The first thrust of Nicholson's stardom coincided with the renaissance of American filmmaking (which may explain how he got into so many interesting pictures, though he's rarely shown as much taste in selecting directors as he has in choosing roles for himself) as well as with the turbulent years of Nixon's presidency. The audience in those years was largely college-age and countercultural, and they shared an unspoken bond with directors (Arthur Penn, Robert Altman, Francis Ford Coppola, Sam Peckinpah) whose work was often an implicit exposé of American myths and American political aggression. Such an audience would naturally identify with the renegade stance, in movie after movie, of an actor like Jack Nicholson, who aimed instinctively at the same myths. His antiauthoritarianism became iconic for American moviegoers.

That great movie era subsided in the mid–1970s, when the audience that had seen Nicholson as a symbol of the countercultural raised fist was superseded by a younger, more passive one. And for a while Nicholson seemed stranded. He gave a fine, unusually understated performance—his brashness still present but reined in, his intensity constant but becalmed—as a horse rustler in Arthur Penn's 1976 *The Missouri Breaks*, opposite Marlon Brando, but hardly anyone cared enough to go see these two generational emblems hash it out on the screen. And then, perhaps in an attempt to make contact with the shifting audience out there, he gave three desperately mannered performances in a row. In the comic western *Goin' South* (1978), which he also directed, he punches up the volume on all the farce tricks he'd used to some effect three years earlier in *The Fortune;* his impression of a scalawag is scenery chewing of the broadest kind. In *The Shining* (1980), he's whipped into a frenzy by Stanley Kubrick, who shoots him in more and more ludicrous close-ups while he snarls and scowls at the camera. These two combine to distort the story's clever comic conceit (a novelist becomes a monster out of the frustrations of writer's block) and turn it into a speed-freak *Dr. Jekyll and Mr. Hyde*. And in the John Garfield role in the attenuated remake of *The Postman Always Rings Twice* (1981), working under his old pal Bob Rafelson (*Five Easy Pieces, The King of Marvin Gardens*), he underscores every line and every gesture with compulsive precision. The energized *anomie* of some of his most memorable early work has dulled into a existential pall.

Nicholson's portrayal of Eugene O'Neill in Warren Beatty's *Reds*, released later the same year, is only a few short scenes in length, but it's assured, controlled; it signals a return to form. In fact it turns out to be a *new* form for Nicholson. In his next film, Tony Richardson's superb *The Border* (1982), he plays Charlie Smith, who leaves southern California for El Paso, where his brother-in-law (Harvey Keitel) lands him a job on the border patrol, hauling in wetbacks. It's a defeating job—Charlie is touched by the distress of the Mexicans who face poverty on one side of the border and exploitation and likely arrest on the other—and at home his spendthrift wife (Valerie Perrine) makes it impossible for him to live a solvent existence. Slumped on the living-room sofa in despair while she's pinned to the TV in the next room, Charlie could be a middle-aged version of Bobby Dupea.

But this Bobby hasn't just aged; he's matured. Charlie cuts through the stagnation in his own life, and the layers of corruption he discovers on his job, by achieving one meaningful act: He helps a young Mexican woman (Elpidia Carrillo) locate the baby stolen from her while she was in detention. Rediscovering nuance and legitimate feeling, Nicholson gives a magnificent performance. His responses are astonishingly fresh; he makes us understand the fullness of Charlie's shock and revulsion at each revelation in the same direct way he communicated fury and passion in his early movies. He's moved from righteous outrage, the young man's emotion, to outraged decency, the hallmark of certain performances by other marvelous actors in the second, deeper flush of their careers (notably Paul Newman in *Fort Apache, The Bronx*, and also Michael Caine in *The Whistle Blower*). And in the final moment of the film, when he hands the baby over to its mother, the smile that crosses Nicholson's face shows us something we've never seen from him before: a sense of deserved self-satisfaction.

The Border was almost entirely ignored by critics and audiences, but it was a breakthrough for Nicholson. You can see its effect in such subsequent movies as *Terms of Endearment, Prizzi's Honor,* and (to a lesser extent) *The Witches of Eastwick, Broadcast News,* and *Batman.* Divorced from the restlessness and alienation of some of the roles that made him famous, his reinstated breezy confidence and self-entertaining mischievousness could now be enjoyed for their own sweet sake, as displays of craft. In *Terms of Endearment,* James Brooks's 1983 weeper, he's cast as Garrett Breedlove, a seedy astronaut, technically a supporting role, but he dominates the picture by playing joyously against the movie's dumb concept. *Terms of Endearment* is essentially a story about the delicate balance that two strong women (Shirley MacLaine and Debra Winger) preserve in their mother–daughter relationship; the men in their lives—husbands and lovers—are rather pathetic. Winger's husband (Jeff Daniels), who can't pull himself out of an affair with a grad student, Winger's overzealous married banker boy friend (John Lithgow), and MacLaine's lover, Garrett, who can't cope with the respectability of a monogamous life style, are really variations on the same character whose sexiness, it appears, derives from undependability and weak-mindedness. But Nicholson refuses to admit Garrett's weakness; he plays this hard-drinking lech as so pleased with the way he runs his own life that anyone who criticizes him ends up looking foolish.

In his first scene, Nicholson falls flat on his face while exiting from a parked car, and proceeds to proposition the undergraduate who has escorted him home as if there were nothing untoward about his position. She hands him a lecture about how his disgraceful behavior has disillusioned her, and he responds by furrowing his brown and brushing his hair across it in a mock attempt at dignity. Brooks probably intended this scene as a deglamorization of the astronaut, but Nicholson shifts it into a comment on the student's callowness. It's an indication of Brooks's lack of sensibility that he clearly doesn't realize that Nicholson's subverting his movie. Brooks uses him again, in an unbilled cameo as a nationally known news anchorman, in *Broadcast News*, where he sends up everybody and everything in the picture every time he makes an entrance.

As Charlie Partanna, the Mafia henchman in *Prizzi's Honor* (1985), Nicholson centers his performance on a stuffed, immobile upper lip, a quizzical look so concentrated that his cerebellum seems to be visible through his forehead, and the slowest comic takes since Oliver Hardy— pure farce controls, to be sure, but brilliantly manipulated. There's nothing to his work in *The Witches of Eastwick* (in which he plays the devil) except flourishes, but they are hilarious flourishes. Absurdly unfit, with a pot belly hanging unceremoniously over his waist, he has the audacity to behave like an oversexed roué in a Feydeau farce, chasing his three female costars (Cher, Susan Sarandon, and Michelle Pfeiffer) around the set with a music-hall leer. His unbridled nasty intentions make him unreasonably sexy. And he's exuberantly funny as the Joker in *Batman*, cackling with self-delight. His delivery of quips about his adversary (Michael Keaton) like "Where does he get those wonderful toys?" can make you explode with laughter. The performance is a *tour de force* in his new style.

The way Paul Newman has realigned his acting in the last fifteen years, and the differences between Lee J. Cobb's Willy Loman and Dustin Hoffman's, demonstrate how the the Method has changed through three generations. So does a look at the disparate styles of Blythe Danner and Jack Nicholson: If these two performers can be said to practice the same approach to acting as Newman and Hoffman, then clearly the Method has expanded, and our definition of it needs to widen accordingly.

When *The Big Chill* came out in 1983, movie-scene commentators were quick to announce that the eclectic agendas at today's most highly thought-of acting schools (like Juilliard and Yale) have overtaken the Method and rendered it obsolete. But I'm not sure what you'd call William Hurt, the star of that movie, if not a Method actor. And, from what I've observed, most of the acting in movies and on stage and TV still has a very strong Stanislavski base. The differences documented in the press reflect the fresh options some of our best actors pursue—options that in no way violate the Method essence of their work. Some find exciting new uses for their training, like John Malkovich evoking Douglas Fairbanks and Olivier's Richard III in *Dangerous Liaisons*. Others have a gift for translating emotional daring into physical fearlessness, like Jessica Lange as a woman confronting the war-criminal father she both loves and hates in *Music Box*. And there are those who filter both the older American theatrical tradition of projecting an immense and powerful personality, and the European ideals of range and adaptability, through the psychological authenticity that the Method teaches, as Morgan Freeman does in *Street Smart, Driving Miss Daisy,* and *Glory*.

Every time we see great new American actors, our idea of what American acting is gets challenged. And if what they do expresses the teachings of Stanislavski and his heirs in this country, we have another opportunity to reconsider what those teachings mean and how far they can be stretched. At the moment of this writing, American Method acting can be defined as the vision that comprehends the work of a Gene Hackman, a Diane Keaton, a Denzel Washington, an Anjelica Huston, a Jeff Bridges, *and* a Nicolas Cage. It's an acting style in constant, glorious flux.

NOTES

◆ ◆ ◆

1. Moving Toward the Method

1. Robert E. Hethmon, ed., *Strasberg at the Actors Studio* (New York: Viking, 1965), p. 67.

2. Konstantin Stanislavski, *An Actor Prepares*, trans. Elizabeth Reynolds Hapgood (New York: Theatre Arts, 1939), p. 122.

3. J. W. Roberts, *Richard Boleslavsky: His Life and Work in the Theatre* (Ann Arbor: UMI Research Press, 1981), p. 130.

4. Edwin Duerr, *The Length and Depth of Acting* (New York and Chicago: Holt, Rinehart & Winston, 1962), p. 223.

5. Ibid., p. 261.

6. William Gillette, "The Illusion of the First Time in Acting," in *Papers on Acting*, ed. Brander Matthews (New York: Hill & Wang, 1958), p. 132.

7. Arthur Gelb and Barbara Gelb, *O'Neill* (New York: Harper, 1962), pp. 322–323.

8. Stanislavski, *An Actor Prepares*, p. 34.

9. Ibid., p. 43.

10. Roberts, *Richard Boleslavsky*, p. 169.

11. Uta Hagen and Haskel Frankel, *Respect for Acting* (New York: Macmillan, 1973), p. 6.

12. Denis Diderot, "The Paradox of Acting," in *The Paradox of Acting and Masks or Faces?: Two Classics of the Art of Acting*, Eric Bentley, advisory ed. (New York: Hill & Wang, 1957), p. 19.

13. William Archer, "Masks or Faces?," in Bentley, *Two Classics*, p. 120.

14. Stanislavski, *An Actor Prepares*, p. 252.

15. Ibid., p. 22.

16. Roberts, *Richard Boleslavsky*, p. 142.

17. Robert Lewis, *Method—or Madness?* (New York and Hollywood: Samuel French, 1958), p. 28.

18. Stanislavski, *An Actor Prepares*, p. 233.

19. Robert Lewis, *Advice to the Players* (New York: Harper & Row, 1980), p. 128.

20. Charles Marowitz, *Stanislavsky and the Method* (New York: Citadel Press, 1964), p. 12.

21. Duerr, *Length and Depth of Acting*, p. 55.

22. Stanislavski, *An Actor Prepares*, p. 166.

23. Ibid., p. 284.

24. Lewis Funke and John E. Booth, *Actors Talk About Acting: Fourteen Interviews with Stars of the Theatre* (New York: Random House, 1961), pp. 282–284.

25. Hagen and Frankel, *Respect for Acting*, p. 28.

26. Clifford Charles Ashby, "Realistic Acting and the Advent of the Group in America: 1889–1922" (Ph.D. diss., Stanford University, 1963), p. 212.

27. Lewis, *Advice*, p. 81.

28. Calvin Tomkins, "The Truth of Appearances," *New Yorker* (9 Sep. 1982): 103.

29. Ibid., p. 108.

30. Joshua Logan, "Introduction," in Konstantin Stanislavski, *Building a Character*, trans. Elizabeth Reynolds Hapgood (New York: Theatre Arts, 1949), pp. xiv–xv.

31. Mel Gussow, "Billie Whitelaw's Guide to Performing Beckett," *New York Times* (14 Feb. 1984): 21.

32. Harold Clurman, "Introduction," in Lewis, *Method*, p. ix.

33. Hal Hinson, "Some Notes on Method Actors," *Sight and Sound* (Summer 1984): 201.

2. Passionate Moderates

1. Clifford Odets, *Awake and Sing!*, in *Six Plays by Clifford Odets* (New York: Grove, 1979).

2. Tillie Lerner, "The Strike," in *Years of Protest*, ed. Jack Salzman and Barry Wallenstein (New York: Pegasus, 1967), p. 144.

3. Clifford Odets, *Waiting for Lefty*, in *Six Plays by Clifford Odets*.

4. Harold Rome and Charles Friedman, "From *Pins and Needles*," in Salzman and Wallenstein, *Years of Protest*, p. 109.

5. Michael Ciment, *Kazan on Kazan* (New York: Viking, 1974), p. 26.

6. Irving Howe, *A Margin of Hope: An Intellectual Biography* (San Diego and New York: Harcourt Brace Jovanovich, 1982), p. 84.

7. Ibid., p. 13.

8. Harold Clurman, *The Fervent Years: The Story of the Group Theatre and the Thirties* (New York: Alfred A. Knopf, 1945), pp. 25–26.

9. Ibid., p. 91.

10. Lewis Funke and John E. Booth, *Actors Talk About Acting: Fourteen Interviews with Stars of the Theatre* (New York: Random House, 1961), pp. 261–262.

11. Clurman, *Fervent Years*, p. 35.

12. Helen Krich Chinoy, ed., "Reunion: A Self-Portrait of the Group Theatre," *Educational Theatre Journal* (Dec. 1976–entire issue): 481.

13. Sam Smiley, *The Drama of Attack: Didactic Plays of the American Depression* (Columbia: Univ. of Missouri Press, 1972), pp. 48–52 and 63–68.

14. Norris Houghton, "Groups on Broadway," *Theatre Arts Monthly* (June 1938): 425.

15. Chinoy, "Reunion," p. 459.

16. Funke & Booth, *Actors Talk About Acting*, p. 262.

17. Chinoy, "Reunion," p. 499.

18. Clurman, *Fervent Years*, pp. 60–61.

19. Ibid., pp. 44–45.

20. Edith R. Isaacs, "Going Left with Fortune," *Theatre Arts Monthly* (May 1935): 328.

21. Robert Lewis, *Advice to the Players* (New York: Harper & Row, 1980), p. 153.

22. Clurman, *Fervent Years*, p. 42.

23. Chinoy, "Reunion," p. 507.

24. Clurman, *Fervent Years*, p. 284.

25. Harold Clurman, "Conversations with Two Masters: From an Informal Diary of a Five-Week Stay in the Soviet Union," *Theatre Arts Monthly* (Nov. 1935): 873.

26. Chinoy, "Reunion," p. 500.

27. Clifford Odets, *Paradise Lost*, in *Six Plays by Clifford Odets*.

28. Clifford Odets, *Golden Boy*, in *Six Plays by Clifford Odets*.

29. Clifford Odets, *Night Music* (New York: Random House, 1940).

30. Margaret Brenman-Gibson, *Clifford Odets, American Playwright: The Years from 1906 to 1940* (New York: Atheneum, 1981), p. 252.

31. This passage can be found only in *Three Plays by Clifford Odets* (New York: Random House, 1935). Odets cut "The Young Actor" from subsequent texts of *Waiting for Lefty*.

32. Clifford Odets, "I Can't Sleep," in *The Anxious Years: America in the Nineteen Thirties—A Collection of Contemporary Writings,* ed. Louis Filler (New York: Putnam, 1963), pp. 214–217.

33. Robert Warshow, *The Immediate Experience* (New York: Atheneum, 1974), p. 56.

34. Ibid., p. 66.

35. Clurman, *Fervent Years,* p. 114.

36. Clifford Odets, *Rocket to the Moon,* in *Six Plays by Clifford Odets.*

37. Brooks Atkinson, "*Golden Boy:* Clifford Odets Rewards the Group Theatre with One of His Best Plays," *New York Times,* 21 Nov. 1937, XI, p. 1.

38. Warshow, *Immediate Experience,* p. 67.

39. Ciment, *Kazan on Kazan,* p. 19.

40. Robert Lewis, *Method—or Madness?* (New York and Hollywood: Samuel French, 1958), p. 46.

41. Clifford Odets, "Democratic Vistas in Drama," *New York Times,* 21 Nov. 1937, XI, p. 1.

3. The Reality Quest

1. Michael Ciment, *Kazan on Kazan* (New York: Viking, 1974), p. 24.

2. Lillian Ross and Helen Ross, *The Player: The Profile of an Art* (New York: Simon & Schuster, 1962), p. 126.

3. Strasberg reports in an interview that the Group worked on Brecht's *He Who Says No* for a week or two, while Brecht himself attended the rehearsals. Strasberg arrived at this fascinating interpretation of Brecht's *Verfremdungseffekt* (alienation effect): "I think what Mr. Brecht wants is reality, but what I call a remembered reality. . . . It's just as real, except it leaves out the emotional present. It's not unemotional, but it tries very clearly to draw attention to what it is that is happening at that moment so that it should be very clear, very believable." Strasberg claims Brecht gave his approval to this interpretation. In any case, his attempt to define epic theater in Method terms is a curious footnote to the history of acting in our century. See Helen

Krich Chinoy, "Reunion: A Self-Portrait of the Group Theatre," *Educational Theatre Journal* (Dec. 1976): 548.

4. Ciment, *Kazan on Kazan*, p. 19.

5. Larry Swindell, *Body and Soul: The Story of John Garfield* (New York: William Morrow, 1975), pp. 67–68.

6. Robert Lewis, *Slings and Arrows: Theater in My Life* (New York: Stein & Day, 1984), p. 61.

7. John Garfield, "Lecture on Film Acting," *Drama Review* (Winter 1984): 74.

4. Psychogropings

1. Richard Schechner, "Working with Life Material: An Interview with Lee Strasberg," in "Stanislavski and America: 1," *Tulane Drama Review* (Fall 1964–entire issue): 118.

2. Robert E. Hethmon, ed., *Strasberg at the Actors Studio* (New York: Viking, 1965), p. 43.

3. Richard Schechner and Theodore Hoffman, "Look, There's the American Theatre: An Interview with Elia Kazan," in "Stanislavski and America: 2," *Tulane Drama Review* (Winter 1964–entire issue): 68.

4. Leslie Fiedler, *The Collected Essays of Leslie Fiedler* (New York: Stein & Day, 1971), p. 68.

5. Ibid., p. 8.

6. Eleanor Clark, "Old Glamor, New Gloom," in Arthur Miller and Gerald Weales, eds., *Death of a Salesman: Text and Criticism* (New York: Viking, 1967), p. 217.

7. David A. Hamburg, ed., *Psychiatry as a Behavioral Science* (Englewood Cliffs, N.J.: Prentice-Hall, 1970), p. 10.

8. Otto Fenichel, *The Psychoanalytic Theory of Neurosis* (New York: W. W. Norton, 1945), p. 4.

9. Ibid., p. 5.

10. Thomas H. Pauly, *An American Odyssey: Elia Kazan and American Culture* (Philadelphia: Temple Univ. Press, 1983), p. 65.

11. David Riesman, with Reuel Denney and Nathan Glazer, *The Lonely Crowd: A Study of the Changing American Character* (New Haven: Yale Univ. Press, 1950), p. 161.

12. Ibid., pp. 71–72.

13. Ibid., p. 160.

14. David Garfield, *The Actors Studio: A Player's Place* (New York: Collier Books/Macmillan, 1984), p. 54.

15. Foster Hirsch, *A Method to Their Madness: The History of the Actors Studio* (New York: W. W. Norton, 1984), p. 122.

16. Garfield, *The Actors Studio*, p. 57.

17. Michel Ciment, *Kazan on Kazan* (New York: Viking, 1974), pp. 47–48.

18. Ibid., p. 41.

19. Hirsch, *Method to Their Madness*, p. 120.

20. Lewis Funke and John E. Booth, *Actors Talk About Acting: Fourteen Interviews with Stars of the Theatre* (New York: Random House, 1961), p. 186.

21. Garfield, *The Actors Studio*, p. 150.

22. Ibid., p. 150.

23. Ibid., p. 151.

24. Theodore Hoffman, "At the Grave of Stanislavsky or How to Dig the Method," *Columbia University Forum* (Winter 1960): 31–32.

25. Ibid., p. 32.

26. Ibid., p. 31.

27. Tyrone Guthrie, "Is There Madness in the 'Method'?" *New York Times Magazine*, 15 Sept. 1957, pp. 82–83.

28. Paul Gray, "Stanislavski and America: A Critical Chronology," in "Stanislavski and America: 2," p. 48.

29. Hethmon, *Strasberg at the Actors Studio*, p. 34.

30. Hollis Alpert, "Autocrat of the Sweat Shirt School," *Esquire* (Oct. 1961): 180.

31. Gray, "Stanislavski and America," p. 48.

32. Hethmon, *Strasberg at the Actors Studio*, p. 170.

33. Ibid., pp. 115–116.

34. Gray, "Stanislavski and America," p. 50.

35. Ibid., p. 50.

36. Paul Gray, "The Reality of Doing: Interviews with Vera Soloviova, Stella Adler, and Sanford Meisner," in "Stanislavski and America: 1," p. 148.

37. Ibid., p. 147.

38. Lawrence Grobel, "*Playboy* Interview: Marlon Brando," *Playboy* (Jan. 1979): 140.

39. Schechner, "Working with Live Material," pp. 132–133.

40. Schechner and Hoffman, "Look, There's the American Theatre," p. 73.

41. Robert Lewis, *Advice to the Players* (New York: Harper & Row, 1980), p. 128.

42. Hirsch, *Method to Their Madness*, p. 77.

43. Gray, "Reality of Doing," p. 144.

44. Hirsch, *Method to Their Madness*, p. 79.

45. Garfield, *The Actors Studio*, p. 176.

46. Personal interview with Drue Bralove, Neighborhood Playhouse student, Aug. 1983.

47. Hethmon, *Strasberg at the Actors Studio*, pp. 136–138.

48. Seymour Peck, "The Temple of 'The Method,' " *New York Times Magazine*, 6 May 1956, p. 42.

49. Robert Lewis, *Method—or Madness?* (New York and Hollywood: Samuel French, 1958), p. 59.

50. Hethmon, *Strasberg at the Actors Studio*, p. 172.

51. Ibid., p. 173.

52. Ibid., p. 66.

53. Ibid., pp. 189–190.

54. Hirsch, *Method to Their Madness*, p. 161.

55. Gray, "Stanislavski and America," p. 52.

56. Robert Brustein, "Are Britain's Actors Better Than Ours?," *New York Times*, 15 Apr. 1973, II, p. 30.

57. Hethmon, *Strasberg at the Actors Studio*, pp. 218–282.

58. Ibid., p. 184.

59. Elia Kazan, "Notebook for *A Streetcar Named Desire*," in *Directors on Directing: A Source Book of the Modern Theatre*, ed. Toby Cole and Helen Krich Chinoy (Indianapolis and New York: Bobbs-Merrill, 1963), p. 371.

60. Schechner and Hoffman, "Look, There's the American Theatre," p. 74.

61. Ciment, *Kazan on Kazan*, p. 41.

62. Schechner and Hoffman, "Look, There's the American Theatre," p. 74.

63. Hoffman, "At the Grave of Stanislavsky," p. 33.

64. Norman Mailer, "Some Dirt in the Talk," in his *Existential Errands* (Boston: Little, Brown, 1972), p. 106.

65. Hethmon, *Strasberg at the Actors Studio*, p. 117.

66. Hirsch, *Method to Their Madness*, p. 220.

67. Ciment, *Kazan on Kazan*, p. 39.

5. Texts for Method Actors

1. Robert Brustein, "The Keynes of Times Square," *New Republic* (1 Dec. 1962): 29.

2. Theodore Hoffman, "At the Grave of Stanislavski or How to Dig the Method," *Columbia University Forum* (Winter 1960): 36.

3. Daniel Walden, "Miller's Roots and His Moral Dilemma: or, Continuity from Brooklyn to Salesman," in *Critical Essays on Arthur Miller*, ed. James J. Martini (Boston: G. K. Hall, 1979), p. 190.

4. Leslie Fiedler, "Jewish-Americans, Go Home!" in his *Waiting for the End* (New York: Stein & Day, 1964), p. 91.

5. George Ross, "*Death of a Salesman* in the Original," in *Death of a Salesman: Text and Criticism*, ed. Arthur Miller and Gerald Weales (New York: Viking, 1967), pp. 259–260.

6. Morris Freedman, *American Drama in Social Context* (Carbondale and Edwardsville: Southern Illinois Univ. Press, 1971), pp. 49 and 52.

7. Julius Novick, "Salesman Redivivus," *The Threepenny Review* (Fall 1984): 18.

8. Arthur Miller, *Death of a Salesman* (New York: Penguin, 1976).

9. Arthur Miller, *All My Sons*, in *Best American Plays, Third Series: 1945–1951*, ed. John Gassner (New York: Crown, 1952), pp. 281–316.

10. Robert Warshow, *The Immediate Experience* (New York: Atheneum, 1974), p. 173.

11. Leslie Fiedler, *The Collected Essays of Leslie Fiedler* (New York: Stein & Day, 1971), p. 397.

12. Michael Paul Rogin, *The Intellectuals and McCarthy: The Radical Specter* (Cambridge, Mass.: M.I.T. Press, 1967), p. 229.

13. Daniel E. Schneider, "Play of Dreams," in Miller and Weales, *Death of a Salesman: Text and Criticism*, p. 252.

14. Lloyd Rose, "Lost in America," *Atlantic Monthly* (Apr. 1984): 130–132.

15. Warshow, *The Immediate Experience*, p. 133.

16. Thomas Allen Greenfield, *Work and the Work Ethic in American Drama, 1920–1970* (Columbia & London: Univ. of Missouri Press, 1982), p. 105.

17. Warshow, *The Immediate Experience*, p. 132.

18. Tennessee Williams, *The Glass Menagerie* (New York: New Directions, 1966).

19. Tennessee Williams, *A Streetcar Named Desire* (New York: New Directions, 1980).

20. Tennessee Williams, *Summer and Smoke*, in *The Theatre of Tennessee Williams, Volume II* (New York: New Directions, 1971), pp. 113–256.

21. Tennessee Williams, *Cat on a Hot Tin Roof* (New York: New Directions, 1975).

22. Elia Kazan, "Notebook for *A Streetcar Named Desire*," in *Directors on Directing: A Source Book of the Modern Theatre*, ed. Toby Cole and Helen Krich Chinoy (Indianapolis and New York: Bobbs-Merrill, 1963), p. 366.

23. Ibid., p. 364.

24. Ibid., p. 369.

25. Frederic Morton, "Actors' Studio," *Esquire* (Dec. 1955): 216.

26. Michel Ciment, *Kazan on Kazan* (New York: Viking, 1974), p. 137.

27. Robert E. Hethmon, *Strasberg at the Actors Studio* (New York: Viking, 1965), p. 67.

28. Normand Berlin, "Complimentarity in *A Streetcar Named Desire*," in *Tennessee Williams: A Tribute*, ed. Jack Tharpe (Jackson: Univ. Press of Mississippi, 1977), p. 99.

29. Ibid., p. 98.

30. Hoffman, "At the Grave of Stanislavsky," p. 36.

31. Edward Dwight Easty, *On Method Acting* (New York: Allograph, 1966), p. 175.

32. Ciment, *Kazan on Kazan*, p. 72.

33. Thomas R. Atkins, "Troubled Sexuality in the Popular Hollywood Feature," in *Sexuality in the Movies*, ed. Thomas R. Atkins (New York: Da Capo Press, 1975), p. 114.

34. Carson McCullers, *The Member of the Wedding* (New York: New Directions, 1951).

35. Harold Clurman, "Some Preliminary Notes for *The Member of the Wedding*," in *Directors on Directing: A Source Book of the Modern Theatre*, ed. Toby Cole and Helen Krich Chinoy (Indianapolis and New York: Bobbs-Merrill, 1963), p. 382.

36. Michael V. Gazzo, *A Hatful of Rain*, in *Best American Plays, Fourth Series: 1951–1957*, ed. John Gassner (New York: Crown, 1958), pp. 179–209.

37. James Roose-Evans, *Experimental Theatre from Stanislavsky to Peter Brook* (New York: Universe Books, 1984), p. 103.

6. The Method Actor as Movie Star:
Montgomery Clift and Marlon Brando

1. Maurice Zolotow, "The Stars Rise Here," *Saturday Evening Post*, 18 May 1957, p. 83.

2. Hal Hinson, "Some Notes on Method Actors," *Sight and Sound* (Summer 1984): 202.

3. Ibid., p. 202.

4. Pauline Kael, *Reeling* (New York: Warner Books, 1976), p. 57.

5. Frederic Morton, "Actors' Studio," *Esquire* (Dec. 1955): 214.

6. Robert Warshow, *The Immediate Experience* (New York: Atheneum, 1974), p. 158.

7. Elia Kazan, "Notebook for *A Streetcar Named Desire*," in *Directors on Directing: A Source Book of the Modern Theatre*, ed. Toby Cole and Helen Krich Chinoy (Indianapolis and New York: Bobbs-Merrill, 1963), p. 375.

8. Ibid., p. 375.

9. Ibid., p. 377.

10. Harold Clurman, *Lies Like Truth: Theatre Reviews and Essays* (New York: Grove Press, 1958), pp. 77–78.

11. Peter Biskind, *Seeing Is Believing: How Hollywood Taught Us to Stop Worrying and Love the Fifties* (New York: Pantheon Books, 1983), pp. 169–182.

12. Michel Ciment, *Kazan on Kazan* (New York: Viking, 1974), p. 105.

13. Thomas H. Pauly, *An American Odyssey: Elia Kazan and American Culture* (Philadelphia: Temple Univ. Press, 1983), p. 191.

14. Lawrence Grobel, "*Playboy* Interview: Marlon Brando," *Playboy* (Jan. 1979): 112.

15. Norman Mailer, "A Transit to Narcissus," *The New York Review of Books* (17 May 1973): 9.

16. Truman Capote, "The Duke in His Domain," in his *The Dogs Bark: Public People and Private Places* (New York: Random House, 1973), p. 324.

17. Hinson, "Some Notes on Method Actors," p. 202.

18. Grobel, "*Playboy* Interview: Marlon Brando," p. 119.

19. Pauline Kael, *Kiss Kiss Bang Bang* (New York: Bantam Books, 1969), p. 238.

20. Ibid., p. 236.

21. Ciment, *Kazan on Kazan*, p. 107.

22. Grobel, "*Playboy* Interview: Marlon Brando," p. 136.

23. Mailer, "Transit to Narcissus," p. 3.

24. Kael, *Reeling*, p. 55.

25. Grobel, *"Playboy* Interview: Marlon Brando," p. 100.

26. Roy Newquist, *Showcase* (New York: William Morrow, 1966), p. 189.

27. Kael, *Reeling*, p. 59.

7. Mystical Communion: James Dean and Julie Harris

1. Stuart Byron and Martin L. Rubin, "Interview with Elia Kazan," *Movie 19* (Winter, 1971–72): 8.

2. David Garfield, *The Actors Studio: A Player's Place* (New York: Collier Books/Macmillan, 1984), p. 94.

3. Michel Ciment, *Kazan on Kazan* (New York: Viking, 1974), p. 123.

4. Tony Richardson, "The Method and Why; au Courant of the Actors' Studio," *Sight and Sound* (Winter 1956/57): 135.

5. Roy Newquist, *Showcase* (New York: William Morrow, 1966), p. 188.

6. Mary McCarthy, *Mary McCarthy's Theatre Chronicles, 1937–1962* (New York: Farrar, Straus, 1963), pp. 174–175.

8. The Neurosis Kids

1. Pauline Kael, *Going Steady* (New York: Bantam, 1971), p. 41.

9. Method Sanity

1. Lewis Funke and John E. Booth, *Actors Talk About Acting: Fourteen Interviews with Stars of the Theatre* (New York: Random House, 1961), pp. 170–171.

2. Robert Warshow, *The Immediate Experience* (New York: Atheneum, 1974), p. 157.

3. Elia Kazan, "Notebook for *A Streetcar Named Desire*," in *Directors on Directing: A Source Book of the Modern Theatre*, ed. Toby Cole and Helen Krich Chinoy (Indianapolis and New York: Bobbs-Merrill, 1963), p. 372.

4. Ibid., p. 372.

10. Jason Robards: The Method as Instinct

1. Richard Schechner and Theodore Hoffman, "Look, There's the American Theatre: An Interview with Elia Kazan," in "Stanislavski and America: 1," *Tulane Drama Review* (Fall 1964): 71.

2. Mary McCarthy, *Mary McCarthy's Theatre Chronicles: 1937–1962* (New York: Farrar, Straus, 1963), p. 81.

3. Ibid., p. 82.

4. Barbara Gelb, "Jason Jamie Robards Tyrone," in *The New York Times Magazine*, 20 Jan. 1974, p. 14.

5. Michael C. O'Neill, "Confession as Artifice in the Plays of Eugene O'Neill," *Renascence* (Spring 1987), p. 434.

6. Normand Berlin, "O'Neill's Shakespeare," in *The Eugene O'Neill Review* (Spring 1989): 5.

11. Submerging Technique and Other Options

1. Alexander Knox, "Acting and Behaving," *Hollywood Quarterly* (April 1946): 262.

2. Hal Hinson, "Some Notes on Method Actors," *Sight and Sound* (Summer 1984): 200.

3. Leonard Probst, *Off Camera: Leveling About Themselves* (New York: Stein & Day, 1975), p. 53.

4. Calvin Tomkins, "The Truth of Appearances," *New Yorker* (9 Sep. 1982): 108.

5. Lloyd Rose, "Lost in America," *Atlantic Monthly* (Apr. 1984): 130.

6. Edward Dwight Easty, *On Method Acting* (New York: Allograph, 1966), p. 148.

7. Elia Kazan, "Notebook for *A Streetcar Named Desire*," in *Directors on Directing: A Source Book of the Modern Theatre,* ed. Toby Cole and Helen Krich Chinoy (Indianapolis and New York: Bobbs-Merrill, 1963), pp. 366–369.

SELECTED BIBLIOGRAPHY

♦ ♦ ♦

Books

Arnold, William. *Shadowland*. New York: McGraw–Hill, 1978.

Barrett, William. *The Truants: Adventures Among the Intellectuals*. Garden City, N.Y.: Anchor Press/Doubleday, 1982.

Basinger, Jeanine, John Frazer, and Joseph W. Reed, Jr. *Working with Kazan*. Middletown, Conn.: Wesleyan Film Program, 1973.

Beaver, James N., Jr. *John Garfield: His Life and Films*. South Brunswick, N.J., and New York: A. S. Barnes, 1978.

Benedetti, Robert L. *The Actor at Work*. Englewood Cliffs, N.J.: Prentice–Hall, 1970.

Bentley, Eric, advisory ed. *The Paradox of Acting and Masks or Faces?: Two Classics of the Art of Acting*. New York: Hill & Wang, 1957.

Bernstein, Barton, and Allen J. Matusow, eds. *Twentieth-Century America: Recent Interpretations*. 2d ed. New York: Harcourt Brace Jovanovich, 1972.

Biskind, Peter. *Seeing Is Believing: How Hollywood Taught Us to Stop Worrying and Love the Fifties*. New York: Pantheon, 1983.

Blum, Daniel. *A Pictorial History of Television*. Philadelphia and New York: Chilton, 1959.

Bogard, Travis. *Contour in Time: The Plays of Eugene O'Neill*. New York: Oxford, 1972.

Boleslawsky, Richard. *Acting: The First Six Lessons*. New York: Theatre Arts, 1933.

Brenman-Gibson, Margaret. *Clifford Odets, American Playwright: The Years from 1906 to 1940*. New York: Atheneum, 1981.

Brockett, Oscar G. *History of the Theatre*. 3d ed. Boston: Allyn and Bacon, 1977.

Cantor, Harold. *Clifford Odets: Playwright–Poet*. Metuchen, N.J.: Scarecrow Press, 1978.

Carnovsky, Morris, with Peter Sander. *The Actor's Eye*. New York: Performing Arts Journals Publications, 1984.

Chekhov, Michael. *To the Actor: On the Technique of Acting*. New York and Evanston: Harper & Row, 1953.

Ciment, Michel. *Kazan on Kazan*. New York: Viking, 1974.

Clurman, Harold. *The Fervent Years: The Story of the Group Theatre and the Thirties*. New York: Alfred A. Knopf, 1945.

———. *Lies Like Truth: Theatre Reviews and Essays*. New York: Grove Press, 1958.

Cole, Toby, and Helen Krich Chinoy. *Actors on Acting: The Theories, Techniques, and Practices of the World's Great Actors, Told in Their Own Words*. New York: Crown, 1970.

Crawford, Cheryl. *One Naked Individual: My Fifty Years in the Theatre*. Indianapolis and New York: Bobbs–Merrill, 1977.

Downer, Alan. *Recent American Drama*. Minneapolis: Univ. of Minnesota Press, 1961.

Duerr, Edwin. *The Length and Depth of Acting*. New York: Holt, Rinehart & Winston, 1962.

Easty, Edward Dwight. *On Method Acting*. New York: Allograph Press, 1966.

Edwards, Christine. *The Stanislavski Heritage: Its Contribution to the Russian and American Theatre*. New York: New York Univ. Press, 1965.

Eustis, Morton. *Players at Work: Acting According to the Actors*. New York: Theatre Arts, 1937.

Fenichel, Otto. *The Psychoanalytic Theory of Neurosis*. New York: W. W. Norton, 1945.

Fiedler, Leslie. *The Collected Essays of Leslie Fiedler*. New York: Stein & Day, 1971.

Freedman, Morris. *American Drama in Social Context*. Carbondale and Edwardsville: Southern Illinois Univ. Press, 1971.

Friedrich, Otto. *City of Nets: A Portrait of Hollywood in the 1940's*. New York: Harper & Row, 1986.

Funke, Lewis, and John E. Booth. *Actors Talk About Acting: Fourteen Interviews with Stars of the Theatre*. New York: Random House, 1961.

Garfield, David. *The Actors Studio: A Player's Place*. New York: Collier Books/Macmillan, 1984.

Gelb, Arthur, and Barbara Gelb. *O'Neill*. New York: Harper & Row, 1962.

Goldstein, Malcolm. *The Political Stage: American Drama and Theatre of the Great Depression*. New York: Oxford Univ. Press, 1974.

Greenfield, Thomas Allen. *Work and the Work Ethic in American Drama, 1920–1970*. Columbia, Mo., and London, England: Univ. of Missouri Press, 1982.

Guthrie, Tyrone. *Tyrone Guthrie on Acting*. New York: Viking, 1971.

Hackett, Alice Payne, and James Henry Burke. *Eighty Years of Best Sellers, 1895–1975*. New York: R. R. Bowker, 1977.

Hagen, Uta, and Haskel Frankel. *Respect for Acting*. New York: Macmillan, 1973.

Hammerton, J. A. *The Actor's Art: Theatrical Reminiscences, Methods of Study and Advice to Aspirants Specially Contributed by Leading Actors of the Day*. New York: Benjamin Blom, 1897; rpt. 1969.

Hayman, Ronald. *Techniques of Acting*. London: Methuen, 1969.

Hethmon, Robert H., ed. *Strasberg at the Actors Studio*. New York: Viking Press, 1965.

Himmelstein, Morgan Y. *Drama Was a Weapon: The Left-Wing Theatre in New York, 1929–1941*. New Brunswick, N.J.: Rutgers Univ. Press, 1963.

Hirsch, Foster. *A Method to Their Madness: The History of the Actors Studio*. New York: W. W. Norton, 1984.

Horney, Karen. *Our Inner Conflicts: A Constructive Theory of Neurosis*. New York: W. W. Norton, 1945.

Howe, Irving. *A Margin of Hope: An Intellectual Biography*. San Diego and New York: Harcourt Brace Jovanovich, 1982.

Kael, Pauline. *Deeper into Movies*. Boston: Little, Brown, 1973.

———. *Kiss Kiss Bang Bang*. New York: Bantam Books, 1969.

———. *Reeling*. New York: Warner Books, 1976.

Kazan, Elia. *A Life*. New York: Alfred A. Knopf, 1988.

Lewis, Robert. *Advice to the Players*. New York: Harper & Row, 1980.

———. *Method—or Madness?* New York and Hollywood: Samuel French, 1958.

———. *Slings and Arrows: Theater in My Life*. New York: Stein & Day, 1984.

McCarthy, Mary. *Mary McCarthy's Theatre Chronicles, 1937–1962*. New York: Farrar, Straus, 1963.

McGaw, Charles. *Acting Is Believing: A Basic Method.* 2d ed. York and Chicago: Holt, Rinehart & Winston, 1966.

Magarshack, David. *Stanislavsky: A Life.* New York: Chanticleer Press, 1951.

Mailer, Norman. *Existential Errands.* Boston: Little, Brown, 1972.

Mangione, Jerre. *The Dream and the Deal: The Federal Writers' Project, 1935–1943.* New York: Avon Books, 1972.

Marowitz, Charles. *The Act of Being: Towards a Theory of Acting.* New York: Taplinger, 1978.

———. *Stanislavsky and the Method.* New York: Citadel Press, 1964.

Matthews, Brander, ed. *Papers on Acting.* New York: Hill & Wang, 1958.

Meisner, Sanford, and Dennis Longwell. *Sanford Meisner on Acting.* New York: Vintage, 1987.

Mendelsohn, Michael J. *Clifford Odets: Humane Dramatist.* Deland, Fla.: Everett/Edwards, 1969.

Miller, Arthur, and Gerald Weales, ed. *Death of a Salesman: Text and Criticism.* New York: Viking, 1967.

Morris, Eric, and Joan Hotchkis. *No Acting Please.* Burbank, Cal.: Whitehouse/Spelling Publications, 1977.

Moss, Leonard, *Arthur Miller.* Rev. ed. Boston: Twayne, 1980.

Nadel, Norman. *A Pictorial History of the Theatre Guild.* New York: Crown, 1969.

Newquist, Roy. *Showcase.* New York: Morrow, 1966.

Pauly, Thomas H. *An American Odyssey: Elia Kazan and American Culture.* Philadelphia: Temple Univ. Press, 1983.

Phillips, Gene D. *The Films of Tennessee Williams.* Philadelphia: Art Alliance Press, 1980.

Probst, Leonard. *Off Camera: Leveling About Themselves.* New York: Stein & Day, 1975.

Rabkin, Gerald. *Drama and Commitment: Politics in the American Theatre of the Thirties.* Bloomington: Indiana Univ. Press, 1964.

Redgrave, Michael. *The Actor's Ways and Means.* London: William Heinemann, 1953.

Ribot, Théodule. *The Psychology of the Emotions.* London: Walter Scott, 1903.

Riesman, David, with Reuel Denney and Nathan Glazer. *The Lonely Crowd: A Study of the Changing American Character.* New Haven, Conn.: Yale Univ. Press, 1950.

Roberts, J. W. *Richard Boleslavsky: His Life and Work in the Theatre.* Ann Arbor, Mich.: UMI Research Press, 1981.

Rogin, Michael Paul. *The Intellectuals and McCarthy: The Radical Specter.* Cambridge, Mass.: M.I.T. Press, 1967.

Roose-Evans, James. *Experimental Theatre from Stanislavsky to Peter Brook.* New York: Universe Books, 1984.

Ross, Lillian, and Helen Ross. *The Player: A Profile of an Art.* New York: Simon & Schuster, 1962.

Salzman, Jack, ed. *The Survival Years: A Collection of American Writing of the 1940's.* New York: Pegasus, 1969.

————, and Barry Wallenstein, eds. *Years of Protest.* New York: Pegasus, 1967.

Shulman, Arthur, and Roger Youman. *How Sweet It Was: Television: A Pictorial Commentary.* New York: Bonanza Books, 1966.

Sievers, David W. *Freud on Broadway: A History of Psychoanalysis and the American Drama.* New York: Hermitage House, 1955.

Smiley, Sam. *The Drama of Attack: Didactic Plays of the American Depression.* Columbia: Univ. of Missouri Press, 1972.

Stanislavski, Konstantin. *An Actor Prepares.* Trans. Elizabeth Reynolds Hapgood. New York: Theatre Arts, 1939.

————. *Building a Character.* Trans. Elizabeth Reynolds Hapgood. New York: Theatre Arts, 1949.

————. *My Life in Art.* Trans. J. J. Robbins. Boston: Little, Brown, 1937.

Steen, Mike. *A Look at Tennessee Williams.* New York: Hawthorn Books, 1969.

Sullivan, Harry Stark. *Conceptions of Modern Psychiatry: The First William Alanson White Memorial Lectures.* 2d ed. New York: W. W. Norton, 1953.

Swindell, Larry. *Body and Soul: The Story of John Garfield.* New York: William Morrow, 1975.

Warshow, Robert. *The Immediate Experience.* New York: Atheneum, 1974.

Weales, Gerald. *American Drama Since World War II.* New York: Harcourt, Brace & World, 1962.

————. *Clifford Odets, Playwright.* New York: Pegasus, 1971.

Wilson, Garff B. *A History of American Acting.* Bloomington: Indiana Univ. Press, 1966.

Plays and Screenplays

Anderson, Maxwell. *Night Over Taos.* New York and Los Angeles: Samuel French, 1932.

Anderson, Robert. *Tea and Sympathy.* In *Best American Plays, Fourth*

Series: 1951–1957, ed. John Gassner. New York: Crown, 1958, pp. 279—314.

Ardrey, Robert. *Thunder Rock*. London: Hamish Hamilton, 1940.

Bertolucci, Bernardo, and Franco Arcalli. *Last Tango in Paris*. London: Plexus, 1976.

Chayefsky, Paddy. *Marty*. In his *Television Plays*. New York: Simon & Schuster, 1955, pp. 133–172.

Costigan, James. *Little Moon of Alban and A Wind from the South*. New York: Simon & Schuster, 1959.

d'Usseau, Arnaud, and James Gow. *Deep Are the Roots*. New York: Charles Scribner's Sons, 1946.

Gazzo, Michael V. *A Hatful of Rain*. In *Best American Plays, Fourth Series: 1951–1957*, ed. John Gassner. New York: Crown, 1958, pp. 179–210.

Green, Paul. *The House of Connelly*. In his *The House of Connelly and Other Plays*. New York and Los Angeles: Samuel French, 1931, pp. 3–119.

———. *Johnny Johnson*. In *Twenty Best Plays of the Modern American Theatre*, ed. John Gassner. New York: Crown, 1939, pp. 137–190.

Inge, William. *Bus Stop*. In *Best American Plays, Fourth Series: 1951–1957*, ed. John Gassner. New York: Crown, pp. 245–278.

———. *Come Back, Little Sheba*. In *Best American Plays, Third Series: 1945–1951*, ed. John Gassner. New York: Crown, 1952, pp. 251–280.

———. *The Dark at the Top of the Stairs*. In *Best American Plays, Fifth Series: 1957–1963*, ed. John Gassner. New York: Crown, 1963, pp. 105–142.

———. *Picnic*. In *Best American Plays, Fourth Series: 1951–1957*, ed. John Gassner. New York: Crown, 1958, pp. 211–244.

Kingsley, Sidney. *Detective Story*. In *Best American Plays, Third Series: 1945–1951*, ed. John Gassner. New York: Crown, 1952, pp. 317–364.

———. *Men in White*. New York: Covici–Friede, 1933.

Laurents, Arthur. *Home of the Brave*. In *Best Plays of the Modern American Theatre, Second Series*, ed. John Gassner. New York: Crown, 1947, pp. 557–596.

Lawson, John Howard. *Gentlewoman*. In his *With a Reckless Preface: Two Plays by John Howard Lawson*. New York: Farrar & Rinehart, 1934, pp. 113–221.

———. *Success Story*. New York: Farrar & Rinehart, 1932.

Levy, Mel. *Gold Eagle Guy*. New York: Random House, 1935.

McCullers, Carson. *The Member of the Wedding*. In *Best American Plays, Third Series: 1945–1951*, ed. John Gassner. New York: Crown, 1952, pp. 173–204.

Miller, Arthur. *All My Sons*. In *Best American Plays, Third Series: 1945–1951*, ed. John Gassner. New York: Crown, 1952, pp. 281–316.

———. *After the Fall*. New York: Boston Books, 1965.

———. *The Crucible*. In *Best American Plays, Fourth Series: 1951–1957*, ed. John Gassner. New York: Crown, 1958, pp. 347–402.

———. *Death of a Salesman*. In *Best American Plays, Third Series: 1945–1951*, ed. John Gassner. New York: Crown, 1952, pp. 1–48.

———. *A View from the Bridge*. In *Best American Plays, Fourth Series: 1951–1957*, ed. John Gassner. New York: Crown, 1958, p. 315–346.

Odets, Clifford. *The Big Knife*. New York: Random House, 1949.

———. *Clash by Night*. New York: Random House, 1942.

———. *Night Music*. New York: Random House, 1940.

———. *Six Plays*. New York: Grove Press, 1979.

———. *Three Plays*. New York: Random House, 1935.

O'Neill, Eugene. *Beyond the Horizon*. In *Representative American Plays*, ed. Arthur Hobson Quinn. 7th ed. New York: Appleton–Century–Crofts, 1953, pp. 929–979.

———. *The Iceman Cometh*. New York: Vintage, 1957.

———. *Long Day's Journey into Night*. New Haven, Conn.: Yale Univ. Press, 1956.

———. *The Long Voyage Home: Seven Plays of the Sea*. New York: Modern Library, 1946.

———. *A Moon for the Misbegotten*. In *Best American Plays, Fourth Series: 1951–1957*, ed. John Gassner. New York: Crown, 1958, pp. 133–178.

———. *Nine Plays*. New York: Liveright, 1932.

Schulberg, Budd. *On the Waterfront*. Carbondale and Edwardsville: Southern Illinois Univ. Press, 1980.

Serling, Rod. *Requiem for a Heavyweight*. In *Great Television Plays*, ed. William I. Kaufman. New York: Dell, 1969, pp. 115–169.

Shaw, Irwin. *The Gentle People*. New York: Dramatists Play Service, 1939.

Sifton, Claire, and Paul Sifton. *1931—*. New York: Farrar & Rinehart, 1931.

Williams, Tennessee. *Baby Doll: A Script for the Film*. London: Secker & Warburg, 1957.

———. *Camino Real*. New York: New Directions, 1953.

———. *Cat on a Hot Tin Roof*. In *Best American Plays, Fourth Series: 1951–1957*, ed. John Gassner. New York: Crown, 1958, pp. 37–90.

———. *The Glass Menagerie*. In *Six Great Modern Plays*. New York: Dell, 1956, pp. 435–512.

————. *The Night of the Iguana*. In *Best American Plays, Fifth Series: 1957–1963*, ed. John Gassner. New York: Crown, 1963, pp. 55–104.

————. *Orpheus Descending*. In *Best American Plays, Fifth Series: 1957–1963*, ed. John Gassner. New York: Crown, 1963, pp. 509–552.

————. *A Streetcar Named Desire*. In *Best American Plays, Third Series: 1945–1951*, ed. John Gassner. New York: Crown, 1952, pp. 49–94.

————. *Summer and Smoke*. In *Best American Plays, Third Series: 1945–1951*, ed. John Gassner. New York: Crown, 1952, pp. 665–702.

————. *Sweet Bird of Youth*. In his *Three Plays by Tennessee Williams*. Norfolk, Conn.: New Directions, 1964, pp. 331–452.

Articles

Alpert, Hollis. "Autocrat of the Sweat Shirt School." *Esquire*, Oct. 1961, pp. 88–89 and 179–185.

Ardrey, Robert. "Writing for the Group: In Which Mr. Ardrey Explains a Mode of Unit Theatre Life." *New York Times*, 19 Nov. 1939, Sec. X, p. 3.

Atkins, Thomas. "Troubled Sexuality in the Popular Hollywood Feature." In his *Sexuality in the Movies*. New York: Da Capo Press, 1975, pp. 109–131.

Atkinson, Brooks. "*Golden Boy:* Clifford Odets Rewards the Group Theatre with One of His Best Plays." *New York Times*, 21 Nov. 1937, Sec. XI, p. 1.

Barthel, Joan. "The Master of the Method Plays a Role Himself." *New York Times*, 2 Feb. 1975, Sec. II, pp. 1, 13.

Ben-ari, R. "Four Directors and the Actor," trans. Harry Elion. *Theatre Workshop*, Jan.–Mar. 1937, pp. 65–74.

Bentley, Eric. "Who Was Ribot? Or: Did Stanislavsky Know Any Psychology?" *Tulane Drama Review*, Winter 1962, pp. 127–129.

Berlin, Normand. "Complementarity in *A Streetcar Named Desire*." In *Tennessee Williams: A Tribute*, ed. Joe Tharpe. Jackson: Univ. Press of Mississippi, 1977, pp. 97–103.

————. "O'Neill's Shakespeare." *The Eugene O'Neill Review*, Spring 1989, pp. 5–13.

Bernstein, Lester. "How the Actors Prepare at the Studio." *New York Times*, 9 Nov. 1947, Sec. II, pp. 1, 3.

Bracker, Milton. "Slow Route to Big Time." *New York Times*, 10 Jan. 1954, Sec. II, p. 3.

Brustein, Robert. "Are Britain's Actors Better Than Ours?" *New York Times*, 15 Apr. 1973, Sec. II, pp. 1, 30.

———. "The Keynes of Times Square." *New Republic*, 1 Dec. 1962, pp. 28–30.

Byron, Stuart, and Martin L. Rubin. "Interview with Elia Kazan," *Movie 19*, Winter 1971–1972, pp. 1–13.

"Candid Conversation with Elia Kazan." *Show Business Illustrated*, Feb. 1962, pp. 26–27.

Capote, Truman. "The Duke in His Domain." In his *The Dogs Bark: Public People and Private Places*. New York: Random House, 1973, pp. 308–353.

Chinoy, Helen Krich, ed. "Reunion: A Self-Portrait of the Group Theatre." *Educational Theatre Journal*, Dec. 1976 (entire issue), pp. 445–552.

Clurman, Harold. "An Answer from the Group Theatre." *Theatre Arts Monthly*, June 1932, p. 507.

———. "Conversation with Two Masters: From an Informal Diary of a Five-Week Stay in the Soviet Union." *Theatre Arts Monthly*, Nov. 1935, pp. 871–876.

———. "The Famous Method." In his *The Divine Pastime: Theatre Essays*. New York: Macmillan, 1974, pp. 74–81.

———. "The Group Theatre Speaks for Itself." *New York Times*, 13 Dec. 1931, Sec. VIII, p. 2.

———. "The Idea Behind Production." *Theatre Guild Magazine*, Dec. 1930, pp. 21–22.

———. "Some Preliminary Notes for *The Member of the Wedding*." In *Directors on Directing: A Source Book of the Modern Theatre*, ed. Toby Cole and Helen Krich Chinoy. Indianapolis and New York: Bobbs–Merrill, 1963, pp. 380–389.

Dunning, Jennifer. "The New American Actor." *New York Times Magazine*, 2 Oct. 1983, pp. 34–37 and 68–74.

Eustis, Morton. "The Director Takes Command, III." *Theatre Arts Monthly*, Apr. 1936, pp. 277–280.

Fagin, N. Bryllion. " 'Freud' on the American Stage." *Educational Theatre Journal*, Dec. 1950, pp. 296–305.

Fiedler, Leslie. "Jewish–Americans, Go Home!" In his *Waiting for the End*. New York: Stein & Day, 1964, pp. 89–103.

Flanner, Janet. "A Woman in the House." *New Yorker*, 8 May 1948, pp. 34–47.

Gassner, John. "The Group Theatre in Its Tenth Year." *Theatre Arts*, Oct. 1940, pp. 729–735.

Gazzo, Michael V. "How to Dig the Method." *Columbia University Forum*, Spring 1960, p. 3.

———. "A Playwright's Point of View." *Theatre Arts*, Dec. 1958, pp. 20–22 and 80.

Gelb, Arthur. "Behind the Scenes at the Actors Studio." *New York Times*, 29 Apr. 1951, Sec. II, pp. 1, 3.

Gelb, Barbara. "Jason Jamie Robards Tyrone: Playing O'Neill in Life and on Stage." *New York Times Magazine*, 20 Jan. 1974, pp. 14–15, 64–68, and 72–74.

Gilliatt, Penelope. "The Actors Studio in London, or, The Broadway Boiler-house Abroad." *Harper's*, Sept. 1965, pp. 32–36.

Gorelik, Mordecai. "I Design for the Group Theatre." *Theatre Arts Monthly*, Mar. 1939, pp. 180–186.

Grobel, Lawrence. "*Playboy* Interview: Marlon Brando." *Playboy*, Jan. 1979, pp. 97–144 and 242.

"The Group Theatre." *The Drama Review*, Winter 1964 (entire issue).

Gussow, Mel. "Actors Studio Thrives at 25 . . . or 26." *New York Times*, 6 Dec. 1973, p. 60.

———. "Billie Whitelaw's Guide to Performing Beckett." *New York Times*, 14 Feb. 1984, p. 21.

Guthrie, Tyrone. "Is There Madness in the 'Method'?" *New York Times Magazine*, 15 Sept. 1957, pp. 23 and 82–83.

Hinson, Hal. "The Naked and the Bred: Winger, Streep, and the New Generation of Actors." *Boston Phoenix*, 2 Oct. 1984, Sec. VI, pp. 11 and 13–14.

———. "Some Notes on Method Actors." *Sight and Sound*, Summer 1984, pp. 200–205.

Hoffmann, Theodore. "At the Grave of Stanislavsky or How to Dig the Method." *Columbia University Forum*. Winter 1960, pp. 31–37.

Houghton, Norris. "Groups on Broadway." *Theatre Arts Monthly*, June 1938, pp. 424–434.

Inge, William. "The Schizophrenic Wonder." *Theatre Arts*, May 1950, pp. 22–23.

"An Interview with Elia Kazan." *Equity*, Dec. 1957, pp. 10–14.

Isaacs, Edith J. R. "At Its Best." *Theatre Arts Monthly*, Feb. 1936, pp. 93–105.

———. "Clifford Odets; First Chapters." *Theatre Arts Monthly*, Apr. 1939, pp. 257–264.

———. "Going Left with Fortune." *Theatre Arts Monthly*, May 1935, pp. 322–332.

————. "Good Plays A-Plenty." *Theatre Arts Monthly*, Dec. 1933, pp. 908–921.

Kantor, Bernard R., Irwin R. Blacker, and Anne Kramer. "Interview with Elia Kazan." In *Focus on Film and Theatre*, ed. James Hurt. Englewood Cliffs, N.J.: Prentice–Hall, 1974.

Kauffmann, Stanley. "Odets's First Film." *New Masses*, 28 July 1936, pp. 12–13.

Kaufman, Wolfe. "Actors Studio Makes Its Bow on Broadway." *New York Times*, 5 Sept. 1948, Sec. II, pp. 1–2.

Kazan, Elia. "Notebook for *A Streetcar Named Desire*." In *Directors on Directing: A Source Book of the Modern Theatre*, ed. Toby Cole and Helen Krich Chinoy. Indianapolis and New York: Bobbs–Merrill, 1963, pp. 364–379.

————. "The Writer and Motion Pictures." *Sight and Sound*, Summer 1957, pp. 20–24.

Knox, Alexander. "Acting and Behaving." *Hollywood Quarterly*, Apr. 1946, pp. 260–269.

Kris, Ernest. "The Contributions and Limitations of Psychoanalysis." In *Art and Psychoanalysis*, ed. William Phillips. New York: Criterion, 1957, pp. 271–291.

Mailer, Norman. "A Transit to Narcissus." *The New York Review of Books*, 17 May 1973, pp. 3–10.

Mendelsohn, Michael J. "Odets at Center Stage." *Theatre Arts*, May 1963, pp. 16–19 and 74–76; June 1963, pp. 28–30 and 78–80.

Morton, Frederic. "Actors' Studio." *Esquire*, Dec. 1955, pp. 107 and 211–218.

Novick, Julius. "Salesman Redivivus." *Threepenny Review*, Fall 1984, pp. 18–19.

Odets, Clifford. "Democratic Vistas in Drama." *New York Times*, 21 Nov. 1937, Sec. XI, pp. 1–2.

————. "I Can't Sleep." In *The Anxious Years: America in the Nineteen Thirties—A Collection of Contemporary Writings*, ed. Louis Filler. New York: G. P. Putnam's Sons, 1963, pp. 214–217.

————. "A Scene from *The Silent Partner*." *New Theatre*, Mar. 1937, pp. 5–9.

————. "Some Problems of the Modern Dramatist." *New York Times*, 15 Dec. 1935, Sec. XI, p. 1.

O'Malley, Suzanne. "Can the Method Survive the Madness?" *New York Times Magazine*, 7 Oct. 1979, pp. 32–40 and 139–141.

O'Neill, Michael C. "Confession as Artifice in the Plays of Eugene O'Neill." *Renascence*, Spring 1987, pp. 430–440.

Paxton, John. "The Fabulous Fanatics." *Stage Magazine*, Dec. 1938, pp. 22–24 and 77–79.

Peck, Seymour. "The Temple of 'The Method'." *New York Times Magazine*, 6 May 1956, pp. 26–27, 42 and 47–48.

Phillips, William. "What Happened in the 30's." In his *A Sense of the Present*. New York: Chilmark Press, 1967, pp. 12–29.

Rahv, Philip. "Proletarian Literature: A Political Autopsy." In his *Literature and the Sixth Sense*. Boston: Houghton Mifflin, 1969, pp. 7–20.

Rainer, Peter. "Dean vs. Pryor: Acting in the Seventies." In *The National Society of Film Critics on the Movie Star*, ed. Elizabeth Weis. New York: Penguin, 1981, pp. 23–34.

Rapoport, I. "The Work of the Actor." *Theatre Workshop*, Oct. 1936, pp. 5–40.

Richardson, Tony. "The Method and Why: au Courant of the Actors' Studio." *Sight and Sound*, Winter 1956/57, pp. 132–136.

Rogoff, Gordon. "The Hidden Theatre: Notes for a Larger Work on The Actors' Studio." *Encore*, Jan.–Feb. 1963, pp. 33–43.

Rose, Lloyd. "Lost in America." *Atlantic Monthly*, Apr. 1984, pp. 130–132.

Salvini, Tommaso. "Some Views on Acting." *Theatre Workshop*, Oct. 1936, pp. 73–78.

Schechner, Richard, and Theodore Hoffman. "Look, There's the American Theatre: An Interview with Elia Kazan." *Tulane Drama Review*, Winter 1964, pp. 61–83.

Schumach, Murray. "Strasberg Fears 'Hams' in Theatre." *New York Times*, 25 Dec. 1970, p. 34.

Seymour, Victor. "Directors' Workshop: Six Years' Activity of the Actors Studio Directors Unit." *Educational Theatre Journal*, Mar. 1966, pp. 12–26.

Shepard, Richard F. "The 'Problems' of Success." *New York Times*, 26 May 1963, Sec. II, pp. 1 and 3.

"Stanislavski in America: 1 & 2." *Tulane Drama Review*, Fall and Winter 1964 (entire issues).

Stanton, Stephen S. "Introduction." In his *Camille and Other Plays*. New York: Hill & Wang, 1957, pp. vii–xxxix.

Strasberg, Lee. "Acting and the Training of the Actor." In *Producing the Play*, ed. John Gassner. Rev. ed. New York: Holt, Rinehart & Winston, 1953, pp. 128–162.

———. "How to 'Be' an Actor." *Saturday Review*, 9 July 1955, p. 18.

———. "In the Words of Less Strasberg." *Cue*, 10 Jan. 1970, pp. 16–17.

———. "Introduction." In *Acting: A Handbook of the Stanislavski Method*, ed. Toby Cole. New York: Crown, 1947, pp. 10–17.

————. "Introductory Note." *Theatre Workshop*, Oct. 1936, pp. 3–4.

————. "Past Performances." *Theatre Arts*, May 1950, pp. 39–42.

————. "Renaissance." *New York Times*, 20 July 1958, Sec. II, p. 1.

————. "View from the Studio." *New York Times*, 2 Sept. 1956, Sec. II, pp. 1 and 3.

Strauss, Theodore. "Group Goes to School: Actors and Playwrights Brush Up on Art Near Smithtown, Long Island." *New York Times*, 13 Aug. 1939, Sec. IX, pp. 1–2.

Strindberg, August. "The Author's Preface to *Miss Julie*." In *Seven Plays by August Strindberg*, trans. Arvid Paulson. New York: Bantam, 1960, pp. 62–75.

Thompson, Howard. "Another Dean Hits the Big League." *New York Times*, 13 Mar. 1955, Sec. II, p. 5.

Tomkins, Calvin. "The Truth of Appearances." *New Yorker*, 9 September 1982, pp. 103–108.

Trilling, Lionel. "Art and Neurosis." In *Art and Psychoanalysis*, ed. William Phillips. New York: Criterion, 1957, pp. 502–520.

Walden, Daniel. "Miller's Roots and His Moral Dilemma: or, Continuity from Brooklyn to Salesman." In *Critical Essays on Arthur Miller*, ed. James J. Martine. Boston: G. K. Hall, 1979, pp. 189–195.

Wasserman, Debbi. "Developing an American Acting Style." *New York Theatre Review*, Feb. 1978, pp. 5–9.

Zola, Emile. "Author's Preface to *Thérèse Raquin*." Trans. Kathleen Boutall. In *From the Modern Repertoire*, ed. Eric Bentley. Bloomington: Indiana Univ. Press, 1956, pp. 515–519.

Zolotow, Maurice. "The Stars Rise Here." *Saturday Evening Post*, 18 May 1957, pp. 44–45 and 83–88.

————. "A Study of the Actors Studio." *Theatre Arts*, Aug. 1956, pp. 70 and 91; Sept. 1956, pp. 95–96.

Dissertations And Theses

Ashby, Clifford Charles. "Realistic Acting and the Advent of the Group in America: 1889–1922." Ph.D. diss., Stanford University, 1963.

Sievers, W. David. "The Group Theatre of New York City, 1931–1941." Masters thesis, Stanford University, 1944.

Wagner, Arthur. "Technique in the Revolutionary Plays of Clifford Odets." Ph.D. diss., Stanford University, 1962.

INDEX

Absence of Malice, 225, 286–87, 288, 292–93
Academy of Motion Picture Arts and Sciences, 294
Acting Is Believing: A Basic Method, 6
"Action," 6, 10, 108–109. *See also* "Objective"
Actor Prepares, An, 3–4, 10, 13, 14, 108
Actors and acting
   in early talkies, 52–53
   Group Theatre, 67–84
   Group Theatre contemporaries, 57–67
   pre-Group Theatre, 52–57, 250
   Romantic, 212
Actors Equity, 29
Actors Laboratory, the, 80, 93
Actors Studio, 1, 6, 58, 114, 115, 127, 129, 136,
   188, 206, 209, 223, 226, 237, 249, 250, 276,
   292, 295
   Actors Studio generation, 19, 74, 83–84, 119,
     132, 133, 143, 148, 235
   first season, 93, 99
   Kazan at Actors Studio, 89, 93, 99, 100, 107,
     109
   Playwrights Unit and workshop productions,
     123, 139–40
   psychiatry and acting, 104–106
   Strasberg at Actors Studio, 13, 20, 92, 99–100,
     100–102, 104–106, 107, 109, 110–11, 212, 301
   style, 86, 100, 102–106, 110–13, 126, 189, 191,
     223–24, 277, 281
"Actors Studio" (TV series), 100
Actors Studio: A Player's Place, The, 101
Actors Studio Theatre, 100, 102, 110, 209
"Adam's Rib," 302
Adding Machine, The, 27
Adler, Jacob, 22, 42
Adler, Luther, 26, 42, 67, 68–69, 70, 72, 73, 75,
   85, 92, 297
Adler, Stella, 5, 15, 22, 26, 30, 35–36, 38, 42, 75,
   92, 106, 108, 111, 243
Adjani, Isabelle, 220
Advice to the Players, 6, 13–14
"Affective memory," 6, 12–14, 105, 107–108. *See
   also* "Emotion memory"; "Emotional mem-
   ory"; "Emotional recall"; "Memory of emo-
   tion"
After the Fall, 119, 121, 302
Agnes of God, 209
Ah, Wilderness!, 269, 300
   revival (1977), 268
   revival (1988), 254, 268
Aiello, Danny, 288
Air Force, 78
Airport, 224–25
Albee, Edward, 139, 218
"Alcoa Hour," 74, 224
Alda, Alan, 243, 305
Alex in Wonderland, 274
Alger, Horatio, 187
Alice Adams, 51, 66–67
Alice Doesn't Live Here Anymore, 275
All Fall Down, 231–32
All My Sons, 87, 92, 116, 117–18, 119–20
   TV (1987), 115
All the President's Men, 250

Allegret, Catherine, 183
Allen, Corey, 194, 195
Allen, Gracie, 177
Allen, Joan, 115
Allen, Woody, 216, 226
Altman, Robert, 17, 112, 115, 215, 216, 218,
   274, 275, 285, 318
American Academy of Dramatic Art, 9, 93
American International Pictures, 316
American Laboratory Theatre, 5, 9, 22, 28, 92,
   129
American Nazi Party, 181
American Psychiatric Association, 88–89
American Shakespeare Festival Theatre and
   Academy, 93
American Theatre Wing, 93
American Tragedy, An
   novel (1925), 30, 147
   film (1931), 147
"Anastasia," 205
"Anatomy of Falsehood, The," 227
Anderson, Edward, 23, 25
Anderson, Maxwell, 30, 54, 58–59, 92, 154
Anderson, Robert, 91, 115
Anderson, Sherwood, 28
Andrews, Dana, 71, 95, 96, 142
Andreyev, Leonid, 27
Angeli, Pier, 278
Angels with Dirty Faces, 191
"Animal exercise," 129–30, 296
Animal Kingdom, The, 53, 56
Ann-Margret, 311
Another Woman, 216, 218
Anouilh, Jean, 205
ANTA Playhouse, 83
Antoine, Andre, 8
Antonioni, Michelangelo, 318
APA-Phoenix Theatre, 304
Apocalypse Now, 180–81
Appaloosa, The, 167–68
Archer, William, 8
Arms and the Man, 302
Arnold, Edward, 61
Arnold, William, 89
"Art and Neurosis," 110
Arthur, Jean, 51, 303, 304
As You Like It, 293, 299
Asther, Nils, 65
Atkins, Thomas, 132
Atkinson, Brooks, 44
Atlantic City, 289
Attenborough, Richard, 211
"Autobiography of Miss Jane Pittman, The," 274
Autumn Garden, The, 92
Awake and Sing!, 22, 40, 41, 42, 44, 45–46, 47,
   49, 115, 118, 122, 123, 140, 250, 299
   Broadway production (1935), 15, 30, 36, 37, 42,
     68, 69, 75, 111, 295

Baby Doll, 94, 96–97, 123, 130, 243
Baby Face, 63, 64–65, 66
Bachelor Mother, 51

Backus, Jim, 194, 195
Baker, Carroll, 94, 197, 243
Balaban, Bob, 216
Baldwin, James, 102, 139
Balsam, Martin, 93, 100
Bancroft, Anne, 232
Bancroft, Squire and Marie Wilton, 8, 17
Band Wagon, The, 26
Bankhead, Tallulah, 95
Barkin, Ellen, 233
Barretts of Wimpole Street, The, 26
Barry, Philip, 27, 53, 303
Barrymore, John, 54–55, 170, 250, 317
Barthelmess, Richard, 65
Baryshnikov, Mikhail, 208
Basserman, Albert, 11, 16
Bates, Kathy, 220
Batman, 166, 320, 321
"Battler, The," 276, 277–78, 280
Beacham, Stephanie, 179
"Beats," 10
Beatty, Warren, 225, 226, 231, 232, 274, 279, 295, 317, 319
Beckett, Samuel, 21, 113, 273
Bedford, Brian, 299
Bedtime Story, 167, 170
Beery, Wallace, 22
Beetlejuice, 62
Before Breakfast, 10
Begley, Ed, 96, 189
Bel Geddes, Barbara, 95, 130
Belasco, David, 251
Belle of Amherst, The, 205
Bellow, Saul, 87, 233
ben Ami, Jacob, 110
Benedek, Laslo, 162
Benedetti, Robert, 14
Bennett, Belle, 66
Bergen, Candice, 318
Berghof, Herbert, 93, 99
Bergman, Andrew, 176, 177
Bergman, Ingmar, 226
Berlin, Normand, 131, 271
Berlin Stories, 200
Bertolucci, Bernardo, 181, 185, 275
Best Years of Our Lives, The, 54, 71, 73, 94, 157, 227
Bettelheim, Bruno, 88
Beyond the Horizon, 252, 255
Big Chill, The, 322
Big Knife, The, 43
   Broadway production (1949), 82
   film (1955), 166, 237, 238
Big Lift, The, 145
Bitter Tea of General Yen, The, 63, 65, 66
Black, Karen, 216, 218, 315, 316
Blackboard Jungle, The, 161
Blackburn, Clarice, 204
Blaze, 291–92
Blithe Spirit, 210, 304
Blondell, Joan, 96
Bloom, Claire, 205
Blues for Mister Charlie, 102
Blues in the Night, 67, 68
Blume in Love, 274
Body Heat, 210
Body and Soul, 78, 79, 80, 82, 83, 163, 282
Bogard, Travis, 253, 255
Bogarde, Dirk, 203

Bogart, Humphrey, 51
Bogart, Paul, 304
Bohnen, Roman, 67, 70–71, 72, 73
Boles, John, 66
Boleslavsky, Richard, 3, 8, 9, 10, 12–13, 22, 28, 32, 92
Bolt, Robert, 241
Bonaparte, Napoleon, 170
Bond, Rudy, 93
Bond, Sudie, 219
Bonnie and Clyde, 195, 274, 295, 317
Booke, Sorrell, 256
Boomerang!, 94, 95, 96
Booth, Edwin, 8
Booth, Shirley, 115
Border, The, 319–20
Borgnine, Ernest, 1, 2, 149, 166
Born to Win, 274
Bostwick, Barry, 304
Bracken, Eddie, 317
Bradlee, Ben, 250
Brand, Phoebe, 69, 93, 107
Brando, Jocelyn, 93
Brando, Marlon, 15, 21, 52, 54, 79, 84, 85, 92, 93, 99, 100, 101, 104, 106, 112, 119, 128, 132, 133, 134, 143, 144, 148, 154–85, 188, 191, 192, 193, 227, 229, 231, 235, 237, 238, 250, 253–54, 267, 272, 275, 277, 278, 292, 293, 305–306, 311, 312, 314, 317, 319
Breaking Point, The, 81, 82
Brecht, Bertolt, 37, 63, 63n
Brenman-Gibson, Margaret, 41
Breuer, Bessie, 99
Brian, Mary, 53
Bridges, Beau, 303
Bridges, Jeff, 275, 303, 322
Britt, May, 168
Broadcast News, 320, 321
Broderick, Matthew, 177
Broken Blossoms, 65, 313
Bromberg, J. Edward, 42, 82, 85, 92
Brooks, James, 320, 321
Brooks, Richard, 208, 278
Brothers Karamazov, The, 27
Brown, Arvin, 268
Brown, Clarence, 247
Brown, Harry, 148
Brustein, Robert, 110, 114, 119
Bryant, Louise, 226
Building a Character, 3, 4, 13
Burn!, 178–79, 184
Burnett, W. R., 57
Burns, George, 177
Burr, Raymond, 148
Burton, Richard, 215
Bus Stop, 92
Butch Cassidy and the Sundance Kid, 276, 284
Byington, Spring, 268

Caan, James, 175, 275
Cabaret, 200
Cage, Nicolas, 322
Cagney, James, 51, 57, 68, 78
Caine, Michael, 320
Caldwell, Erskine, 23
California Split, 274
Camille, 63, 199

Camino Real, 100, 123, 124, 126, 127, 129, 132, 139, 250
Candida, 58, 302
Candy, 167
Cantwell, Robert, 23
Canty, Marietta, 194
Capek, Karel, 27
Capote, Truman, 167
Capra, Frank, 63, 65, 288, 303, 304
Capri, Ahna, 245
Carnal Knowledge, 318
Carnegie, Dale, 88
Carney, Art, 304
Carnovsky, Morris, 15, 26, 29, 30, 32, 42, 69–70, 71, 72, 73, 74, 85, 92, 93, 111, 295, 297
Carpenter, Don, 244
Carradine, Keith, 216, 274
Carrie, 217
Carrillo, Elpidia, 320
Carroll, Sidney, 281
Case of Clyde Griffiths, The, 30, 63, 92
Casella, Alberto, 54
Cassavetes, John, 184
Casualties of War, 94
Cat on a Hot Tin Roof, 123–24, 126, 130, 132
    Broadway production (1955), 95, 130–31
    film (1958), 278–79, 280, 286
    TV (1985), 213, 243–44
Catcher in the Rye, 91, 134
Cattle Annie and Little Britches, 239, 242
Caught, 249
Chaliapin, Feodor, 110
Chaney, Lon, Jr., 59
Chaplin, Charles, 167, 300
Chase, The, 167, 170
Chatterton, Ruth, 55, 56
Chayefsky, Paddy, 1–3, 115, 119, 201, 210, 238
Chekhov, Anton, 3, 5, 16, 43–46, 49, 110, 114, 155, 188, 202, 210, 215, 218, 306
Chekhov, Michael, 14, 128
Cher, 218, 321
Cherry Orchard, The, 306
Chinatown, 316, 318
Chopin, Frederic, 316
Christie, Julie, 241, 306
Circle in the Square, 235, 254, 300, 306, 313
City for Conquest, 67, 68
Civic Repertory Company, 28
Clark, Eleanor, 87
Clark, Walter Van Tilburg, 87
Clash by Night, 249
Claudel, Paul, 27
Cleveland Playhouse, 85
Clift, Montgomery, 86, 92, 93, 99, 112, 132, 142–54, 155, 158, 188, 223, 224, 292, 314, 317
Clurman, Harold, 42, 106, 243
    as critic, 159–60
    as director, 48, 52, 92, 127–28, 134, 139, 197–98
    Group Theatre, 21, 22, 26, 27, 28–29, 30, 33, 34, 35, 36, 48, 58–59, 61, 75, 102, 109, 301
Cobb, Humphrey, 23
Cobb, Lee J., 67, 71–75, 83, 95, 96, 123, 163, 276, 295–99, 301–302, 321
Cocteau, Jean, 127
Cohen, Leonard, 245
Cohen, Robert, 286
Collector, The, 216
Collins, Russell, 85

Colman, Ronald, 66
Color of Money, The, 289–91, 292
Columbia Pictures, 57
Come Back to the 5 & Dime, Jimmy Dean, Jimmy Dean, 115, 215, 217–22
Come Back, Little Sheba, 115, 120
Come and Get It, 60–61
"Comedian, The," 201, 236
Coming Home, 275
Communist Manifesto, The, 39
Communist Party, 23, 47
Congreve, William, 171
Conrack, 275
Conrad, Joseph, 61, 180
Conte, Richard, 175
Contour in Time, 253, 255
Conversation, The, 274
Converse, Frank, 313–14
Cook, George Cram, 9
Cool Hand Luke, 276, 280, 283–84
Cooper, Gary, 51
Copeau, Jacques, 27
Coppola, Francis Ford, 17, 139, 174, 175, 177, 180–81, 274, 318
Coquelin, Constant-Benoit, 11, 12
Corman, Roger, 316
Cornered, 68–69, 70
Corsaro, Frank, 140
Costigan, James, 201, 202
Counsellor-at-Law, 54, 55
Count of Monte Cristo, The, 10
Countess from Hong Kong, A, 167, 170
Country Girl, The, 43
Courtenay, Tom, 241
Coward, Noel, 26, 210, 310
Craig, Edward Gordon, 252
Crawford, Cheryl, 22, 29, 75, 93, 101
Crawford, Joan, 82, 207
Creating a Role, 3
Crichton, Michael, 303
Cronyn, Hume, 203
Crosby, Bing, 177
Cross Creek, 246–48
Crouse, Lindsay, 285
Crucible, The, 162–63
Cruise, Tom, 289
Curtis, Tony, 238
Curtiz, Michael, 76
Cyrano de Bergerac, 69

Dahlberg, Edward, 23
Dangerous Liaisons, 322
Dangling Man, 87
Daniels, Jeff, 320
Danner, Blythe, 208, 217, 275, 276, 302–15, 321
Dark at the Top of the Stairs, The, 135–36
Daughters Courageous, 77, 78–79, 81
Davalos, Richard, 186
David, 172
Davidovich, Lolita, 291
Davis, Bette, 51, 52, 170
Day of the Locust, The, 59, 60
De Havilland, Olivia, 145, 271
De Niro, Robert, 15, 21, 166, 274, 275, 278, 288, 292, 294, 304–305, 318
De Sica, Vittorio, 96, 143, 146
de Wilde, Brandon, 232, 282, 283
Dead End, 61, 163, 191

Dead End Kids, 171, 275
Dead of Night, 257
Dean, James, 19, 52, 84, 86, 95, 100, 112, 121,
    134, 144, 148, 156, 186–97, 201, 217, 218,
    219, 220, 221, 223, 237, 277, 278, 279, 317
Dean, John, 216
Death of a Salesman, 42, 50, 87, 116–18, 119–22,
    124, 136, 185, 259, 278, 282, 301
    Broadway production (1949), 71, 120, 123, 295
    film (1951), 301
    TV (1966), 71, 74, 295–99, 301–302
    revival (1984), 15, 276, 293–302
    TV (1985), 295
"Death of Socrates," 277
Death Takes a Holiday, 54
Death in Venice, 143
Deep Are the Roots, 87, 92
Defector, The, 152
Deliverance, 275
Deluge, The, 128
Demme, Jonathan, 272
Dennis, Sandy, 206, 209, 214–22, 223, 224
DePalma, Brian, 217
Desire Under the Elms, 120
Desiree, 167, 170, 171
Destry Rides Again, 51
Detective Story, 87, 120
Devlin, Don, 233
Dewhurst, Colleen, 254, 264, 268, 269, 271, 304
Dickens, Charles, 172, 187, 249
Dickinson, Emily, 205
Diderot, Denis, 7, 11
Dillon, Melinda, 225, 286, 287
Diner, 233
Dinner at Eight, 29
D.O.A., 68, 69
Dr. Jekyll and Mr. Hyde, 319
Doctor Zhivago, 238, 239, 240–41
Dodsworth, 55–56, 63
Dog Day Afternoon, 274
Doll's House, A, 9, 18
    TV (1959), 203–204
Donaldson, Ted, 96
Don't Look Now, 275
Doran, Ann, 194
Dos Passos, John, 23
Dostoevski, Feodor, 27, 159, 270
Double Indemnity, 64, 94
Douglas, Melvyn, 115, 283
Dovzhenko, Alexander, 128–29
Dowd, Harrison, 257
Dowd, Nancy, 285
Dowling, Eddie, 252
Drama of Attack, The, 30
Dramatic Workshop, 92, 106
Dreiser, Theodore, 19, 30, 147, 252
Driving Miss Daisy, 322
Dru, Joanne, 143, 144
Dry White Season, A, 179
Duchess of Malfi, The, 176
Duerr, Edwin, 7
Duke, Daryl, 244
"Duke in His Domain, The," 167
Dummar, Melvin, 272
Dunaway, Faye, 317
Duncan, Isadora, 215
Dunn, James, 95
Dunnock, Mildred, 93, 99, 100, 298
"DuPont Show of the Month," 72, 202

Duse, Eleanora, 109, 110, 306
Dust Be My Destiny, 78
Duvall, Robert, 175, 244, 275, 305
Duvall, Shelley, 274

Eakins, Thomas, 19–20, 292
"Early Frost, An," 62
East of Eden, 95, 96, 97–98, 100, 121, 144, 186–
    87, 189, 190, 192–193, 196, 197, 200
Easty, Edward Dwight, 6, 104–105, 132, 296
Easy Living, 51
Easy Rider, 315, 316–17, 318
Eccentricities of a Nightingale, The, 124, 308
    TV (1976), 208, 217, 306, 308–10
Edison, Thomas Alva, 60
Edison the Man, 60
Edwards, Ben, 271
Eichmann, Adolf, 178
"Eighty-Yard Run, The," 278, 279, 280, 286, 292
Eisenhower, Dwight, 91, 102, 161
Eldridge, Florence, 95
Elmer Gantry, 256, 260
Emmich, Cliff, 245
"Emotion memory," 75, 211. *See also* "Affective
    memory"; Emotional memory"; "Emotional
    recall"; "Memory of emotion"
"Emotional memory," 14. *See also* "Affective
    memory"; "Emotion memory"; "Emotional
    recall"; "Memory of emotion"
"Emotional recall," 6, 107, 129. *See also* "Affective
    memory"; "Emotion memory"; "Emotional
    memory"; "Memory of emotion"
Emperor Jones, The, 251, 262
End as a Man, 91, 136, 139
Enemy of the People, An, 261
Entertainer, The, 172, 258, 300
"Ethan Frome," 204–205
Evans, Walker, 97
Ewell, Tom, 93
Exodus, 231
Expressionism, 37, 62, 97, 251, 253, 262

Face in the Crowd, A, 94, 96, 97–98
Fairbanks, Douglas, 322
Fallen Sparrow, The, 81
Farentino, James, 297
Farewell to Arms, A, 51, 57
Farmer, Frances, 60–61, 63, 89, 233
Farrell, James T., 252
Farrow, Mia, 274
"Father Knows Best," 91, 305
Faulkner, William, 207
Fearing, Kenneth, 23
Fechter, Charles, 8
Federal Theatre Project, 28
Feiffer, Jules, 318
Fellini, Federico, 96, 160
Fenichel, Otto, 88
Fervent Years, The, 27, 30
Feydeau, Georges, 321
Fiddler on the Roof, 116
Fiedler, Leslie, 86, 90, 116, 119
Field, Sally, 287
Fields, W. C., 177, 317
Fifty Million Frenchmen, 26
Fine, Morton, 239
Finney, Albert, 112, 247

Fiske, Minnie Maddern, 16
Five Easy Pieces, 315–16, 317, 318, 319, 320
Fletcher, Louise, 316
Flying High, 26
Fonda, Henry, 62
Fonda, Jane, 274, 275, 306
Fonda, Peter, 303, 317
Fontanne, Lynn, 16
Foote, Horton, 201
Force of Evil, 79, 81
Ford, John, 57, 94
Foreman, Carl, 157
Formula, The, 181
Forster, Robert, 173
Forsythe, John, 93, 249
Fort Apache, the Bronx, 287–88, 292–93, 320
Fortune, The, 319
Fosse, Bob, 274
Four Daughters, 76–77, 78, 79
"Fourth wall," 7–8, 37
Fox, The, 214
Frances, 213–14
Franciosa, Anthony, 227, 228
Frank, Harriet, Jr., 282
Frankenheimer, John, 54, 201, 207, 236, 254
Freedman, Morris, 116
Freeman, Morgan, 322
French Connection, The, 274
Freshman, The, 176–77
Freud, 152
Freud, Sigmund, 88, 106, 107, 120, 152, 187, 206, 253
Freudian drama, post-World War II, 130, 136. *See also* Psychological drama, post-World War II
Friedkin, David, 239
From Here to Eternity, 94, 143, 144, 145–46, 148–50, 153
Front Page, The, 53
Fugitive Kind, The, 167, 168–69, 169–70, 185, 223, 224
Fury, 61
Futureworld, 303–304

*G*able, Clark, 51, 64, 153, 154, 236
"Gangster as Tragic Hero, The," 121–22
Garbo, Greta, 187
Gardenia, Vincent, 281
Garfein, Jack, 139
Garfield, David, 101, 102, 105, 188
Garfield, John, 21, 26, 41, 42, 52, 75–84, 85, 91, 92, 96, 99, 121, 142, 147, 150, 154, 163, 182, 249, 278, 282, 292, 319
Garfunkel, Art, 318
Garner, Peggy Ann, 96
Garrick, David, 7
Garrick Gaieties, The, 27
Garson, Greer, 310
Gazzara, Ben, 139, 140
Gazzo, Michael V., 139–41, 227, 228, 275
Gehrig, Eleanor, 305
Gehrig, Lou, 305
Gelb, Arthur, 10
Gelb, Barbara, 10, 254–55
Gentle People, The, 29, 61
Gentleman's Agreement, 80, 81, 92, 95, 96
Gentlewoman, 29, 108
George, Gladys, 71
George White's Scandals, 68

Ghosts, 18
Giant, 188, 195–97, 218, 220
Gigi, 241
Gillette, William, 9, 251
Gish, Dorothy, 189
Gish, Lillian, 187, 232, 313
Glaspell, Susan, 9
Glass Menagerie, The, 42, 87, 123, 124, 125, 126, 128, 130, 131, 132, 184, 208, 212
Glenville, Peter, 208
Goddess, The, 210, 212, 214
Godfather, The, 17, 139, 167, 172, 174–78, 181, 272
Godfather, Part II, The, 17, 109–10, 139
Goethe, Johann Wolfgang von, 27
Goetz, Augustus, 145
Goetz, Ruth, 145
Gold, Michael, 23
Gold Eagle Guy, 29, 34, 35
Golden Boy, 29, 37, 40, 43, 46, 47, 48–50, 82, 83, 91, 116, 121, 150, 163, 196–97
Broadway production (1937), 48, 49, 61, 67, 68, 69, 70, 75
film (1939), 49–50, 64, 71–72
TV (1950), 83
revival (1952), 83
Goldman, Bo, 272
Goldman, Emma, 224, 225, 226
Goldwyn, Samuel, 55
Gone with the Wind, 236
Goodman, Paul, 91
"Goodyear Television Playhouse," 1, 238
Gorelik, Mordecai, 26, 29
Gorki, Maxim, 3
Gould, Elliott, 216
Graczyk, Ed, 115, 217–18, 221
Grand Hotel, 75
Grant, Cary, 51, 52, 61, 231
Grant, Lee, 100
Grapes of Wrath, The, 25, 87
Grasso, Giovanni, 110
Graves, Ralph, 63–64
Gray, Paul, 104
Great God Brown, The, 251, 252–53, 255, 262
Green, Paul, 29, 63
Green Grow the Lilacs, 27
Green Pastures, The, 26
Greenfield, Thomas Allen, 122
Grobel, Lawrence, 178
Group Theatre, 5, 10, 13, 20, 21, 25, 27–29, 38, 43, 44, 46, 51, 53, 54, 55, 57, 58–59, 60, 61, 63, 63n, 86, 89, 99, 102, 105–107, 108, 112–13, 128, 301
actors, 67–84, 249
Awake and Sing!, 15, 42
background of Group members, 85
contemporaries, 57–67
ensemble, 17, 34–35, 41, 52
founding of, 22–23
Golden Boy, 49, 61
influences on, 23–27, 35–36, 56
Men in White, 31–34, 35
Odets in the Group Theatre, 36–37, 115, 250
post-Group careers, 92–93
selection of plays, 27, 29–31, 67
Strasberg in the Group Theatre, 33–34, 34–35, 41, 100–101, 104, 129
Waiting for Lefty, 37
Groupstroy, 35–36

Growing Up Absurd, 91
"Guilty Is the Stranger," 191
Guthrie, Tyrone, 104
Guys and Dolls, 79
  film (1955), 167, 170–71
Gymnase, 8

Hackman, Gene, 115, 274, 275, 295, 318, 322
Hagen, Uta, 6, 10–11, 16
Hailey, Arthur, 75
Hairy Ape, The, 82, 251, 252, 262
Haley, Alex, 181
Hall, Peter, 294
Haller, Ernest, 193
"Hallmark Hall of Fame," 202, 203
Hamburger Hill, 94
Hamlet, 8, 176, 252
Hammett, Dashiell, 250
Hapgood, Hutchins, 9
Harder They Fall, The, 237–38
Harding, Ann, 56
Hardy, Oliver, 300, 321
Harlow, Jean, 56
Harper, 283
Harrigan, Edward, 8
Harris, Julie, 19, 86, 93, 100, 128, 132, 134, 143,
  184, 186–87, 197–205, 237, 305–306
Harry and Son, 292
Hart, Dolores, 152
Hart, Lorenz, 27
Hart, Moss, 80, 95, 304
Hart, Tony, 8
"Harvest," 189–90
Harvey, Laurence, 201, 208
Hatful of Rain, A, 140–41, 275
  Broadway production (1955), 100, 110, 139–40,
    228
  film (1957), 227–28, 231
Haunting, The, 205
Havoc, June, 93
Hawks, Howard, 94, 142, 143
Hawn, Goldie, 274
Hayden, Sterling, 201, 204, 207
Hayes, Helen, 56–57, 304
Hays Code, 145, 162, 311
He Who Says No, 63n
Hearn, George, 268
Heart of Darkness, 180, 181
Heart Is a Lonely Hunter, The, 87
Hearts of the West, 275, 302, 303
Hecht, Ben, 53, 54
Heckart, Eileen, 203, 279
Hedda Gabler, 9, 16, 18, 204
Heflin, Van, 224
Heilveil, Elayne, 245
Heiress, The, 144–45
Helburn, Theresa, 22
Hellman, Lillian, 92
Hellman, Monte, 316
Hemingway, Ernest, 23, 82, 277
Hepburn, Katharine, 15, 51, 52, 56, 66–67, 96,
  171, 219, 261, 262–63, 303
Herne, James, 251
Herrman, Edward, 305
Hethmon, Robert, 104–105, 109
Heyward, Dorothy, 27
Heyward, DuBose, 27
Higgins, Michael, 190

High Sierra, 51
Hiken, Gerald, 209
Hill, Dana, 247
Hill, George Roy, 284, 285, 286
Hill, Steven, 93
Himmler, Heinrich, 178
Hinson, Hal, 21, 143–44, 150, 170, 275
Hirsch, Foster, 99, 112
Hitchcock, Alfred, 61, 150, 231
Hitler, Adolf, 88
Hobson, Laura Z., 80
Hoffman, Dustin, 15, 111, 112, 274, 276, 293–302,
  306, 318, 321
Hoffman, Theodore, 102–103, 111, 132
Holden, William, 72, 142
Holiday, 302
  film (1930), 53, 56
  film (1938), 51, 303
Holm, Celeste, 96, 101
Hombre, 283
Home of the Brave, 87, 120, 279
  film (1949), 94
Hondo, 206–207
Hope, Bob, 177
Hopper, Dennis, 316
Hopper, William, 194
Hotchkis, Joan, 317
Hotel Universe, 27
Houghton, Norris, 30
House Committee on Un-American Activities, 86,
  163
House of Connelly, The, 29, 30, 32, 34
Howard, Sidney, 27
Howard, Trevor, 171
Howe, Irving, 26, 102
Howland, Beth, 304
Hud, 276, 281, 282, 283
Hudson, Rock, 196
Hughes, Howard, 272, 273
Hughie
  revival (1964), 254
  TV (1984), 254, 267–68
Humoresque, 76, 80, 82
Hunter, Kim, 86, 93, 100, 128, 132, 158, 160,
  201, 223, 235–37
Hurst, Fannie, 76, 82
Hurt, William, 276, 322
Hustler, The, 281, 282, 289, 290, 291
Huston, Anjelica, 322
Huston, John, 94, 110, 153, 154, 167, 172, 272,
  285, 316
Huston, Walter, 55–56, 63, 74, 250

I Am a Camera
  Broadway production (1952), 200
  film (1955), 200–201
I Am a Fugitive from a Chain Gang, 53, 163
"I Can't Sleep," 41–42
I Confess, 150
"I, Don Quixote," 72–73
I Got the Blues, 41, 42, 47
I Never Sang for My Father, 115
Ibsen, Henrik, 7, 9, 17, 18, 27, 114, 116, 119–20,
  203–204, 218, 261–62
Iceman Cometh, The, 87, 115, 121, 250, 251–52,
  253, 264, 265, 266, 268, 273, 289
  Broadway production (1946), 250, 252, 255
  revival (1956), 254

TV (1960), 250, 254, 255–59, 260, 265, 270, 271, 272
film (1973), 54, 249, 254, 255, 275
revival (1985), 259–60
Illustrated Man, The, 242
Immoralist, The, 188
impressionism, 126–27, 133, 225, 251
improvisation, 6, 16–17, 98–99, 129, 140–41, 184–85, 187, 275
In the Heat of the Night, 237, 238, 241–42
Indiscretion of an American Wife, 144, 145, 146, 151–52
Inge, William, 89, 91, 92, 115, 119, 120, 218
Inside of His Head, The, 120
Interiors, 207–209, 224, 226
International Ladies' Garment Workers' Union, 24
Isaacs, Edith, 33
Isherwood, Christopher, 200
It Happened One Night, 51
Ives, Burl, 243, 244

Jackson, Anne, 93
James, Henry, 144, 179
James Dean: The First American Teenager, 189
Jandl, Ivan, 143
"Jason Jamie Robards Tyrone," 254–55
Jewison, Norman, 241
Jezebel, 51
Johnny Johnson, 29, 34, 63
Johnson, Lamont, 239
Johnson, Lyndon, 291
Jones, James, 149
Jones, James Earl, 181
Jones, Jennifer, 143, 146, 151
Jones, Robert Edmond, 9, 120
Jones, Tommy Lee, 213, 244
Jonson, Ben, 27
Jourdan, Louis, 188
Joyce, James, 153
Jubilee, 142
Judgment at Nuremberg, 151, 152, 153
Juilliard Drama School, 322
Julia, 250, 272
Julius Caesar, 160–61
Juno and the Paycock, 224, 225
"Justification," 6, 10–11

Kael, Pauline, 154–55, 170, 183, 184, 214
Kaiser, Georg, 27
Kaufman, Boris, 96
Kaufman, George S., 304
Kazan, Elia, 47, 48, 51, 82, 113, 163, 172, 186, 249, 312
as actor, 41, 67–68
at Actors Studio, 86, 93, 99–100, 101, 109
background and influences on, 25, 26, 85
as film director, 80, 81, 83–84, 92, 94–98, 128–29, 132, 151, 152, 157, 160, 162, 187, 192
as stage director, 71, 83–84, 89, 92, 111, 116, 123, 126, 127–28, 130–31, 154, 157, 158, 159, 235, 236, 311
work with actors, 92–99, 107, 109, 111, 141, 187
Kean, Edmund, 8
Keaton, Diane, 15, 112, 226, 276, 306, 322
Keaton, Michael, 321
"Keep Our Honor Bright," 189, 190
Keitel, Harvey, 275, 319

Keith, Brian, 174, 205, 277
Kelly, Grace, 231
Kennedy, Arthur, 96, 192
Kershner, Irvin, 233, 274
King Lear, 43, 73, 176, 184, 267, 271, 296, 297, 299
King of Marvin Gardens, 319
Kingsley, Sidney, 31–33, 34, 35, 120
Kirk, Phyllis, 232
Kirkland, Alexander, 32
Klute, 274, 275, 306
Knox, Alexander, 274
"Kraft Television Theatre," 189, 211
Kramer, Stanley, 151
Kramer vs. Kramer, 294
Kromer, Tom, 23
Kubrick, Stanley, 319

La Motta, Jake, 166, 275, 294
La Strada, 160
Ladies of Leisure, 63–64
Lady Eve, The, 64
Lady L, 284
Lahr, Bert, 60
Lancaster, Burt, 149, 176, 225, 289
Lane, Lola, 76
Lane, Mike, 238
Lane, Priscilla, 76, 77, 78
Lane, Rosemary, 76
Lang, Fritz, 61
Lang, Stephen, 297, 300
Lange, Jessica, 213, 233, 293, 322
Langella, Frank, 306, 309, 310
Lark, The, 201
TV (1957), 201
Last American Hero, The, 275
Last Detail, The, 316, 317
Last Mile, The, 26
Last Picture Show, The, 274, 275, 283
Last Tango in Paris, 168, 172, 175, 176, 179, 181–85, 267, 275, 293
"Laugh-In," 275
Laughton, Charles, 179
Laurel, Stan, 300
Laurents, Arthur, 120, 279
Laurie, Piper, 217, 282
Lawrence, D. H., 181
Lawson, John Howard, 23, 44, 108
Lazarus Laughed, 251, 252
"LBJ: The Early Years," 291
"Le Bourgeois Gentilhomme," 85
Le Gallienne, Eva, 28, 85
Le Mat, Paul, 272
Leachman, Cloris, 93, 100
Leadbelly (Huddie William Ledbetter), 169
Lean, David, 239, 241
Learned, Michael, 115
"Leave It to Beaver," 91
Left Handed Gun, The, 276, 279
Lehman, Ernest, 278
Leigh, Vivien, 158, 220, 235, 236, 311, 312, 313
Length and Depth of Acting, The, 7
Lenny, 294
Leopard, The, 176
Lerner, Tillie, 24
Letter, The, 51
Levant, Oscar, 76, 82
Levene, Sam, 96

Lewis, Robert, 6, 13–14, 16–17, 21, 26, 34, 41, 68, 92, 93, 99, 101, 106, 107, 109, 111, 128, 195
Lewis, Sinclair, 55, 181
Lie of the Mind, A, 207–208, 209
Life, A, 95
Life and Times of Judge Roy Bean, The, 285
Lithgow, John, 320
Little Caesar, 57
Little Moon of Alban, 202
    TV (1958), 202–203
    TV (1964), 203
Little Richard (Richard Tenniman), 91
Little Shop of Horrors, The, 316
Little Women, 51
Litvak, Anatole, 68
Living Newspaper, The, 28
Lloyd, Harold, 187
Lloyd, Kathleen, 180
Logan, Joshua, 20
Loggia, Robert, 209
London, Jack, 78
Lonely Crowd, The, 89–90
Lonely Passion of Judith Hearne, The, 203
Lonelyhearts, 151, 152, 153, 223, 224
Long, Earl, 291
Long Day's Journey into Night, 115, 121, 250, 251, 253, 254, 261–62, 264, 265, 266–67
    Broadway production (1956), 250, 254, 255, 261
    film (1962), 56, 219, 250, 252, 254, 261, 262–64, 265, 266, 270, 272
    revival (1971), 270
    TV (1973), 270
    revival (1976), 254
    revival (1977), 268
    revival (1988), 254, 268–71
"Long Time Till Dawn, A," 189, 190–91
Longest Yard, The, 285
Look Homeward, Angel, 136
Lord, Pauline, 110
Lost Weekend, The, 94
"Love Affair: The Eleanor and Lou Gehrig Story, A," 305
Lovin' Molly, 275, 302, 303
Loving, 233–35, 274
Lower Depths, The, 275
Lucia de Lammermoor, 261
Luedtke, Kurt, 287
Lumet, Sidney, 93, 169, 201, 239, 254, 261, 277, 289
Lumpkin, Grace, 23
Lunt, Alfred, 16
Lupino, Ida, 78
Lynn, Jeffrey, 76

MacArthur, Charles, 53, 54
MacArthur, James, 236
McCabe and Mrs. Miller, 274
McCambridge, Anita, 285
McCambridge, Mercedes, 196
McCarthy, Joseph, 91, 119, 163
McCarthy, Kevin, 93, 100, 209, 211, 306
McCarthy, Mary, 203–204, 252
McCormick, Myron, 256, 281
McCoy, Horace, 25
McCrane, Paul, 259
McCullers, Carson, 87, 92, 127–28, 133–39, 141, 167, 197, 198

Macdonald, Ross, 283
McDormand, Frances, 235
McGaw, Charles, 6
Macgowan, Kenneth, 9
McGuane, Thomas, 179, 180
McGuire, Dorothy, 95, 96
McGuire Sisters, 219
Macklin, Charles, 7
MacLaine, Shirley, 320
McLiam, John, 179
McMurtry, Larry, 283, 303
Macpherson, Aimee Semple, 65
Macready, W. C., 8, 11
Made for Each Other, 274
Madorsky, Bryan, 216
Magnani, Anna, 168, 169
Mailer, Norman, 87, 91, 112, 143, 164, 183
Malden, Karl, 93, 94, 159, 164, 229, 243
Malkovich, John, 297, 300, 301, 322
Maltese Falcon, The, 51
Maltz, Albert, 23
Mamet, David, 288
Man with Two Brains, The, 209–210
Man Who Cheated Himself, The, 71
Mankiewicz, Joseph L., 160
Mann, Delbert, 1
Manners, David, 65
Man's Castle, A, 60
Marathon Man, 294
March, Fredric, 53–54, 301
Marco Millions, 27, 251, 252, 262
Marine Workers Industrial Union, 41
Mark, The, 238
Mark Taper Forum, 224
Marked Woman, 51
Marowitz, Charles, 14
Marquez, Evaristo, 178
Marsh, Marian, 55
Marshall, E. G., 93, 100, 226
Martin, Dean, 225
Martino, Al, 175
Marty
    TV (1953), 1–3, 115, 201, 238
    film (1955), 1–2, 166
Marvin, Lee, 162, 254, 255
Marx, Harpo, 54, 216
Marx Brothers, 177
M*A*S*H
    film (1970), 275
    TV series, 302
Massey, Raymond, 95, 186
Master Builder, The, 11
Mastrantonio, Mary Elizabeth, 290
"Max Schmidt in a Single Scull," 19
May, Elaine, 275
Mazursky, Paul, 274
Mean Streets, 274, 275
Meet John Doe, 64
Meiningen Players, 5, 8, 17
Meisner, Sanford, 42, 92, 100, 106, 107, 109
Melvin and Howard, 272–73, 306
Member of the Wedding, The, 115, 133–39
    Broadway production (1950), 92, 127–28, 134, 197–98
    film (1952), 94, 134, 143, 198–200, 201, 202
"Memory of emotion," 13. See also "Affective memory"; "Emotion memory"; "Emotional memory"; "Emotional recall"
Men, The, 94, 143, 155–57, 159

Men in White, 31, 32, 35
  Broadway production (1933), 29, 30, 31, 32–35, 36
  film (1934), 32
Menjou, Adolphe, 53, 72
Merchant of Venice, The, 294
Meredith, Burgess, 20, 58–60, 70
Merrily We Go to Hell, 61, 62–63
Method—or Madness?, 6, 13, 16, 195
"Method of Physical Actions," 108, 109
Method to Their Madness, A, 99, 113
Michelangelo, 172
Midnight Cowboy, 274, 275, 294
Midsummer Night's Dream, A, 51
Mielziner, Jo, 120
Milestone, Lewis, 53, 59, 71
Millay, Edna St. Vincent, 23
Miller, Arthur, 50, 89, 92, 115–22, 123, 124, 127, 153, 163, 185, 250, 259, 261, 296, 297, 299, 300
Miller, Henry, 181
Miller, Penelope Ann, 177
Minciotti, Esther, 2
Mineo, Sal, 194
Minnelli, Liza, 200, 274
Miracle Woman, The, 63, 65
Miranda, Carmen, 154
Misfits, The, 110, 153–54
Miss Julie, 18
Miss Lonelyhearts, 152
Missouri Breaks, The, 179–80, 319
Molnar, Ferenc, 27
Moniz, Antonio, 89
Monroe, Marilyn, 101, 110, 153, 154, 210
Montigny, Adolphe, 9
Moon Is Down, The, 71
Moon for the Misbegotten, A, 87, 121, 250, 251, 254, 261, 264
  Broadway production (1947), 250
  revival (1973), 254
  TV (1975), 250, 252, 254, 264–67, 270, 272
Morituri, 167
Morris, Clara, 8–9, 12
Morris, Eric, 317
Moscow Art Theatre, 3, 5, 43, 275
Mosel, Tad, 191, 201, 279
Moses, 172
Mostel, Zero, 59–60
"Motorcyclists' Raid, The," 161
Mourning Becomes Electra, 27, 251, 252, 262
Mr. Deeds Goes to Town, 51
Mr. Smith Goes to Washington, 51
Muni, Paul, 53, 110
Murphy, Mary, 161
Murray, Don, 227–28
Music Box, 322
Mutiny on the Bounty, 167, 170, 171–72, 180, 184
My Heart's in the Highlands, 195
My Son John, 57

Naked and the Dead, The, 87, 143
Nash, Ogden, 92
Nashville, 17
Nasty Habits, 209–10, 215–16
National Committee for Mental Hygiene, 89
National Mental Health Act, 88
National Mental Health Foundation, 89
National Theatre of Britain, 270

Nazimova, Alla, 9
Naturalism, 6, 8, 36, 63, 115, 252, 253, 269. See also Realism
Naughton, James, 312
Neal, Patricia, 93, 132, 276, 282
Neighborhood Playhouse, 92, 106, 109
Nelson, Ruth, 92
Nemirovich-Danchenko, Vladimir, 3, 5
New Kind of Love, A, 284
New Theatre League, 28, 37, 75
New Theatre Magazine, 28
New York Times Magazine, 254
New Yorker, The, 19
Newman, Paul, 86, 123, 191, 201, 209, 232, 276–93, 320, 321
Nichols, Mike, 275, 318
Nicholson, Jack, 180, 195, 226, 274, 276, 315–21
"Night Club," 100
Night of the Following Day, The, 167
Night of the Iguana, The, 124, 129, 130
Night Music, 30, 37, 40–41, 45, 67, 68
Night Nurse, 63, 64
Night Over Taos, 29, 35
Night Rider, 87
Night They Raided Minsky's, The, 271
Nightcomers, The, 179
1931—, 29, 34, 63
Nixon, Richard, 318
No Acting Please, 317
"No Deadly Medicine," 73, 74–75
"No License to Kill," 224
No Way to Treat a Lady, 242
Nolan, Lloyd, 228
Nolte, Nick, 276
"Nonsense" exercise, 165
"Noon Wine," 271–72
Norris, Frank, 19
North by Northwest, 231
Not I, 21
Nothing in Common, 231
Novick, Julius, 116

Oates, Warren, 242
Ober, Philip, 149
"Objective," 6, 109. See also "Action"
O'Brien, Jack, 115
O'Brien, Pat, 53
O'Casey, Sean, 48, 202, 203, 225
Odets, Clifford, 15, 23, 24, 25, 26, 29, 30, 31, 32–33, 36–50, 61, 67, 68, 75, 76, 77, 82–83, 91, 115–16, 117, 118, 122, 123–24, 128, 163, 166, 197, 238, 250, 278, 299
Of Mice and Men, 59, 70–71, 73
Okada, Eiji, 169
O'Keefe, Michael, 305
Old Globe Theatre, 306
"Old Man," 201, 207
Olivier, Laurence, 21, 111, 172, 249, 258, 270, 300, 322
Olson, James, 209
On Method Acting, 6, 105, 132
On the Waterfront, 73, 94, 96, 97, 100, 121, 161, 162–66, 167, 168, 170, 172, 174, 176, 177, 183, 184, 227, 228–31, 232, 233, 277
Once in a Lifetime, 26
One Eyed Jacks, 167, 168, 170, 171
One Flew Over the Cuckoo's Nest, 316, 317, 318
One Touch of Venus, 92

O'Neill, Eugene, 9, 10, 27, 54, 56, 82, 120–21, 184, 218, 226, 250–72, 300, 306, 319
O'Neill, James, 10
O'Neill, James, Jr., 254–55
O'Neill, Michael, 264
"O'Neill's Shakespeare," 271
Ontkean, Michael, 285
Organization of the League of Workers Theatres, 28
Orlenev, Paul, 9
Orpheus Descending, 92, 124, 130, 167
Oscarsson, Per, 272
Ostrovsky, Alexander, 4
Othello, 14, 290
"Other People's Houses," 238
Our Town, 138, 200
    TV (1955), 232, 279–80
Ouspenskaya, Maria, 5, 129
Out of Towners, The, 215–16
Overton, Frank, 152
Ox-Bow Incident, The, 87
"Ozzie and Harriet," 91

Pacino, Al, 109, 274, 275, 288, 292, 318
Page, Gale, 76
Page, Geraldine, 123, 188, 201, 206–10, 223, 224, 226, 243, 281
Palance, Jack, 166, 236, 238, 277
Palcy, Euzhan, 179
Palmer, Lilli, 79, 83
Panic in the Streets, 96
Paradise Lost, 30, 38–39, 40, 41, 44–45, 46, 47–48, 49, 116, 118, 128, 278
    Broadway production (1935), 36, 37–38, 41, 68, 69, 70, 75
Paradox of Acting, The, 11
Paramount Pictures, 177
Parents, 216
Paris Blues, 281
Parks, Michael, 216
Parsons, Estelle, 110
Partisan Review, 26, 87
Party Girl, 73, 74
Passenger, The, 317–18
Pasteur, Louis, 53
"Patch on Faith, A," 74
Patton, Mark, 218
Pauly, Thomas, 89, 163
Pavlov, Ivan, 107, 108
Pawnbroker, The, 182, 238, 239–40
Paxton, John, 161, 162
Payday, 244–46, 248
Peale, Norman Vincent, 88
Pearce, Donn, 285
Pearson, Beatrice, 79
Peck, Gregory, 80, 96
Peckinpah, Sam, 271, 274, 318
Peer Gynt, 267
Pellicer, Pina, 168
Pelly, Farrell, 257
Pendleton, Austin, 306
Penn, Arthur, 98, 179, 180, 201, 274, 277, 279, 318, 319
Penn, Sean, 276
Peppard, George, 202
Perelman, S. J., 92
Performance Group, 141
Perkins, Anthony, 132, 303
Perrine, Valerie, 319

"Perry Mason," 194
Persoff, Nehemiah, 93, 100
"Personalization," 14–16, 110–112, 127
Peters, Jean, 168
Petrie, Daniel, 287
Petrified Forest, The, 58
Pfeiffer, Michelle, 321
Philadelphia Story, The, 51, 303
"Philco-Goodyear Playhouse," 232
Phillips, Nancie, 234
"Philoctetes: The Wound and the Bow," 110
Photoplay, 218
Picnic, 91, 135, 277
Pidgeon, Walter, 268
Pierson, Frank, 284
Pinero, Arthur Wing, 8, 306
Pins and Needles, 24
Pinter, Harold, 117, 224
Pirandello, Luigi, 27, 187
Piscator, Erwin, 92, 106
Place in the Sun, A, 144, 145, 146–48, 150, 151
Planet of the Apes, 235
Plato, 277
Platt, Edward, 194
"Play of the Week," 59, 69
Playboy, 164, 178, 181, 184
Player, The, 58
"Playhouse 90," 70, 207, 236, 278
"Playrights '56," 277
"Plot to Kill Stalin, The," 70
Plummer, Christopher, 202, 203
Poitier, Sidney, 241
Polanski, Roman, 318
Pollack, Sydney, 98, 287, 293
Polonsky, Abraham, 81
Pontecorvo, Gillo, 178
Pope of Greenwich Village, The, 207, 209
Porgy, 27
Porter, Cole, 142
Porter, Katharine Anne, 271, 272
Portrait of a Madonna, 100
Postman Always Rings Twice, The
    film (1946), 77, 78, 79, 80
    film (1981), 319
"Pot," 140
Presley, Elvis, 91
Price, Richard, 289
Pride of the Marines, 75–76
Prince of the City, 288
Prince of Wales Theatre, 8
Private Lives, 26
"Private moment," 105, 173, 211
Prizzi's Honor, 320, 321
"Problem play," 18, 31–32, 120, 201. See also "Social play"; "Well-made play"
Probst, Leonard, 285
"Producer's Showcase," 232, 279
Proletbuhne, 28
Proust, Marcel, 19, 107, 126
Prouty, Olive Higgins, 66
Provincetown Players, 9–10, 251. See also Provincetown Playhouse
Provincetown Playhouse, 22, 28. See also Provincetown Players
Psacharopoulos, Nikos, 302, 306, 311, 313, 315
Psychiatric Foundation, 89
psychological drama, post-World War II, 87–88, 119–121. See also Freudian drama, post-World War II

"Psychological gesture," 128, 166
Public Enemy, 51
Public Health Service, Mental Health Division, 88
Puccini, Giacomo, 187
Pumpkin Eater, The, 232
"Pygmalion," 205

Quaid, Randy, 291, 316
Quinn, Aidan, 115, 314–15
Quinn, Anthony, 160, 166–67, 237
Quintero, Jose, 254, 259, 264, 268, 269, 271
Quintilian, 14

Rafelson, Bob, 319
Raging Bull, 15, 166, 275, 278
Rain Man, 294
Rains, Claude, 81
Raintree County, 151, 152, 153, 231
Rally 'Round the Flag, Boys, 284
Ravetch, Irving, 282
Rawlings, Marjorie Kinnan, 246
Ray, Nicholas, 193
Realism, 17–18, 19–20, 63, 206, 227, 236–37, 251,
    292, 298–99. *See also* Naturalism
Rebel Without a Cause, 91, 121, 144, 161, 190,
    191, 193–95, 196
Red and the Black, The, 147
Red River, 142, 144, 145
Red Rust, 22, 75
Redfield, William, 93
Redford, Robert, 256, 276, 284
Redgrave, Michael, 257
Redgrave, Vanessa, 240, 272, 306
Reds, 224, 225–26, 319
Reed, Donna, 145
Reed, John, 225, 226
Reeve, Christopher, 306
Reflections in a Golden Eye, 167, 172–74, 178–79,
    181, 205
Reid, Kate, 297, 300
Remember the Night, 64
Remick, Lee, 152, 153
Renoir, Jean, 175
Requiem for a Heavyweight
    TV (1956), 163, 166, 236–37, 277
    film (1962), 166–67, 237
Respect for Acting, 6, 16
Revere, Anne, 146
Ribot, Theodule, 12
Rice, Elmer, 27, 31, 32, 251
Richard III, 322
Richardson, Ralph, 56, 145, 261, 270
Richardson, Tony, 319
Ride in the Whirlwind, 316
Riesman, David, 89–90, 91
Riggs, Lynn, 27
Right Stuff, The, 213
Riskin, Robert, 57, 304
Ritt, Martin, 93, 98, 238, 246, 281–82, 283
Robards, Jason, 184, 203, 249–50, 252, 254–73,
    304, 306
Robbins, Jerome, 93
"Robert Montgomery Presents," 189
Robertson, Thomas, 8, 17
Robinson, Edward G., 57–58, 60, 63, 78
Robson, Mark, 94
Robson, May, 78

Roche, Eugene, 304
Rocket to the Moon, 37, 43, 69
Rockwell, George Lincoln, 181
Rockwell, Norman, 77
Rocky, 59, 166, 278
Rodgers, Richard, 27
Rogers, Ginger, 51
Rogin, Michael Paul, 119
Rogoff, Gordon, 102
Rome, Harold, 24
Rooney, Frank, 161
Rooney, Mickey, 201
Roosevelt, Franklin, 25, 83
"Roots: The Next Generations," 181
Rose, Lloyd, 121, 295
Rose, Reginald, 74, 201
Rose Tattoo, The, 100, 123, 126, 139
Rosenberg, Stuart, 284
Ross, George, 116
Ross, Helen, 58
Ross, Lillian, 58
Rossellini, Roberto, 96
Rossen, Robert, 281, 282
Rowlands, Gena, 216
Rudman, David, 297, 300
Runyon, Damon, 68, 170, 197, 284
Rush, Barbara, 280
Ryan, Robert, 152, 249, 270

S. *S. Glencairn* cycle, 251
Sabotage, 61–62
Sacco and Vanzetti, 58
Saint, The, 22
Saint, Eva Marie, 86, 100, 143, 162, 168, 201,
    223, 227–35, 279
"St. Elsewhere," 302
St. Petersburg Players, 9
Salinger, J. D., 91, 134
Sally's Irish Rogue, 201
Salvini, Tommaso, 12
Sanchez, Jaime, 240
Sand, Paul, 304
Sarandon, Susan, 321
Sardou, Victorien, 17
Saroyan, William, 195, 250
Saxe-Meiningen, Duke of, 8
Sayonara, 167, 169, 171
Sbarge, Raphael, 268
Scarecrow, 274
Scarface (1932), 53
"Scarlet Letter, The," 211, 212, 213
Schaefer, George, 202, 204, 205
Schaffner, Franklin, 201
Schary, Dore, 153
Schechner, Richard, 85, 107, 141
Schlondorff, Volker, 295
Schmid, Al, 75–76
Schneider, Alan, 59
Schneider, Benno, 58
Schenider, Daniel, 120
Schneider, Maria, 168, 182
Schulberg, Budd, 162
Scorsese, Martin, 274, 275, 278, 289
Scott, Campbell, 269
Scott, George C., 102, 249, 281, 282, 300, 301
Scribe, Eugene, 17–18
Sea of Grass, 96
Sea Gull, The, 5, 16, 45, 188, 202

361

Sea Gull, The (continued)
  Actors Studio workshop production (1948), 99
  TV (1974), 306–308, 310
Sea Wolf, The, 78
Seance on a Wet Afternoon, 210, 211, 212, 213
Search, The, 94, 142–43, 145, 154
Secret Agent, The, 61
Secret War of Harry Frigg, The, 284–85
Seduction of Joe Tynan, The, 243
Segal, Alex, 71, 295, 301
Segal, George, 215, 233, 274, 301
"Sense memory," 10, 107, 115, 129. *See also* "Sensory recall"
"Sensory recall," 129. *See also* "Sense memory"
Sergeant, The, 242
Serling, Rod, 163, 166, 191, 201
Serpico, 288
1776, 302
Shadow of a Doubt, 157
Shakespeare, William, 8, 69, 160, 261, 271, 296, 299
Shampoo, 274
Shatner, William, 74
Shaver, Helen, 289
Shaw, George Bernard, 18, 27
Shaw, Irwin, 61, 251, 278
Sheeler, Charles, 252
Shelton, Ron, 291
Shepard, Sam, 209
Sheridan, Jamey, 269
Sherlock Holmes, 9
Sherman, Vincent, 277
Sherwood, Madeleine, 123
Sherwood, Robert, 71
Shining, The, 319
Shire, Talia, 278
Shoot the Moon, 113, 233, 247
Shooting, The, 316
Shop Around the Corner, The, 51
Sidney, Sylvia, 61–63, 64, 78, 249
Silliphant, Stirling, 242
Silver Cord, The, 27
Silvera, Frank, 140
Simon, Neil, 215
Sinatra, Frank, 145, 232
Siodmak, Robert, 94
Skin of Our Teeth, The, 92, 95
Slap Shot, 285–86, 288, 292
Slither, 275
Sloane, Everett, 155
Smiley, Sam, 30
Smith, Betty, 92
Smith, Maggie, 203, 293
Snake Pit, The, 89
"Social play," 18, 29–30, 61, 62, 67, 123. *See also* "Problem play"; "Well-made play"
Socialist Party, 23, 26
Soloviova, Vera, 110
"Some Notes on Method Actors," 143–44, 275
Somebody Up There Likes Me, 276, 277, 278, 279, 280, 284, 292
"Song and dance," 105
Sons of Guns, 26
Sounder, 274
Spacek, Sissy, 276
Spark, Muriel, 209, 215
"Speaking out," 105
"Spine," 6, 10, 127. *See also* "Super-objective"; "Through-line"

Splendor in the Grass, 97, 279
Stage Door, 51
Stalin, Josef, 86
Stallone, Sylvester, 166, 278
Stanislavski, Konstantin, 3–5, 7, 8, 9, 10, 11, 12, 13, 14–15, 16, 17, 18, 19, 20, 21, 36, 43, 63, 85, 105, 108, 110, 114, 128, 188, 297, 322
  Stanislavski "system," 3–5, 8, 9, 10–11, 12, 28, 35, 44, 75, 112, 113, 206, 275, 322
Stanley, Kim, 83, 201, 206, 209, 210–14, 215, 223, 224, 235
Stanwyck, Barbara, 20, 63–67, 78, 249
Stapleton, Jean, 304
Stapleton, Maureen, 86, 92, 93, 99, 100, 101, 123, 201, 223–26
Star Is Born, A, 54
Starr, Blaze, 291
Steenburgen, Mary, 246
Steiger, Rod, 1–3, 86, 92, 115, 132, 165, 182, 201, 223, 237–42
Steinbeck, John, 23, 25, 59, 70, 81, 160, 168, 186
Steiner, Ralph, 94
Stella Dallas
  film (1925), 66
  film (1937), 66–67
Stendhal, 147
Stern, Isaac, 76
Stern, Stewart, 193
Stevens, George, 143, 148, 195–96
Stevens, Warren, 93
Stewart, James, 51, 304
Sting, The, 276, 284
Stockwell, Dean, 261
Story of Adele H., The, 220
Story of G. I. Joe, The, 59, 94
Stradling, Harry, 96
Straight, Beatrice, 93
Straight Time, 294
Strange Interlude, 27, 251, 253, 255
Strange One, The, 139
Strasberg, John, 101
Strasberg, Lee, 1, 52, 85, 92, 128, 129, 141, 142, 156, 302
  as actor, 109, 275
  at Actors Studio, 6, 20, 86, 92, 99–100, 100–102, 104–109, 110–11, 112, 114, 132, 139, 173, 188, 280, 301
  "affective memory" debate, 12, 13, 107–109
  detractors, 102, 106, 107, 108, 249
  as director, 33, 34–35, 41, 82, 110, 209, 215
  in the Group Theatre, 5, 22, 26, 28, 29, 32, 33–35, 42, 63n, 301
  "personalization," 110–111
  psychoanalytic approach to acting, 104–106, 110, 210, 212
Strasberg, Paula, 110
Strasberg at the Actors Studio, 104
Stratford Shakespeare Festival, Ontario, 299
Streep, Meryl, 15, 276
Street Scene, 31, 32
  film (1931), 61, 62, 95
Street Smart, 322
Streetcar Named Desire, A, 14, 42, 87, 111, 115, 124, 125–26, 127, 128, 129–30, 131–32, 135, 212, 308, 309
  Broadway production (1947), 99, 100, 104, 123, 127, 154, 159–60, 166, 235, 311

film (1951), 96, 97, 123, 128, 157–60, 172, 173, 182–83, 184, 191, 220, 235–36, 236–37, 253–54, 277, 311
   TV (1984), 311
   revival (1986), 302, 306, 310–13
   revival (1988), 235, 306, 313–15
Streisand, Barbra, 274
Strictly Dishonorable, 26
Strindberg, August, 7, 18, 114, 182
"Studio One," 73
Sturges, Preston, 94, 317
Success Story, 29, 44
Suddenly, Last Summer, 130
   film (1959), 152, 153
Sullavan, Margaret, 51, 303
Summer and Smoke, 87, 124, 125, 126, 128, 129, 130, 132, 308
   revival (1953), 206, 208
   film (1961), 208
Sundown Beach, 99, 100
Sunset Boulevard, 94, 209
Sunshine Boys, The, 299
Superman, 181
"Super-objective," 6, 10–11, 127. *See also* "Spine"; "Through-line"
Sutherland, Donald, 179, 275
Svengali, 54, 55
Swann's Way, 107
Sweet Bird of Youth, 123, 124, 130
   Broadway production (1959), 208
   film (1962), 208, 209, 243, 279, 280–81
Sweet Smell of Success, 238
Swerling, Jo, 57, 64, 65
Swinburne, Algernon Charles, 271
Swindell, Larry, 75
Symbolism, 251
Synge, John Millington, 202

"Taking a minute," 103–104
Talma, Francois-Joseph, 11
Tandy, Jessica, 100, 123, 127, 311
Tarita, 184
Tarkington, Booth, 66
"Tattinger's," 302
Taxi Driver, 274, 275
Taylor, Elizabeth, 143, 146, 148, 151, 153, 173, 196, 215, 278, 279, 280
Taylor, Laurette, 79, 110, 184
Taylor, Renee, 274
Taylor, Vaughn, 189
Tea and Sympathy, 91, 135
Teahouse of the August Moon, The, 167, 169, 171
Tell Me How Long the Train's Been Gone, 102
Tempest, The, 176
Tender Mercies, 244
Terms of Endearment, 320–21
Terror, The, 316
Terry, Ellen, 8
That Certain Feeling, 231
That Cold Day in the Park, 215, 216–17
"Theater in America," 302, 306
Theatre Arts Monthly, 33
Theatre Collective School, 29
Theatre Guild, 22, 26–27, 52, 85
Theatre Guild Studio, 22, 75
Theatre Libre, 8
Theatre Union, 28, 29
Theatrical Syndicate, 5

They Knew What They Wanted, 27
They Made Me a Criminal, 78, 81, 83
They Shoot Horses, Don't They?
   novel (1935), 25
   film (1969), 274
Thieves Like Us, 25
Three Comrades, 51
Three Sisters, The, 30–31, 45
   Actors Studio production (1964), 102, 110, 209, 210
   film (1966), 209, 210, 211–12, 213, 215, 218
   Williamstown production (1976), 302
Three into Two Won't Go, 242
Threepenny Review, The, 116
"Through-line," 6, 137. *See also* "Spine"; "Super-objective"
Thunder Rock, 30
Ticotin, Rachel, 292
Till the Day I Die, 29, 37, 48
Time of Your Life, The, 250
To Have and Have Not, 82
Toast of New York, The, 61
Toland, Gregg, 56
Toller, Ernst, 27
Tomkins, Calvin, 19–20, 292
Tomlin, Lily, 274
Tone, Franchot, 34
Tootsie, 15, 111, 293–94, 295
Torme, Mel, 236
Torn, Rip, 123, 223, 243–48
Tortilla Flat, 81
Touch of the Poet, A, 254
Towne, Robert, 318
Tracy, Spencer, 60, 63, 96
Treasure of the Sierra Madre, The, 94
Tree Grows in Brooklyn, A, 92, 95, 96
Trelawny of the "Wells," 8
   Williamstown production (1982), 302, 306
Trilling, Lionel, 110
Trip to Bountiful, The, 232
   TV (1953), 232
   film (1985), 209
Trojan Women, The, 240
Truckline Cafe, 87, 92, 154–55
Truman, Harry, 88, 91
Trumbo, Dalton, 23
Truth About Women, The, 201
"Truth of Appearances, The," 19–20
Turgenev, Ivan, 27
Turn of the Screw, The, 179
Turner, Kathleen, 209–210
Turner, Lana, 78, 79
Turturro, John, 289
Twelfth Night, 173
Twelve Angry Men, 72, 73, 74
Twentieth Century, 54
Tyson, Cicely, 274

Ugly American, The, 167, 168, 169, 179
Uncle Vanya, 108
   Williamstown production (1972), 302
Under My Skin, 68, 69, 81–82
Up the Down Staircase, 214, 215
"U.S. Steel Hour, The," 202

Van Fleet, Jo, 100, 123, 152, 186
Van Gogh, Vincent, 126, 129

Verdict, The, 288–89, 292
Verfremdungseffekt, 63n
"Verisimilitude, 6, 7–10, 21, 33
"Victoria Regina," 205
Vidor, King, 66
View from the Bridge, A, 119
Vigo, Jean, 96
Visconti, Luchino, 176
Viva Zapata!, 96, 97–98, 160, 166, 168, 169
Voight, Jon, 275
Vorse, Mary Keaton, 23

Waiting for Godot, 273
   TV (1961), 59–60
Waiting for Lefty, 24, 29, 31, 32, 36–37, 39–40,
   41, 43, 48, 118, 140
   original New York productions (1935), 23, 34,
   36, 37, 67, 75
Walken, Christopher, 311–12
Walker, Robert, 57
Wallach, Eli, 97, 100, 123, 132, 153
Wallant, Edward Lewis, 239
War and Peace, 241
Ward, Mary Jane, 89
Warhol, Andy, 243
Warner Brothers Pictures, 49, 57, 68, 76, 81, 82,
   122, 163, 278
Warren, Robert Penn, 87
Warshow, Robert, 42, 45–46, 119, 121–22, 157,
   227
Washington, Denzel, 322
Washington Square, 144
Waters, Ethel, 198
Wayne, David, 93, 99, 100, 249
Wayne, John, 144, 207
Weaver, Sigourney, 311, 312
Webster, John, 176
Weill, Kurt, 63, 92
Welles, Orson, 51, 94
"Well-made play," 18, 119. See also "Problem
   play"; "Social play"
Wellman, William, 94
West, Nathanael, 152
West Side Story, 161
Westley, Helen, 34
Westworld, 303
Wharton, Edith, 204
What a Way to Go!, 284
Whistle Blower, The, 320
Whistler, James McNeill, 19
Whitaker, Forest, 291
White Heat, 191
"White Negro, The," 91
White Nights, 208
Whitelaw, Billie, 21, 113
Whitman, Stuart, 238
Whitmore, James, 93, 115
Whole Town's Talking, The, 57–58, 60, 303
Who's Afraid of Virginia Woolf?, 214–15
Widowers' Houses, 18
Wild Bunch, The, 249
Wild Duck, The, 18, 204
Wild One, The, 121, 144, 159, 161–62, 183,
   193
Wild River, 94, 151, 152–153
Wild Strawberries, 216

Wilder, Billy, 94
Wilder, Thornton, 92
Williams, Tennessee, 89, 92, 97, 100, 123–33,
   139, 141, 158, 160, 167, 169, 172, 182, 208,
   217, 218, 236, 243, 244, 250, 278, 281, 306,
   308, 313
Williamstown Theatre Festival, 302, 306, 311, 313
Willingham, Calder, 91, 139
Wilson, Edmund, 110
Wilson, Elizabeth, 268
Wilson, Michael, 148
Wind, The, 313
"Wind from the South, A," 202
Winger, Debra, 320
Winters, Shelley, 140, 147, 228
Winter's Tale, The, 267
Winterset, 58–59
   film (1936), 58
Wise, Robert, 278
"Wish on the Moon," 232–33
Witches of Eastwick, The, 320, 321
Witness for the Prosecution, 179
Wolfert, Ira, 81
Wood, Natalie, 194
Woods, Donald, 202
Woodward, Joanne, 123, 280
Wordsworth, William, 11
Workers' Laboratory Theatre, 28
Works Progress Administration, 28
"World of Sholom Aleichem, The," 69–70
Wright, Richard, 23
Wright, Teresa, 155, 157, 227
Wyatt, Jane, 95
Wyler, William, 55, 71, 94, 143, 144, 227
Wynn, Ed, 237
Wynn, Keenan, 166, 237

Yale Drama School, 85, 277, 322
Yale Repertory Theatre, 268–69
Yankee Doodle Dandy, 51
Yearling, The, 247
Yeats, William Butler, 252
Yiddish Theatre, 22, 42, 85, 237
"You Are There," 277
You Can't Take It with You
   film (1938), 304
   revival (1965), 304
   TV (1979), 304–305
   revival (1983), 304
You and Me, 63
You Only Live Once, 61, 62, 63
Young, Gig, 189
Young, Janis, 233
Young, Neil, 245
Young, Stark, 22
Young Lions, The, 153, 167, 168, 169, 171
Young Philadelphians, The, 277, 279, 280
Young Stranger, The, 236
You're a Big Boy Now, 207, 209

Zapata, Emiliano, 168
Zinnemann, Fred, 94, 134, 143, 149, 155, 156,
   198, 227
Zola, Emile, 17, 53
Zorich, Louis, 299

364